Descartes's Theory of Mind

Descartes's Theory of Mind

Desmond M. Clarke

CLARENDON PRESS · OXFORD

OXFORD
UNIVERSITY PRESS

Great Clarendon Street, Oxford OX2 6DP

Oxford University Press is a department of the University of Oxford.
It furthers the University's objective of excellence in research, scholarship,
and education by publishing worldwide in

Oxford New York

Auckland Cape Town Dar es Salaam Hong Kong Karachi
Kuala Lumpur Madrid Melbourne Mexico City Nairobi
New Delhi Shanghai Taipei Toronto

With offices in

Argentina Austria Brazil Chile Czech Republic France Greece
Guatemala Hungary Italy Japan Poland Portugal Singapore
South Korea Switzerland Thailand Turkey Ukraine Vietnam

Oxford is a registered trade mark of Oxford University Press
in the UK and in certain other countries

Published in the United States
by Oxford University Press Inc., New York

© Desmond M. Clarke 2003

British Library Cataloguing in Publication Data

Data available

Library of Congress Cataloging in Publication Data

Data available

ISBN 0-19-926123-7   978-0-19-926123-9

ISBN 0-19-928494-6 (Pbk.)   978-0-19-928494-8 (Pbk.)

Typeset by SNP Best-set Typesetter Ltd., Hong Kong
Printed in Great Britain
on acid-free paper by
Biddles Ltd.
King's Lynn, Norfolk

ACKNOWLEDGEMENTS

I am grateful to University College, Cork, for leave of absence for the Michaelmas Term, 2001, during which the initial drafting of this book was completed. I presented early versions of some of the arguments at the British Society for the History of Philosophy meeting at Keele, and at the Philosophy Departments at the University of Utrecht; University College, Cork; the University of Massachusetts, Amherst; and University College, Dublin. I am grateful to participants at these gatherings for critical comments and helpful suggestions. A few of these ideas also emerged inchoately in Clarke (2001) and in my contribution to Randall E. Auxier and Lewis E. Kahn (eds.), *The Philosophy of Marjorie Grene* (Open Court, 2002, 471–85). The reports of three anonymous readers were very helpful, especially one that made detailed and critical comments on the whole text. I did not always accept the readers' suggestions, but the text was much improved in the process of trying to defend my original thesis. Finally, I presented a general outline of this interpretation for the first time in the process of applying for the Chair of Philosophy at University College, Cork, in July 2000. The unusual circumstances of my subsequent appointment were such that I failed to deliver an inaugural lecture. This monograph might be offered as a substitute.

Desmond M. Clarke

Cork
October 2002

CONTENTS

A NOTE ON TEXTS

I have used the standard edition of the works of Descartes, originally edited by Adam and Tannery, for all quotations. I provide a reference, in parentheses, for each quotation by giving the volume and page number in roman and arabic numerals respectively (although I have omitted the traditional 'AT' as redundant). Volumes viii and ix are each divided into two parts, and these are designated as viii-1, viii-2, etc. In common with anyone else writing in English, I have benefited from the standard three-volume edition of *The Philosophical Writings of Descartes*, trans. and ed. J. Cottingham, R. Stoothoff, D. Murdoch, and A. Kenny. However, to avoid possible commitments to traditional dualist interpretations and to achieve consistency in translating key terms such as 'thought', 'mind', etc., I have translated all quotations from the original texts, with the exception of *The World*. Some of my own translations have already appeared in a two-volume selection of Descartes's writings, published by Penguin. Citations from the latter (adjusted in some cases for consistency of style), and from the English translation of *The World*, are abbreviated as follows:

D.   R. Descartes, *Discourse on Method and Related Writings*, trans. and ed. D. M. Clarke (Penguin, 1999)

M.   R. Descartes, *Meditations and Other Metaphysical Writings*, trans. and ed. D. M. Clarke, rev. edn. (Penguin, 2001)

W.   R. Descartes, *The World and Other Writings*, trans. and ed. Stephen Gaukroger (Cambridge University Press, 1998)

Introduction

There is a standard account of Cartesian dualism that is so familiar that it almost needs no introduction. According to this account, human beings are composed of two distinct substances, a material substance and an immaterial substance, and the latter is a necessary and sufficient condition for (most) mental events. Despite its familiarity and longevity, however, there are good reasons to doubt that Descartes ever proposed such a theory as an *explanation* of the human mind. The most fundamental reason for doubting the standard account was made explicit in one of Hobbes's objections to the *Meditations*. The English philosopher had been convinced that Descartes was an unrelenting critic of the style of explanation used by scholastic philosophers, and he drew the conclusion that such explanations are irremediably flawed even in metaphysics. Hobbes was therefore understandably surprised to find that, when attempting to explain how we think, Descartes seemed to revert to precisely the kind of faculties and powers that he had categorically rejected in natural philosophy: 'If Descartes were to show that the agent who understands is identical with the understanding, we would return to the scholastic way of speaking: the understanding understands, vision sees, the will wills, and, according to the best analogy, walking—or at least the faculty of walking—walks' (vii. 177). Although I later argue that Descartes did not in fact make this mistake, Hobbes's caution is an appropriate response to what I think is a plausible misreading of the *Meditations*. He deserves recognition as the first to object that, if faculties are non-explanatory in natural philosophy, they cannot do any genuine explanatory work in philosophizing about human minds or God.

The second reason for reconsidering the standard account is the almost universally acknowledged failure of this kind of Cartesian dualism. Generations of students in introductory courses in philosophy of mind have sharpened their critical skills by refuting the position caricatured by Gilbert Ryle (1949: 17) in the memorable phrase 'the dogma of the Ghost in the Machine'. According to the standard account, the two substances of which we are composed have no properties in common, or at least none that is relevant to explaining their interaction. Nonetheless, these substances seem to interact when some of our thoughts cause bodily motions or when external stimuli cause us to have perceptions, although we cannot understand how such interaction is possible.

Thus what seems to have begun as a theory of the human mind and its functions turns out to be an obvious dead end. Given the magnitude and predictability of the theoretical failure involved, the only appropriate comment today is to explain how this misguided ontology of substances developed in the history of ideas.[1] In other words, we can make sense of Descartes's mistake historically, even if we cannot make sense of substance dualism as a theory of the mind. However, a closer reading of the texts suggests that Descartes did not endorse the understanding of substances, and its implicit category mistake, on which Ryle's version of Cartesian dualism depends. If any philosopher were to use the concept of a substance to explain the familiar realities of consciousness, thinking, willing, and so on, they should claim to understand what substances are and offer some account of how they could discharge the theoretical role assigned to them. Descartes is, at best, confused about what substances are. Secondly, he consistently argues that we have no independent knowledge of substances apart from knowing their properties. This raises significant doubts about the extent to which he relied on the traditional scholastic concept of a substance as the central theoretical term in an allegedly futile explanation of the human mind.

The third reason for doubting the standard account is that Descartes's attempts to explain perception, memory, and imagination point in a completely different direction. Despite the technical and theoretical obstacles that impeded his research, Descartes announced very early in his scientific career that he would look for a theory of human mental abilities by beginning with animal physiology. He wrote to Mersenne in 1632 that he was 'dissecting the heads of various animals, so that I can explain what imagination, memory, etc. consist in' (i. 263). He may not have actually performed all the experiments from which he claims to have derived evidence and, most probably, he observed personally or

---

[1] Although I have found many points of contact with Baker and Morris (1996) and have learned much from reading their book, I disagree with the suggestion that Descartes's ontology or the basic categories within which he philosophized are a feature of the underlying grammar of his language, and that we cannot ask for any further explanation of why he apparently adopted them. For example, Baker and Morris (1996: 202) argue that 'none of his doctrines are hypotheses, and it makes no sense to subject them to any form of empirical confirmation or disconfirmation, however indirect'. Once the underlying assumptions of his ontology are made explicit, one cannot dispute them; to do so is 'to replace his concepts with our *different* ones' (1996: 204). Carried to its logical conclusion, this implies that 'what Descartes called the mind (*mens*, *esprit*) is definitely not the subject-matter of twentieth-century philosophy of mind, and he definitely did not propound his dualism as a solution to what is now called the "mind–body problem"' (1996: 119). While accepting the suggestion that we should not replace Descartes's concepts or language with our own and then delude ourselves that we are discussing Descartes, it would be helpful to acknowledge the extent to which Descartes had at his disposal a range of concepts, some of which were borrowed from scholastic philosophy (and even here, from different incompatible sources), and that he was trying to extend the range of scientific explanation in a way that challenged the resourcefulness of the conceptual framework that he inherited from his teachers.

directly only some of what he subsequently described. The relevant point here, however, is that he began his quest for an explanation of human sensation, memory, and imagination by looking inside the brain of a sheep.

Of course these objections are scarcely enough on their own to displace what is almost an established tradition of reading Descartes's works. One might respond to them cautiously by pointing out that the philosophical writings of any author are bound to show up various inconsistencies. Thus, if we encounter exegetical problems in Descartes, in texts that were written over a period of almost twenty-five years, we might give priority to certain well-known texts and their standard interpretation and then try to accommodate other awkward texts as well as possible. For example, one might give priority to the *Meditations* as Descartes's official position and then attempt a consistent reading of other texts accordingly. However, that strategy has resulted in attributing to its author a theory that simply does not work; hence the motivation to reread the texts and to look for a more plausible interpretation.

The alternative approach adopted here is to put Descartes's account of *explanation* (rather than substance dualism) at the centre of his philosophy of mind, and in particular his negative evaluation of the merits of scholastic explanations. With this starting point, it makes sense that a young natural philosopher living in the Netherlands would have looked inside animal brains to begin to understand sensation, memory, and imagination, and that he would have stretched to their limits the resources of such a novel research programme. Those limits, both conceptual and experimental, were very obvious in the 1630s. While Descartes was not unduly modest about the conceptual limits of his project, he frequently acknowledged the extent to which the development of his natural philosophy was frustrated by a lack of observational or experimental results. On this reading, Cartesian natural philosophy and the kinds of explanation that it requires are the guiding principle in reading his work. This may reveal different exegetical problems that are avoided by the standard account, but the obvious failure of the latter supports the necessity of considering alternatives.

The challenge, then, is to find a coherent reading of all the texts that survive from Descartes's pen, including those that we describe today as science, which avoids the spectre of Ryle's ghost. This requires a significant change in perspective about which texts are more or less central to the Cartesian intellectual enterprise, and it may be helpful at the outset to provide the reader with some advance notice of the shift in perspective involved.

PHYSICS AND METAPHYSICS IN DESCARTES'S WRITINGS

The chronology of Descartes's writings is sufficiently uncontentious to show that, from about the late 1620s, he hoped to emulate the great instauration of knowledge that Bacon had already proposed some years earlier. His initial efforts resulted in a number of unfinished texts, many of which remained unpublished during his lifetime. These included *Rules for Guiding one's Intelligence in Searching for the Truth* (c.1628), *The World*, and *A Treatise on Man* (c.1632), and other even more inchoate texts such as a short essay on metaphysics that is lost. Among these, only the manuscript of *The World* was close to being ready for publication. However, when Descartes heard about the condemnation of Galileo in 1633, he feared that his own endorsement of heliocentrism in *The World* would attract a similar censure from Rome and he decided accordingly not to publish the book. Descartes's first published book in 1637 included the *Discourse on the Method for Guiding one's Reason and Searching for Truth in the Sciences*, together with three scientific essays that were supposed to illustrate such a method in practice: *The Dioptrics, the Meteors, and the Geometry*. This book reflects the concerns that had prevented publication of *The World* four years previously. The author's name is omitted from the title page, and part six of the prefatory *Discourse* outlines the reasons why he changed his mind on more than one occasion about the wisdom of publishing the book. The *Meditations* was published in 1641, and here for the first time Descartes's name appeared on the title page of one of his books. This was followed, three years later, by *The Principles of Philosophy* (1644), which included a summary of the issues already presented in the *Meditations* and, in Parts II–IV, explanations of natural phenomena that had been outlined in earlier essays, both published and unpublished. Finally, Descartes published *The Passions of the Soul* in 1649. One of the questions raised by this chronology is the role and significance of the *Meditations* in the Cartesian œuvre as a whole, and the sense in which Descartes claimed that all human knowledge depends on metaphysics.

It is well known that Descartes says that metaphysics provides the foundation for his physics, but he does not explain adequately what that means. The metaphor about building knowledge on firm foundations is complemented by an equally revealing metaphor about a tree of knowledge in the French edition of the *Principles* (1647): 'Thus the whole of philosophy is like a tree, of which the roots are metaphysics, the trunk is physics, and the branches that emerge from this trunk are all the other sciences, which reduce to three principal sciences, namely: medicine, mechanics and morals' (ix-2. 14). The foundational metaphor might mean that one must establish one's metaphysics before doing physics, that metaphysics is more certain than physics, or perhaps that it sets the conceptual limits within which physics may be developed.[2] Although some texts seem to support this reading, it unfortunately involves Descartes in speaking with more confidence about God and his causal influence in nature than about the natural events whose ultimate explanation, he claims, points in the direction of God. It also conflicts with his usual account of how we acquire metaphysical or theoretical concepts; according to this, we construct them by analogy with simpler, more familiar concepts that derive from perception and experience. That suggests an inversion of the foundation metaphor, at least when describing Descartes's order of discovery. He seems to have constructed a natural philosophy first and then addressed the epistemological and metaphysical issues that emerge in the course of that construction.

The context in which Descartes wrote in the seventeenth century was such that it was impossible to separate completely natural philosophy from metaphysics or theology. Whether he wished to or not, he could not avoid addressing questions about the implications of his physics for theologically sensitive doctrines. Galileo had been confronted by the same challenge, and had argued that the Bible does not teach physics and that scientific theories are not designed to teach theology.[3] He notoriously lost that battle, at least temporarily. Descartes repeated Galileo's strategic error and, perhaps reluctantly, tried to explain the complementarity of his natural philosophy with orthodox Christian teaching. In this spirit, for example, he refers to the Lateran Council in the letter dedicating the *Meditations* to the theology faculty at the Sorbonne:

As regards the soul, many people thought that its nature cannot easily be investigated, and some have even dared say that human reason shows us that the soul dies with the body and that the contrary view is held by faith alone; however, the Lateran Council, held under Leo X (Session 8), condemns them and explicitly commands Christian philosophers to defeat their arguments and to prove the truth to the best of their abilities, and therefore I too have not hesitated to take on this challenge.   (vii. 2–3; M. 9)

The Lateran Council was a general council of the Roman Catholic Church held in 1512–17. Pope Leo X issued a bull in December 1513, condemning various neo-Aristotelians who claimed, among other things, that if the human soul is an Aristotelian form it must cease to exist with the death of the individual.[4] The official teaching of Lateran borrowed a philosophical language that had not

---

[2] This is a very inadequate summary of what is involved, but it gives a sense of the interpretative perspective adopted, for example, in Garber (1992).

[3] The literature on this topic is extensive; see especially Blackwell (1991).

[4] Denziger (1960: 272): 'damnamus et reprobamus omnes asserentes, animam intellectivam mortalem esse, aut unicam in cunctis hominibus . . .'.

been used in the New Testament.[5] By thus assimilating Christianity to scholastic philosophy the Council bound its understanding of the Christian doctrine of personal salvation to a philosophical theory about the human soul, and it adopted the language of substances as the official expression of its religious faith. This set the context within which Descartes attempts to explain how his natural philosophy is consistent with the Church's teaching about the immortality of the soul. This attempt at reconciliation is reflected in the subtitle of the *Meditations*; although it was significantly altered between the first and second editions (1641 and 1642), it remains explicit about the two principal objectives of the essay. In the first edition, the subtitle reads: 'in which God's existence and the immortality of the soul are demonstrated', while the second edition is modified to read: 'in which God's existence and the distinction between the human soul and the body are demonstrated.'[6] The clear distinction between the soul and the body that is mentioned in the amended subtitle is a much weaker conclusion than the soul's immortality, but, if demonstrated, it would at least be consistent with the teaching of the Church.[7]

Thus one reason why Descartes became involved in metaphysical discussions is clear. The intellectual climate in which he wrote was such that he was expected to explain how his novel natural philosophy was consistent with the teaching of various Christian churches and the philosophical language in which they expressed their teaching. Once he had accepted that challenge, wisely or otherwise, it still remained an open question whether Descartes would simply adjust his physics so that it was consistent with scholastic philosophy, or whether he would engage with the latter to adapt it as much as possible to his physics. Evidently, there was no such thing as a single 'scholastic metaphysics' that was universally adopted in the early seventeenth century. Disputes within school philosophy were as frequent and acrimonious as later objections, by scholastics, to the apparent implications of the new sciences. Thus any genuine engagement with scholastic philosophy implied a selective negotiation with those elements of that tradition that were likely to be compatible with the new sciences and, even more seriously, with theological views that were widely

---

[5] The extent to which scholastic forms and qualities are foreign to the Scriptures was emphasized by Descartes in his letter to Regius (Jan. 1642) (iii. 502).

[6] Cf. the books written by Jean de Silhon, in which the same two questions about the existence of God and the immortality of the soul are the main focus: *Les Deux Véritez de Silhon* (Paris, 1626), and *De l'immortalité de l'âme* (Paris, 1634).

[7] Despite his wish to console Princess Elizabeth by discussing the happiness enjoyed in the afterlife, Descartes admits that 'natural philosophy by itself makes us hope that our soul will be in a happier state after death than now'. If we rely on 'natural reason alone we can make many favourable conjectures . . . but we cannot have any certainty' about the afterlife (Descartes to Elizabeth, 1 Sept. 1645 and 3 Nov. 1645 (iv. 263, 333)).

accepted as the official teaching of various Christian churches. In this context, Descartes had reason to be concerned by Calvinists at Utrecht as much as Roman Catholics at the Sorbonne.

For these reasons, I read Descartes's discussion of theological and metaphysical issues as the engagement of a reluctant participant with the politically dominant ideologies of his time. What he actually says about God is closer to the modesty of Aquinas' *via negativa* than to the theologically confident claims of his contemporaries. More generally, his understanding of the limited role of metaphysics in the reconstruction of human knowledge is summarized in this advice to Princess Elizabeth:

Although I think it is very necessary to have understood well, once in a lifetime, the principles of metaphysics . . . I also think that it would be very harmful to occupy one's understanding frequently in thinking about them because the understanding would find it difficult to leave itself free to use the imagination and the senses. It is best to be satisfied with retaining in one's memory and one's belief the conclusions that have once been drawn from the principles of metaphysics, and to devote one's remaining study time to those thoughts in which the understanding acts together with the imagination and the senses. (iii. 695; M. 154)

The minimal metaphysics and modest theology required for a renewed natural philosophy is reflected in Descartes's relatively uncreative use of elements from Augustine, Aquinas, or Suarez as the need arose.[8] One of these borrowed scholastic concepts is that of a substance. It would be inconsistent with the textual evidence to pretend that Descartes does not refer frequently to substances, especially when describing the human mind and God. However, the fundamental question is whether, in talking about substances, Descartes is trying to construct a theory of mind by using scholastic metaphysics, or whether he is selectively exploiting the resources of the latter to open up enough conceptual space for his primary objective—namely, a renewal of natural philosophy.

READING DESCARTES'S WORKS

As already indicated above, almost all Descartes's writings in the period 1626–40 were concerned with natural philosophy, and they were withheld from publication or published only reluctantly and anonymously. This kind of natural philosophy appears to many modern readers as quaint, primitive, or just

---

[8] Recent studies of the extent to which Descartes borrowed liberally from Augustine and Suarez include Des Chene (1996), Menn (1998), and Secada (2000).

ill-informed.[9] In contrast with the proto-science of other writings, however, the *Meditations* addresses issues that appear familiar to modern philosophers, in a book that has the added authority of the author's name on its title page. This suggests that, from the perspective of modern readers, Descartes's work might divide naturally into two genres: (1) outdated scientific treatises, and (2) philosophical arguments, such as those found in the *Meditations*, that resonate with at least some modern philosophy. It also suggests that there is little likelihood that the former could teach us anything significant about the human mind and its operations.[10]

However, I think that one should argue, in exactly the opposite direction, that Cartesian science is so different from theories that are current in the twenty-first century that we should attempt to see things from Descartes's radically different perspective. Once we remember that Descartes's experiments and observations were done before the invention of the microscope, we can hardly be surprised that his descriptions of the anatomy of the brain are as primitive as they appear to us.[11] If one accepts this perspective, with its emphasis on the role of natural philosophy in the Cartesian project, it implies a re-evaluation of the relevance of his theory of matter for contemporary discussions of what is now called the mind–body problem. When Descartes wrote about matter, the matter in question was a theoretical construct of Cartesian natural philosophy. Whatever *corpus* or *materia* may have meant in that system, these terms certainly did not mean the same as 'matter' today. Thus we cannot assume without serious anachronism that, when Descartes writes about matter and its limited powers and, by implication, about the irreducibility of mental events to matter in motion, his matter–mind distinction is conceptually isomorphic with what is now called the mind–body problem.

This emphasis on the historicity of Descartes's concepts, and their embeddedness in his natural philosophy, implies that it is a mistake for readers today to read selectively and ahistorically those sections of his work (such as the *Meditations*) that seem to be philosophically interesting to us, while ignoring the wider intellectual context in which they were written. Given this conclusion, some

---

[9] The gap between Cartesian natural philosophy and contemporary science is underlined by the comments of a recent critic (Des Chene 2001: 153), who points out that Descartes would have needed 'organic chemistry, the cell theory, the discovery of mitosis, the identification of genes, the analysis of DNA and of the mechanism of replication' even to understand the 'inheritance of characters'.

[10] Is the criticism that Descartes was correct to attempt a scientific account of the mind, but that he lacked the theories we now have? That would be equivalent to denigrating old science for not being new. Or is the objection that any scientific effort is doomed to failure, in principle? In that case the relative underdevelopment of Cartesian science is irrelevant to determining the success or otherwise of Descartes's theory of mind.

[11] Bitbol-Hespériès points out in her Introduction to Descartes (1996: p. iv) that the inventor of the microscope, Leeuwenhoek, was born only in 1632, the same year in which *Le Monde* was completed.

reluctant readers may abandon Descartes's philosophy in its entirety to a respectful oblivion. I hope the following pages may help persuade them of the opposite conclusion. Descartes was among the first of those who used creatively the language of the schools to subvert the philosophical principles with which its protagonists fashioned a failed theory of the soul. We could at least learn from him not to lapse into the same Aristotelian categories that he considered philosophically bankrupt and, following the Lateran Council, theologically dangerous.

The central concept on which this interpretation depends is a theory of explanation that was shared more or less explicitly by many natural philosophers of the seventeenth century from Galileo to Newton. According to this, any account of human mental experiences or activities in terms of faculties of the soul is merely a redescription of what needs to be explained, and it makes no progress towards providing an explanation. This insight motivated Descartes, from his earliest work in the 1630s, to direct his research towards physiology with a view to explaining animal behaviour. The results of this rather speculative work were subsequently applied to human beings in a number of early works: *The World, A Treatise on Man*, and *A Description of the Human Body*. These writings, together with *The Dioptrics*, proposed accounts of perception, imagination, and memory that rely heavily on the rather primitive (by our standards) neurology and physiology of his time. In particular, they depend on the ways in which a subtle fluid called 'animal spirits' flows through the ducts that constitute the nerves.

It was most unlikely that such a scientific project could have produced the results that we expect today from neurology, psychology, linguistics, and related sciences. Descartes conceded that every scientific theory, sooner or later, exhausts its theoretical fertility and, at that point, it reverts to (hypothetical) claims about how things are. He also acknowledged that some theories might encounter insurmountable difficulties much sooner than expected, because they lack the observations or empirical data required to develop them adequately. It is not surprising, then, if the projected Cartesian explanation of human mental powers met with limited success prior to 1650, and if its limits were marked by references to faculties, dispositions, or powers that are described exclusively in terms of the effects that they cause. On this reading, the Cartesian theory of mind is a first rather bold step in the direction of removing souls completely from explanations of human behaviour, because they are mere non-explanatory redescriptions of the phenomena to be explained. The reappearance of soul or faculty language in Descartes's project, therefore, marks the place where genuine explanation comes to a provisional halt rather than the limits, in principle, of what can be explained. Alternatively, it marks a distinction, frequently drawn by Descartes, between a description of the first-person experience of thinking and its objective explanation. This is consistent with the fact that Descartes adopts two apparently inconsistent attitudes towards substantial forms. His fundamental argument is that they are non-explanatory. However, he also retains the human soul as the only residual substantial form in his philosophy. But the reason for its survival is not that it does any explanatory work in the case of human beings, when it manifestly does none elsewhere. It is merely a marker, a stop-gap measure, which indicates where an extremely ambitious Cartesian theory of the mind encounters apparently insurmountable obstacles.[12]

TWO LANGUAGES: DESCRIBING AND EXPLAINING

Wilfrid Sellars (1963) popularized a way of thinking about scientific theories in terms of two images, which he called the 'manifest image' and the 'scientific image'. The manifest image is our way of describing the world by using the ontology of ordinary language. Despite its historical origins in theories of which modern ordinary-language users may be completely unaware, this ontology of macroscopic bodies and their familiar properties fits comfortably with our ordinary experience of the world in which we live. In this manifest image, we describe our experience of the world in ways that give priority to how realities appear to us. In fact, 'the primary objects of the manifest image are *persons*' (Sellars 1963: 9), although it also includes animals, rivers, stones, and so on. From this perspective, the sun is a relatively small, circular, moving object in the sky. In contrast, the scientific image is unashamedly theoretical. By using the language of a scientific theory, we describe and explain our experience of the world in terms of the theoretical entities that are postulated by the best current theory for the reality in question. From this perspective, the sun is an extremely large, spherical, stationary object in space and familiar objects, such as tables and chairs, are complex structures of unobservable particles in constant motion. As a scientific realist, Sellars argued that the scientific image provides our most reliable access to reality and the best reasons for adopting one ontology rather than another.

---

[12] This point is also made, but as a criticism of Descartes, by Alan Gabbey (1990: 279, 282): 'So it is not surprising . . . that the mechanists' explanations of sensations and certain other phenomena . . . were either exercises in extending the traditional Peripatetic qualities to the particles of the explanatory structure, or were circular or tautologous, to varying degrees of sophistication, or were empirically uncheckable—defects they shared with the corresponding Peripatetic explanations they were intended to replace . . . The mechanists were usually clear about the hypothetical nature of their explanatory structures, but it seems to me they were incognizant of the circularity that often attended the explanations themselves.'

Descartes also adverts to these alternatives in the Third Meditation, in which he considers two contrasting ideas of the sun.

For example, I find that I have two different ideas of the sun. One idea, which seems to have been acquired from the senses and is a paradigm example of an adventitious idea, makes the sun appear very small. The other idea, however, is derived from astronomical reasoning . . . and it makes the sun appear to be several times greater than the earth. They cannot both be truly similar to the same sun that exists outside me, and reason convinces me that the one that seems to have originated more directly from the sun resembles it the least.   (vii. 39; M. 34)

This text contrasts the idea of the sun that we spontaneously acquire by looking at the heavens without the aid of a telescope, and a different idea of the sun that emerges from attempts to explain our visual experiences. As a scientific realist, Descartes endorses the latter as the more accurate idea. The same contrast and the same conclusion should apply in other contexts. For example, the sine law of refraction explains why straight sticks immersed in water appear bent, and here again it is the familiar experience that is deceptive while the scientific theory is endorsed as most reliable.

There is a more general and basic issue underlying this apparently simple choice between competing descriptions or explanations of the sun or an apparently bent stick. The fundamental issue is whether Descartes's ontology was inherited uncritically from his predecessors, or whether he was constructing a new ontology while revising more or less radically the categories in which his critics conducted theological and metaphysical debates. Descartes may not have been as clear as we might wish about which of these options he chose. But, if he adopted the second one, then we can discover his fundamental ontology only from the theories or explanations that he actively supported. In other words, the kinds of things that exist in a Cartesian universe are the theoretical entities that are required for an adequate explanation of all the realities in that universe, including human mental events. According to this criterion, substances are redundant.

Thus the special circumstances in which the *Meditations* appeared were unique in several respects. Descartes had done a significant amount of work before 1641 on his fundamental project of constructing a new, comprehensive natural philosophy, though much of it remained unpublished primarily because of fear of church censure. He then published the *Meditations*, including lengthy replies to objections that had been submitted prior to publication. However, despite the care exercised in meeting his critics' objections and despite the request for corrections addressed to 'the dean and professors of the faculty of sacred theology' (vii. 1; M. 8), this book was put on the Roman index of forbidden books in 1663. The *Meditations* fulfilled what Descartes called 'my duty to attempt something in this area' (vii. 3; *M.* 9). While it was an honest attempt to support the teaching of the Lateran Council, Descartes could not have been unaware in 1641 of the conflict between his unpublished scientific treatises and his dutifully submissive efforts to write something in metaphysics that would satisfy inquisitive theologians. The *Meditations* therefore can be seen, not as the most authoritative expression of Descartes's philosophy, but as an unsuccessful attempt to reconcile his theologically suspect natural philosophy with an orthodox expression of scholastic metaphysics.

This divided allegiance is reflected in the way in which Descartes discusses mental powers and functions in two completely different languages. One is the newly emerging language of the scientific revolution, which is evident in most of his writings apart from the *Meditations*. The other is the dualistic language of the scholastic tradition, which is most evident in his efforts to support the Lateran Council, and which is used in that context to demarcate those features of human behaviour and experience that seemed to be immune to scientific explanation. When pressed by critics, Descartes identified the use of language as the critical property that distinguishes human beings from other members of the animal kingdom and he developed this argument in support of the real distinction of mind and matter. However, even if the irreducibility of mental properties is accepted, substance dualism could not provide any extra contribution to a theory of the human mind. Anticipating subsequent Lockean reservations about the concept of a substance, Descartes implied that the language of substances, instead of explaining qualities, merely classifies them by the contingencies of their co-occurrence. We do not know substances independently of their properties. Therefore, even if we borrowed them with a generous line of epistemic credit, they would explain nothing about the mental phenomena that they are expected to explain.

Cartesian theory, after 1641, includes an emerging scientific explanation of human mental powers and, in parallel, a recognition that some of those powers appear to be immune to scientific explanation. Thus mental powers under some descriptions are irreducible to the properties of Cartesian matter, and this irreducibility prevents the construction of a unified theory of human beings that explains all their properties. The property dualism for which Descartes had provided arguments was then translated into the language of substance dualism, for which he lacked independent arguments. The years after 1641 testify to the conceptual confusion that this situation produced. Descartes never resolved the conceptual problems that were endemic to the language of substance dualism, and he seems to have abandoned the effort to construct a coherent theory of human persons in that language.[13] Despite this failure, or, possibly, because of it, Descartes continued as late as 1649 to develop a scientific explanation of other mental properties, especially of human emotions, and he approached this task as usual from the perspective of a natural philosopher.

The subsequent history of Descartes's theory of mind, beginning with La Forge's *Treatise on the Human Mind*, reproduces the ambivalence that I attribute to Descartes. La Forge decided to fulfil Descartes's original promise and to supply an account of the human mind and its relation to the body, based on various published and unpublished Cartesian texts. He tried to establish beyond doubt the theological orthodoxy of Descartes's theory in a preface replete with lengthy quotations from St Augustine, and he struggled as best he could with the unresolved parallelism of Cartesian mind and matter by integrating it into a theory of occasional causality. La Forge's efforts helped crystallize Descartes's theory of mind into what we now recognize as Cartesian dualism. With the passing of time, philosophical readers omitted the natural philosophy that was central to La Forge's synthesis and accepted the simplified and extremely implausible position that was caricatured by Ryle. At the same time, subsequent advances in scientific theory have long overtaken Descartes's 'old science'. The result of these parallel developments, for the most part involving two different sets of readers, was the emergence of Descartes the metaphysician who was a substance dualist, rather than Descartes the natural philosopher who flirted briefly with substance dualism only when dutifully making his contribution to the Catholic Counter-Reformation.

The primary aim of this monograph is to restore the integrity and ambiguity of the original Cartesian account of how human mental abilities may be explained partly by reference to the brain and other relevant physiological systems, and of why human thought displays properties that are irreducible to the properties of matter. This approach does not assume that Descartes was dishonest in the views he presented in the *Meditations*, or that he held a secret doctrine that he was afraid to make public but that is somehow available to sympathetic commentators today. The reality was and remains much simpler. Descartes required any genuine explanation of the human mind to avoid scholastic pseudo-explanations and to be consistent with the new natural philosophy that he supported. Once he began that project, however, it emerged clearly that Cartesian matter in motion could not deliver the kind of

---

[13] Stephen Voss (1994) examines all the texts in which Descartes attempts to describe human beings, coherently, as either two substances joined together (which maintain their original identities) or as a single substance that results from joining what are, conceptually, two distinct substances. His conclusion is that Descartes 'has no answer at all' to the question: what is a human being?

explanation that was required. Some mental properties are not reducible to the properties of Cartesian matter.[14]

The problem with which Descartes struggled in the 1640s is not much closer to resolution today, despite significant advances in our understanding of the properties of matter. In the final chapter below I review briefly the ways in which apparently irreconcilable features of our mental life are accommodated within Donald Davidson's 'anomalous monism' or in Thomas Nagel's distinction between subjective descriptions of experiences and objective explanations of their occurrence. One of the central issues here is whether the irreducibility of two languages implies the impossibility of having common referents for some of their terms, and whether the plausibility of an identity theory is an exclusively conceptual question that can be resolved a priori or whether it is partly an empirical question whose resolution depends on future scientific developments. I argue that the identity or otherwise of mental experiences with processes that fall within the scope of the sciences is a scientific question, although it seemed extremely improbable to any informed natural philosopher of the early seventeenth century that an appropriate theory could be constructed. Our scientific knowledge has progressed in ways that would have seemed almost unimaginable in 1650, but our understanding of human consciousness is still little more than a promissory note. Thus the construction of a theory or explanation of human mental states and processes, which seemed impossible to Descartes, remains almost as problematic today as it was in the early seventeenth century.

According to this interpretation, Descartes embarked on an attempt to construct an explanation of animal and human behaviour, including a theory of the human mind. The relatively undeveloped state of the relevant sciences in the seventeenth century was such that his efforts were almost predictably unsuccessful. The lack of success, however, does not prove that the project is incapable of success. It shows rather that it originated from philosophical views that, in principle, implied the redundancy of the human soul rather than its immortality, and that the logical culmination of the Cartesian approach was Locke's query about the feasibility of God super-adding thought to a material body or La Mettrie's *Machine Man*.[15] Many of Descartes's contemporaries, who

---

[14] Margaret Wilson (1978: 182–3) acknowledges that one reason for Descartes's dualism 'may be found in his commitment to mechanistic explanation in physics, together with the perfectly creditable belief that human intelligence could never be accounted for on the available mechanistic models'. However, Wilson understands Descartes's dualism, not as a form of parallelism, but as claiming that 'bodily states are not merely not *identical* with mental states: they are not even *relevant* to a subclass of such states . . . any physiological study will necessarily be irrelevant to' pure understanding (Wilson 1978: 180–1).

[15] See John Yolton (1983, 1991) for a survey of some of this literature, and La Mettrie (1996). Locke's query is found in Locke (1975: IV. iii. 6).

were sensitive to the implications of his natural philosophy, suspected that it would more likely lead to atheism than to the clear separation of the soul from the body that he promised to deliver in the *Meditations*. The evidence, I think, supports the accuracy and insight of their concerns.

Cartesian Explanation

One of the defining features of the scientific revolution in the seventeenth century was its radical reform of the concept of explanation. Natural philosophers of this period, including Descartes, criticized trenchantly and consistently the style of explanation that was widely attributed to the scholastics and proposed instead a new ideal of what is often called, somewhat misleadingly, mechanical explanation. The success of this critique was such that, by the close of the century, the concept of explanation had been effectively redefined. In this chapter I review some of the arguments that supported this fundamental change in our understanding of what constitutes an explanation, with particular reference to their implications for a Cartesian theory of mind. In doing so I shall not quote extensively from the many writers who enthusiastically embraced the new ideal during this period. They are both too numerous and too well known. However, to avoid giving the impression that Descartes was particularly reductionist or that his methodological assumptions depended significantly on an atypical metaphysics, I shall refer briefly to comparable views that were espoused with equal conviction by Robert Boyle (1626–91). Boyle evidently belonged to a slightly later generation of natural philosophers. Although familiar with Descartes's work, he was an independent natural philosopher whose primary intellectual circle was the Royal Society in England. I refer to Boyle's parallel and similar critique of scholasticism to illustrate the extent to which this new model of explanation was widely shared by natural philosophers in the seventeenth century. In fact, if one allows for slight variations in emphasis or expression, this is almost the unanimous view about explanation held by all the principal proponents of the scientific revolution from Galileo (1564–1642) to Newton (1642–1727).

Despite this near unanimity, however, it is usually assumed that the scope of the new model of explanation was restricted to natural phenomena, and that phenomena associated with the mind—such as thinking, remembering, or consciousness—are an exception, in principle, to its otherwise universal application. In the case of Descartes, the reason usually offered for this differential approach to nature and the human mind is that he first established a dualistic ontology, and that the substance dualism for which he is renowned in the history of philosophy decides the question about how to construct a theory, and especially how not to construct a theory, of the human mind. If mind and body are completely different kinds of substance, then the style of explanation that is appropriate to the latter may be completely inappropriate in the case of the mind.

There are two good reasons for not assuming this division of labour a priori. One is that Descartes and his contemporaries were particularly convinced of the negative evaluation of scholastic explanations, even if they continued to debate the competing merits of alternative proposals. They were convinced that the objections against scholastic 'explanations' were so fundamental that they were never genuinely explanatory. Such explanations did not work in the case of natural phenomena, and the problems that rendered them useless there did not disappear if one simply changed the phenomena to which they were applied. If anything, the debilitating flaws of scholastic explanations became more apparent when applied to mental phenomena, which, then as now, constituted a particularly intractable challenge to our attempts at explanation. The second reason was that the plausibility of substance dualism depends on the success or otherwise of applying the new scientific methods to the human mind. Unless Descartes is understood as inheriting substance dualism uncritically from his predecessors, he needs convincing arguments to persuade readers that the mental life of some biological machines is not amenable to the new style of explanation and, consequently, that we should think of human beings as combinations of two radically different types of reality. Substance dualism should follow from, rather than precede, a thorough examination of the feasibility of explaining the human mind scientifically. We should therefore expect that, in constructing a theory of mind, Descartes would not revert spontaneously to the failed concept of explanation against which he had argued so successfully, and that he would at least test the applicability of the novel explanatory strategies that he proposed with almost evangelical zeal from his earliest writings.

When this approach is tried and reaches its limits—and one would expect those limits to emerge rather quickly, given the minimal knowledge of the human brain with which Descartes was working—Descartes has a number of options available (although the following suggestions are not meant to exhaust the list). One is simply to acknowledge the boundaries of his success to date and to talk about the mind as what remains unknown. A modified version of the same response is to describe the mind as what is partly known and understood, and to signal the limits of his success in explaining mental phenomena by relying on dispositional explanations whose apparent circularity and other limitations (discussed below) are acknowledged. A third option is to argue for a much stronger conclusion—namely, that the failure of one's explanatory efforts vis-à-vis the human mind implies a compelling, a posteriori, justification for ontological dualism.

The most plausible interpretation of the Cartesian solution can be decided only after considering the relevant texts and arguments. In this chapter, I outline the very strong reasons that should prevent any committed natural philosopher of the seventeenth century from reverting to empty scholastic explanations. If followed to their logical conclusion, these criticisms require Descartes to look for an alternative, less unsatisfactory, response to the genuine problems encountered in explaining mental phenomena. At the conclusion of this chapter, I indicate one 'way out' adopted by Digby, and I defer to later chapters any final interpretation of Descartes's solution.

CRITIQUE OF SCHOLASTIC EXPLANATIONS

The most fundamental issue on which most natural philosophers in the seventeenth century agreed was their rejection of the style of explanation that was widely shared in the schools. Some of the principal objections to 'substantial forms' and 'real qualities' in an explanatory context were articulated at length by Boyle, sixteen years after Descartes's death, in *The Origin of Forms and Qualities* (1666):

First, That I see no necessity of admitting in Natural things any such substantial Forms, Matter and the Accidents of Matter being sufficient to explicate as much of the Phaenomena of Nature, as we either do or are like to understand. *The next,* That I see not what use this Puzling Doctrine of substantial Forms is of in Natural Philosophy . . . the *third,* which is, That I cannot conceive, neither how Forms can be generated . . . nor how the things, they ascribe to them, are consistent with the Principles of true Philosophy . . .   (Boyle 1999–2000: v. 340)[1]

The second objection, that forms make no contribution to our understanding of any phenomenon, follows from the alleged incomprehensibility of the forms in

---

[1] Rozemond (1998: 102–11) points out that many commentators today conflate substantial forms and real qualities, although they were different theoretical entities for the scholastics. Substantial forms were introduced to explain substantial change, as when an object of a certain kind either comes into existence or ceases to exist. Since, according to this account, a substance is a combination of a substantial form and matter, a substance comes into existence by the arrival into undifferentiated matter of the relevant form. Descartes understood qualities as features of things that are not themselves things or substances, and he claimed that scholastic philosophers introduced so-called real qualities because they believed that, 'without them, sense perception could not be explained' (vii. 435).

question, and from the claim that we know nothing more about forms than what is already known about the phenomena to be explained.

I do not remember, that either *Aristotle* himself . . . or any of his Followers, has given a solid and intelligible solution of any one Phaenomenon of Nature by the help of substantial Forms: which you need not think it strange I should say, since the greatest Patrons of Forms acknowledg their Nature to be unknown to Us, to explain any Effect by a substantial Form, must be to declare (as they speak) *ignotum per ignotius* [i.e. what is unknown by what is more unknown], or at least *per aeque ignotum* [i.e. by what is equally unknown]. And indeed, to explicate a Phaenomenon, being to deduce it from something else in Nature more known to Us, then the thing to be explain'd by It, how can the imploying of Incomprehensible (or at least Uncomprehended) substantial Forms help Us to explain intelligibly This or That particular Phaenomenon? For to say, that such an Effect proceeds . . . from its substantial Form, is to take an easie way to resolve all difficulties in general, without rightly resolving any one in particular.   (Boyle 1999–2000: v. 351–2)

These three objections, concerning: (1) the redundancy of forms, (2) their lack of explanatory value, and (3) the way in which their proponents fail to account for their origin, are typical of many corpuscularian philosophers of this period. One is not surprised to find that Descartes and many Cartesians expressed the same objections in almost identical terms.

Descartes raised the question about the redundancy of forms, as theoretical entities, in Chapter 2 of *The World* (1632). In the course of elaborating his own preferred explanation of what happens when a fire burns a piece of wood, he wrote:

When it [a fire] burns wood or other similar material we can see with our eyes that it moves the small parts of the wood, separating them from one another . . . Someone else may if he wishes imagine the 'form' of fire, the 'quality' of heat, and the 'action' of burning to be very different things in the wood. For my own part, I am afraid of going astray if I suppose there to be in the wood anything more than what I see must necessarily be there . . . For you can posit 'fire' and 'heat' in the wood and make it burn as much as you please . . . provided only that you grant me that there is some power that violently removes its more subtle parts and separates them from the grosser parts, I consider that this alone will be able to bring about all those changes that we observe when the wood burns.   (x. 7–8; W. 6–7)

Thus, in contrast with the style of explanation that prevailed among scholastics, Descartes limits his conceptual repertoire in this context to the size, shape, and motion of small parts of matter. If he can construct a viable explanation of natural phenomena by using only those properties, he argues, then the various forms and qualities to which scholastic philosophers appeal are redundant. In fact, not only are such forms and qualities redundant; they themselves also need to be explained.

> If you find it strange that, in explaining these elements, I do not use the qualities called 'heat', 'cold', 'moistness', and 'dryness', as the Philosophers do, I shall say that these qualities appear to me to be themselves in need of explanation. Indeed, unless I am mistaken, not only these four qualities but all others as well, including even the forms of inanimate bodies, can be explained without the need to suppose anything in their matter other than [the] motion, size, shape and the arrangement of its parts.   (x. 25–6; W. 18)[2]

The same opinion, slightly qualified by the irenic motives of its author with respect to his Dutch correspondent, is expressed ten years later in a letter to Regius in 1642. On this occasion Descartes is counselling Regius about how best to avoid needless controversy with scholastic theologians at the University of Utrecht. He advises his protagonist that it is best not to reject explicitly the real qualities and substantial forms to which Reformed theologians appeal, and even to retain them in name while offering new arguments that imply their redundancy. This was the strategy that he had adopted, he claims, in *The Meteors*: 'Do you not remember that, in the *Meteors* (page 164), I warned in the most explicit terms that I did not reject or deny them in any way, but only that I did not need them to explain my theories? If you had followed the same plan, no one among your listeners would have failed to reject them as soon as they saw that there was no use for them' (iii. 492).[3] Even more explicitly, Descartes recommends that Regius write to Voetius, the quarrelsome rector of the University of Utrecht, that the 'harmless entities' in dispute should not rashly be rejected and that Cartesians merely claim that 'we do not need them in order to provide the causes of natural things' (iii. 500).

It should be acknowledged that, despite this apparently conciliatory advice to Regius, Descartes denies that substantial forms have any genuine function when explaining natural phenomena. However, he also makes an exception of the human soul in the very same context in which he urges the elimination of all substantial forms from natural philosophy. This coincides with the explicit

---

    [2] Cf. Descartes to Morin (13 July 1638), where Descartes appeals to the relatively few theoretical entities he needs compared with the almost unlimited range of forms and qualities required by scholastic philosophers (ii. 199–200; D. 76–7).
    [3] Cf. *The Meteors*, First Discourse (vi. 239): 'Know also that, to maintain the peace with the philosophers, I do not at all wish to deny what they imagine in bodies over and above what I have claimed, such as their substantial forms, their real qualities, and similar things; for it seems to me that my explanations ought to be approved so much more readily in so far as I make them depend on fewer things.' See also Descartes to Mersenne (28 Jan. 1641), in which Descartes claims to have included all the foundations of his physics in the *Meditations*, but asks his correspondent not to mention this fact to supporters of Aristotle. Instead he hopes that readers may become accustomed to Cartesian principles and recognize their truth 'before noticing that they destroy the principles of Aristotle' (iii. 298).

exception made for the human mind or soul by Boyle (1999–2000: v. 300): 'When ever I shall speake indefinitely of Substantial forms, I would always be understood to except the Reasonable Soule, that is said to inform the humane Body; which Declaration I here desire may be taken notice of, once for all.'[4] I return to the justifiability and implications of this exception below.

The second reason for excluding substantial forms from explanations of natural phenomena is that they are obscure realities that are poorly understood even by their proponents, and are so specifically tailor-made or ad hoc that they provide a facile pseudo-explanation of every conceivable phenomenon without making any progress in genuine understanding.

proponents [of substantial forms] admit that they are occult and that they do not understand them. If they say that some action results from a substantial form, that is the same as saying that it results from something that they do not understand; which explains nothing. . . . In order to provide explanations easily of everything (if indeed an explanation of anything is provided when what is obscure is explained by what is more obscure), they have invented substantial forms and real qualities; in this enterprise their ignorance is not at all learned, but ought to be described instead as vain and pedantic. (iii. 506, 507)[5]

The core of this objection was not simply that the terms used by the scholastics appeared obscure to others who worked outside that philosophical tradition; that type of objection could be made by an unsympathetic critic of any theory. The objection was much more fundamental: that one cannot *explain* any phenomenon merely by attributing a quality or form to it which is named after the effect to be explained.[6] Otherwise, we could equally well 'explain' why houses

---

[4] Cf. Boyle 1999–2000: v. 340: 'But the summe of the Controversy betwixt Us and the Schools is this, whether or no the Forms of Natural things, (the Souls of Men always excepted) be in Generation educed, as they speak, *out of the power of the Matter*, and whether these Forms be true *substantial Entities*, distinct from the other substantial Principle of Natural Bodies, namely Matter.'

[5] Cf. Letter to Father Dinet (vii. 592), and *A Description of the Human Body* (xi. 243; W. 181): 'Now supposing that the heart moves in the way that Harvey describes, not only must we imagine some faculty which causes the movement, the nature of which is much more difficult to conceive than what it is invoked to explain; we must also suppose the existence of yet other faculties that alter the qualities of the blood while it is in the heart.'

[6] Cf. Locke (1975: II. xxi. 20) for the same objection to attributing faculties to either the mind or the body. 'But the fault has been, that Faculties have been spoken of, and represented, as so many distinct Agents. For it being asked, what it was that digested the meat in our Stomachs? It was a ready, and very satisfactory Answer, to say, That it was the *digestive Faculty*. What was it that made any thing come out of the Body? The *expulsive Faculty*. What moved? the *motive Faculty*: And so in the Mind, the *intellectual Faculty*, or the Understanding, understood; and the *elective Faculty*, or the will, willed or commanded . . . Which ways of speaking, when put into more intelligible Words, will, I think, amount to thus much: That Digestion is performed by something that is able to digest; Motion by something able to move; and Understanding by something able to understand. And in truth it would be very strange, if it should be otherwise; as strange as it would be for a Man to be free without being able to be free.'

with structural defects collapse simply by saying that they have a 'collapsing form', or why successful therapies cure people by saying that they have a 'therapeutic form'. In the caricature borrowed from Cartesian philosophy and made famous by Molière, we would explain why sleeping pills have their desired effect by saying that they have a 'dormitive power'.[7] Thus forms and qualities are obscure entities that are equally in need of explanation as the phenomena they are designed to explain.

Malebranche suggested that the willingness of scholastics to endorse 'occult qualities or imaginary faculties' was due to a lack of confidence in their powers of observation and a failure to understand the need to hypothesize unobservable causes. When natural philosophers fail to see, by the unaided eye, the unobservable particles that, according to Malebranche, are the real causes of natural phenomena, they tend to have recourse to faculties and powers that explain nothing: 'They resort to qualities in the moon, rather than to the pressure of the air surrounding the earth in order to explain the tides, and to forces of attraction in the sun, rather than to the impulses caused by the particles of subtle matter it continuously diffuses, in order to explain the rising of vapours' (Malebranche 1997: 30). Here the Oratorian's objection assumes the viability of some kind of corpuscular theory, and contrasts its superior explanatory resourcefulness with the alleged deficiencies of the scholastic alternative. However, the central Cartesian objection could have been expressed just as easily without seeming to beg the question of which theoretical framework is most likely to succeed. Even if the new corpuscular philosophy were to fail completely, there could be no justification for reverting to scholastic explanations in terms of real qualities and substantial forms.[8]

It is clear that 'occult', in this context, does not mean simply 'hidden' or 'unobservable'. Neither Descartes nor other corpuscularians of the seventeenth century objected to postulating the existence of extremely small parts of matter that, because of their size, were unobservable and therefore hidden or occult. The theoretical entities of the scholastic tradition were rejected as occult in a very different sense. From the perspective of their critics, they were not too small to be observable, but too obscure to be intelligible.

Finally, Descartes argues that, even if one granted the existence of what scholastics called real qualities and substantial forms, one would still not under-

---

[7] In the closing scene of *Le Malade imaginaire*, Doctor Bachelierus explains how opium makes one fall asleep by saying that it has a 'virtus dormitiva, cujus est natura sensus assoupire' (Molière 1971: ii. 1173).

[8] Rozemond (1998: 116) suggests that 'the rejection of real qualities and substantial forms depends significantly on the virtues of Descartes's mechanistic explanations'. I argue that the objections to scholastic explanations were independently valid.

stand how such entities interact with other features of physical bodies that we can understand unproblematically, such as their size, shape, or motion.

However, we cannot in any way understand how something that is completely different from them in nature is produced by these same things (namely, by size, shape, and motion), such as those substantial forms and real qualities that many people assume in things; nor how subsequently these same qualities or forms would be able to cause local motion in other bodies.   (viii-1. 322)

This conceptual or explanatory chasm between substantial forms and the kind of qualities that are described and explained in Cartesian natural philosophy—such as the size or motion of bodies—does not diminish over time, nor does it lose its significance when the explanandum in question is mind–body interaction.

Thus Descartes's consistent attitude throughout his mature philosophy was to object to the explanatory framework to which many scholastic philosophers of the period appealed. Granted, the objection was articulated from the perspective of an alternative explanatory framework, one in which only parts of matter and a very limited number of their properties were admitted. The explanatory superiority of the latter and the obviousness of its appeal were so taken for granted that, towards the conclusion of the seventeenth century, one finds John Locke giving an otherwise surprising answer to a question about how external objects cause ideas in the human mind: 'The next thing to be consider'd, is how bodies produce Ideas in us.' He answers: 'manifestly by impulse, the only way which we can conceive bodies operate in' (Locke 1975: II. viii. 11). This attitude to the very conceivability of the ways in which material bodies interact was matched by correspondingly exaggerated claims, on the part of proponents, about the degree of success already achieved by the new corpuscular philosophy. The rhetoric of success camouflaged the need to engage in a genuine evaluation of the limited progress in scientific explanation that had been made to date, and especially of the possible need to expand the range of variables required for a successful scientific research programme. In this respect, Descartes shared the unwarranted confidence of his contemporaries in the new sciences and in the fruitfulness of the conceptual framework within which they were developed.

However, even if all these qualifications are conceded, the fundamental objection to scholastic explanations remains valid. This objection hinges on the minimal value of appealing to forms and qualities when what is needed is an explanation of some phenomenon. What was at issue at this juncture was the concept of explanation itself.

STRUCTURAL EXPLANATION

Cartesian natural philosophy represented a fundamental challenge to the assumption that any phenomenon is explained by inventing a corresponding quality or form. The task of articulating what precisely was defective about scholastic explanations was almost overlooked in the unanimity with which they were rejected. Boyle, for example, takes on this task by appealing to an implicit standard of *structural* explanation.

to explicate a phenomenon, it is not enough to ascribe it to one general efficient [cause], but we must intelligibly show the particular manner how that general cause produces the proposed effect. He must be a very dull inquirer who, demanding an account of the phenomena of the watch, shall rest satisfied with being told that it is an engine made by a watchmaker, though nothing be thereby declared of the structure and coaptation of the spring, wheels, balance and other parts of the engine, and the manner how they act on one another, so as to co-operate to make the needle point out the true hour of the day. (Boyle 1996: 150)

The effectiveness of this objection depends, to some extent, on how little the listener or reader already knows about watchmakers. If all they know is that the word 'watchmaker' means 'someone who makes watches', then the emptiness of the proposed account is doubly debilitating. It tells us nothing about (1) the specific skills of a watchmaker, or about (2) how the various parts of a watch work together to move the hands. In an obvious way, it merely names the relevant cause as 'the kind of cause that can give rise to the effect to be explained', without telling us anything about either the cause itself or how it works.

Boyle's reference to a watchmaker makes explicit a central assumption of Cartesian explanation, in contrast with the deductive–nomological model of explanation that has been widely discussed in philosophy of science in the twentieth century. According to that model, the occurrence of a particular event or phenomenon is explained by deducing a description of a single event from a universal law and relevant descriptions of initial conditions. Thus a phenomenon is said to be explained simply by showing how it is a particular instance of a more general pattern in nature. One is hesitant to claim that such an account has absolutely no explanatory power, but its limits are evident. There is little progress made in explaining why a piece of metal conducts electricity if we are told simply that all pieces of copper conduct electricity (and that this metal is copper). In fact, the explanatory limitations involved here are very similar to those to which Cartesians objected.[9]

---

[9] The contrast between Cartesian and deductive-nomological explanations is made explicitly by Baker and Morris (1996: 149 ff.).

In the rush to expose the vacuity of explanations in terms of forms and, in the case of natural phenomena, to substitute structural explanations, even Cartesians had to acknowledge that there might be a limited role for an appeal to fundamental dispositional qualities whose description involves the kind of circularity that had been alleged against forms. Antoine Arnauld, who, in this respect at least, was an orthodox Cartesian, assumed the task of articulating when forms or qualities were acceptable, and when they were not. In *On True and False Ideas* (1683), he distinguished between their correct and incorrect usage.

But why do the Cartesian gentlemen have such an aversion to the general terms 'nature' and 'faculty' when the Peripatetics use them? . . . these are words which can be used correctly or incorrectly. The word 'faculty' is used incorrectly when one understands by it something distinct from the thing to which one attributes the faculty . . . when one claims to have given an explanation of an effect that is known . . . as when one says that the magnet attracts iron because it has this faculty . . . the abuse of the word consists principally in this: before knowing what is involved in iron being attracted to a magnet . . . one is satisfied with saying that the magnet [has an attractive force].   (Arnauld 1990: 153)

The objection to such ad-hoc forms was that they involved a premature short-circuiting of the work required to construct an explanation. Without knowing or even guessing the cause of a given phenomenon, one says simply that it has the kind of form that can cause the effect in question. This is trivially true rather than false, and if the triviality of the claim were recognized there could be little objection to it apart from the waste of time involved. But many proponents of forms and qualities seem to have thought of them as real entities of some kind that were distinct from the phenomenon to be explained.[10]

Isaac Newton argued, for similar reasons, against what he described as occult qualities while recognizing their limited role in scientific explanation. In Query 31, at the conclusion of the *Opticks*, Newton was anxious to distinguish the mathematical and experimental character of his own work from what he took to be the unsubstantiated speculation of the Cartesian tradition. In particular, he wished to explain that inertial force and 'certain active principles, such as is that of Gravity', were not occult in any objectionable sense of the term.

Such occult Qualities put a stop to the Improvement of natural Philosophy, and therefore of late Years have been rejected. To tell us that every Species of Things is endow'd

---

[10] A similar analysis is offered by Boyle (1996: 32–3). He had no objection, he said, to using the phrase 'concocting faculty' if it were used 'compendiously [to] express several things together by one name' (namely, all the bodily functions involved in eating and digesting food), on condition that it did not imply the existence of a distinct 'real existent being'.

with an occult specifick Quality by which it acts and produces manifest Effects, is to tell us nothing: But to derive two or three general principles of Motion from Phaenomena, and afterwards to tell us how the Properties and Actions of all corporeal Things follow from those manifest Principles, would be a very great step in Philosophy, though the Causes of those Principles were not yet discover'd.   (Newton 1952: 401–2)

The accuracy or otherwise of Newton's description of his own scientific method is a complicated issue that need not be pursued here. But one part of his objection in the *Opticks* is clear enough. To explain every specific natural phenomenon in terms of a form that is tailor-made for that particular case is to make no progress in explanation, 'to tell us nothing'.[11] In contrast, he argues, it is acceptable to identify a range of phenomena that may be explained by reference to a single force or active principle, even if the nature of that active principle remains unexplained. That would represent some progress in explanation in the following sense: we would have discovered that a single principle or force is active in a number of disparate phenomena, even if the principle in question is described in terms of the phenomena to be explained. At the same time, one might also anticipate that, in time, the provisionally adopted principle would be further explained.

Arnauld suggests that forms or faculties may have a legitimate if limited use in natural philosophy, similar to Newton's defence of what he called 'principles', but only a provisional function:

But if, after having explained, as Descartes does . . . what the attraction of iron by a magnet is and what the magnet contributes to it, one then asked how it comes about that . . . the magnet has screw-shaped pores, then it would be perfectly acceptable to reply by saying that it is because such is the nature of the bodies that we call . . . magnets . . . if one asks in general terms why matter is able to move, it is perfectly proper to reply by saying that this is its nature, and that God, in creating it, has given to its parts this faculty by which one of them can be moved closer to, or further from, another.   (Arnauld 1990: 153–4)

In other words, an appeal to forms or qualities signals an impasse, more or less temporary, in constructing an explanation. In the case of Newton, he assumed that he could eventually discover more fundamental theoretical entities than the forces to which he appealed in the *Principia* and *Opticks*.[12] In the case of

---

[11]   This central objection is also found, for example, in Newton's unpublished manuscripts: 'what certainty can there be in a Philosophy which consists in as many Hypotheses as there are Phaenomena to be explained' (quoted in Westfall 1980: 643).

[12]   Newton's various hypotheses about what those principles might be, and whether they would ultimately be mechanical, spiritual in some sense, or discovered from his researches into alchemy, were the object of his continued research over a long time. See McGuire (1968), McMullin (1978b), and Westfall (1980: 298–307, 638–48).

Arnauld, he wished to acknowledge that our explanations must come to a stop at some point and, wherever that is, it is not objectionable to say that phenomena occur as they do because of some ultimate dispositions in matter. It may be that these dispositions, in turn, are identifiable only by reference to the observable properties that they cause, and in this respect they exhibit a circularity that resembles scholastic explanations.

Thus there is no absolute ban among natural philosophers of the seventeenth century on an appeal to ultimate features or dispositions of matter, even if such qualities are described in terms of the effects that they explain. However, this solution cannot be adopted, on a case-by-case basis, for every specific phenomenon for which an explanation is sought. Likewise an appeal to 'nature' may legitimately signal the limit—or the limits to date—of an explanatory programme, but one cannot explain every specific natural phenomenon simply by a reference to its nature. If these qualifications are not observed, one's explanations in terms of occult faculties, powers, or natures are trivially circular and uninformative.

Another assumption built into the theory of explanation adopted by Cartesians is that, if theoretical entities are introduced, they should be understood at least as well as the phenomenon to be explained. Once this is accepted as a general principle, it is then a contingent matter of fact to determine which realities are understood at a particular point in time, and which are still beyond our comprehension. This requirement applies both to the kind of realities to which one appeals in an explanation, and to the manner in which they act as causes (or as part of a viable explanation) of whatever phenomenon one wishes to explain. The objection to substantial forms and real qualities in this context was that, as theoretical entities, they fail on both counts. Cartesians claimed that they could neither understand what substantial forms were nor, even if their existence were provisionally conceded, how they could be put to work to cause the relevant phenomena.

In contrast, the kinds of theoretical entity that seventeenth-century natural philosophers were willing to endorse were a function of their limited understanding, at that time, of the range of variables required for an adequate natural philosophy. Without being able to stipulate in advance what would be unacceptable, they could offer paradigm examples of what fell unambiguously within the scope of their understanding. For example, Descartes argued that everyone knows that one body in motion can cause another body to move as a result of impact between the two. This does not presuppose any theoretical understanding of the forces involved, or of the mathematical calculations required to quantify the results of a particular impact. It is simply an everyday experience that, when two relatively hard bodies collide, unless one body collapses or disintegrates on impact, they either spring back from each other or continue their motions with a modified speed or direction.[13] Since this is a phenomenon with which we are already familiar from our ordinary experience, we could equally well understand if something like this were to occur at the level of extremely small, unobservable pieces of matter. As Descartes writes in reply to Morin, in 1638: 'In the analogies I use, I compare only some movements with others, or some shapes with others, etc.; that is, I compare those things that because of their small size are not accessible to our senses with those that are, and that do not differ from the former more than a large circle differs from a small one' (iii. 67–8).[14] There is no justification in this argument for claiming that nothing apart from the size, shape, and movements of small parts of matter could possibly be accepted as variables in a theory. However, the way in which the concept of explanation developed during the scientific revolution was constrained by the haunting spectre of regressing to the occult qualities of the scholastic tradition, so that any theoretical entity that was either less familiar or less well understood than the impact of colliding pieces of matter, or that had worrying connotations of occultness, was pre-emptively excluded from consideration as part of a viable theory. The fate of forces in the history of dynamics in this period is sufficiently well documented to illustrate the point. Even 'the incomparable Mr Newton', as Locke described him, was sufficiently concerned about the taint of occultness that he searched for some acceptable explanation of gravitational effects and preferred not to publish his more speculative hypotheses about active principles and the ether.

One of the most immediate consequences of this concept of explanation was a significant reduction in the complexity and sophistication of the concept of matter with which natural philosophers of the seventeenth century worked. The matter included in theories from Descartes to Locke was one that could be described adequately in terms of very few fundamental properties, all of which were familiar to observers from their everyday experience. The relatively meagre explanatory success of this concept of matter was a function of the conceptual limitations adopted by its proponents. It would make no sense to transpose such a concept from the seventeenth century to the twenty-first, and to assume that the term 'matter' had not changed meaning during the very significant developments in scientific theory that have occurred in the intervening cen-

[13]   As is well known, some of Descartes's impact rules seemed to contradict our everyday experience. The only relevant point here is that we know from experience that bodies bounce off each other on impact, whatever the details of the subsequent redistribution of their original motions.

[14]   This suggestion was first made in the *Cogitationes privatae*: 'Human knowledge of natural things is acquired only by analogy with those things that fall within the scope of the senses. Indeed, we consider that the one who has philosophized best is the person who has most successfully assimilated what is sought to what is known by sensation' (x. 218–19).

turies.[15] Therefore, when Descartes speaks about what matter can or cannot do, or what may or may not be explained by reference to the powers of matter, he must be understood as talking about the matter of Cartesian theory, or what might be called *matter_c*

Descartes does not claim that matter_c lacks all active qualities, or that matter_c has no ultimate dispositions by reference to which its phenomenal properties may be explained. The predominant limiting feature of his theory is that such qualities or dispositions of matter may not be thought of as something other than *modes*, and that the relevant dispositions required for explanations in natural philosophy must be modes of a *material object*. Thus he advises Regius:

> However, we do not deny active qualities, but we deny that any degree of reality greater than that of modes should be attributed to them, since that cannot be done without conceiving of them as substances. Nor do we deny dispositions, but we understand them as being of two kinds. Some are purely material, and depend only on the configuration or other arrangement of the parts. Others, however, are immaterial or spiritual, such as the theologians' dispositions of faith, grace, etc., which do not depend on matter, but are spiritual modes that exist in a mind in the same way that motion or shape are corporeal modes that exist in a body.   (iii. 503)

This still leaves open the possibility, as indicated above in the case of Boyle, that there are two distinct types of reality—one 'purely material' and the other 'immaterial or spiritual'—and that explanations in natural philosophy are irrelevant to the task of explaining mental operations such as thinking or remembering. Before considering that option, it may be helpful to clarify what Descartes meant by the term 'real', in the phrase 'real qualities and substantial forms', and to mention his independent reasons for rejecting real qualities.

REAL QUALITIES AND SUBSTANTIAL FORMS

Descartes's concept of explanation was motivated partly, as indicated above, by the models of explanation or intelligibility that he borrowed from everyday experience, and partly by widely shared objections to the vacuity of scholastic explanations. One feature of the latter that attracted independent objections was their appeal to so-called real qualities. As Stephen Menn has shown, Descartes was not claiming that qualities such as the colour or shape of something are unreal, but that they are not 'real' qualities. 'A quality can really belong to something, and be really a quality, without being a real quality' (Menn 1995: 184). The linguistic clue to understanding what was meant by 'real qualities' is

---

[15] Cf. McMullin (1978*b*).

the Latin word *res* (a thing). To ask whether a quality is real is to ask whether it has the status of a thing, and this in turn is equivalent to asking whether a quality could be thought of as existing apart from the reality of which it is predicated. Although this interpretation of real qualities may not have been widespread among scholastics, it was adopted at least by some of them, including Suarez (to whom Descartes often looked as a source of metaphysical concepts). Descartes, therefore, understood 'real qualities' as entities that had the same status as substances or things. It was for this reason, he explains in the Sixth Replies to objections, that he had rejected the scholastic account of heaviness. 'When, for example, I conceived of gravity as if it were a real quality of some kind which inhered in solid bodies, although I called it a "quality", in so far as I attributed it to the bodies in which it inhered, I also added, nevertheless, that it was "real" and thus I was thinking of it as a genuine substance' (vii. 441).[16] The same point is made two years later, in a letter to Mersenne (26 April 1643), where Descartes emphasizes the distinction between denying the reality of motion, which he is not remotely tempted to do, and denying that motion is a real quality of moving bodies.

I do not assume that there are any *real qualities* in nature, which would be added to a substance, like little souls to their bodies, and which could be separated from it by God's power; and thus I do not attribute to motion, or to all the other variations of substance which are called qualities, any more reality than philosophers usually attribute to shape, which they do not call a real quality [*qualitatem realem*] but only a mode [*modum*].   (iii. 648–9)

The motion of a body is just as real as its shape, or as any of the other features that philosophers usually call a mode. But it should not be thought of by analogy with a soul that is added to bodies and would therefore be separable from matter, if only by divine power.

One of the objections to understanding qualities as real is that the concept of a real quality involves a contradiction in terms. 'It is completely contradictory to claim that there are real accidents, because whatever is real can exist apart from any other subject and whatever is capable of existing separately in this way is a substance rather than an accident' (vii. 434). The principal reason, however, for rejecting so-called real qualities was that they are both unintelligible and redundant in the explanation of natural phenomena. Returning to a claim already mentioned above and frequently repeated in the texts, Descartes writes to Mersenne:

---

[16] Cf. Descartes to Elizabeth (21 May 1643): 'various qualities . . . that we imagined as real, that is, as having an existence that is distinct from that of the body and, consequently, as being substances even though we called them mere qualities' (iii. 667).

The principal reason that makes me reject these real qualities is that I do not see that the human mind has any notion in itself or any particular idea with which to conceive of them; thus in naming them and in claiming that they exist, one believes in something that is not conceived and that one does not understand oneself. The second reason is that philosophers have assumed these real qualities only because they believed that they could not otherwise explain all the phenomena of nature; for my part, I find on the contrary that one can explain natural phenomena much better without assuming them. (iii. 649)

The objection to so-called substantial forms is exactly the same, and for this reason the two categories are often linked together in a single phrase as the target of Descartes's objections: 'real qualities and substantial forms'. Accidental forms, however, do not raise comparable difficulties. Scholastic writers used the term 'accidental form' to describe a feature of something that could change without any fundamental change in the thing itself. In this sense, the colour of a door or the weight of a person is said to be an accidental form, and a new coat of paint on the door or a change in someone's weight will not convert the former into a non-door, nor turn the latter into a non-person or a different person. Descartes adverts to such changeable qualities in the discussion of the piece of wax in the Second Meditation. 'It loses what remains of its taste, its smell is lost, the colour changes, it loses its shape, increases in size, becomes a liquid, becomes hot and can barely be touched. Nor does it emit a sound if tapped. But does the same wax remain? It must be agreed that it does; no one denies that, no one thinks otherwise' (vii. 30; M. 27). A piece of wax can present itself to us in 'different modes' without ceasing to be wax, and the traditional Latin term for a non-essential quality, *forma*, was used by Descartes in this context without any ontological commitments that might subsequently embarrass him. If the need arises, he could distinguish the wax itself 'from its external forms [*formis*]' and could think about it 'as if it were bare and without its clothes on'. However, in contrast with such accidental forms, it is impossible to accommodate the language of substantial forms within Cartesian natural philosophy without making ontological commitments that would compromise the coherence of the conceptual framework used.

Descartes understands a substantial form as something that satisfies the conditions necessary for being a substance and therefore, even if joined with something else, would have the status of an independent thing and would be capable of existing without being predicated of something else. In a letter to Regius (January 1642) he makes this explicit: 'Lest there be any ambiguity in terms, it should be noted here that, when we reject substantial forms, the term should be understood as some kind of substance that is joined with matter . . . which is a genuine substance, or something that exists of itself . . .' (iii. 502). Thus substantial forms suffered from a fundamental objection similar to that raised against real qualities: they involved a contradiction of being and not being independent entities in their own right.

Descartes may have other metaphysical reasons for rejecting the traditional scholastic concept of a substantial form. If so, the appropriate place to discuss them is in Chapter 8 below, which reviews his more general reservations about the concept of a substance. For present purposes, it is enough to acknowledge that the Cartesian model of explanation requires that one explain some features of a given phenomenon (the *explanandum*) by reference to other features that are better understood (the *explanans*). This would be impossible if he were to classify some characteristics of a given phenomenon as 'real qualities or substantial forms', because Descartes understood both of these expressions as implying that the features in question are distinct substances. The implications of this insight emerged, even more explicitly, when addressing the conceptual disparity between the mental and the physical.

The extent to which mental phenomena constitute a significant and possibly insurmountable challenge to the Cartesian model of explanation is best approached by degrees. The first step is to consider how Descartes proposed to explain living things. Then, among living things, conscious or thinking beings raise even more challenging difficulties. In the case of living things, Descartes's commitment to structural explanation holds firm. When confronted by conscious experiences, however, one has to ask whether he admits defeat and reverts to ontological dualism, or whether he merely acknowledges the limits, in the 1640s, of the success of his explanatory programme.

EXPLAINING A LIVING BODY

The style of explanation proposed by seventeenth-century corpuscularians was applied to living creatures with a degree of rigour that must have appeared to many contemporaries as unwarranted dogmatism. Descartes was no more unique in this respect than he was in proposing a new concept of explanation. Traditional explanations of living creatures were borrowed from commentaries on Aristotle's *De anima*. According to Aristotle, 'the soul is, so to speak, the first principle of living things' (1986: 402a). While all living things had souls, human beings were thought to have a complex soul that was divisible into three 'parts' or basic functions, the vegetative, the sensitive, and the intellective. Souls, in turn, were understood as special cases of the more general metaphysical category of forms. Therefore those who maintained that forms, substantial or otherwise, and natures were non-explanatory were required to look elsewhere for an alternative account of living things.

Boyle was typical of those who made the direct inference from abandoning forms and qualities to forging a new account of living things. In *A Free Enquiry*, he addressed the plausibility of the traditional argument that the spontaneous response of the human body to 'fever, pleurisies, etc.' is a good reason to believe in the independent efficacy of 'nature'.

In order to this [i.e. to address this objection], I desire it may be kept in mind that I do not only acknowledge, but teach, that the body of a man is an incomparable engine, which the most wise author of things has so skilfully framed for lasting very many years, that if there were in it an intelligible principle of self-preservation (as the naturists suppose there is) things would not in most cases be better or otherwise managed for the conservation of the animal's life than they generally are. So that the question is not, whether there is a great deal of providence and wisdom exercised in the crises of diseases, but upon what account it is that these apposite things are performed.   (Boyle 1996: 92–3)

Many physicians wished to explain the phenomenon of spontaneous life-preserving reactions in our bodies—accepted as a reality by all concerned—by reference to an 'intelligent principle they call nature'. In contrast, Boyle preferred to invoke 'the wisdom and ordinary providence of God, exerting itself by the mechanism, partly of that great machine of the world, and partly of that smaller engine the human body' (Boyle 1996: 93). This might seem initially like a mere dispute about terminology, especially since Boyle had already conceded, earlier in the same text, that animals are 'furnished with faculties or powers and other requisites to enable them to preserve themselves and procure what is necessary for their own welfare' (Boyle 1996: 74). However, such faculties and powers had to be explained without understanding them as distinct theoretical entities, apart from 'what regularly, or what most usually, happens to beings of that species'. In other words, God's providence is the ultimate principle, for Boyle, by reference to which we can understand how bodies are self-preserving. But the detailed explanation of how God's design is implemented must be provided in terms of the chemical and physical mechanisms that are found in animals themselves and in the wider environment in which they survive.[17]

Despite his spirited defence of the 'engine' analogy, Boyle was also anxious to acknowledge its limitations. He was not therefore proposing that the human body is like a watch because it is much more flexible and organic than the term

---

[17] Boyle acknowledges the scruples that readers may have about explaining 'the bodies of animals, though not the rational souls of men' by mechanical laws, but he reminds them that an earlier generation of readers was equally reluctant about rejecting the intelligences that allegedly moved the 'celestial orbs' (Boyle 1996: 98–9).

'engine' might suggest: 'And here I desire to have it taken notice of . . . that I look not on a human body as on a watch or a hand mill—i.e. as a machine made up only of solid or at least consistent parts—but as a hydraulical, or rather hydraulo-pneumatical, engine, that consists not only of solid and stable parts, but of fluids and those in organical motion' (Boyle 1996: 127–8). As usual, Boyle adds a second qualification to the effect that the human body also has a rational mind to guide it.[18] Since this is absent in the case of other animals, the significance of the mechanical model is obvious, and its disanalogies with the *explanandum* are accepted. In summary, Boyle's machine analogy is a methodological proposal to the effect that we should try to construct explanations of living things without postulating souls in them, because such explanations are vacuous.

Cartesians were equally enamoured of animal machines for the same methodological reasons. The best way to understand their reliance on a machine analogy is from the perspective of a theory of explanation. From this perspective, the negative motivation for proposing that model is clearer than its positive content. Fundamentally, the analogy between living bodies and machines represented a rejection of animal souls as non-explanatory, rather than a limitation imposed a priori on the content of explanations in biology or embryology to what is analogous to clocks. Thus the project outlined in Descartes's early works, including the posthumously published *World*, included a programmatic statement of how to construct an explanation of the human body. As is well known, Descartes borrowed the theoretical model used in *A Treatise on Man* from machines that had been developed in the sixteenth and seventeenth centuries and had aroused expressions of wonder in observers. He refers, for example, to the hydraulically activated machines in the royal gardens at Saint-Germain-en-Laye: 'Similarly, you may have observed in the grottoes and fountains in the royal gardens that the force that drives the water from its source is all that is needed to move various machines, and even to make them play certain instruments or pronounce certain words, depending on the particular arrangements of the pipes through which the water is conducted' (xi. 130; W. 107). As visitors walk through the gardens they may unwittingly trigger a reaction in one or more of the statues, directly as a result of the sensitivity of the statues to objects in their environment. 'For they cannot enter without stepping on certain tiles which are arranged in such a way that, for example, if they approach a Diana bathing they will cause her to hide in the reeds, and if they

---

[18]   Boyle also relied on the metaphor of a pilot in a ship, in the case of human bodies: 'a man is not like a watch or an empty boat . . . but like a manned boat, where, besides the machinal part (if I may so speak), there is an intelligent being that takes care of it, and both steers it or otherwise guides it . . .' (1996: 135). I discuss Descartes's use of this metaphor in Chapter 5.

move forward to pursue her they will cause a Neptune to advance and threaten them with his trident . . . and other such things depending on the whim of the engineers who constructed them' (xi. 131; W. 107). In *A Treatise on Man*, Descartes proposed that non-human animals be explained as complex biological machines, with the qualification that they are vastly more complex than human artefacts such as clocks, because they were created by God: 'as I am supposing that this machine is made by God, I think you will agree that it is capable of a greater variety of movements than I could possibly imagine in it, and that it exhibits a greater ingenuity than I could possibly ascribe to it' (xi. 120; W. 99). In making the machine of the body, God provides it with 'all the parts needed to make it walk, eat, breathe, and imitate all those functions we have which can be imagined to proceed from matter and to depend solely on the disposition of the organs' (xi. 120; W. 99).

One could read this as a radically misconceived proposal that disingenuously omits from its list of explananda precisely those features of genuine, living animals that are most difficult to explain, such as their sensations, memories, and so on.[19] That would amount to reducing the complexity of the explanandum to the conceptual limitations of one's explanatory model. But the way in which Descartes develops the suggestion implies something quite different. The project is motivated, not by a priori limits on the kinds of theoretical entities that it may include, but by a rejection of the scholastic style of explanation that it is designed to replace. The Cartesian approach to explaining living creatures depends on the same principle of ontological parsimony that excluded forms and qualities, and on the same ideal of explanation that implied their redundancy. In this context, the methodological proposal was to omit all souls in so far as they are neither necessary nor useful in constructing a genuine explanation, and to push to its limits the resourcefulness of the new model of structural explanation. The extent to which this project was successful can be decided only by subsequent historical developments both in scientific theory and in empirical methodology. Whatever the degree of success achieved at any particular time, it was a firm conviction of the Cartesian view that one should never revert to vacuous explanations in terms of souls.

Why then does Descartes do precisely this when he discusses the powers and faculties usually associated with the human mind? Hobbes articulates this challenge sharply, in his Objections to the *Meditations*: 'If Descartes were to show

---

[19] The assumed necessary link between 'life' and 'soul' has led some commentators to describe Cartesian animal-machines as not being alive. See Des Chene (2000: 12): 'Descartes's animal-machine, perhaps the most influential image of the living in the new science, has no life.' A similar claim is made in the introduction to Des Chene (2001: 2–3): 'The science of life is henceforward to be, not the science of a special part of nature consisting in those things that live, and that therefore have souls, but an extension of physics.'

that the agent who understands is identical with the understanding, we would return to the scholastic way of speaking: the understanding understands, vision sees, the will wills, and, according to the best analogy, walking—or at least the faculty of walking—walks' (vii. 177). Even if one prescinds from Hobbes's commitment to materialism, this point is well taken. What progress in explanation or understanding of the relevant phenomena is made by attributing to human beings various faculties, such as the understanding and the will, that are described precisely and exclusively as powers to perform the kind of actions that require an explanation?

It is appropriate to recall that one of Descartes's objections to the use of forms and qualities in natural philosophy was that they were introduced as soul-like or spiritual realities in a context where something physical or material was needed and that, once introduced, it seemed impossible to explain how they could interact with the kinds of physical properties for which they were intended as an explanation. Some commentators have assumed that this objection is irrelevant to constructing a theory of mind, on the assumption that the mind is spiritual.[20] That misses the point, however, about the alleged inconceivability of a link between the mental and the physical. Descartes was correctly concerned about the viability of any explanation that relies on theoretical entities for the interaction of which we lack any model or even an elementary understanding. However, the more fundamental objection to forms and qualities was that they were non-explanatory, and this objection remains valid even when explaining mental phenomena.[21] Descartes implicitly acknowledges this in the *Meditations*, in a context where he describes our thinking and our decision making as resulting from two distinct faculties or powers, the intellect and the will. But even here he was mindful of Occam's razor. Although human beings characteristically make mistakes, one could not explain this reality by reference to a 'mistake-making faculty [*facultas ad errandum*]' (vii. 54).

Thus there is a general, principled objection to invoking faculties or powers in order to explain anything, and there is a further specific objection that we do

---

[20] Paul Hoffman (1986: 350) argues that one of Descartes's principal reasons for rejecting substantial forms and real qualities is that such explanations are anthropomorphic: 'Obviously, this objection that explanations appealing to substantial forms are anthropomorphic does not apply to an explanation which takes the human soul to be a substantial form.' M. Rozemond (1998: 152) also argues that the charge of anthropomorphism 'obviously does not apply to the human soul'.

[21] Paul Hoffman (1986: 351) argues that the soul or mind is not a theoretical entity at all. 'The human soul, in contrast, is not a mere theoretical entity. That he exists and that he is a thinking thing are the first two propositions Descartes claims to know with certainty in the *Second Meditation*.' Evidently, the fact that Descartes exists and thinks does not imply that he is equally certain about having an immaterial mind. Unless the term 'mind' merely redescribes the reality it is intended to explain, it must be treated as a theoretical entity that is introduced to explain those features of our experience about which even Descartes expressed no doubts, such as the fact that we think.

not understand how such faculties, if conceived as real entities of some kind, could interact with well-known features of bodies, such as their size, shape, and so on. The question, then, is whether a theory of mind is a general exception to these fundamental objections, or whether the admission of a human mind, as a spiritual substantial form, exemplifies all the objections outlined earlier in this chapter. Descartes confronts this issue most explicitly in his correspondence with Princess Elizabeth in the 1640s.

EXPLAINING BODY–MIND INTERACTION

When Descartes published the first two editions of *Meditations* in 1641 and 1642 (which included the lengthy sets of objections and replies), the titles included clear references to the immortality of the human soul or its distinction from the body, the implications of which were not lost on his readers. Among the first to challenge explicitly whether this new way of talking about the mind and the body could provide an explanation of our mental experiences was Princess Elizabeth of Bohemia. Her correspondence with Descartes provided confirmation of the problems that arise when one deviates from the criteria for what counts as a viable explanation and reverts to the discredited language of the schools. Elizabeth's first attempt to clarify the issue (16 May 1643) was expressed as follows:

How can the human soul, which is only a thinking substance, determine the movement of the animal spirits in order to perform a voluntary action?[22] It seems as if every determination of movement results from the following three factors: the pushing of the thing that is moved, the manner in which it is pushed by the body that moves it, and the quality and shape of the latter's surface. The first two presuppose that the bodies touch, while the third presupposes extension. You exclude extension completely from your concept of the soul and, it seems to me, it is incompatible with being an immaterial thing. That is why I am asking for a more specific definition of the soul than what is provided in your *Metaphysics*, that is, of the substance of the soul when it is separated from its action of thinking.   (iii. 661; M. 148)

Descartes's reply relies on a claim that we have a limited number of fundamental concepts by reference to which we can explain successfully phenomena of different categories. He suggests (21 May 1643) that there are two different features of the soul that require explanation: 'one is that it thinks and the other is that, since it is united with the body, it can act and be acted on in conjunction

---

[22] The term 'determine' is a technical term in Cartesian physics, which refers to modifying the direction and velocity of a moving body.

with the body' (iii. 664; M. 148). His excuse for failing to address the second question in the *Meditations* was that it was less relevant to his primary objective in that book—namely, to demonstrate the immortality of the soul. But, once his royal correspondent had raised the question of mind–body interaction, Descartes accepts the challenge. It is in this context that he offers a threefold classification of explanatory categories, or what he calls 'primitive notions':

I think that there are certain primitive notions in us which are like originals, on the model of which we construct all our other knowledge. There are very few such notions. For apart from the most general notions of being, number, duration, etc. which apply to everything that we can conceive, we have only the notion of extension that is specifically for the body, and from that follow the notions of shape and movement; and for the soul on its own we have only the concept of thought, which includes perceptions of the understanding and inclinations of the will. Finally, for the soul and body together, we have only the concept of their union, on which depends the notion of the soul's power to move the body and the body's power to act on the soul by causing its sensations and passions. (iii. 665; M. 149)

It is not clear what Descartes meant by this claim.[23] One implication, made explicit by Descartes himself, is that the clusters of concepts that depend on these primitive notions do not overlap and that it is impossible to explain one primitive notion in terms of another. No argument is offered on this occasion to support that claim; the kind of argument assumed will be considered in Chapter 9. It follows that it would be a mistake to attempt to explain any phenomenon by applying an inappropriate set of concepts, and it would be equally misguided to attempt to explain one primitive notion in terms of another. 'For if we try to resolve a particular difficulty by using some notion that does not apply to it, we cannot fail to go wrong. The same thing happens if we try to explain one of these notions by reference to another; since they are primitive notions, each of them can be understood only through itself' (iii. 665–6; M. 149). When applied to the mind–body problem, this implies that we have different primitive notions available for thinking of the soul on its own, and for thinking of it as united and interacting with a body. Descartes illustrates his point by referring back to a reply to one of the Sixth Objections. We are pre-theoretically aware of the fact that the soul can move the body, and we also know from experience that heavy

---

[23] For an alternative reading, see Garber (2001: 168–88). Garber argues 'that Descartes is just not *entitled* to the answer he gives Elizabeth' (2001: 169). Since God is involved as the ultimate cause of the agency of occasional causes, the explanation of all motion in Cartesian physics presupposes the intelligibility of the interaction of God (a pure spirit) with matter. Thus mind–body causal connections, rather than the concept of extension, provide the primitive notion for understanding all motion, and Descartes therefore gave Elizabeth the wrong answer to her question by assuming that body–body causal relations are intelligible and that mind–body connections are problematic. I prefer to read Descartes as if he understood the conceptual foundations of his physics, and that we should reject Garber's interpretation rather than Descartes's.

bodies move towards the centre of the earth. If we were to think of the motion of heavy bodies as being caused by some kind of soul in each heavy body, that would amount to applying the wrong primitive notion. It would mean applying mental concepts to something that is extended and that should be explained, however it is done, by appeal to the concept of extension and to other concepts that are compatible with that basic concept.[24]

Elizabeth was not convinced by Descartes's initial response. She rephrased her original objection (20 June 1643) by confessing that 'it would be easier for me to attribute matter and extension to the soul than to attribute the ability to move a body, and to be moved by a body, to an immaterial being' (iii. 685; M. 151). Evidently, the mechanism by which two entities can interact, when they have as little in common as the mind and the body, remained as unintelligible to her as it had been earlier. Descartes tries once more to address the underlying issue in his reply. He concedes that one might wish to conceive of the soul as material, 'which is, strictly speaking, to conceive of its union with the body', but even in that case the problem remains once we acknowledge that it is separable from the body. The new factor in this letter (28 June 1643) is that we not only have three distinct primitive notions, but that they are acquired in different ways. Their distinct origins help to explain the fact that there is no overlap in the phenomena to which they may legitimately be applied.

the soul is conceivable only by pure understanding; the body, that is extension, shapes and movements, may also be conceived by pure understanding on its own, but it can be conceived much better by the understanding assisted by the imagination; and finally, things that pertain to the union of the soul and body are known only obscurely by the understanding on its own or even by the understanding assisted by the imagination, but they are known very clearly by the senses.   (iii. 691–2; M. 152)

Descartes draws the conclusion that people who never philosophize and who use only their senses 'have no doubt that the soul moves the body and the body acts on the soul'. However, they also think that body and soul are one and the same thing; 'in other words, they conceive of their union. For to conceive of the union of two things is to conceive of them as one thing' (iii. 692; M. 152). This might seem like a misguided concession by Descartes simply to appease an importunate royal correspondent who could not easily be ignored or dismissed. But Descartes goes on to explain that metaphysical thoughts are likely to mislead us when we conceive of the unity of the human being, and they may be responsible for obfuscating rather than clarifying 'the notion we have of the union of mind and body'. The reason is that we find it difficult to conceive 'very

---

[24] The conceptual confusion involved in the analogy between gravity and the soul's power to move the body is found in vii. 442, and Descartes to Elizabeth (21 May 1643) (iii. 667).

distinctly, and simultaneously, both the distinction and union of body and soul'. In other words, we find it difficult to conceive of mind and body as a single reality and at the same time to conceive of them as two distinct realities, 'which is self-contradictory' (iii. 693; M. 153).

It remains to be seen, in subsequent chapters, whether this correspondence with Elizabeth can be combined with Descartes's model of explanation to provide a coherent theory of the human mind. The most familiar interpretation of these letters is that they represent an honest recognition of the consequences of ontological dualism. However, they may also be read as a discussion of what happens when Cartesian science reaches the limits of its explanatory success and acknowledges that it cannot provide, in the 1640s, a unified theory of mental powers in terms of properties that are described as material (in the Cartesian sense of that term).

CONCLUSION

The interim conclusion from this chapter is that Descartes's project in natural philosophy is motivated primarily by his concept of explanation and, in particular, by his systematic critique of the widely established style of explanation that was prevalent in the schools. The principal claims made in this context were: (1) we can explain some phenomenon only by reference to something else that is already adequately understood; (2) it is not an explanation at all to postulate a specific 'form' or 'faculty' for every phenomenon that needs to be explained; (3) when constructing an explanation, we must not postulate more theoretical entities than are strictly necessary (Occam's razor); (4) there is no objection to postulating the existence of unobservable theoretical entities, on condition that they are described by analogy with well-known properties of macroscopic bodies; (5) the explanation of any phenomenon must be developed by relying on a set of concepts that are relevant to that type of phenomenon (though the implications of this vague rule remain to be made explicit); and (6) the explanation of all natural phenomena must ultimately come to a stop somewhere and there is no alternative, at that stage, but to appeal to fundamental dispositions of matter that are described in terms of the relevant *explananda*.

Neither Descartes nor his contemporaries can establish the first condition in an atemporal manner, as if what we can understand were completely independent of the current state of our best theories. However, this condition constitutes a standing challenge to anyone who wishes to introduce new theoretical entities: to explain what they mean by them and, especially, to explain how the adoption of such entities would contribute to an improved understanding of some phenomenon. Thus, without being committed uncritically to the fruitfulness of corpuscular theories, Cartesian objections to real qualities and substantial forms remain valid. Such occult entities failed the most basic requirements of a good explanation because they were not adequately understood, were redundant, and were fundamentally non-explanatory. There is a real sense in which these objections represent a watershed in the history of ideas; there could be no going back to substantial forms, faculties, natures, or their equivalent in a genuine explanation of any phenomenon, including the human mind.

Descartes also accepted that any explanation must come to at least a temporary end at some point, at which one simply specifies those fundamental features of some reality that must be postulated in order to explain its manifest appearances. If this point is to avoid being premature or arbitrary, one needs some account of why one's explanatory progress happens to stop there rather than elsewhere. Descartes's correspondence with Princess Elizabeth presupposes, rather than explains, one of the points at which explanations of natural phenomena encounter a conceptual impasse. It remains to be seen whether he can provide a reason for this without relying on a metaphysics that is either discredited or unsupported by independent arguments.

One option available to Cartesian natural philosophy is to accept the limits of its chosen model of explanation by linking 'mechanical explanation' and 'material bodies' together, and then to face with an open mind the implications for what were generally classified as immaterial realities. Much would depend, at this juncture, on what Descartes wishes to claim about what is described as 'immaterial'. He could adopt Boyle's suggestion, in the *Christian Virtuoso* (Part 2), that 'immaterial' is a name not for another kind of reality that we know, but for something that (by definition or otherwise) we do *not* know or that we know very inadequately.

For though superficial considerers take up with the vulgar definition, that *a spirit is an immaterial substance*, yet that leaves us exceedingly to seek, if we aim at satisfaction in particular inquiries. For it declares rather what the thing *is not*, than what *it is*; and is as little instructive a definition, as it would be to say, that *a curve line is not a strait one*, which sure will never teach us what is an ellipsis, a parabola, an hyperbola, a circle, or a spiral line, etc.   (Boyle 1999–2000: xii. 474)[25]

This suggestion, if carried further (as it is by Hobbes), would result in an explicit denial that we know what we are talking about when we speak of immaterial

---

[25] Boyle illustrates his point by reversing the definition in favour of immaterial substances. If one knew only that 'a body is an unspiritual substance', one would know little about 'the distinct and particular natures of the sun, or a cloud, or of the stars, elements, minerals, plants, animals' (Boyle 1999–2000: xii. 475).

substances.[26] But one could also stop short of this conclusion and claim that, while we have some knowledge of material things and have a promising model for explaining them, our knowledge of what is immaterial is either too indirect or limited to provide an appropriate foothold for applying the same model of explanation. Kenelm Digby, who, like Descartes, set himself the task of establishing the immortality of the human soul, adopted this solution.

Digby published his *Two Treatises* in the same year as Descartes's *Principia* (that is, in 1644). In the *Treatise of Mans Soule*, Digby argues: 'Here we have passed the Rubicon of experimentall knowledge: we are now out of the boundes that experience hath any iurisdiction over: and from henceforth, we must in all our searches and conclusions rely only upon the single evidence of Reason' (1644: 415–16). Digby argues that everything material, including the motions and sensations of animals, falls in principle within the scope of mechanical explanation.[27] When one reaches the limits of explanation, one could invoke forms as place-holders for various features of a material body that one hopes to specify subsequently. Scholastic philosophers, however, misunderstood the function of forms and thought of them as entities that are distinct from the realities to be explained and comparable to immaterial souls.

But later Philosophers, being very disputative, and desiring to seeme ignorant of nothing (or rather, to seeme to know more than any that are gone before them and to refine their conceptions) have taken the notions, which by our first Masters were sett for common and confused explications of the natures, (to serve for conveniency and succinctenesse of discourse) to be truly and really particular Entities, of thinges of themselves . . . for in truth, they turne all bodies into spirits, making (for example) heate, or cold, to be of it selfe indivisible, a thing by it selfe, whose nature is not conceivable; not the disposition or proportion of the partes of that body which is said to be hoat or cold, but a reall thing, that hath a proper Being and nature peculiar to it selfe; whereof they can render you no account.   (Digby 1644: 351–2)

The damaging consequence of this strategy was that they collapsed the distinction between bodies and spirits by conflating the distinction between our ways of knowing them. For Digby, the introduction of faculties and powers is appropriate once we go beyond material things and attempt to know something about what is non-material.

For wee having very slender knowledge of spirituall substances, can reach no further into their nature, then to know that they have certaine powers, or qualities; but can

---

[26] Hobbes (1991: 34): 'And therefore if a man should talk to me of . . . *Immateriall Substances* . . . I should not say he were in an Errour; but that his words were without meaning; that is to say. Absurd.'

[27] Digby (1644: 366): 'all the actions of sensible bodies may be reduced to locall motion, and to materiall action of one body unto another (in a like manner (though in a different degree) as the motion which we see in liveliest bodies.'

seldome penetrate so deepe, as to descend to the particulars of such Qualities, or Powers. Now our moderne Philosophers have introduced such a course of learning into the schooles, that unto all questions concerning the proper natures of bodies, and their operations, it is held sufficient to answere, they have a quality, or a power to doe such a thing. And afterward they dispute whether this Quality or Power, be an Entity distinct from its subiect, or no; and how it is seperable, or unseperable from it, and the like. (Digby 1644: preface)

Digby's concern is that if some feature of material bodies is explained by reference to a 'qualitie occult, specificall, or incomprehensible', and if these occult qualities turn out to be nothing more than features of material bodies that were misunderstood or poorly named, the mental properties from which he concludes the immateriality of the soul may be likewise explained by 'a corporeal occult quality'. In a word, the viability of any argument for the immateriality of the soul presupposes agreement about a significant distinction between (1) our knowledge of material things and their properties, and (2) our ignorance about what is classified as immaterial. It follows that the strategy that is inexcusable in the case of material bodies, including animals—namely, the introduction of occult powers—may be appropriate in the case of the immaterial, because of the indirectness of our knowledge of the latter and the lack of empirical information to support our reasoning.

Of course this move merely defers the problem of explaining the 'immaterial' unless it is supported by supplementary reasons. It suggests that we construct genuine explanations of what is material and that we offer only provisional explanations of what is immaterial.[28] There are two ways in which Descartes could justifiably adopt this option. One is to accept that all our explanatory efforts must eventually reach some limit. At that point, we cannot further explain the realities postulated to account for the explanandum with which we began, and we may appeal to explanatory entities that are described purely dispositionally in terms of their effects. Given the limited development of all the relevant sciences in the 1640s, it would have been reasonable for a natural philosopher to concede that, at that time, the human mind was beyond the 'Rubicon' of which Digby wrote. But even then we would not be reduced to complete silence; we could argue that human beings have faculties or powers that are identified merely as the kind of faculties that give rise to our mental experiences. A second option is to think of mental phenomena as not being completely natural events because they are not explained adequately by causal

---

[28] Cf. MacIntosh (1983: 333), on the tension caused for those who are both corpuscularian natural philosophers and Christians: 'This makes it difficult for them in dealing with humans, since they want to explain all the animal functions mechanically, while offering non-mechanical (non)-explanations for the rest.'

interactions between material bodies. Such events could be described as non-material and therefore not subject to structural explanations because, like human language, they involve *conventional* signs, the meaning of which cannot be analysed merely in terms of causal relations. I discuss the somewhat vaguely perceived significance of this option for Descartes's theory of mind in Chapter 6. Both options would allow Descartes to think of the scope of the material as being co-extensive with those natural phenomena for which we can, at least in principle, provide a scientific explanation, and to classify whatever lies outside the scope of the latter as 'immaterial'. It may be that mental phenomena are immaterial in both senses. This interim conclusion also leaves open the question whether the mind is explained, in any sense of the term, by reference to substance dualism.

CHAPTER 2

Sensation: Ideas as Brain Patterns

The activity of sensing is, in Cartesian language, a form of thinking.[1] In fact, sensation is not only one form of thinking but it is also the model according to which Descartes conceives of all acts of perceiving or consciousness. Thus the phenomenon of sensing should feature prominently in any theory of the human mind that is consistent with the Cartesian account of explanation. From the time of drafting the *Rules for Guiding one's Intelligence in Searching for the Truth* (*c.*1628) to the publication of the *Meditations* in his mature period, Descartes developed and actively supported such a project, in which he conceived of ideas as characteristic patterns in the brain. The sophistication of this account is evidently a function of the relatively underdeveloped state of physiology and neurology in the early part of the seventeenth century, and of Descartes's familiarity with the work of his contemporaries. However, it is also true that, even with the publication of Thomas Willis's *Cerebri Anatome: cui accessit Nervorum Descriptio et Usus* (1664), the fundamental principles of the Cartesian account remained unchanged, as evidenced by Louis de la Forge's *Traité de l'esprit de l'homme* (1666). Part of the reason is that none of the experimental work in the seventeenth century came remotely close to providing a detailed analysis of the relevant brain functions. Thus minor variations in degrees of sophistication among proto-neurologists of the early modern period were almost unobservable. The other reason is that Descartes was arguing from our experience of thinking, and from the evidence available even to non-scientists that the brain is involved in a significant way in our thought patterns, to hypothetical claims about the activity in the brain that would be required to explain its role in human thought. In that sense, the viability of his approach to brain patterns was not significantly affected by the limited scientific knowledge about the brain to which he had access in constructing his theory. What was at stake was a matter of principle rather than of detail.

---

[1] For example, in the *Meditations*: 'By the term "thought" I mean everything that is in us in such a way that we are immediately conscious of it. Thus all operations of the will, intellect, imagination, and the senses are thoughts' (vii. 160; M. 85). The implications of this definition are discussed in Chapter 7.

In this chapter I describe the steps by which the Cartesian account of sensation was developed, beginning with the *Rules*. The subsequent sections follow the development of this account through *The World* and *The Dioptrics*, and examine the impact of this theory on the philosophy of sensation that appears in the *Meditations* and the *Principles*. Finally, the closing section examines the textual evidence that seems to imply a denial of genuine sensation in animals. I argue that the focus of the Cartesian position is not whether all animals have sensations, but whether the linguistic competence of human beings implies more than a difference of degree between their thinking and that of other animals.

THE *RULES*

The *Rules* should probably be read as a transitional essay written by its author when he was moving from the scholastic theories that he had learned in college, at La Flèche, to a natural philosophy that was designed to supersede their limitations. It is thus a programmatic statement of a new method for searching for the truth about things, but one whose articulation still relied on the Latin terminology of the schools. The first attempt on Descartes's part towards constructing a theory of how perceptions occur is found in Rule Twelve, which acknowledges the hypothetical and conditional nature of its speculation. The reader is advised: 'Do not believe that things are as I describe them unless you want to; but what would prevent you from following these assumptions [*suppositiones*] if it seems that they take nothing away from the truth of things but rather make everything clearer?' (x. 412; D. 152). This suggests that we may invent models for anything we wish to understand, on condition that we are not committed to believing that our models correspond to reality. After all, it may be possible to construct alternative models that are superior.[2]

Having adopted this theoretical licence, Descartes assumes that external perceptions are caused by the action of objects on our external senses, in a manner that is analogous to the way in which a seal impresses an image on wax:

First, then, one must understand that all the external senses, in so far as they are parts of the body—although we apply them to objects through an action, viz. through local motion—have sensory perceptions in the strict sense by means of a passion, in the same way as wax receives an impression from a seal. One should not think that I am speaking

---

[2] Admittedly, this presupposes relevant criteria for assessing models, depending on what one hopes to do with them. I assume that, in the *Rules*, Descartes needs a model that allows him to abstract some epistemological features of perception that are relevant to constructing a method for acquiring knowledge.

by analogy here; clearly, it should be understood that the external shape of the sentient body is really changed by the object, in exactly the same way as that which is on the surface of the wax is changed by the seal.   (x. 412; D. 152)

One might misread this text and conclude that Descartes is talking only about the sense of touch. But the claim is general in scope: 'the same applies to other senses.' Thus, in the case of hearing, seeing, and tasting, the relevant sensory organ in each case 'assumes a new shape' from a sound, an illumination, an odour, or a flavour.

Descartes's justification for linking sensation with shapes derives partly from the intelligibility and accessibility of the concept of shape: 'nothing is more accessible to the senses than shape, for it is both touched and seen' (x. 413: D. 153). It also relies on the assumption that everything material must have some shape or other, even if we do not happen to know what it is: 'the concept of shape is so common and simple that it is involved in everything that is capable of being sensed.' Thus Descartes did not claim that he already had the knowledge required to explain, for example, different colours in terms of various shapes. The suggestion was merely that colours could be conditionally modelled onto shapes and that, by doing so, we would at least avoid the mistake of imagining new theoretical entities that are unrelated to sensations.

For example, you may imagine colour to be anything you wish, but you will not deny that it is extended and that it therefore has a shape. As long as we take care not to invent any new entity uselessly and foolishly, while not denying anything that others have pre-ferred to claim about colour, what difficulty could result if we merely abstract from everything else apart from the fact that colour has the nature of shape and if we conceive the difference between white, blue, red, etc., as being like that between the following shapes [see Fig. 1], or similar ones.   (x. 413; D. 153)

Accordingly, natural philosophers may continue to differ about what light really is, or about which feature of light causes colour perceptions. At the time of writing the *Rules*, Descartes was unable to offer any theory about the nature of

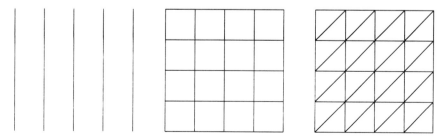

Fig. 1

the physical reality that causes perceptions of light, apart from claiming in Rule Eight that light must be some kind of 'natural power'. However, while reserving the right of natural philosophers to disagree about the physical nature of illumination, he suggests that they could model colours onto various shapes because there is an indefinite number of shapes available to correspond to all possible colours.

Once a shape or pattern is impressed on an external sensory organ, it is subsequently transmitted to the so-called common sense (*sensus communis*), the internal organ in the brain in which all incoming sensory stimuli are synthesized. The common sense, in turn, must act like a seal when it forms on the passive, waxlike material of the phantasy or imagination all the shapes or ideas (*figuras vel ideas*) that result from external stimuli. Descartes is particularly anxious to emphasize that the shapes or ideas that are transmitted from external stimuli to the phantasy are not some kind of distinct entity (that is, distinct from the motions involved), something like the discredited intentional species that were introduced in scholastic theories of perception. The relevant shape or pattern (*figura*) is transmitted from the external senses to the brain 'without any real entity moving from one to the other', just as, by moving the tip of a pen when writing, the other end of the pen is moved simultaneously without any distinct entity passing along the length of the pen. Moreover, when shapes or ideas are transmitted from the sensory organs to the brain, they arrive there in a state that is described as 'pure and without a body [*purae et sine corpore*]' (x. 414). This is not to suggest that the shapes in question are incorporeal or immaterial. The point is rather that a pattern is transmitted along a material connector that is already in place—namely, through the nerves—without physically transmitting some extra body or thing. The part of the brain called the phantasy must have sufficient capacity to be able to store a very large number of distinct impressions: 'This phantasy is a genuine part of the body, and it is big enough for various parts of it to assume many shapes that are distinct from each other, and to retain them usually for some time; in that case, it is the same as what is called memory' (x. 414; D. 154).[3]

Finally, the patterns or shapes that are present in the phantasy may in turn cause motions in various parts of the body without there being images (*imagines*) of those motions in the brain. The lack of a representational similarity (1) between external stimuli and internal brain patterns, and (2) between these patterns and the motions in the body that they cause, is an important qualification to distinguish this theory from scholastic alternatives. According to the latter, the forms of external realities are transmitted to the mind by means of form-

[3] John Sutton (1998: 63–4) has pointed out that this limitation is subsequently relaxed, in the 1630s, when Descartes began thinking of a distributed model of memory.

preserving entities of some kind. In the Cartesian account, there need be nothing more than a one-to-one correspondence between members of either pair—for example, between an external stimulus and the pattern it causes in the phantasy—in the same way that the motion of the top of a pen corresponds to, but may not resemble, the motion of the nib.[4] In this way one readily understands 'how all the motions of other animals [apart from man] can occur, even granting that there is absolutely no knowledge [*cognitio*] of things in them . . . [and] how all the operations that we perform without any assistance from reason occur in ourselves' (x. 415; *D*. 154).

Before we trace the development of this theory in subsequent Cartesian writings, it should be acknowledged that, immediately after the passages quoted above from Rule Twelve, Descartes reverts to a traditional dualist language when describing the various faculties that we use in acquiring knowledge. 'The power by which we know things in a strict sense is completely spiritual [*vim illam . . . esse pure spiritualem*].' What he means by 'completely spiritual' remains to be decided, and is discussed further in Chapter 7. He also argues that this cognitive ability is a single power rather than, for example, a number of distinct faculties.

It is one and the same power which, together with the phantasy, receives shapes [*figuras*] from the common sense or applies itself to those that are stored in memory, or forms new shapes which so occupy the imagination that it is incapable of receiving ideas [*ideas*] coming from the common sense, or of transmitting them to the force responsible for motion . . . In all these things this cognitive power [*vis cognoscens*] is sometimes passive, at other times active . . . But it is one and the same power which, if it applies itself together with the imagination to the common sense, is said to see, to touch, etc.; if it applies itself to the imagination alone, in so far as it is endowed with various shapes, it is said to remember . . . Finally, if it acts alone, it is said to understand. . . . The same power therefore is called 'pure intellect', 'imagination', 'memory' or 'sensation', depending on its different operations. But it is called 'intelligence' [*ingenium*] in a strict sense when it forms new ideas in the imagination [*ideas in phantasia novas format*] or applies itself to those already formed there.   (x. 415–16; *D*. 154–5)

Even these ideas that are formed in the imagination by intelligence in a strict sense are understood as brain patterns or shapes. Thus Descartes assumes that a single, cognitive power can be the passive recipient of information transmitted through the external senses by means of a process called 'sensation'. The same cognitive power can also be applied to images stored in the brain; when performing this function, it is called 'memory'. Finally, if it becomes creative and

---

[4] 'Nor is the whole pen moved in the same way as its lower part; on the contrary, most of it seems to be affected by a very different and opposite movement' (x. 415; *D*. 154).

causes the occurrence of new brain patterns, it is called 'imagination' when it depends on previously stored images, and 'pure intellect' when it acts independently of perceptions or impressions.

The fact that there is only one power at work here, and that it is named in different ways as if it were a series of interconnected but distinct faculties, suggests that the phrases 'pure intellect' and 'completely spiritual' must be read with caution. When Descartes writes, in this context, about something that is a part of the brain, he emphasizes how physical it is. In contrast, when he needs to warn readers against assuming that every meaningful word denotes a distinct physical entity of some kind, he has recourse to adjectives such as 'pure' (*pura*) or 'incorporeal' (*sine corpore*). The patterns that are transmitted from our external senses to the centre of the brain are described as pure and incorporeal in the sense that they are not themselves distinct bodies or things of some kind, but are features that cannot exist apart from the bodies in which they inhere.

Perhaps the various distributed functions performed by the brain could be described in the same language. The plausibility of this suggestion remains to be assessed later, when discussing 'pure understanding' in Chapter 7.

THE WORLD (1632)

The close connection between brain patterns and cognitive functions is further developed in the second part of *The World*, entitled *A Treatise on Man*. This book was part of a larger project in natural philosophy that Descartes had prepared for publication prior to the condemnation of Galileo's *Dialogue Concerning the Two Chief World Systems* (1632). Once Descartes became aware of this news from Italy, he decided not to publish a work in which he had supported the same heliocentric theory as Galileo and which was likely to raise similar theological objections. As a result, Descartes's *World* was never published during the author's lifetime.[5] However, *The World* had been finalized and prepared by its author for the publisher in a way that the *Rules* had never been, and it therefore represented the first sustained attempt on Descartes's part to implement a research programme in natural philosophy that emulated the ambitions of Bacon's earlier 'great instauration'.

The first sentence of *The World* introduces one of the fundamental themes of the Cartesian account of sensation—namely, the lack of any necessary resemblance between external stimuli that cause our sensations and the ideas or

---

[5] *Le Monde de Mr Descartes ou la Traité de la Lumière* was first published in 1664; a Latin version of *A Treatise on Man* had appeared two years earlier.

images that arise in the mind as a result of appropriate (external or internal) stimulation. 'Since my plan here is to discuss light, the first thing that I want to bring to your attention is that there may be a difference between our sensation of light, i.e. the idea [in French: *idée*] which is formed in our imagination by means of our eyes, and whatever it is in the objects that produces that sensation in us, i.e. what is called "light" in a flame or in the sun' (xi. 3; *D*. 85). Descartes acknowledges that most people assume that our ideas 'are completely similar to the objects from which they originate' in sensation, but there is no evidence to support that assumption. On the contrary, there are many experiences that seem to point in the opposite direction. However, it is not necessary at this juncture to prove that ideas do not resemble the stimuli that cause them, or even to explain what the term 'resemble' might mean if the thesis were supported. It is enough to show that such an assumption is unnecessary in a viable theory of perception.

One of the arguments used against the assumption of resemblance is that 'words do not in any way resemble the things they signify' (xi. 4; *D*. 85). The word 'cat' does not resemble a cat—that is, it has none of the properties of a cat, such as its size, shape, and so on. Nonetheless, that does not prevent words from unerringly causing us to think about the appropriate things, even when we do not advert to what language was spoken (when we are competent in more than one language) or what specific words were used. The argument from this familiar experience is: if words succeed in signifying realities without resembling what they signify, 'why is it not possible that nature may have established a particular sign which would make us have the sensation of light, even though such a sign contains nothing in itself that resembles the sensation?' (xi. 4; *D*. 85). However, it is agreed that words have meaning 'only as a result of a human convention'. Descartes seems to suggest that, if a mere human convention can establish such reliable word–thing relations, why could God or nature not have established equally dependable connections between external stimuli and sensations? There are already some cases of such natural signs in the way that nature 'has established laughter and tears to make us read joy and sorrow on people's faces' (xi. 4; *D*. 85).

The argument for not assuming a resemblance between stimuli and sensory experiences is further supported by examples derived from sensations of sound and touch. The consensus among natural philosophers in the seventeenth century was that unspecified vibrations in the air cause the experience of sound. If this were accepted for the sake of argument, and if our sensation of a sound reported 'the real image of its object', then our sensation would resemble the motion of particles of air as they vibrate against our ears. But, of course, the phenomenological features of sounds have nothing in common with vibrating air. Someone could easily hear and appreciate a musical tune without ever knowing anything about the physical causes of the perceived sounds. This insight is confirmed by two other arguments about the sense of touch, the first of which had previously been used by Galileo in *The Assayer* (Galilei 1957: 275). If one lightly rubs a feather 'over the lips of a sleeping child', the child experiences a tickling sensation. In such circumstances, the child is likely to scratch his or her lip or to move, without even waking or seeing what caused the sensation, but no one is tempted to claim that the sensation resembles anything in the feather or its motion. Likewise, after a battle a soldier may experience pain in some part of his body that is protected by armour. Given the weight of the armour, he may need assistance to take it off before inspecting the site of the pain. It may turn out that the pain was caused merely by a buckle or strap pressing against his skin, rather than by a wound sustained in battle, as he may have feared. However, if the pain he experienced had resembled the cause of the pain, he would have been able to identify the pressure of the buckle as the cause of the pain without any assistance from others. He could have relied on the resemblance between the pain and its cause to infer the latter from his experience of the former. Our inability to do this implies that, even in the case of touch, 'which is, among all our senses, the one that is thought to be least deceptive and most reliable', no one assumes any resemblance between our sensations and their objective causes. And, if 'touch makes us conceive many ideas that do not in any way resemble the objects which produce them' (xi. 5; D. 85), then we have no reason to assume otherwise in the case of sight.

These examples do not show that our sensations never resemble the stimuli that cause them, but merely that we have no guarantee of such a resemblance and that we should not assume it in constructing a theory of sensation. 'I see no reason to make us believe that whatever is in the objects, from which we get a sensation [*sentiment*] of light, resembles this sensation any more than the actions of a feather or a strap resemble tickling or pain' (xi. 6; D. 86–7).

The primary focus of Descartes's comments about non-resemblance is the lack of similarity between the causes of sensations and the subjective experiences that we have when we sense something.[6] Pains do not resemble a cut caused by a sword, no more than words resemble the realities that they denote. This account of non-resemblance could be extended to include a more general contrast between the objective and the subjective. A theorist of perception may describe, in objective terms, the air vibrations that cause us to hear sounds and

---

[6] I agree with Arbini (1983: 332–6) that there is a distinction between perceptions and physical images. While the latter have a shape, the former do not. As is evident in this whole chapter, I also agree with Arbini's thesis (1983: 317–18) that the appropriate place to look for a Cartesian theory of sensation is in *The Dioptrics* and other scientific works.

may analyse such vibrations into their frequency and amplitude in ways that match variations in our perception of the pitch and volume of sounds. However, to give a scientific explanation along these lines is not to describe, from the perspective of an observer, features of the world that resemble our subjective experiences, but to identify the processes that allegedly cause them. When the relevant causes are traced into the body of the perceiver, similar Cartesian arguments would imply that the brain states involved in causing sensations might not resemble the subjective experiences of the perceiving subject. This distinction is fundamental to the type of objection, raised by Thomas Nagel, against the viability of an objective explanation of subjectively experienced states of consciousness, to which I return in Chapter 9. For present purposes, it is enough to acknowledge that Descartes is consistent, in his later writings, about this basic insight.[7]

A Treatise on Man, which was planned as an integral part of *The World*, is mostly a treatise on the brain and its operations. Here Descartes claims to explain 'how ideas of objects are formed in the place assigned to the imagination and to the common sense, how these ideas are retained in the memory, and how they cause the movement of all the bodily parts' (x. 174; W. 46). Descartes illustrates his account by considering the inverted image that forms on the retina of someone who looks at an arrow. His theory is that the brain includes a very large number of long thin tubes, which connect various parts of the body to the brain (see Fig. 2). These tubes are similar to coaxial cables, in which central fibres (called the marrow) pass through the tubes from end to end. The marrow is surrounded by a subtle fluid called animal spirits, which helps to maintain it in a taut condition, and which makes it possible to transmit a pressure from one end to the other almost instantaneously. The back of the eye is connected by a number of optic nerves to the centre of the brain. Thus any

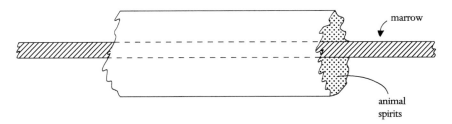

Fig. 2

---

[7] See the *Meditations*: 'The principal error, however, and the one most likely to occur here, consists in the fact that I judge that the ideas that are in me resemble or conform to things that are outside me' (vii. 37; M. 32–3); the *Principles* (1. 71): 'the mind had different sensations, namely those that we call the sensations of taste, smell, sound . . . which did not represent anything located outside these thoughts' (viii-1. 35; M. 141).

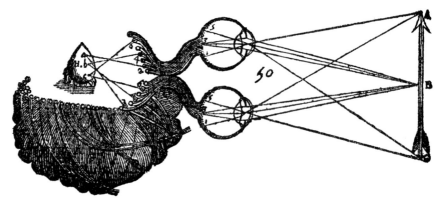

Fig. 3

patterned pressure on the retina, which results from the image of an arrow appearing there, is transmitted through the nerves to produce a corresponding pattern in the centre of the brain. Animal spirits are constantly emerging from the pineal gland, and they enter more or less easily into those pores that are appropriately oriented towards the gland and are more or less open. Descartes speculates that the animal spirits enter the nerves in a pattern that corresponds in some systematic way to the shapes impressed on the retina, where the term 'corresponds' means simply that there is a one-to-one correlation between both events. The shape, pattern, or form adopted by the animal spirits in their emergence from the pineal gland, in order to enter the appropriately disposed nerve tubes, is what he wishes to call an idea (see Fig. 3).

Thus, just as the figure [*figure*] corresponding to the object ABC is traced on the inside surface of the brain depending on the different ways in which tubes 2, 4, 6 [which connect the retina with the centre of the brain] are opened, so that figure is traced on the surface of the gland depending on the ways in which the spirits issue from points *a*, *b*, and *c* [which are on the surface of the pineal gland]. That is to say, only these should be taken as the forms or figures [*formes ou figures*] which . . . the rational soul will consider directly when it imagines some object or senses it.   (xi. 176–7; W. 149)

Since Descartes wrote *The World* in French, the term *figure* in this passage corresponds to the Latin term *figura* in the *Rules*. Descartes advises his readers that this term should not be understood too narrowly or literally, as if it meant only a geometrical shape: 'note that by "figures" I mean, not only things that somehow represent the position of the edges and surfaces of objects' but anything that provides an opportunity for the perceiver to sense movement, size, distance, and so on. Among figures understood in this wider sense, 'it is not those imprinted on the organs of sense, or on the inside surface of the brain, that should be taken as ideas, but only those traced in the spirits on the surface of the gland H, where the seat of the imagination and the common sense is' (xi. 176; W. 149).[8]

In developing this rather speculative account of how a patterned sensation might be transmitted through the optic nerves and stored for subsequent use by the memory, Descartes applied the French term *idée* to the characteristic pattern in which animal spirits flow out from the pineal gland. 'I wish to apply the term "idea" generally to all the impressions which the spirits are able to receive as they issue from the gland H' (xi. 177; W. 149–50). It must be acknowledged that, although ideas are defined as brain patterns in this context, Descartes does not preclude the possibility that the 'rational soul' also has ideas of a different type. But at least his theory of sensation initially postulates brain patterns that do not resemble the external stimuli that cause them, and these occur in the brain as a direct result of the patterned impressions on our sensory organs. The only condition that is imposed by the Cartesian theory on ideas, understood as patterns in the flow of animal spirits, is some kind of one-to-one correlation, without similarity, between impressions on the relevant sensory organ and the consequent activity in the brain.

Despite the decision to suppress publication of *The World*, Descartes continued his scientific studies of human physiology and optics during the 1630s. He eventually decided somewhat reluctantly to publish three scientific essays, which appeared in 1637 as *Discours de la Méthode. Pour bien conduire sa raison et chercher la vérité dans les sciences. Plus La Dioptrique, Les Météores, Et la Géométrie. Qui sont des essais de cette Méthode.* The possible ramifications of the Galileo affair were still fresh in his mind, and Descartes's first book appeared without the author's name on the title page.

THE DIOPTRICS (1637)

The term 'dioptrics' was used in the seventeenth century for studies of light refraction—for example, through lenses—in contrast with the word 'catoptrics', which referred to a study of light reflection. In constructing an account of refraction, Descartes comments in Discourse VI on the way in which the lens in the human eye functions and, more generally, the multiple ways by

---

[8] The text continues immediately: 'That is to say, only these should be taken as the forms or images that the rational soul, when it is united to this machine, will consider directly when it imagines some object or senses it.' This text evidently assumes that a rational soul has a role in sensation. It remains to be seen whether this merely describes the function of the mind or soul, or implies the kind of substance dualism against which I argue in Chapters 8 and 9.

which information is transmitted through the eye to the brain. Understandably, in a treatise on dioptrics, the senses of touch, taste, and so on are not discussed directly. However, the discussion of the transmission of information through sight provides a model for thinking about how the other senses work. Despite the limitation in scope suggested by the title, therefore, *The Dioptrics* includes the author's most fully developed general theory of sensation.

It would also be a mistake to assume that Descartes is concerned exclusively in *The Dioptrics* with the optical features of the visual sensory system, or that he thinks of the retinal image as the exclusive source of the information that becomes available to the brain. In *The Senses Considered as Perceptual Systems*, J. J. Gibson argued that traditional theorizing about the senses failed to acknowledge that our sensory organs are normally movable in space, and that much of the information that we gather through the senses is a function of slight variations in perception, which result from changes in the disposition of our sensory organs in relation to objects of perception. Thus, in the case of visual perception, the fact that we have two eyes, that we can move them in their sockets, and that we can move about in space and get different perspectives on many objects of perception, provides a lot more information than could possibly be gleaned from a fixed visual image. Gibson (1966: 172) summarizes the limited role of the visual image, in the context of all this extra sensory information, as follows: 'The retinal image is a stimulus for a retina but not the stimulus for an eye and certainly not for an ocular system.' Even if one narrows attention to the retinal image, it should not be understood as a small picture that has to be seen or observed. What are important about it are its structural properties rather than its visible properties. These structural features of the retinal image can best be incorporated into the structural features of the whole sensory experience that is available to a perceiver on the occasion of looking at an object.[9] This suggests that the information that can be conveyed by the whole ocular system, when functioning normally, far exceeds the information provided by an optical image. This is also the way in which Descartes analyses visual perception in Discourse VI of *The Dioptrics*.

The Dioptrics assumes that the relative sharpness of an optical image on the retina initially determines the quality of the information available to a perceiver, and that it makes sense to claim that this image resembles, more or less, the

---

[9] 'If we could think of an image in the derived sense as a complex of relations, as the invariant structure of an arrangement, in short as information, there would be no great harm in extending the original meaning of the term. But this is hard to do, for it carries too much weight of history . . . It would surely be false to say that there is a phonograph record in the ear, and the same error tempts us when we say that there is an image in the eye' (Gibson 1966: 226–7).

external visual object. However, Descartes cautions that we should not assume that the mind perceives the visual object as a result of a resemblance between object and optical image. 'We must not hold that it is by means of this resemblance that the picture causes us to perceive objects, as if there were yet other eyes in our brain with which we could perceive it' (vi. 130). This indicates that Descartes was at least aware of, and was attempting to avoid, what Anthony Kenny (1972: 65–74) called the 'homunculus fallacy'.[10] *The Dioptrics* argues that the concept of resemblance applies literally only to a picture (*une peinture*). But one cannot assume that this type of literal resemblance is maintained when an impression is transmitted through the sensory organs to the brain, and in the subsequent occurrence of an idea as a mental event. On the contrary, all the 'qualities of objects of perception' can be perceived as a direct result of their differential effects on the appropriate senses. The qualities in question may be classified, according to Descartes, into six principal features: colour, brightness, location, distance, size, and shape.

In order to perceive the colour of a visual object, Descartes suggests that 'one must think that the nature of our soul is such that the force of the movements that occur in that part of the brain from which the narrow fibres of the optic nerves originate causes it to have a sensation of light, and the way in which such movements occur causes it to have a sensation of colour' (vi. 130–1). This hypothesis is then generalized for all the other senses, so that the different features of hearing sounds, tasting flavours, and so on are all correlated with patterns in the movement of nerve fibres in the brain. However, as already indicated in discussing *The World*, it is not necessary 'that there be any resemblance between the ideas that the mind conceives and the movements that cause these ideas' (vi. 131). This is confirmed, for example, by cases where we see bright lights as a result of an eye injury, even when there are no lights present, or when we see an after-image from a light source even when we close our eyes or know independently that the visual object is no longer present.

The quantity of motion in the optic nerves varies in proportion to the quantity of light that strikes the retina. For Descartes, light is not a thing of some kind but a force or pressure that is transmitted, through particles of the second

---

[10] Kenny is aware of Descartes's evasive moves; despite them, he argues that Descartes is still guilty of this fallacy. 'I shall call the reckless application of human-being predicates to insufficiently, human-like objects the homunculus fallacy, since its most naïve form is tantamount to the postulation of a little man within a man to explain human experience and behaviour' (1972: 65–6). Although Descartes avoids this most naïve form, he is said to have faltered in the *Passions* (1. 35) where images on the gland are said to cause the soul to see or perceive something (xi. 356). However, I think this is shorthand for a human being perceiving by means of the faculty called the soul.

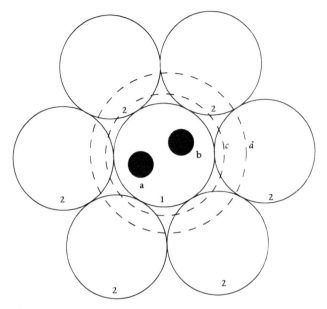

Fig. 4

element, in the same direction as light seems to travel from a source to some illuminated body.[11] Thus a higher quantity of illumination corresponds to a greater pressure or tendency to move that is transmitted to the eye and subsequently to the optic nerves. However, the intensity of one's visual sensation is not a function exclusively of the quantity of illumination that is emitted by an object. It also varies in proportion to the extent to which the pupil is open and the surface area of the retina is stimulated, and inversely in proportion to the distance of the object. A similar analysis applies in the case of colour perception. Descartes argues that our powers of discriminating different parts of a visual object depend on our being able to differentiate between variations in the ways that its parts appear coloured. This in turn depends on a number of factors, including the area of the retina that is stimulated, the net effect on each distinct nerve fibre of all the illumination that affects it, and the relative size of those fibres in relation to the pressure points that affect them. For example, Fig. 4 represents a cross section of the retina and each circle depicts an enlarged cross section of an individual nerve fibre.[12] Descartes is arguing that it would be impossible to discriminate between two stimuli, *a* and *b*, that are so small that they simultaneously affect the same nerve fibre, 1. Likewise, for a stimulus *c* that affects both fibre 1 and those that surround it and are numbered 2, if the intensity of the illumina-

---

[11] *Principles* (iii. 55–64).   [12] This is adapted from *The Dioptrics* (vi. 146).

Fig. 5

tion is strong enough we would be unable to discriminate between *c* and other stimuli (such as *d*) that affect a larger fraction of the fibres at 2. In other words, objects that affect the retina will be perceived as similar if the difference between their effects on the retina, like *c* and *d*, is too fine to be discriminated.

The location of an object in relation to our bodies is perceived by using our eyes 'in the same way as we would do so by using our hands' (vi. 134). Here Descartes appeals to the example of a blind person who can identify the position of objects by using two sticks (Fig. 5). The blind man's location of an object does not depend on any image arriving from the object, but on his perception of the disposition of his own arms and hands from information supplied from his muscles. Similarly, when our eyes turn in the direction of some visual object, we become aware of this by perceiving changes 'in the muscles that are used for this purpose' (vi. 135), which, in turn, affect the corresponding nerves in the brain.

Judgements about the distance of a visual object are equally independent of any image emitted by the object. They depend, instead, on a number of factors. One is the familiar experience of adjusting the shape of our eye, or the focal length of the ocular lens, to produce a sharp image of a visual object on the retina. Secondly, we can judge distance by the adjustments we experience in binocular vision. There is a kind of spontaneous triangulation involved in the simultaneous focusing by the two eyes of an observer on a single object of perception. Given the distance between the two eyes, and the deviation from parallel focusing required to get both eyes looking at the same object, one can estimate the distance of the object from the observer.[13] Thirdly, we can estimate the distance of an object (1) from the relative distinctness or indistinctness of the object perceived, and (2) from the strength or weakness of the light by which it is seen. This involves an unconscious comparison with other objects in the same visual field. Distant objects appear less distinctly and less well illuminated than nearer objects in similar conditions of illumination. In all three cases, the muscular and other physical motions in the sensory organs are the source of internal sensations, and these are correlated with distinctive brain patterns that assist us in making a judgement of the distance between the observer and the object of perception.

This account of visual perception provides a basis for understanding the ubiquitous Cartesian phrase 'clear and distinct', which applies originally and literally to visual perceptions and is subsequently used, by analogy, in reference to all perceptions. For example, if we see or hear something, we cannot be said to have a clear perception if the light or sound involved is too faint. In either such case, a lack of clarity is a function of the low intensity of the light or sound, even if the reality to be seen or heard is close to the perceiver and otherwise relatively easy to perceive. Thus, lack of clarity is a feature of one's perception that results from weak stimuli, but it may also result from inhibiting features in one's sensory system. It is the force of the incoming signal received in the ear or the retina that determines the clarity of a perception. It can fail to be clear because, for example, of a constriction in the pupil of the eye or any obstruction in the sensory organ. But a strong visual or auditory signal, though necessary, is not sufficient to guarantee a distinct perception. In fact, an incoming signal that is too strong in relation to the sensitivity of the sensory organ could equally be a cause of indistinctness. Distinctness is, like clarity, a feature of our perception rather than of the object perceived. An indistinct perception is such that we are unable to separate the boundaries of what is perceived from other things in its environment. Whatever the cause of this phenomenon on a particular occasion—whether the small size of the object to be perceived relative to our sensory organs, the strength of the incoming signal that produced an unfocused image on the eye or other sensory organ, or the weakness of the signal and the consequent blurring of the received image—the result of an indistinct percep-

---

[13] In the simplest geometrical example, the distance between the two eyes is fixed as the length of the base of an isosceles triangle, and the size of the angles at the base is known by the extent to which the eyes are turned inwards from parallel focusing. From this information, the distance of the apex of the triangle from the base can be calculated. If the distance between one's two eyes is d, and the angle of deviation from parallel focusing is α, the distance of an object from the observer is $d \sin (90 - \alpha)/2$.

tion is that we are unable to delineate sharply the boundaries of the object perceived and to demarcate it from other objects in its environment.

Descartes exploits all these elements, which are originally derived from an analysis of visual perception, in his definition of clear and distinct perception in the *Principles*. It should be noted that he refers not to clear and distinct ideas in this context, but to perceptions; this illustrates how the term 'perception' extends from visual sensing to seeing things in a wider, metaphorical sense:

I call a perception [*perceptio*] clear when it is present and accessible to an attentive mind, in the same way as we say that we see things clearly when they are present to our eye when it is looking and, while it is open, they strike it strongly enough. However, I call a perception distinct which, when it is clear, is so separated and so disconnected from all other perceptions that it evidently contains nothing that is not clear.   (viii-1. 22; M. 128–9)[14]

One of the immediate consequences of having a clear and distinct perception is that the perceiver can make a reliable judgement about an object of perception. The image received is not too faint, nor does it have such vague boundaries that one is unsure where the object ends and its neighbours begin. In other words, one is unlikely to confuse the object of perception with others or to merge a number of distinct objects into a single object of perception.

This hypothesis provides an explanation, not only of successful perceptions, but also of how our senses deceive. 'It is the soul that sees, and not the eye, and it sees immediately only through the intervention of the brain' (vi. 141). Therefore the judgements we make about visual objects depend both on the quality of the original impressions on the sensory organs and on the accuracy with which they are transmitted to the brain. The former depends on the sensitivity of the tiny fibres that are stimulated by motions in the environment. The fact that Descartes has only one generic type of cause with which to explain all sensations—the motion of bodies that impinge on our sensory organs—means that he had to invoke as many variables as possible in the motion of bodies to account for all discriminations between different sensations. Accordingly he explains how, for example, if the sensitive fibres in a particular sensory organ were very small, they would be inadequately sensitive to minute variations in the movement of stimulating bodies.[15] Likewise, the general condition of the

---

[14] The French edition of the *Principles*, which maintains the term *perception* in the subheading, speaks in the first sentence about perceiving things clearly enough to support sound judgements. But the definition of 'clear and distinct' refers to the kind of knowledge (*connoissance*) (ix-2. 44) on which reliable judgements may be based.

[15] Cf. Descartes to More (5 Feb. 1649), which explains how material objects might become completely imperceptible if all particles of matter were too small or moved too quickly to affect nerve endings with the

tubes that carry information through the nerves to the brain, and the degree to which they are already moved by other stimuli, affect their ability to transmit finely discriminated information.

Descartes's discussion of perception in the *Dioptrics* moved freely from detailed descriptions of the optics of the eyes and the physiology of their controlling muscles to suggestions about how the mind (*nôtre âme* (vi. 137)) perceives the distance of a visual object without reflection, and how a judgement of distance, 'although only a simple act of imagination, implicitly contains a reasoning that is very similar to that performed by surveyors'.[16] These spontaneous estimations of distance involve a judgement, an estimation based on prior knowledge or belief.[17] The conclusion of Discourse VI is a summary of how judgements of distance (*'pour ce qui est de juger de la distance . . .'* (vi. 147)), which are based on size, shape, colour, or light, may be mistaken.

The apparently casual variation between mind and brain, and between sensations, judgements, and reasoning, might arouse suspicions about the clarity of the author's project or his commitment to disambiguating the common usage of such terms in the construction of his theory. It also raises questions about the applicability of this account of perception to animals, for, according to his theory, they lack a mind or soul. I return to the status of animals' perception at the conclusion of this chapter. First, I need to comment on the apparent conceptual confusion.

One of the standard ways of reading the Cartesian theory of mind is to give priority to substance dualism, to adopt it as a first principle of Descartes's philosophy, and then to read all the texts so that they are consistent with that basic premiss. On this approach, one should apply substance dualism to the 'muddled' account of perception that is offered in *The Dioptrics* so that there is a clear distinction between the mind and its intellectual operations (such as judging and reasoning) and bodily events that are associated with mental operations. One should also expect that Descartes's subsequent, 'more careful' or more explicitly dualistic work in the *Meditations* would provide an urgently needed opportunity to remove latent confusions. However, when one reads the *Meditations* with such anticipations, the text disappoints. Instead of rejecting or

kind of stimulation required for perception. 'There is no matter that would not be obviously imperceptible if it were divided into parts much smaller than the particles of our nerves and if the individual parts were moved quickly enough' (v. 268).

[16] 'It is the mind [*l'âme*] that sees, and not the eye' (vi. 141). The French text for the quotation about reasoning is: *'par une action de la pensée, qui, n'étant qu'une imagination toute simple, ne laisse point d'envelloper en soi un raisonnement tout semblable à celui que font les arpenteurs . . .'* (vi. 138).

[17] Here the verb *juger* is used; for example: 'nous le jugeons' (vi. 138), 'qui nous la fait juger' (vi. 140). Estimates of distance are based on prior beliefs: 's'estime par la connoissance, ou l'opinion, qu'on a' (vi. 140); 'la figure se juge par la connoissance, ou l'opinion, qu'on a . . .' (vi. 140).

disambiguating *The Dioptrics*, Descartes continues to appeal to its results and even retains the underlying primitive understanding of an idea as a brain pattern that denotes, without resembling, a quality of some perceived object. Against our expectations, perhaps, the *Meditations*, the *Principles*, and *The Passions of the Soul* presuppose and consolidate the theory of perception outlined in the 1630s. They develop a distinction between internal and external sensation and distinguish, within sensation, various levels or stages in which mind and judgement are more or less involved. From this perspective, *The Dioptrics* is not conceptually confused; it merely fails to separate adequately various features of our perception that usually occur together, including the spontaneous judgements that arise on the occasion of having sensory experiences that are more or less 'clear and distinct'.

THREE LEVELS OF SENSATION

The texts considered so far, from the unpublished *Rules* (1628) to *The Dioptrics* (1637), establish brain patterns as a basic element of the Cartesian account of sensation. They also leave room for the addition of a human mind or rational soul, to complete the theory of sensation as a form of thinking. The replies to objections to the *Meditations* provided an appropriate opportunity to address some of the implications of *The Dioptrics* for traditional philosophical accounts of perception, and to define some of the key concepts in Descartes's philosophical repertoire. One of these is the concept of an idea, which is defined as follows in the Replies to Mersenne:

By the word 'idea' I understand the form [*forma*] of any thought by the immediate perception of which I am conscious of the thought itself. Hence I cannot express anything in words or understand what I am saying without, by that very fact, being certain that I have an idea of whatever is meant by those words. Thus I do not apply the term 'ideas' only to the images that are depicted in the imagination; in fact, I do not call them ideas at all here, in so far as they are depicted in the bodily imagination, that is, in some part of the brain, but only in so far as they inform [*informare*] the mind itself when it turns towards that part of the brain.   (vii. 160–1).

The Latin term used in the *Rules* (*figura*) and its transformed French equivalent from *The World* (*figure*) have been replaced here by the traditional philosophical term *forma*. When applied to physical ideas in the brain, *figura* meant literally the shape or characteristic structure of a brain pattern, in virtue of which a creature with sensory organs reacts to different stimuli in a discriminating way. When defining ideas in a more general and abstract way, Descartes needs a new term with similar connotations. There must be something about any thought in virtue of which the thinking subject perceives its content in a differential manner. In keeping with the linguistic strategy outlined in the *Rules*—namely, to adapt words that were already in use in scholastic Latin to express his own thoughts[18]—Descartes exploits the nearest best term in scholastic Latin— namely, *forma*—to define an idea as that feature of a thought (similar to the structure of a brain state) that determines its specific content.[19] However, even though this definition was designed to refer to ideas in general, the reader is reminded that 'idea' is also applied correctly to brain patterns in so far as they 'inform' the mind—that is, in so far as they cause the subject to think of a specific content. There is no indication here that brain patterns have become redundant or that they are no longer ideas. The focus in the *Meditations* is on the conceptual content that is determined by, among other things, ideas as brain patterns.

This reflects a theme that is consistent throughout the *Meditations* (including the Objections and Replies): that we may conceptualize ideas by analogy with images. For example, Descartes distinguishes in the Third Meditation between two different kinds of thought (*cogitationes*): (1) ideas in a strict sense, and (2) mental acts such as judgements and volitions. The former are characterized by the fact that they 'are like images of things [*tamquam rerum imagines sunt*]', while the second class includes thoughts that involve something more than 'a resemblance [*similitudo*] of some thing, which we fear, for example, or about which we make a judgement' (vii. 37; M. 32). In other words, both types of thought include some kind of image or similitude of whatever is thought about, although the second type involves an extra feature. The extent to which ideas are in some sense an image or similitude is taken for granted and frequently repeated throughout the *Meditations*. For example, Descartes wonders whether ideas that originate outside the mind are similar (*similes*) to the things of which they are ideas. He argues that, even if some ideas are caused by external objects or events, it does not seem to follow that the ideas must be similar to their external causes (vii. 38, 39). He claims that it is evident, by the natural light of reason, that my ideas 'are like images of some kind [*velut quasdam imagines*]', and that ideas represent (*repraesentare*) and exhibit (*exhibere*) to the mind other people, angels

---

[18] Rule Three: 'I am not thinking at all about the way in which certain words have been used in recent times in the schools . . . All I do is to notice what particular words mean in Latin, so that, whenever I lack appropriate words, I shall transfer to my own meaning whatever words seem most suitable' (x. 369; D. 123).

[19] A. Kenny considered this usage of the term *forma* as puzzling because it does not coincide with any recognizable scholastic usage. 'The word "form" is a piece of scholastic jargon, but no scholastic theory seems to be involved' (1969: 110). This puzzle disappears if 'form' is a substitute for shape or pattern, since for Descartes none of these terms is used in a scholastic sense.

and even God (vii. 43). In the Fifth Meditation, the idea of God is said to be 'the image [*imago*] of a true and immutable nature' (vii. 68), and in the Sixth Meditation Descartes recalls how it seemed natural to him to believe, before his sceptical doubts began, that ideas that are acquired through the senses are similar (*similes*) to the realities that cause them (vii. 72).[20]

Despite this consistent use of the metaphor of an image, Descartes was notoriously explicit in the Sixth Meditation in drawing a distinction between two different ways of thinking, which he called imagination and pure understanding (*pura intellectio*). Here he argued that, since one can understand complex geometrical figures that are impossible to imagine clearly, there must be a distinction between the two operations. However, when he attempted to explain this distinction, he resorted to a contrast between two different kinds of *image*, one in the mind and the other in a part of the brain. 'Thus this way of thinking [i.e. imagining] differs from pure understanding only in the sense that the mind, when it understands, turns back on itself in some way and reflects on one of the ideas that are inside itself; however, when it imagines, it turns towards a body and sees something in it that resembles the idea that had been understood by itself or perceived by sensation' (vii. 73; M. 58). This suggests a parallel between the mind looking into itself and seeing some kind of mental image, and looking at a physical image in the brain. In both cases, the mind relies on something like an image that specifies the content of one's idea, but in the case of pure understanding the mind is independent of the imagination's limited capacity.

The clearest opportunity for Descartes to revise or qualify the theory proposed in The Dioptrics occurs in the Sixth Objections, which had been collected from various sources by Mersenne. The objection was made, for example, that, in the case of a stick that is partly submerged in water and appears to be bent, we do not correct our sensations by using our intellect but by using other senses, such as the sense of touch (vii. 418). Descartes's reply introduced a distinction between three levels or degrees of sensation. The first level is the sum total of motions caused in the sensory organs and the brain by the impact of external stimuli. To obviate any misunderstanding of this, especially by some of the scholastic theologians and philosophers who had raised the objection, Descartes refers them to the work already done in The Dioptrics, Discourse VI:

For example, when I see a stick one should not imagine that various 'intentional species' fly from the stick to my eye, but simply that rays of light are reflected from the stick and trigger certain motions in the optic nerve and, as a result, in the brain (as I explained at

---

20 The use of images as models for ideas was made explicit in Gassendi's objections, where he writes to Descartes about ideas 'that you wish to be thoughts, in so far as they are like images' (vii. 279).

sufficient length in *The Dioptrics*). The first level of sensation consists in this motion of the brain, which we have in common with brute animals.   (vii. 437)

This first degree or level of sensation spontaneously gives rise to a perception of the colour and light that is reflected from the stick, and this is a second level of sensation. Descartes makes a rather strange claim that 'nothing more than this should be included in sensation if we wish to distinguish it carefully from the intellect [*ab intellectu*]' (vii. 437). He refers to the theory developed in *The Dioptrics*, where he showed that judgements about the size, shape, and distance of an object of perception depend on information provided by the sensory organs. These spontaneous judgements may be classified in two different ways, depending on how clearly one wishes to demarcate the role of the intellect and of reasoning.

However, if I judge that the stick, which is located outside me, is coloured as a result of the sensation of colour by which I am affected; likewise, if from the extension of the colour, and from its boundary and its position in relation to parts of my brain, I reason about the size of the stick, its shape and its distance from me; even though this is commonly attributed to sensation and I have classified it under the third level of sensation, it is evident that it depends on the intellect alone [*a solo intellectu*].   (vii. 437–8)

In the *Meditations*, therefore, Descartes acknowledges that the extension of the term 'sensation' may include judgements that we spontaneously make about external objects that cause sensations in us. When the text attributes these judgements to the 'intellect alone', it is likely to mislead the reader and may even have misguided the author. Descartes had already acknowledged in *The Dioptrics* that there is an element of estimation or calculation involved in many perceptions, and that we perform such calculations so spontaneously that we are often unaware of them. There is no reason to deny that this is also a feature of perception that human beings share with other animals, for animals make the kind of calculations of distance, and so on, that were discussed in *The Dioptrics*. Thus it was appropriate to include such spontaneous calculations, in *The Dioptrics* and in the *Meditations*, as part of sensation or as the third level of sensation.

The relevant new suggestion in the *Meditations*, in response to sceptical concerns, is that such spontaneous judgements are often mistaken, and that we cannot correct them without noticing how they are made and without applying to them some kind of critical reflection or evaluation. The distinction that Descartes is attempting to draw here is not between bodily and mental events, between merely having impressions in the brain (which is the first level of sensation), and making judgements (which may be called the third level of sensation but is actually a function exclusively of the understanding). The distinction being made is between: (1) the spontaneous judgements that follow naturally on our perceptions and are correctly included in the *Dioptrics* discussion as an integral part of sensation, even in animals; and (2) the reflective judgements that we make, based on sensations, following our realization that our sensations may not resemble their objective causes and that the spontaneous judgements we have made since our infancy are often mistaken. It is such reflective judgements that depend on the 'intellect alone' (whatever that phrase may turn out to mean). Descartes seems to endorse this interpretation and to rescue himself from incoherence by a comment later in the same text. When we say that 'intellectual certainty is much greater than the certainty of sensation, that means simply that the judgements that we make in our maturity as a result of new observations are more certain than those we made uncritically in our earliest years, and that is undoubtedly true' (vii. 438).[21]

The account of sensation presented in the *Principles* is consistent with that found in the *Meditations* three years earlier. Part IV (Articles 189–98) provided an opportunity to summarize the Cartesian theory of sensation and to make more explicit than previously a distinction between internal and external sensations.

INTERNAL AND EXTERNAL SENSATIONS

The Cartesian account of sensation was based, as indicated above, on the impact of environmental events on our sense organs and the transmission of the results of these nerve stimulations to the brain. Descartes distinguished seven principal groups of nerves that provide stimuli for sensations, five of which are external and two internal. He reminds readers that external senses are usually distinguished into five different sensory sources 'by the five different kinds of object that move the corresponding nerves' (viii-1. 318). For example, the nerves that terminate in the skin all over the body provide the input for sensations of touch 'in the mind [*in mente*]'. With variations in intensity of the relevant stimuli, the same sense of touch can give rise to contrary sensations of pleasure or pain. The sensation of pain, therefore, occurs when the body is injured by the strength or intensity of the action by which our nerve endings are affected. The sensation of pain is caused in the mind (*menti*) by what amounts to a bodily injury (*laesio*). In a similar way, taste, smell, hearing, and sight refer to sensations caused by different external objects on nerve endings in our tongue, our nose, the membrane of the tympanum, and the retina. These nerve endings

---

[21] The same distinction is made in the final sentence of Part I of the *Principles*, which advises that it is inappropriate for a philosopher to trust 'in the senses, that is, in the uncritical judgements of their childhood, rather than in their mature reason' (viii-1. 39; M. 144).

can be stimulated only by appropriate external bodies in motion. Thus the size and shape of particles are very important for smell and taste, vibrating air is required for hearing, and the pressure of globules of the second element is appropriate in the case of sight.

The internal senses are those networks of nerve endings that transmit information from inside the human body to the brain. One group of nerves extends from the brain to the stomach, throat, and so on—those internal organs that are designed to satisfy our natural desires or wants. A sensation produced by these is called a 'natural appetite [*appetitus naturalis*]' (viii-1. 316). The nerves that connect the brain with the heart and the surrounding area give rise to another kind of internal sensation, which includes all the emotions or passions such as joy, sorrow, love, or hatred. However, the distinction between internal and external sensations cannot be coherently made by reference to the bodily location of the nerve endings that are stimulated. For, according to that criterion, the inner ear or the retina is just as internal to the body as the throat, although the sensations that result from the former are classified as external. Besides, pain is often used as an example of an internal sensation, although it can be experienced in the same site as touch (which is an external sense) on the periphery of the body, even on the skin. The distinction between internal and external senses must be made, therefore, as it is in the *Passions* (1. 23, 24), because we refer some sensations to external causes (that is, external to one's own body), while others are referred to causes that are internal to the perceiver's body.[22] We can even refer the same type of sensation—for example, the sensation of heat or cold— to either internal or external causes. Thus, when our hands are very cold and we put them close to a fire, we attribute the sensation of cold to our hands and the sensation of heat to the fire.[23]

Descartes had already acknowledged, in the Sixth Meditation, that both internal and external sensations could give rise to mistaken judgements. For example, he acknowledged that towers that appeared, from a distance, to be round were discovered to be square when viewed from close by. 'In countless other similar things I discovered that the judgements of the external senses were

---

[22] Cf. Descartes to Elizabeth (6 Oct. 1645): 'Thoughts that result from external objects, or from internal dispositions of the body, such as the perception of colours, sounds, odours, hunger, thirst, pain, and so on, are called sensations, some of which are external and others internal' (iv. 310–11).

[23] *Passions*: 'The perceptions we refer to things outside us, namely to the objects of our senses, are caused (at least when our belief is not false) by these objects . . . The perceptions we refer to our body or to some of its parts are those of hunger, thirst, and of our other natural appetites. To these we may add pain, heat, and other conditions that we feel as if they were in our limbs and not in objects that are outside us' (xi. 346–7). Descartes goes on to say that we may feel heat in our hand or in an outside body, 'without there being any difference between the actions' that cause us to feel either one. The distinction between internal and external sensations is also mentioned in the *Passions*, ii. 85 (xi. 391), and in *A Treatise on Man* (xi. 176; W. 149).

mistaken' (vii. 76; M. 60). He had the same experience with judgements based on internal sensations. 'For what can be closer to me than pain? But I once heard, from those who had had a leg or arm amputated, that they still seemed to feel pain in the part of their body that was missing. Likewise, it did not seem certain in my own case that I had a pain in some limb even if I felt a pain in it' (vii. 76–7; M. 61). The arguments are exactly parallel for both internal and external sensations. In each case the perceiver has a sensation that is caused by the effects of relevant bodies in motion on nerve endings in the eye, ear, stomach, and so on. The perceiver spontaneously makes a judgement based on the information received from both kinds of stimuli, and both types of judgement may be faulty. In the case of external sensations, the perceiver judges that an external object has some property (such as a square shape) that it does not in fact have. In the case of internal sensations, such as a pain or hunger, the perceiver judges that a part of the body is injured or that the stomach is empty enough to need more food.[24] The mistake on the perceiver's part occurs in a judgement about the condition of part of the perceiver's body.[25]

Descartes sketched the mechanism by which these misleading internal sensations are caused in the Sixth Meditation. If I feel a pain in my foot, the sensation is caused because the nerves in my foot send a signal through the leg, the spine, and eventually to the brain. When these nerves are pulled like a cord,

they also pull the inner parts of the brain, where they terminate, and they stimulate a certain motion there, which was established by nature to affect the mind [*mentem*] with a feeling of what seems like a pain in the foot. Since these nerves have to pass through the leg, the thigh, the loins, the back, and the neck to reach from the foot to the brain, it can happen that, even if that section of the nerves which is in the foot is not affected but only some other intermediate section, evidently the very same motion occurs in the brain as when the foot is hurt, from which it will necessarily follow that the mind feels the same pain. The same thing must occur in the case of other sensations.   (vii. 87; M. 68)

The mistaken judgement might be described as mislocating the pain, which evidently cannot occur in an amputated foot. But this is an expression in ordinary language that fails to capture adequately the implications of Descartes's

---

[24] Baker and Morris claim (1996: 50) that Descartes 'took pain, hunger and fear to be objects of *sense-perception*. Hence they must in some sense be modes of extension . . . that have the power to modify local motions within the appropriate sense-organs.' While sympathizing with the motive for this claim, I disagree that pain is an object of perception for Descartes. 'Feeling a pain' is not comparable to 'hearing a sound'. The word 'sound' may apply to a sensation or to what is heard, and the link between the sensation and the reality sensed is problematic. However, in the case of pain, the term 'pain' applies only to our sensation, but a similar problematic relation obtains between the feeling and what is felt. The ambiguity in phrases such as 'hearing a sound' was admirably discussed by Jacques Rohault (1723: 183–96).

[25] Descartes also has a theory to the effect that internal sensations are designed by nature to trigger an appropriate response by the perceiver. I return to this question in Chapter 4.

analysis, because the mistake seems to depend on the fact that one cannot have a pain in a missing limb. In the example that is quoted above and is familiar to people who suffer from damaged or dislocated disks in their spine, one can just as easily mislocate pain from a spinal disk and feel the pain in one's leg (when the leg is still very much there). The mistaken judgement, in each case, is in concluding that a pain in the leg or foot is caused by an injury to the leg or foot rather than, for example, one's spine or the nerves that transmit sensations from the foot. In both cases, the mistake occurs in assigning a sensation that is genuinely experienced to an incorrect cause (that is, an injury in part of the body). Descartes summarizes this conclusion in the *Principles*, as follows: 'we sometimes feel pain as if it were in certain limbs; however, there is no cause of pain in those, but in other parts of the body through which pass the nerves which extend from those limbs to the brain' (viii-1. 320).

Descartes's discussion of the perception of pain in the *Principles* (1. 66–67) suggested to some commentators that he thought of pain as a purely mental event. However, the issue at stake in these articles is not whether pains are purely mental but whether our sensations are known clearly and distinctly enough to support reliable judgements. The marginal heading for Article 66 reads: 'How sensations, emotions and appetites are known clearly, although we often make incorrect judgements about them.' The conclusion proposed is that they are often known clearly enough, but that we should not make precipitate judgements about the true causes of external sensations. 'For all of us have judged from our childhood that all the things that we sense are things existing outside our mind and are exactly similar to our sensations' (viii-1. 32; *M.* 138). Descartes argues, in the next article, that similar care is required when drawing conclusions about the causes of internal sensations, including pleasure and pain. In these cases we are not tempted to suppose that our pain resembles some *object* that exists outside us (that is, outside our body). However, we may also fail to understand that pains exist only in our mind or our perception (*in sola mente sive in perceptione nostra*), and we may believe instead that they exist in the hand, the foot, or some other part of the body. This is almost a matter of definition, since the term 'pain' is used here to denote a very specific internal sensation.[26] Descartes's conclusion parallels the case of colour mentioned in the previous article. 'When, for example, we perceive a pain as if it were in our foot, it is not

---

[26] There is room for confusion, of course, in the apparent parallelism of 'I perceive a house' and 'I perceive a pain'. In the former, 'house' is the cause of my sensation, whereas in the second example 'pain' refers to the perception itself. Descartes is concerned here, not with the linguistic muddle, but with the assumption that, in either case, we may draw conclusions invalidly about the cause of our sensations from the phenomenological character of the experience itself.

certain that the pain is something that exists outside our mind, in our foot, any more than when we see a light as if it were in the Sun, the light exists outside us in the Sun' (viii-1. 33; *M.* 138–9).[27] The implication of these two articles is not that pain must be classified merely as a mental reality, whatever that might mean. Rather, sensations are inner experiences that are caused either by objects that are outside our bodies or by conditions of our body. In neither case may we assume that our sensory experience provides an image that resembles its cause. Thus, although our sensations provide information that can be used reliably, if carefully, it is always a mistake to assume naively that the causes of our sensations—for example, a perception of a colour or a pain—correspond exactly to the sensations themselves.

SENSATIONS IN ANIMALS

For the sake of brevity I use the term 'animals' in this section to refer to non-human animals. Descartes is often taken to have denied that animals have sensations, including the sensation of pain. For example, he wrote to Mersenne in June 1640: 'in my view pain exists only in the understanding [*dans l'entendement*]' (iii. 85).[28] Since animals completely lack thought, they must also lack the experience of pain.[29] The significance of this objection is difficult to exaggerate. If Descartes were to deny the reality of pain in animals despite their unambiguous pain behaviour, that would constitute for many critics a *reductio ad absurdum* of his whole account of sensation. To avoid this interpretation, it may not be sufficient to quote texts that explicitly state the contrary, although I exploit that option below. One also needs an understanding of the historical context within which Descartes's brief and apparently unambiguous negative comments about animals may be understood.

The historical context of the debate is made explicit in a letter to Newcastle in 1646, in which Descartes discusses 'the understanding and thought that

[27] Here the term used for light is *lumen*, and Descartes is relying on his theory that the cause of our sensation of light is not simply some objective feature of the sun but the force or pressure that is transmitted from the sun to our eyes. If we thought that there is some feature of the sun that resembles our perception of light, we would be making the kind of mistake that Descartes is trying to correct.

[28] The full text shows that this remark occurs in the context of explaining pain: 'I do not explain the feeling of pain without a soul; for, in my view, pain exists only in the understanding. But I explain all the external movements that accompany this feeling in us; it is these movements alone that are found in animals, and not pain in a strict sense' (iii. 85).

[29] In the Sixth Replies: 'But not only did I claim that there is no thought [*cogitatio*] at all in animals, but . . . I proved it with the strongest arguments' (vii. 426).

Montaigne and others attribute to animals' (iv. 573). The 'others' in this context includes Pierre Charron (iv. 575). One clue, therefore, to what Descartes rejects is whatever Montaigne and Charron share in their discussion of animal faculties. That is, undoubtedly, the claim that the linguistic competence of animals is comparable (or superior) to that of human beings.

In *An Apology for Raymond Sebond*, Montaigne discusses human ignorance and pride and, in this context, provides a lengthy and rhetorical exposition of the superiority of animals to human beings. For Montaigne (1991: 520), 'there is a greater difference between one man and another than between some men and some beasts'. In the course of recounting stories about entertaining cats (1991: 505),[30] sympathetic, loyal and affectionate dogs (1991: 525), fish that are mathematical experts (1991: 534),[31] a lion that would rather starve than eat a friendly slave (1991: 532–3), and 'blackbirds, ravens, magpies and parrots' that can be taught to speak (1991: 518), Montaigne frequently claims that animals use language. Animals 'have means of complaining, rejoicing, calling on each other for help or inviting each other to love; they do so by meaningful utterances: if that is not talking, what is it?' (1991: 512).[32] Together with an extraordinary array of references to poetic fables and almost incredible feats attributed to trained animals, Montaigne also introduces a general philosophical argument to support this claim. 'There is, I say, no rational likelihood that beasts are forced to do by natural inclination the selfsame things which we do by choice and ingenuity. From similar effects we should conclude that there are similar faculties. Consequently, we should admit that animals employ the same method and the same reasoning as ourselves when we do anything' (1991: 524). Perhaps it is a poetic or rhetorical flourish that brings the author of the *Essays* to ask: 'Why do we deprive the heavenly bodies of souls, life or rationality?' (1991: 504). However, even if one stops short of attributing rationality and souls to planets, the fundamental challenge of Montaigne's query is unambiguous. We 'explain' human competence by postulating appropriate faculties in ourselves. When animals exhibit comparable behaviour, why do we not attribute similar faculties to them? Why do we explain animal behaviour by instinct, when human behaviour seems to require an immortal soul?

Pierre Charron was equally unambiguous in his analysis of the linguistic abilities of animals.[33] Charron examines four bases on which human beings claim

---

[30] 'When I play with my cat, how do I know that she is not passing time with me rather than I with her?'

[31] 'Three parts of Mathematics are particularly well known to tunny-fish: the way they live shows that.'

[32] Montaigne also quotes, with approval, from Lucretius: 'animals customarily make sounds having various meanings, when they feel fear or pain or when joy overflows' (1991: 506).

[33] Charron's discussion of the status of animals is found in Bk. I, Ch. viii, of *De la sagesse trois livres*, and in Bk. I, Ch. 34, of the English edition of 1729, *Of Wisdom Three Books*. I have provided new translations of all quotations from the French text.

to be superior to animals: (1) the faculties of mind possessed by humans; (2) their power to dominate animals; (3) their liberty; and (4) their virtue. Following Montaigne's example, he disputes the conclusiveness of all four of these as signs of superiority. In particular, he claims, animals have an ability to speak that is comparable to ours.

Just as we speak by gestures and by moving our eyes, our head, our hands, and our shoulders (by which those who are mute become wise), animals do the same, as we observe in those that have no voice but nonetheless engage in mutual exchanges; and just as animals understand us to some extent, we likewise understand them. . . . We speak to them, and they speak to us, and, if we do not understand each other perfectly, who is responsible for that? They could easily judge, by the same reasoning by which we judge them, that we are animals; however, they also reproach us that humans do not understand each other. We do not understand the Basques, the Bretons . . .   (Charron 1654: 56)

Thus the lack of verbal communication between humans and animals is reciprocal. But in the case of human beings, we are even less competent than animals because we fail to understand other members of the same species who happen to speak a different language. Charron argues that there is an unresolved and fundamental question about whether animals completely lack all spiritual faculties. According to him, they 'derive universals from particulars', they exhibit virtues such as fidelity to their (human) masters, but, despite that, some people 'maliciously attribute all these things to a natural inclination that is determined and servile' (1654: 58, 60). He concludes that, even though human beings may be superior because they possess some specific abilities that animals lack, the consequences of this are not necessarily favourable to human beings.

The conclusion of this comparison is that man vainly and wrongly elevates himself so much above animals. For if man possesses something more than animals, such as primarily the liveliness of his mind and understanding, and the major faculties of the soul, on the other hand he is subject to a thousand ills that animals avoid completely, such as inconstancy, fickleness, superstition, a painful concern about future events, ambition, avarice, envy, curiosity, etc.   (1654: 65)

While Charron's arguments in favour of animals are much less prolix than those of Montaigne, they are sufficiently similar to merit their joint classification by Descartes as his opponents on this issue. Given the significance, in the *Discourse*, of language as a defining characteristic of human understanding, the primary focus of his argument is the alleged failure of both Montaigne and Charron to distinguish adequately between animal communication and human language. I return to this issue in Chapter 6. For present purposes, the interim conclusion is that Descartes disagrees with Montaigne and Charron primarily because he rejects their claims about the linguistic abilities of animals.

However, there is still a lingering suspicion that Descartes also denies that animals have sensations, and it would help mitigate this concern if Descartes explicitly rejected the objection that he denies animals have sensations, especially in texts where the focus of the discussion is specifically animal faculties. For example, in reply to queries from Henry More (5 February 1649), Descartes summarizes his arguments for claiming a difference in species between human and non-human animals, most of which rely, as already indicated, on his account of language use. He acknowledges that, although we cannot demonstrate the positive thesis that there is any thought in animals, 'I do not think that it is therefore possible to prove that there is none.' Given the lack of proof, Descartes proposes to investigate 'what is most probable about this question', and concludes in the negative. He then adds, writing in Latin:

For the sake of brevity I omit the other reasons for denying thought [*cogitatio*] to animals. However, I would like to point out that I am speaking of thought, not about life or sensation [*de sensu*]. For I do not deny that any animal has life—which, I claim, consists only in the heat of the heart. Nor do I even deny sensation to animals, in so far as it derives from a bodily organ. Thus my view is not so much cruel to animals as respectful to human beings . . . whom it absolves from any suspicion of crime whenever they kill or eat animals.   (v. 278–9)[34]

This suggests a distinction between sensation and thought, despite Descartes's standard classification of sensation as a form of thought. Alternatively, Descartes could use a distinction between having a sensation of which the subject is not aware, and having a similar sensation accompanied by reflective awareness. He proposed such a distinction in reply to Plempius (3 October 1637), rejecting the suggestion that he believed that animals see things in the same way as we do—that is, 'while sensing or thinking that they see': 'I do not think that animals see as we do when we are aware of seeing, but only as we do when our mind is distracted, such as when the images of external objects are depicted on our retinas and, perhaps, the impressions they make in the optic nerves even determine our limbs to make various movements but we are not aware of any of this. In such circumstances, even we move like *automota*' (i. 413–14).[35] Thus, when Descartes denies that animals have thoughts (*cogitatio, pensée*), he assumes

---

[34] Cf. *Meditations*, Sixth Replies: 'But not only have I said that there is no thought [*cogitatio*] at all in animals, as is assumed here, but I also proved it by very strong arguments that no one so far has refuted . . . I have not denied that animals have what is commonly called life, a bodily soul, and organic sensation' (vii. 426).

[35] The phenomenon of blindsight, though unknown in the seventeenth century, would provide an empirical instantiation of unconscious sensation. Cf. Greenfield (2000: 29) and Zeki (1993: 347–50).

that they have sensations that guide their behaviour automatically, but that they are not conscious of having those sensations and are therefore not capable of reflecting on them and guiding their behaviour intentionally.

The same kind of argument was used in a letter to the Marquess of Newcastle (23 November 1646). Here too the conclusion drawn was about what is most probable: 'this seems to me a very strong argument . . .'; 'this is unlikely . . .'. The argument hinged on a comparison between human linguistic abilities and the inability of animals to use language in a similar way. The conclusion drawn was not that animals lack sensation, but that their actions 'are not guided by thought'. Descartes contrasts two ways in which human agents act, one in which their actions are guided by thought and one in which they result from instinct.

It often happens that we walk or eat without thinking at all about what we are doing; and similarly, without using our reason [*raison*], we reject things that are harmful for us and parry blows aimed at us. Indeed, even if we expressly willed not to put our hands in front of our head when we fall, we could not prevent ourselves from doing so. I consider also that, if we had no thought [*pensée*], we would eat as the animals do without having learned to do so; and it is said that those who walk in their sleep sometimes swim across streams in which they would drown if they were awake. As for the movements of our passions, even though in our case they are accompanied by thought because we have the ability to think, it is nevertheless very clear that they do not depend on thought, because they often occur in spite of us. Consequently they can occur in animals, even more violently than in human beings, without being able to conclude from that that animals have thoughts.   (iv. 573)

It seems clear enough that Descartes readily concedes to animals everything that takes place in us apart from thought or reasoning. This includes those passions that are typically expressed in 'cries of joy or sadness and the like'. In the case of a talking magpie, its repetition of words is attributed to an 'expression of one of its passions' (for example, 'the hope of eating'), and, in the case of other trained animals, their actions 'are only expressions of their fear, their hope and their joy; and consequently they can be performed without any thought' (iv. 574).

Having accepted that animals perform some actions much better than we do, just as clocks also keep the time better than us, Descartes has no objection to the suggestion that animals have a 'natural cunning' or 'instinct' by which they often surpass us. Indeed, since their bodily organs are similar to ours, 'one might conjecture that there is attached to these organs some thought [*quelque pensée*] such as we experience in ourselves, but of a very much less perfect kind'. He is reluctant to accept that this level of thought is sufficiently similar to ours ('this is unlikely') to support postulating mental faculties in all animals, including even oysters or sponges. On the contrary, there seems to be a decreasing level of complexity from man to sponges, and the degrees of complexity are most probably matched by corresponding degrees of what one may call 'thought'. But we have no reason to believe that even sponges have the kind of reflective awareness that we enjoy, and therefore we need not postulate in them any faculty that is comparable to the human mind.

A similar argument is used in Descartes's final work, *The Passions of the Soul* (1649), in a context devoted to the apparently automatic link between certain passions and the usual way of expressing these passions in action. The possibility of retraining human passions is supported by the experience of training animals. 'For, although they lack reason, and perhaps even thought [*la pensée*], all the movements of the spirits and of the gland that produce passions in us are nevertheless present in them too' (xi. 369). The argument is that if, with a little effort, we are able 'to change the movement of the brain in animals devoid of reason', we should be able to achieve the same result even more effectively in the case of human beings.

Animal rights defenders may baulk at the grudging acknowledgement of sensation in animals with the qualification: '*quatenus ab organo corporeo dependet.*' But that results from oversimplifying the machine model to which Cartesians appealed in the context of explanation. Given the three degrees of sensation that were distinguished in the *Meditations*, it is impossible for Descartes to deny sensation to animals. However, the three degrees are still not sufficiently clear to provide him with a completely unambiguous language, and the close conjunction between thought or reasoning and many human sensations facilitates the kind of terminological carelessness that shows in some of his comments. If one concedes that there is some unresolved ambiguity in the use of relevant terms such as 'thought' (to which I return in Chapter 7), the core of the Cartesian theory seems to be the following. Both animals and human beings have sensations, including the sensation of pain. Human sensations spill over spontaneously into calculations and judgements, many of which we are unaware of making, and into appropriate actions that are often automatic reactions that bypass our conscious decisions. Many animals seem to act similarly. However, a fully developed account of sensation would require a language that could distinguish various elements of sensation that occur together in human experience but are not duplicated fully in the case of animals. Descartes began this process, somewhat confusingly, in the distinction between various degrees of sensation, but a satisfactory account required much more work.

For present purposes it is enough to record that the position adopted by Descartes in relation to animals was widely shared in the middle of the seventeenth century and that it was not inconsistent with our experience of animal behaviour.[36] The subsequent history of the debate about the capacities of animals helped to focus attention, not on whether animals feel pain or have other sensations, but on what kind of theory is most appropriate to explaining their behaviour.[37] It became apparent quickly that many of the defenders of the reality of animal sensations were not disputing facts about animal sensations and behaviour, but were attempting to defend the relevance of souls for explaining both animal and human behaviour. Descartes's apparent stubbornness in the face of the evidence is a symptom of the extent to which he rejected the necessity or utility of souls as an explanation of animal behaviour. What was frightening, for many, about Descartes's theory of the animal machine was not the apparent denial of animal sensations, but the theoretical possibility of explaining all human behaviour by using the same model of a biological machine interacting with its environment. In the choice of explanatory strategies, Descartes had abandoned Aristotle and his scholastic followers and, unwittingly, had anticipated La Mettrie.

In conclusion, Descartes approaches the task of explaining sensations, both in human beings and in other animals, by postulating various mechanisms in the sensory organs, nerve connections between the organs and the brain to relay information, and ways in which the core of the brain may respond to the incoming signals that it receives. The logic of this research agenda was to stretch this type of explanation to its limits. There is a clear acknowledgement, based on human experience, that we often respond to information provided by the senses by a purely automatic response over which we have little control and which does not require any conscious decision on our part. There remains a question, then, about the resourcefulness of this type of explanation, and about the limits of such an explanatory model. There is also an unresolved question about how best to map traditional language about thought, reason, consciousness, and so on onto the proposed account of brain activity. Descartes struggled with this issue, with some success, in the proposed three degrees of sensation. He also struggled with the same issue when combating what he took to be the manifestly false view of Montaigne that the linguistic competence of animals is comparable to ours. It remains to be seen whether his theory of sensation can do justice to the twin demands of providing a scientific explanation without reducing animals to insensate automata.

---

[36] Cf. Pierre Chanet (1646) and Marin Cureau de la Chambre (1648).
[37] The standard account is Rosenfield (1968).

CHAPTER 3

Imagination and Memory

Descartes's *World* was already in manuscript form when he wrote to Mersenne, in late 1632, that the book would include a more comprehensive discussion of various human functions than he had originally anticipated. He then added the following sentence, to identify one of the sources of his investigations: 'I am dissecting the head of various animals at present to explain what the imagination, memory, etc. consist of' (i. 263).[1] It is not surprising that these anatomical observations yielded minimal results. Whatever Descartes may have observed with the naked eye in 1632 was completely inadequate for constructing a scientific explanation of how memory and imagination work. What is surprising, however, is that he decided to examine animal brains to develop an account of imagination and memory because it implies, despite his subsequent references to an intellectual memory, that he thought of memory and imagination as functions of the brain. This attempt at a scientific explanation of these mental faculties is consistent with the account of perception developed in the years 1630–40.

As indicated in Chapter 2, Descartes claimed in *A Treatise on Man* that ideas are those figures that are 'traced in the spirits on the surface of the gland H [the pineal gland], where the seat of the imagination and the common sense is' (xi. 177; W. 149). The patterns assumed by animal spirits as they emerge from the pineal gland, in response to the dilation of nerve endings, are correlated with the patterns of relative ease or resistance with which the spirits enter at the end of neural tubes. These in turn are determined by incoming impressions from stimuli that affect the senses, or by various conditions of the brain and other parts of the body. 'When they depend on the presence of objects they can all be

---

[1] When writing to Mersenne in 1639, Descartes mentions on two occasions that he had spent considerable time doing dissections. On 20 February, he wrote that he had spent 'much time in doing dissections' during the previous eleven years (i.e. since 1628). On 13 November he recalled a winter he had spent in Amsterdam, during which 'I went almost daily to the butcher's house to see him kill the beasts, and I used to carry home with me those parts that I wished to anatomize at my leisure. This is something I did a number of times in all the places where I lived' (ii. 525, 621). Cf. Descartes 1859–60 (i. 162, 170), where Descartes describes the results of dissecting the brain of a calf.

attributed to the common sense; but they may also proceed from other causes
. . . they should then be attributed to the imagination' (xi. 177: W. 150). In other
words, the ideas that occur on the pineal gland are caused either by objects that
are currently affecting the senses, or by various conditions of the brain (among
which are included the after-effects of earlier sensations). Descartes claims at
this point that he could explain how these patterns can be communicated
through the arteries to the heart, and how they may be passed from a mother's
brain to a foetus in her womb. However, without providing even a hint of the
proposed explanation, he writes instead: 'I shall content myself with telling you
more about how the traces are imprinted on the internal parts of the brain . . .
which is the seat of memory.'

This hypothesis about relevant brain functions implies a unified explanation
of sensation, imagination, and recollection, in which 'the brain [is] . . . the
organ or the seat of the common sense, of the imagination, and of the memory'
(xi. 227; W. 172). In all three cases, an idea in the brain is a characteristic pattern
in the outflow of animal spirits from the pineal gland, in direct response to
the condition of various parts of the brain. Different kinds of thinking result
from the ways in which these brain patterns are caused, either by an object of
perception that is currently present to the sense organs or by other states of
the brain. Memory and imagination are forms of thinking that do not presuppose the presence of a perceptual object, although they share a common
source of ideas in sensation. They both presuppose the capacity of the brain
to store the results of earlier perceptual experiences and to reuse them in
various ways subsequently. However, while memory is limited to the recollection of earlier brain patterns, imagination can also act creatively to construct
novel ideas.

There is a remarkable consistency over time in the way in which Descartes
classifies various cognitive faculties and explains them in terms of relevant brain
activities, beginning with the *Rules*. For example, he acknowledges in Rule Eight
that 'the intellect alone is capable of scientific knowledge, but it can be aided
or hindered by three other faculties, namely, by imagination, sensation, and
memory' (x. 398: D. 143). Rule Twelve provides a summary of the contents and
implications of the first set of twelve rules, and again lists the same four faculties
for acquiring knowledge, 'the intellect, imagination, sensation, and memory'
(x. 411; D. 151). While he assumes that the 'power by which we know things in a
strict sense is completely spiritual' (x. 415; D. 154), it is one and the same power
that operates through sensation, imagination, and memory. Descartes does not
develop, in the *Rules*, an account of the degree of abstraction involved in so-
called scientific knowledge; but he invariably links it with the ways in which
ideas are manipulated or processed in the brain, where the different processes

are described as faculties of sensation, imagination, and memory, depending on the source or novelty of the ideas involved.[2]

This unified account of the activity of the brain and its contribution to knowledge by means of different faculties is summarized in Part V of the *Discourse on Method*, in which the reluctant author reveals some of the conclusions reached in the unpublished *World*:

I had explained all these things in sufficient detail in the treatise that I had planned to publish earlier. Then I had shown . . . what changes must be made in the brain to cause waking, sleep, and dreams; how light, sounds, odours, tastes, warmth and all the other qualities of external objects can impress different ideas on it through the senses . . . what part of the brain should be taken as 'the common sense', where these ideas are received; what should be taken as the memory [*la mémoire*], which stores the ideas, and as the imagination [*la fantaisie*], which can vary them in different ways and compose new ones and, by the same means, distribute the animal spirits to the muscles and cause the limbs of the body to move in as many different ways as our own bodies can move without the will directing them, depending on the objects that are present to the senses and the internal passions of the body.   (vi. 55; *D*. 40)

Thus sensation, imagination, and memory are all functions of the brain and its operations. They are also forms of thought.[3] Descartes did not see any difficulty in accepting that they could be both at the same time. Accordingly he wrote to Gibieuf (19 January 1642): 'I also see no difficulty in understanding that the faculties of imagining and sensing belong to the soul, because they are thoughts of some kind; and that they nevertheless belong to the soul only in so far as it is joined to the body, because they are types of thought without which one can conceive of the soul completely apart' (iii. 479). In the following pages, I summarize Descartes's account of how imagination and memory are forms of thinking that are explained by related activities of the brain. Imagination is discussed first, because the brain processes that are responsible for it are similar to those involved in sensation, although it would be equally appropriate to discuss memory first since images stored in memory are sometimes relevant to explaining imagination.

In developing these explanations, Descartes often refers to distinctions between imagination and pure understanding, and between corporeal memory and intellectual memory. Thus both of these faculties, the imagination and the memory, reflect a form of dualism similar to that mentioned in the earlier dis-

---

[2] The continued use of the traditional faculty language should not be misunderstood as if the faculties are really distinct. Wolf-Devine (1993: 17–18, 51) draws attention to the 'vestigial' faculty psychology in the *Rules* and its gradual elimination even as early as *The Dioptrics* (1637).

[3] Imagining is classified as a form of thought in the *Meditations* (vii. 28, 73, 78), while both imagination and memory are identified as forms of thought in the *Principles* (i. 65) (viii-i. 32).

cussion of sensation. In this context we are also provided the first hints of a theoretical basis for such dualistic descriptions—namely, the way in which we can
generate universals from the images of particulars by using the resources of
language.

IMAGINATION

Many recent discussions of the Cartesian account of the imagination have
been so concerned with epistemological problems, especially with the extent
to which the unwary may be misled by their imagination, that they have overlooked both the inchoate theory of imagination developed by Descartes and its
unique role in how we acquire knowledge.[4] The latter features are interdependent. They were first analysed in the *Rules*, and the schematic overview presented
there was repeated throughout Descartes's mature work. Evidently, our first-
person experiences of imagining, of daydreaming, or of dreaming while asleep,
are all available to us without having any explanation of how imagining takes
place. It would, therefore, be possible to provide a phenomenology of the experience of imagining, or to analyse the epistemological issues raised by the imagination, without trying to explain how the imagination functions. But this was
not how Descartes worked. From his earliest reflections on the imagination, he
discussed together the experience of imagining, its explanation as a function of
the brain, its status as a form of thinking, and the epistemological implications
of its special status.

The first significant reference to imagination in the *Rules* (Rule Three) contrasts the reliability of intuition (*intuitus*) with the false judgements that result
from the imagination when it combines images inappropriately.[5] This caution
should not mislead readers of the *Rules*, as if the imagination were always a
source of mistaken judgements. In fact Descartes balances this initial warning
with a comprehensive discussion of how the imagination provides necessary
data for reliable judgements about physical reality. Thus, despite the familiar
contrast between reliable intuition and unreliable imagining, Descartes's final
position is that the imagination is a cognitive faculty and, like any other instrument, it may be used properly or improperly. The distinction between appropriate and inappropriate use depends on the type of reality that we are
investigating. Imagination has a specific, important role in natural philosophy,

---

[4] Sepper (1996) is a notable exception.

[5] However, the role of memory traces in the brain is mentioned earlier, in the *Cogitationes privatae* (x. 230).

but a much more limited use in metaphysics. Before assessing what Descartes says about imagination in any given text, therefore, it is important to distinguish its supporting role in acquiring knowledge of the physical world from its allegedly obstructive or misleading influence when applied to the objects of metaphysical speculation—namely, the soul and God. For example, Rule Eight claims that the intellect is the first object of our knowledge and is known directly by reflection or intuition. Apart from that, 'there are only two' other instruments by the use of which we can gain knowledge, 'the phantasy and the senses' (x. 396; D. 141).[6] The same rule later enumerates three other faculties, rather than two, that can assist or hinder the intellect, 'imagination, sensation, and memory' (x. 398; D. 143).[7]

As indicated in Chapter 2, the inputs from the sensory organs are transmitted to the brain, and the knowing subject exploits the capacities of the brain to sense, to imagine, and to remember. The shared brain functions explain how the imagination interacts with the senses, with memory, and with the intellect. Thus the intellect can cause various things to be depicted in the imagination and, in the opposite direction, the imagination can cause ideas to arise in the intellect. Likewise the senses can imprint images on the imagination, and the latter can help direct our sensory organs in ways that make it possible to have new sensations. The various faculties may also impede each other as they vie for use of the limited processing capacity of the brain. For example, the creative use of the imagination can so overload the brain's capacity that it may become temporarily incapable of receiving new inputs from the sense organs or triggering appropriate actions in the muscles. In these circumstances our knowing power 'forms new shapes that so occupy the imagination that it is often no longer capable of receiving ideas coming from the common sense, or of transmitting them to the force responsible for motion in the way in which purely bodily motions take place' (x. 415; D. 154).

One of the special functions of the imagination, in this context, is to help the intellect to acquire distinct ideas of physical things. This endorsement of the role of the imagination had been made earlier, in the *Cogitationes privatae*, where Descartes compared unfavourably the success of philosophers, in contrast with poets, in forging concepts of spiritual realities by analogy with observable things. 'Just as the imagination uses shapes to conceive of bodies, so likewise the

---

[6] Descartes usually reserves the Latin term *phantasia* (rather than *imaginatio*) to refer to brain functions that support imagining, although he sometimes uses the terms interchangeably; for example, in Rule Twelve he refers to 'the phantasy or the imagination [*in phantasia vel imaginatione*]' (x. 414).

[7] The discrepancy is explained by the fact that the same part of the brain can function as either memory or imagination; 'memory, at least that which is physical and similar to the recall of brute animals, is not distinct from the imagination' (x. 416; D. 155). Cf. Rule Twelve, where he lists four faculties for acquiring knowledge: 'intellect, imagination, sensation and memory' (x. 411; D. 151).

understanding uses certain sensible bodies, such as the wind or light, to model spiritual realities' (x. 217). The same suggestion is repeated in the *Rules*. In order to acquire ideas of physical things, 'the idea of that thing should be formed in the imagination as distinctly as possible' (x. 416–17; D. 155). Although this proposal is made in a draft, unpublished text and might therefore be thought not to represent Descartes's mature philosophy, it remained central to the Cartesian account of theory construction in science. Clear and distinct ideas of extended or physical objects are possible only with the aid of reliable images in the imagination.[8]

Of course, the reason why the imagination can provide this essential service is that, as a part of the brain, it is itself an extended body. 'The phantasy itself, together with the ideas it contains, [are] nothing but a real body that is really extended and has a shape' (x. 441; D. 171). There is a detailed example of how the imagination plays this role in Rule Fourteen, in which the author explains that 'we shall undertake nothing from here on without the help of the imagination' (x. 443; D. 173). Even a cursory familiarity with the work of Descartes suggests that the identification of body and extension is an enduring feature of his natural philosophy. This identification is explained for the first time, in the *Rules*, where the argument depends essentially on an appeal to what we can *imagine*. 'Extension' is defined as whatever has length, breadth, and depth, and no further explanation is needed 'because there is absolutely nothing that is perceived more easily by our imagination' (x. 442; D. 172). Here the reader is warned about the dangers of abstraction—in this particular case, the illusion that extension is something distinct from an extended thing—and Descartes draws the general conclusion that one should reject 'the kinds of philosophical entity which do not really fall within the scope of the imagination' (x. 442; D. 173). For example, some people might convince themselves that they can make a genuine distinction between extension *per se* and an extended body, but 'they would not use a physical idea to conceive this'. The proposed remedy for such an unjustified abstraction is 'to reflect carefully on the image of extension that they attempt to depict at that time in their phantasy. For they would notice that they do not perceive it as deprived of every subject, but that the way in which it is imagined is completely different from what they think' (x. 443; D. 173). In other words, in

---

[8] In the *Rules* Descartes claims that 'the sciences, no matter how hidden they may be, are to be deduced not from lofty and obscure things, but merely from those that are easy and most evident' (x. 402; D. 145). He then quotes as an illustration of such an approach how we could learn what a 'natural power' is by reflecting 'on the local motions of bodies, because there could be nothing easier to perceive in this whole area'. Cf. Descartes's summary account of his early mathematical work in Part II of the *Discourse on Method*, where he claims to have concentrated his attention on proportions between lines 'because I found nothing simpler nor anything that I could represent more distinctly to my imagination and senses' (vi. 20; D. 17).

order to discover whether extension is really distinguishable from extended bodies, we should consult our image of a real body and we should attempt to separate, within the image, the extension from the body to which it belongs. Our efforts are bound to fail, which implies that extension is not really distinguishable from body.[9]

This test of the true meaning of the terms 'extension' and 'body' is repeated for each of the three propositions that are analysed in Rule Fourteen: 'extension occupies a place', 'a body has extension', and 'extension is not a body'. In the second proposition, it might seem as if 'extension' means something other than the term 'body'. Descartes argues against this, however, because 'we do not form two distinct ideas in our phantasy—one of a body and the other of extension—but only one idea, that of an extended body' (x. 444; D. 173–4). In the case of the third proposition, which asserts that extension is not a body, Descartes warns that the term 'extension' is used in such a way that 'there is no characteristic idea in the imagination that corresponds to it'. He concludes that, if this proposition makes sense, the term 'extension' must be understood as denoting some abstract entity that is generated by the pure intellect. 'This is an occasion of error for many people, who fail to recognize that extension understood in this way cannot be comprehended by the imagination, and who represent it to themselves as a true idea' (x. 444; D. 174). The imagination is the faculty that is used here to form true ideas and to correct the mistakes of the understanding that result from unwarranted abstraction.[10]

Is this the same Descartes, familiar to readers of the *Meditations*, who constantly recommends the importance of pure understanding and warns about the epistemological snares associated with the senses and the imagination? One might be forgiven for thinking that these endorsements of the imagination are the objections of some critic rather than genuine Cartesian texts or, perhaps, that they represent merely their author's first (and subsequently abandoned) reflections while he was still working within a scholastic framework. The opposite is in fact the case. Descartes draws a general conclusion from his examination of these three propositions that is subsequently a central feature of his mature philosophy.

---

[9] Descartes uses the concept of a real distinction here without explaining the concept explicitly. He returns to this issue in the *Principles*, (1, 60–1), which is discussed in Chapter 9.

[10] The link between matter and the imagination is such that it supports the following claim in *A Treatise on Light*: 'The idea of that matter is such a part of all the ideas that our imagination can form that you must necessarily conceive of it, or you can never imagine anything at all' (xi. 35; W. 24). The resulting concept of matter is the same as that proposed in the *Rules*: 'the quantity of the matter that I have described does not differ from its substance any more than number differs from the things numbered. Nor should they find it strange if I conceive of its extension, or the property it has of occupying space, not as an accident, but as its true form and essence' (xi. 35–6; W. 24).

It should be carefully noted that, in all other propositions in which these terms retain the same meaning and are used in the same way . . . we can and ought to use the assistance of the imagination. For in that case even though the intellect attends precisely only to what a word means, the imagination ought to form a true idea of the thing [*veram rei ideam*], so that the same intellect can turn to other conditions that are not expressed by the word, if the need arises, and without ever judging foolishly that they have been excluded.   (x. 445; *D*. 174–5)

The intellect evidently operates by abstracting features of some reality in such a way that only such abstracted features are reflected in the meaning of a word. It follows that we could not decide questions about the attributes of a physical reality by simply consulting the words used to describe it. That would be a seventeenth-century version of a misleading style of argument that became familiar in twentieth-century ordinary language philosophy. We need, instead, what the text describes as a 'true idea' of the reality in question. The *Rules* suggest that the appropriate corrective for intellectual abstraction is provided by the imagination, and that such a remedy is essential for scientific method. If investigators adopted this suggestion, they would no longer think of extension as something that is distinct from real bodies or of number as something distinct from numbered things. In a word, they would avoid the pitfalls of what Descartes describes as 'wonderful mysteries and sheer nonsense' or, in the words of Rule Five, the fundamental mistake of philosophers who neglect expe-rience and believe 'that the truth will spring from their own brains as Minerva did from the head of Jove' (x. 380; *D*. 131).

The irreplaceable contribution of the imagination to our knowledge of material things should therefore complement the caution, first mentioned in Rule Three, about the possible deceptiveness of imagination. Rule Twelve pro-vides a way of reconciling these apparently incompatible suggestions in its analysis of how we come to know what are called 'composite things'. Com-posite realities may be known by acquaintance (from some direct experience of them), or they may be composed from simpler parts by the imagination. This kind of composition is admittedly a possible source of error, but it is also a unique source of knowledge in certain cases. The function of the imagination in synthesizing discrete items of sensory experience was acknowledged, for example, in the *Compendium of Music*. The problem addressed there was how to hear a tune from a series of discrete notes that are separated in time. This is pos-sible only because one can use one's imagination to remember the notes long enough to join them together to form a tune. 'Thus our imagination proceeds to the end, where it eventually conceives the entire song as a single thing that is constituted from many equal parts' (x. 94). Dennis Sepper (1996: 45) comments on this passage that 'imagination is portrayed here as an extraordinarily active power that is responsible for the ability to perceive the complex unity of sounds as a whole rather than as simply a congeries of unconnected tones'. Once the imagination is credited, as it is here, with the task of synthesizing discrete sensory inputs, it raises a question about a possible lack of fit between the composite idea formed by the imagination and the reality to which it is attributed. The fallibility of the imagination, therefore, derives from its synthesizing role in the perception of composite realities. Descartes argues in the *Rules* that there is no danger of being deceived as long as one does not judge 'that the imagination faithfully represents the objects of the senses or that the senses are endowed with the true shape of things' (x. 423; D. 159). This is a familiar problem, that we may perceive or imagine things other than they really are, with the consequent risk of error if we make judgements without due caution. For example, if we are told a story, we should not believe without further evidence that the events happened exactly as they are described. We are equally liable to error 'when the imagination is malfunctioning, as happens in the case of melancholics, if we judge that its disturbed images represent real things' (x. 423; D. 160). However, such compositions by the imagination 'will not deceive the intellect of someone who is wise, because they will judge that whatever they accept from their imagination is really represented there, but they will never claim that the very same thing was transmitted in its integrity and without any modification from external things to the senses and from the senses to the phantasy, unless they know this independently on the basis of some other evidence' (x. 423; D. 160). Thus the analytical work attributed to the imagination, in assisting us to acquire an accurate idea of what is meant by 'body' or 'extension', remains immune to sceptical concerns. In the case of composite realities, however, the mere fact that a particular image of a composite reality is presented to our imagination does not guarantee that our image faithfully reflects the reality in question. This was the source of the concern that prompted the apparently unfavourable contrast with *intuitus* in Rule Three.

The most significant feature of the discussion of the imagination in the *Rules*, almost independently of what is actually said in detail about it, is how much this cognitive faculty features in the analysis of method and knowledge proposed by the young Descartes. Here the imagination emerges as a major contributor to the acquisition of genuine, scientific knowledge whose role cannot be replaced by some kind of purely intellectual knowing. If one includes both the hypotheses about how the imagination works in the brain, and the epistemological analysis of its role, the *Rules* includes the following suggestions:

1. There is a real part of the brain of all animals in which images of things are imprinted.

2. Since the same part of the brain is involved in sensation and in memory, what is usually described as three distinct faculties is actually the processing of information derived from current sensations, from brain traces that assist the recollection of earlier experiences, and from the more or less spontaneous interaction of neural impulses from disparate sources.

3. Sensation, memory, and imagination are all equally likely to mislead, whenever we naively assume that external composite realities correspond exactly to our internal images of them. However, if we avoid making this unwarranted assumption, all these faculties may guide our judgements; in some cases it is impossible to acquire the relevant knowledge without recourse to these brain-dependent faculties.

4. Imagination is particularly relevant to acquiring knowledge of physical realities. The best way to acquire such knowledge is to make the realities themselves, or distinct images of them, available through sensation or imagination.

5. The knowledge of particulars that we acquire in this way can be generalized by abstraction, and we can also draw inferences from it by reasoning. The latter operations are functions of what is called 'pure intellect' (to which I return in Chapter 7).

The *Rules* unambiguously locates the activity of imagining in the brain, even if there is some slippage between the words used to describe (*a*) a faculty or function of imagining, and (*b*) the part of the brain in which it takes place. Some of this ambiguity is avoided in later writing, but without any diminution of the fundamental Cartesian insight that imagining really does involve the depiction of images of some kind in the brain of the subject. Despite this continuity, however, readers who are more familiar with the *Meditations* might assume that there is a very significant change in emphasis from the earlier work to the well-known publications of Descartes's mature period, that the latter highlight the necessity of leading the mind away from the errors to which the imagination is prone, and that the early Cartesian theory of the imagination suffers the same fate as the theory of ideas as brain states: they are both superseded by a theory of purely incorporeal ideas in a non-material mind.

One cannot deny that there is a change of emphasis from the *Rules* to the *Meditations*, but the change is not in Descartes's theory of what the imagination is or how it functions. It is a change in focus from a scientific explanation of this 'faculty' to problems in epistemology that result from its misapplication to the study of metaphysical realities. In other words, the *Meditations* is unequivocally an attempt on Descartes's part to explain how we can acquire reliable knowledge of God and the soul, and how such knowledge is possible despite the familiar sceptical arguments that are rehearsed in the First Meditation. Knowledge of these elusive realities is possible, he argues, for those who complete the course of meditative exercises proposed to readers of the *Meditations*. These exercises show how it is possible to lead the mind, step by step, away from its usual way of knowing to a kind of knowledge that is very difficult to achieve but, once realized, is such that its benefits last a lifetime. The *Meditations* do not tell us how to acquire scientific knowledge of the world; nor do they imply that we should ignore the irreplaceable contribution of sensation and imagination to the task of acquiring knowledge. As Descartes himself makes abundantly clear, the *Meditations* provide a specialized method that is suitable for a very specific task: to make reliable claims about God and the soul. When not engaged in this task, we should not shy away from an appropriate use of the imagination.

I mentioned above that, in the *Rules*, Descartes addresses three related sets of questions about the subjective experience of imagining, the epistemology of the imagination as a cognitive faculty, and the fundamental reality of what the imagination is or how it functions. The *Rules* says little about the third issue beyond assuming that imagining is some kind of brain functioning similar to perception, one that may occur in the absence of any object of perception. *A Treatise on Man* takes up the challenge again, with only marginally better results. Here Descartes contrasts the brain of a sleeping person with that of someone who is awake in terms of the force with which animal spirits course through its various cavities. When this happens, the matter of the brain is extended in all directions, 'causing it to expand and tighten all the tiny nerve fibres coming from it, in the same way that a moderate wind can fill the sails of a ship and tighten all the ropes to which they are attached' (x. 173; W. 146). With a less forceful flow of spirits, only some parts of the brain are fully distended while others are relaxed, 'as happens in various parts of the sail when the wind is too feeble to fill it'. The latter represents the body of someone who is asleep and dreaming. Whatever the mechanism involved in perceiving an object, as outlined in Chapter 2, Descartes assumes that similar processes occur in the brain even when the perceptual object is no longer present. In those cases the motion of animal spirits through nerve fibres may be stimulated simply by the ebb and flow of such spirits in a body when the cavities of the brain are not completely closed and when external stimuli are absent or not dominant. Thus, when impressions or brain states 'depend on the presence of objects they can all be attributed to the common sense; but they may also proceed from other causes . . . and they should then be attributed to the imagination' (x. 177; W. 150).

This suggests that imagining is some kind of spontaneous brain activity that is similar to what happens in sensation, except that there is no perceptual object present. As long as the brain fibres are sufficiently open to allow animal spirits to flow through, the patterns of animal spirits may resemble those associated with parts of different perceptual objects. 'It is in this way that chimeras and hippogriffs are formed in the imagination of those who dream while awake, that is, those who let their fancy nonchalantly wander here and there without external objects diverting it, and without being directed by reason' (x. 184; W. 56–7). Apart from the suggestion that the imagination may sometimes be controlled by the will, Descartes assumes here that the kinds of things we imagine depend on images that originated in sensations. If we are daydreaming, he assumes that our brains process incoming information from the senses and spontaneously generate other imagined images. However, if we are asleep, it is more likely that the complete lack of incoming information will facilitate the activity of the imagination, with the result that we dream things with greater clarity and force; hence 'the images formed in dreams can be more distinct and more lively than those formed during waking' (x. 198; W. 165).

  If the imagination relies on this kind of brain activity, which is similar to what happens when we have veridical perceptions, it is consistent with Descartes's epistemology of the imagination and supports the caution recommended when making judgements based on imagined compound objects. It also implies or anticipates the extent to which physical images in the brain are less important in Descartes's metaphysical writings. However, despite the limited role of the imagination in metaphysics, this faculty is still understood there in the same way as in earlier writings. Thus the imagination is defined in the *Meditations* as 'the contemplation of the shape or image of a physical thing' (vii. 28; M. 26). It is described in the Replies to Objections as relying on 'an image depicted in the phantasy [*imago in phantasia depicta*]' (vii. 165), and on 'the images of material things depicted in the corporeal phantasy' (vii. 181). Such references often involve a sharp contrast between (1) imagining and (2) thinking about abstract ideas. For example, in reply to Hobbes's objections, Descartes argues that we have a genuine idea of the human soul despite the fact that 'there is no image of it depicted in the phantasy' (vii. 183). Even this contrast presupposes the account of imagination that had been proposed in earlier writings and by comparison with which the functioning of the intellect is to be explained. In doing so, Descartes consistently denies the equivalence between ideas and the images that occur in the part of the brain called the 'phantasy'. For example, in discussing the idea of God, he argues: 'Nor do I think that that idea is of the same nature as the images of material things that are depicted in the phantasy' (vii. 139). Likewise, when Gassendi challenged the distinction made in the Sixth Meditation between imagining and understanding, Descartes replied that the powers of understanding and imagining are not simply different in degree, but are two completely different ways of thinking. 'For the mind alone is used in understanding whereas, in imagining, a corporeal form is contemplated. And although geometrical figures are completely corporeal, it does not follow that we should think about those ideas by which we understand them as corporeal, as long as they do not fall within the scope of the imagination' (vii. 385).

One way of expressing this argument is: even if an image is necessary in order to have a 'true idea' of a physical thing, this does not preclude us from having an idea of other realities of which we have no image, such as the human mind or God. The latter are, in a strict sense, unimaginable (vii. 385). The distinction between these two ways of thinking is explained in the Sixth Meditation.

When I imagine a triangle, for example, I do not merely understand that it is a figure bounded by three lines but, at the same time, I also see those three lines with the mind's eye as if they were present, and that is what I call imagining. However, if I wish to think about a chiliagon, I understand equally well that it is a figure that consists of one thousand sides, just as I understand that a triangle is a figure that consists of three sides; but I cannot imagine a thousand sides in the same way, that is, I cannot see them as if they were present.   (vii. 72; M. 57–8)

There were a number of objections to this distinction, but Descartes's replies, in the *Meditations*, add little to the persuasiveness of the original claim. However, there are sufficient indications in his correspondence and elsewhere to clarify the distinction between imagination and understanding in terms of the level of abstraction involved in each.

The twin benefits and limitations of imagination had been aptly summarized, four years previously, in the *Discourse on Method* (Part IV), where Descartes writes about the reason why many people experience great difficulty in forming an idea of their own soul or of God. 'They are so used to not thinking of anything without imagining it—which is an appropriate way of thinking of material things—that anything that is not imaginable seems to them to be unintelligible' (vi. 37; D. 28). Descartes wrote to Mersenne two years later (13 November 1639) about the role of the imagination in doing mathematics. 'That part of the mind that is most useful for mathematics, namely the imagination, is more of a hindrance than a help in metaphysical speculations' (ii. 622). This reflects both the significance of imagination for doing mathematics, as suggested originally in the *Rules*, and the importance of not being limited to images when we wish to abstract from individual physical things and their properties in order to speculate about what is not material. Consequently the intellect, rather than the imagination, is especially suited to thinking about universals, as Descartes explained to Regius (24 May 1640): 'I do not see why you wish to attribute the perception of universals to the imagination rather than to the intellect. I attribute this exclusively to the intellect, which applies an idea that, in itself, is singular to many things' (iii. 66). Without begging the question about the status of such abstract knowledge, it is clear that the Cartesian approach to acquiring knowledge of material things relies necessarily on information acquired through the senses, and that any subsequent analysis of our concepts presupposes that we consult either the realities themselves or images of them that are imprinted on the phantasy. However, as soon as we abstract from individuals or exploit the universals made available by language use, we are no longer limited to images and we can engage in the kind of metaphysical speculation that is necessary in order to think about the soul or God.

The same evaluation of the role of the imagination is found in Part I of the *Principles*. Imagination is appropriate for thinking about physical things but inappropriate for thinking about abstract or non-material realities. 'Many people do not understand any substance unless it is imaginable and physical, and even unless it is capable of being sensed. Nor do they realize that the only things that are imaginable are those that involve extension, motion, and shape, even though there are many other things that are intelligible' (viii-1. 37).

One should not conclude that the superiority of metaphysical speculation (in its degree of abstraction), or the familiar negative evaluation of the limits of the imagination, implies that we should devote our time primarily to metaphysics. It was not simply an unwarranted sympathy for the distractions experienced by his royal correspondent that prompted the following reply to Princess Elizabeth (28 June 1643):

> I can also say truthfully that the main rule that I followed in my study—and the rule that I believe has helped me most to acquire some knowledge—is that I never gave more than very few hours a day to thoughts that occupy the imagination, and very few hours a year to thoughts that occupy the understanding on its own; I spent all the rest of my time in relaxing the senses and reposing my mind.   (iii. 692–3; M. 153)

Apart from the element of consolation or personal reassurance involved, Descartes was conceding the relative abstractness and difficulty of metaphysics, and the extent to which we might survive a whole lifetime on the memory of the conclusions once drawn in such speculations.[11] Our normal experience is that we rarely exercise the intellect without at the same time picturing something in the imagination;[12] this is characterized as a defect by Descartes, but only when he is trying to do metaphysics. Having made his contribution to that

---

[11] See *Conversation with Burman*: 'It should be noted that one should not be so taken up with the *Meditations* and with metaphysical things, nor should they be developed in commentaries and the like. Much less should one repeat the work already done by the author, as some try to do, for he has delved into them sufficiently. It is enough to have known them once in a general way, and then to remember the conclusions' (v. 165).

[12] Cf. Sixth Replies (vii. 441), although here Descartes is describing how he thought in his infancy.

esoteric discipline, he is content in 1643 to recommend that we devote most of our time 'to those thoughts in which the understanding acts together with the imagination and the senses' (iii. 695).

The central role of the imagination, not only in acquiring knowledge, but equally in the emotional life of the individual, was developed by Descartes in correspondence with Princess Elizabeth. In a letter in May or June 1645, he discusses the difference between the intellect and the imagination in terms of their impact on our emotional equanimity. We are emotionally affected by plays or stories, he suggests, even when we know (intellectually) that they are merely theatrical inventions. Likewise, if someone has many independent reasons for being sad, they can ameliorate their emotional condition by focusing the imagination on less distressing images. The reason why the imagination is so efficacious here, where the understanding fails, is that imagination works through the brain, so that its influence on the emotions is direct and physical. It affects the blood that circulates through the body and causes different emotional states, in exactly the same way that medical remedies could thin the blood and provide beneficial results (iv. 220).

These reflections on the beneficial uses of the imagination are summarized in *The Passions of the Soul*, in which the status of imagining is distinguished from sensations and memories, and the limited degree to which imagination comes under the control of the will is made explicit. The soul can cause us to imagine something that does not exist, such as 'an enchanted palace or a chimera'. But the imagination can also be activated solely by the body, when images are formed 'simply from the fact that, when the spirits are agitated in different ways and encounter traces of various impressions which preceded them in the brain, they move through the brain by chance through certain pores rather than others' (xi. 344–5). In those cases, we are subject to 'the illusions of our dreams, and also of the daydreams we often have while we are awake as our thought wanders idly without applying itself to anything on its own'.[13] Given this account of brain functioning, it follows that we may have images or memories that are presented to the mind in much the same way as our sensations. 'All the things that the soul perceives by means of the nerves [i.e. by sensation] may also be represented to it by the fortuitous movement of the spirits' (xi. 348), and hence the familiar question about deciding the origin and veridicality of such brain-induced ideas. Descartes's suggestion in Part I of the *Passions* is that the only difference between genuine perceptions that are triggered by real phenomena and similar brain states that result from the imagination is that 'the impressions that come into the brain through the nerves are usually more lively

---

[13] Cf. Descartes to Elizabeth (6 Oct. 1645) (iv. 311).

and more distinct than those stimulated in the brain by the spirits' (xi. 348). He had offered a different criterion at the conclusion of the *Meditations*, to the effect that our sensory experiences cohere better with all our other experiences (vii. 89–90).

The unity of the cognitive and affective functions in the same part of the brain, and the interrelationship between the mind or soul and the centre of the brain that is assumed by Descartes, make it possible for the subject not only to will certain things, but to affect directly the emotions they experience by willing to have appropriate images in the brain. The role of the will and the imagination, in this context, is discussed further in Chapter 5.

MEMORY

The Cartesian account of memory is that an animal's brain, following the impressions made on it by sensations, acquires dispositions that facilitate the flow of animal spirits in patterns corresponding to the original pattern associated with the occurrence of a particular idea (where 'idea' means a brain state). Thus if a retinal image stimulates a specific flow of spirits from the pineal gland, which results from the way in which nerves connecting the retina to the centre of the brain are opened by the impact of light, the same tubes will be more disposed than otherwise to facilitate subsequent similar flows of spirits. The more frequently this pattern is repeated, the stronger the acquired disposition and thus the stronger the 'memory' of the earlier idea. Descartes develops this hypothesis without questioning the reality of animal spirits, and without being able to observe the tiny ducts through which the spirits allegedly flow in characteristic patterns. This is his summary statement of the theory in *A Treatise on Man* (see Fig. 6):

To this end [i.e. to explain memory], imagine that after issuing from gland H spirits pass through tubes 2, 4, 6 and the like, into the pores or gaps lying between the tiny fibres making up part B of the brain. And suppose that the spirits are strong enough to enlarge these gaps a little, and to bend and arrange any fibres they encounter in various ways, depending on the different ways in which the spirits are moving and the different openings of the tubes into which they pass. And they do this in such a way that they also trace figures in these gaps, corresponding to those of the objects. At first they do this less easily and perfectly here than on gland H, but they gradually improve as their action becomes stronger and lasts longer, or is repeated more often. Which is why in such cases these patterns are no longer easily erased, but are preserved in such a way that the ideas that were previously on this gland can be formed again long afterwards without requiring the presence of the objects to which they correspond. And this is what memory consists in. (xi. 177–8; W. 150)

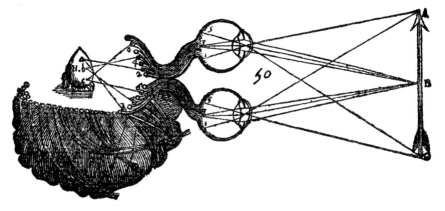

Fig. 6

Apart from the obvious assumptions already mentioned, such as the flow of animal spirits, the role of the pineal gland, and the unobservable ducts through which the spirits flow, Descartes also assumes here a new factor in parts of the brain, namely some kind of non-permanent dispositional properties to reopen or to open more easily to subsequent flows of animal spirits. These dispositions are 'explained', as is often the case in Cartesian science, by analogy with what we experience in familiar everyday objects. 'Similarly, if one were to pass several needles or engraver's points through a linen cloth as you see in the cloth marked A, the tiny holes that would be made there would stay open . . . after the needles are withdrawn; or if they did close again, they would leave traces in the cloth . . . which would make them very easy to open again' (xi. 178–9; W. 151) (see Fig. 7).

This tendency or disposition in the 'substance' of the brain to undergo similar subsequent flows of spirits is also illustrated by another analogy used by Descartes when writing to Meysonnier in 1640: 'As regards the impressions that are preserved in the memory, I imagine that they are simply like the folds that remain in this paper once it has been folded, and thus I believe that they are received principally in the whole substance of the brain, although I do not deny that they may also be found in some sense in this [pineal] gland, especially in those who have a more sluggish mind' (i. 20).[14]

It would be a mistake to think that the role of traces in the brain, in explaining memory, is merely a feature of Descartes's early scientific work, and that it

---

[14] Cf. Descartes to Mesland (2 May 1644): 'the traces in the brain make it capable of moving the mind in the same way that it had been moved earlier, and in this way to cause it to remember something, just as the folds made in a piece of paper or in a piece of cloth make it easier to fold it again subsequently, in the same way as it had been earlier, than if it had never been folded in that way' (iv. 114–15).

Fig. 7

was abandoned or diluted in later years. The dispositions in the brain to open to flows of animal spirits are repeatedly invoked throughout his career and mentioned in letters to numerous different correspondents. For example, he wrote to the correspondent identified as Hyperaspistes in 1641 about the ways in which the mind interacts with the body, and the ways in which sensory impressions or thoughts that originate in the subject move certain parts of the brain. 'And from the motion of those parts of the brain is formed a trace on which recollection depends' (iii. 425). This response was contemporaneous with Descartes's replies to objections to the *Meditations*. In this text, there is relatively little said about memory, although it is appropriately linked with imagination in the Fourth Meditation, where the author refers to 'the faculty of remembering or imagining [*facultas recordandi vel imaginandi*]' (vii. 57). However, in replies to the Fifth Objections from Gassendi, Descartes appeals to his standard account of recollection, which presupposes the role of brain traces. 'As long as it is joined with the body, it is necessary for the mind, in order to recall thoughts that it had in the past, that some traces of those thoughts be imprinted in the brain; by turning itself towards those, or by applying itself to them, it remembers. Is it surprising, then, if the brain of an infant or of someone who is sleepy is not appropriate to receive such traces?' (vii. 357). Evidently, our ability to recall what happened in the past depends, among other factors, on the condition of our brain at the time of having the original thoughts, and on its capacity at that time to store the traces that are subsequently needed to remember something. A lethargic brain provides a poor receptor for receiving and storing ideas or brain traces.

In a similar vein, Descartes wrote to Father Mesland (May 1644): 'As regards memory, I think that the memory of material things depends on the traces that remain in the brain, after an image has been impressed on it' (iv. 114). The discussion of memory in correspondence with Arnauld, in 1648, drew particular attention to the role of intellectual memory, to which I return below. But even here the fundamental prerequisite for memory remained the traces in the brain that result from prior motions of animal spirits. 'It is not enough, in order to remember something, that the thing in question should have been formerly observed by our mind and have left some traces in the brain, on the occasion of which the very same thing would recur in our thought' (v. 219–20).

One of the most significant implications of this schematic account of how memory works is that ideas are not stored individually in exactly the same condition in which they originally occurred, like pictures in a gallery awaiting the gaze of a mental homunculus. However, although ideas as such are not stored, the modifications of the brain that occur during sensation must be retained in some sense. According to the Cartesian hypothesis, what is stored in the brain is merely a disposition to give rise to other ideas that are similar to, and occur subsequent to, the perceptual impression that initially affected the brain. In this sense, what is stored is not so much an idea but a capacity or disposition to come to have similar ideas at a subsequent time. Surprisingly, the bodily dispositions that facilitate the reimpression of ideas on the gland are not located exclusively in the brain. In following up this insight, Descartes wrote to Mersenne (1 April 1640) about the way in which the muscles of a lute player could help the musician to remember a musical tune:

But I believe that it is all the rest of the brain [apart from the pineal gland] that is most useful for memory, especially its innermost parts, and that even all the nerves and muscles can also be used. Thus, for example, lute players have part of their memory in their hands, because the facility to bend and move their fingers in various ways, which they have acquired by habit, helps them to remember passages that require them to move their fingers in that way in order to play them.   (iii. 48)[15]

The way in which fingers or muscles might contribute to one's memory is exactly analogous to the way in which the folds of the brain assist in recollection.

---

[15] Cf. Descartes to Meysonnier (29 Jan. 1640): 'I also think that some of the impressions that are used by the memory can be located in various other parts of the body, just as the skill of a lute player is not only in his head but also partly in the muscles of his hands, etc' (iii. 20).

A new input of spirits from the brain to the fingers will find it easier to move through those channels that had previously been used for familiar finger movements than in others that are completely new, and in this way the habit of playing a musical passage will tend to reinforce one's skill and facilitate the playing of a piece of music that had been practised.

Since memory does not store actual ideas, but mere dispositions to reacquire similar ideas and even to perform skilled actions on subsequent occasions, one might expect that this account would also exploit the familiar experience of consolidating memories by frequent instances of recall or repetition; as we recall ideas more often or repeat a complex action, we reinforce the bodily dispositions that make it possible to do so. Descartes makes exactly this claim, in a letter to Mersenne in August 1640. Here he rejects the suggestion, as he often does, that we remember best the things that we did when we were young. However, if we succeed in recalling some events from our infancy, they are remembered 'principally because we have repeated them since then and have renewed our impressions of them by reminding ourselves of them often' (iii. 143–4). In this way the dispositional theory of memory is consistent with our experience of improving or consolidating a specific memory by repetition.

The problem of adequate storage capacity in the brain, which was mentioned in the previous chapter as a possible limitation on what we can remember, is partly resolved by the dispositional account of how memory works. However, the problem does not disappear completely and it is evidently still in the background as Descartes distributes the storage function to parts of the body other than the brain and even, at the limit, to various aids to memory such as written records.[16] Descartes mentions on a number of occasions, in correspondence with Mersenne in 1640, that the total number of 'memory folds' in the brain is relatively few. 'There cannot be an infinite number of such folds in the brain' (iii. 84). On 6 August, he apologized for not replying to all the queries he had received, including one about the number of folds of the memory. 'I do not believe that there must be a very large number of them to support all our recollections, because the same fold is linked with all the things that resemble each other' (iii. 143), and because intellectual memory can help compensate for

---

[16] The offloading of unnecessary items from the memory is first suggested in the *Rules*. 'Nature seems to have provided memory for this purpose [of storing what is not immediately required for an intuition]. But, since memory is often unreliable, and to avoid having to dedicate some of our mind's attention to repairing it while we are occupied with other thoughts, method has very appropriately invented the use of writing' (x. 454; D. 182). The usefulness of written records is also discussed in a letter to Hogelande (8 Feb. 1640): 'There are many things that are much better kept in books than in the memory, such as astronomical observations, tables, rules, theorems, and whatever does not spontaneously remain in the memory as soon as someone learns it once. For the less we fill it, the more apt will we retain our intelligence for increasing our knowledge' (iii. 723).

the limitations involved. However, the implied economy of this storage system has both negative and positive consequences. On the negative side, the super-imposition of memory traces on each other in the same part of the brain helps explain why memories of distinct events can become confused with each other. 'There is no doubt that the folds of memory impede each other' (iii. 84). On the positive side, the superimposition of memory traces explains how the recollection of one event may trigger a memory of other events associated with it in the past.

If people have at some time in the past enjoyed dancing while a certain tune was being played, then as soon as they hear a similar tune again the desire to dance will return to them; on the contrary, if some have never heard the music for a galliard without some misfortune befalling them, they would infallibly become sad as soon as they hear it again. This is so certain that, if you whipped a dog five or six times to the sound of a violin, I believe that it would begin to howl and run away as soon as it hears that music again.   (i. 134)

This is Pavlovian conditioning, long before Pavlov did the research associated with his name. It is explained by the limited storage capacity of the brain, and the fact that dispositions to generate otherwise unrelated ideas may be stored in the same part of the brain because the original impressions that caused them occurred together. As a result, whatever triggers one memory trace is likely to activate all the other memory traces that are stored together in the same folds of the brain.

The association of ideas through conditioning and the establishment of connections between brain states and thoughts that underpin the Cartesian account of memory, provide a way in which a subject can exploit innate mind–brain connections and thereby extend the control exercised through the mind over their body. This is taken up again in Chapter 5, where the Cartesian account of the will is discussed.

Descartes also offers an explanation of how memory and imagination may be impeded by current sensations. Sensations may make a more or less forceful or dominant impression on the gland, depending on the intensity of stimuli that affect our sensory organs and the transmission of this information to the centre of the brain. The flexibility and creativity of the imagination are therefore inversely proportional to the strength of incoming signals from the senses. If the input from external sources is either limited or weak, it will require less force for the spirits that spontaneously issue from the gland and their passage will be facilitated by dispositions in the brain that result from previous sensations. In those circumstances the corresponding images or ideas are formed sponta-neously on the gland, and they may include elements of different former ideas that happen to have been traced there with equal force. 'It is in this way that chimeras and hippogriffs are formed in the imagination of those who dream while awake, that is, those who let their fancy nonchalantly wander here and there without external objects diverting it, and without being directed by reason' (xi. 184: W. 156–7).

This account of memory, in terms of a dynamic system of dispositions in the brain that associate similar previous perceptions and that give rise to subsequent occurrences of the same ideas even when our senses are not being stimulated by the appropriate sensory objects, also explains Descartes's well-known concerns about false memories. The brain states that are common to sensation, imagination, and memory make it appear, to the thinking subject, that ideas that are caused by our memory are the result of a previous reliable perception and they prompt us to assent to a mistaken judgement based on false memories. The epistemological caution required by this account of memory and imagination is expressed as follows in the *Principles*: 'However, we are often mistaken in thinking that many things were formerly perceived by us and, once they are entrusted to memory, we assent to them as if they were fully perceived even though, in fact, we never perceived them' (viii-1. 21; M. 128). The epistemological problems associated with false memories result from an uncritical use of what seems to be remembered, in a way that resembles the imagination when it falsely combines elements into a non-veridical image. From the point of view of the subject who exercises their imagination or their memory, therefore, their conscious experiences may be sufficiently similar to having a current reliable sensation or a veridical recollection that they are inclined to make an intemperate judgement. Such mistaken judgements cannot be avoided by examining closely the phenomenology of the experience itself. Comparative criteria, provided by reason, are necessary to decide whether one's current inner experience is reliable.

INTELLECTUAL MEMORY

Descartes acknowledges in a number of contexts that, besides the corporeal memory that depends on the brain and other parts of the body, we each have what he calls an 'intellectual memory'. One of the first references to this type of memory is found at the conclusion of his discussion of corporeal memory, when writing to Mersenne in 1640: 'But apart from this memory that depends on the body, I acknowledge another memory that is completely intellectual [*du tout intellectuelle*] and depends only on the soul' (iii. 48). It is significant that this brief allusion to an intellectual memory is the final sentence of a comparatively lengthy discussion of body-dependent memory, and that Descartes merely acknowledges its existence without any argument or further explanation of its function. This pattern of brief, non-explanatory allusions is repeated in other cases. The acceptance of an intellectual memory is usually included, almost as an afterthought, in a discussion of how corporeal memory functions.

For example, in a lengthy letter to Mersenne (11 June 1640), which is concerned almost exclusively with replying to scientific queries from his correspondent, Descartes devotes one short paragraph to a query about memory, and one phrase to intellectual memory. Having explained the role of the folds of memory in the brain, he adds: 'intellectual memory has its own separate traces [*especes*], which do not depend in any way on these folds [in the brain]' (iii. 84–5). He wrote to Mersenne the same year (6 August 1640), about other scientific queries, and once again added the usual concession that, besides our corporeal memory, we also have an intellectual memory. 'Besides bodily memory [*la mémoire corporelle*] . . . I judge that there is another type of memory in our understanding that is completely spiritual and that is not found in animals' (iii. 143). The relative insignificance of intellectual memory is underlined in Descartes's letter to Hyperaspistes in 1641. Here, writing in Latin, he provides a summary of his standard account of memory as depending on traces in the brain, and acknowledges that purely spiritual beings have no genuine recollection at all (*nulla proprie recordatio est*) (iii. 425), because, in their case, there is no difference between thinking about something on the first occasion or on subsequent occasions. This implies that it is a necessary condition for a genuine recollection that the same thought occur a second time in the mind, and that the cause of its recurrence is some kind of trace or vestige of the previous thought that remains in the brain. Descartes later adds a third necessary condition, to exclude cases where a thought recurs as a result of earlier thoughts but without any recognition on the part of the subject that the later occurrences are not novel.[17]

Descartes wrote to Huygens in 1642, to extend condolences on the recent death of his brother and to console him with the belief in an afterlife in which

---

[17] Cf. Locke's problem in the *Essay*, once he had defined ideas exclusively as the objects of current acts of thinking: 'having *Ideas*, and Perception being the same thing' (1975: ii. i. 9). Since he rejected any dispositional account of ideas, Locke's theory raised the same problem as the Cartesian reference to angelic thought: how to distinguish between merely thinking about *X* and remembering *X*. Locke defined remembering *X* as having a thought of *X* together with a supplementary thought that one had previously thought of *X*. 'But our *Ideas* being nothing, but actual Perceptions of the Mind, which cease to be any thing, when there is no perception of them, this *laying up* of our *Ideas* in the Repository of the Memory, signifies no more than this, that the Mind has a Power, in many cases, to revive Perceptions, which it has once had, with this additional Perception annexed to them, that it has had them before' (1975: ii. x. 2).

Christian believers hope to rejoin the departed dead. On this occasion Descartes is uncharacteristically hesitant about what he can claim with conviction. In speaking about our souls, he tells Huygens that he thinks he can know clearly enough that they ought to survive longer than the body. However, although religion teaches us many things about an afterlife, Descartes admits to a weakness common to most people of not being able to believe very strongly what is taught by faith unless it is supported by 'very evident natural reasons'. In the course of this letter, he mentions the hope of having some memory, in the afterlife, of our earthly existence 'because I acknowledge in us an intellectual memory that is certainly independent of the body' (iii. 798). This acknowledgement merely repeats the standard theological belief that part of our enjoyment in the afterlife involves meeting again with our relatives and friends, and that we could not do this unless we were able to remember them even though, without a body, the usual brain traces required for memory are not available. Thus the reality of an 'intellectual memory' is a tentative conclusion from a theological doctrine about the afterlife, and about the kind of human happiness that was traditionally promised to those who benefit from the Christian doctrine of salvation, rather than a conclusion derived from the Cartesian theory of mind.

The letter to Father Mesland, in 1644, addresses a range of issues raised by this sympathetic Jesuit correspondent, following his reading of the *Meditations*. One query concerning memory was answered both with the standard account of memory that depends on traces in the brain, and with a reference to an intellectual memory that uses some other kind of traces.

As regards memory, I believe that the memory of material things depends on traces that remain in the brain, once some image has been imprinted on it; and that the memory of intellectual things depends on some other traces [*vestiges*] that remain in thought itself. But these latter traces are of a completely different type than the former, and I would not be able to explain them by any example borrowed from corporeal things that would not be very different from them.   (iv. 114)

All the texts quoted so far merely mention the existence of an intellectual memory in theological contexts that assume the existence of separated souls. However, none of these texts makes any effort to explain how such a memory works, while the letter to Hyperaspistes suggests that there is no genuine recollection if we merely think of the same thought a second time. The suggestion seems to have been that we can think of ideas at any time we wish and that no residue from earlier thoughts is required to think, a second or subsequent time, about something that we had thought about in the past. However, when questioned by Burman in 1648 about the kind of intellectual memory that angels and disembodied spirits have, Descartes replied with both a weaker endorsement of the usual concession and a hint of an explanation:

I do not deny intellectual memory; that is taken for granted. For example, when hearing that the word 'king' signifies the supreme power, I commit this to memory and if subsequently, by means of my memory, I repeat that signification, that is certainly realized by means of intellectual memory. For there is no similarity between these four letters (k, i, n, g) and their meaning from which I derive the meaning. It is by means of intellectual memory that I remember that those letters have that meaning. It is true that this intellectual memory is of universals rather than particulars, and thus we cannot use it to recall all the details of our lives.   (v. 150)

The content and structure of this argument are unclear. The idea seems to be that, without the appropriate learning involved in acquiring a new language, one could never discover the meaning of a string of letters in some language simply by inspecting them when they are presented for the first time. In the case of someone who does not speak English, therefore, the letters 'KING' have no meaning. We have to learn their meaning first, and then to remember it if we are to interpret this word later. But the recollection required here is not between two concrete items the traces of which might be linked together in one's brain, but between a string of symbols (which is capable of having a brain trace) and a universal. Thus intellectual memory is required in order to remember the meanings of words. This reflects a much more fundamental thesis held by Descartes, to the effect that language use is what distinguishes human beings from other animals and therefore it is not surprising if, when pressed by Burman, he links intellectual memory with the understanding or the mind as the faculty responsible for language acquisition and use. I return to this in Chapter 6 below.

The role of intellectual memory is also acknowledged in two letters to Arnauld in 1648. In both cases Descartes concedes that memory involves brain traces that cause us to recollect—that is, to have an idea or thought that we had previously. The additional feature suggested in these letters is an ability to recognize a thought as being novel or, alternatively, as being merely a recurrence of a thought that we had previously. Intellectual memory is said to be involved in the reflective recognition of novelty or otherwise. Accordingly, Descartes writes to Arnauld (4 June 1648) about why we do not remember many of the experiences that we had as infants. He accepts 'that there are two different powers of memory'. The minds of young children are impressed by many sensations that leave behind traces in the brain that could provide a basis for memory. But these traces are usually insufficient to remember the earlier sensations. The reason suggested is that we would have to recognize that our sensations as adults resemble sensations of infancy, which 'presupposes a certain reflection of the intellect or of intellectual memory, which was not functioning at all in the womb' (v. 193). In other words, the lack of reflective consciousness available to a foetus in the womb removes one of the necessary conditions for subsequently recognizing that a thought that recurs in the mind had been present to it earlier.

This is made more explicit, though not more clear, the following month (29 July 1648), when Descartes argues as follows:

> If we are to remember something, it is not sufficient that the thing should previously have been before our mind and that it should have left some traces in the brain that provide an occasion for it to occur in our thought again. It is also necessary that we should recognize, when it occurs the second time, that this is happening because it had already been perceived by us earlier . . . Thus it is clear that, for memory, it is not enough that certain traces are left in the brain from previous thoughts; the only adequate traces are those that the mind recognizes as not having been in us always, and as having arrived on some occasion for the first time. But if the mind is to be able to recognize this, I think that when these traces are first imprinted the mind must have made use of pure intellect in order to recognize that the thing, when it was first observed, was novel or that it had not been observed before. But there could be no corporeal trace of that novelty. There-fore, if I wrote somewhere that the thoughts of an infant leave behind no traces in its brain, I understood this as applying to traces that would be sufficient for memory, i.e. those that we recognize as novel when they are imprinted, by using a pure under-standing.   (v. 220)

One could conceive of an organism in which sensory ideas occurred a second time without resulting from new sensations but from traces left in the brain as a result of earlier sensations. This would be similar to the example given by Descartes (omitted from the quotation above) of how verses might occur in a poet's mind. If the poet fails to realize that they had read them previously, they are likely to believe mistakenly that they had composed a new poem. In that case, the verses occur in the poet's mind as a result of an earlier similar occur-rence, but the subject is not aware of the lack of novelty in the apparently new poem and is not said to remember the verses in question. It follows that it is a necessary condition for a genuine recollection that a thought occur in a subject as a result of traces remaining from an earlier occurrence of the same thought, and that the subject be aware that the subsequent occurrence is a repetition of an earlier similar thought.

Descartes's argument suggests that, when he thinks about something—for example, the house where he lived as a child in the town that is now named Descartes—he would have to be able to decide whether this thought is occur-ring for the first time (as a novel event in his mental life) or as a recurrence of an earlier thought (which must result from brain traces or something similar). If he is not aware of having had a thought previously, he cannot be said to remember it. But he could not be aware of this without being able to decide, for any thought that occurs to him, whether it is a novel thought or a remembered one. However, Descartes also argues that, once we recognize a thought as occurring for the first time, we must be able subsequently to recall that initial recognition of novelty. Otherwise, we would merely realize on subsequent occurrences of that thought that we had had it before, but we would not be in a position to identify the events or circumstances in which it originally occurred and we could not be said, therefore, to be remembering its first occurrence.

This argument could be made explicit as follows. Assume an event E occurs to a subject S at a given time T_1. When E first occurs, S is aware of E and realizes that this is the first occasion on which S had such a thought or experience. Some trace or vestige of E remains in S, together with a vestige of the recognition of its novelty. Without the latter, any subsequent recollection of E would be too vague to enable S to remember E. Instead S would merely recognize the same thought on subsequent occasions as having occurred to S before, in much the same way in which we often realize that we have seen someone before but cannot identify where, when, or who they are. When S subsequently remembers E, in a strict sense, the following conditions must be satisfied:

1. S is thinking about E at time T_2 as a result of some vestige of an earlier thought remaining in S, and thus S is not simply thinking about E a second time;
2. at time T_2 S realizes that he/she had previously thought about E, and thus is aware of the fact that this is a case of remembering;
3. S can identify the first occasion on which he/she thought about E at time T_1 and, consequently, can be said to be *remembering E* rather than merely having a thought about an event that is recognized as not being novel.

Although this is a plausible analysis of what it means to remember something, it is difficult to see why Descartes claims that either the initial recognition of novelty or its memory trace requires an intellectual memory. In fact, there are reasons for claiming the opposite if one takes seriously the suggestion, in *The Passions of the Soul* (II. 69) that there are only six primitive passions. The first of these is wonder (*admiration*), which is defined as a feeling of surprise in the soul that is generated, as other passions are, by specific motions of animal spirits. The characteristic features of flows of spirits associated with wonder include two factors, one of which is their novelty (*la nouveauté*) (xi. 382). The definition of wonder that is offered in the *Passions* and its explanation in terms of characteristic flows of animal spirits presuppose the capacity of a subject to recognize the novelty of, for example, a perceptual experience because it causes the spirits to flow in unusual ways. Presumably, familiar experiences are associated with flows of spirits in patterns that are already well established and benefit from the inertial dispositions mentioned above, whereas a novel experience will direct the spirits in ways that encounter more resistance. This suggests, in a very schematic form, a physical basis for recognizing novelty or its absence.

The Cartesian account of the mechanism by which we remember something that we are attempting to recall is equally physicalist. In the *Passions* (1. 42), Descartes suggests that, once we try to remember something, the established links between volition and the pineal gland cause the gland to tilt in different directions until it encounters a pathway which contains traces of what we wish to remember (xi. 360). As already mentioned, these traces consist simply in the fact that 'the pores of the brain, through which the spirits flowed previously as a result of the presence of the object [to be remembered], have thereby acquired a greater facility than other pores to be similarly opened subsequently by other flows of spirits that come towards them' (xi. 360).

It seems then as if Descartes has not satisfactorily made a case, in response to Arnauld, for the necessity of an intellectual memory to explain either the recognition of novelty in thoughts or the recollection of novelty in subsequent experiences. It also seems as if most of his other references to an intellectual memory are philosophical reflections on a theological doctrine (about the afterlife), rather than conclusions from a theory of how various mental powers work. It is hardly surprising if a seventeenth-century philosopher is forced by circumstances to test his natural philosophy against the litmus of religious orthodoxy. However, it would reverse the order in which we acquire and use concepts if we were to test our physics against theology. For Descartes, our concepts are acquired and have their primary use in the ordinary experiences that help to generate them, and they are later applied to God, angels, and separated souls only by analogy and with due caution. For this reason, I have suggested that we focus primarily on the Cartesian account of corporeal memory and then examine the relatively weak considerations that are said to support the acceptance, not of another memory, but of another power of memory that functions less dependently on the brain traces that are always involved in human recollection.

CHAPTER 4

Passions of the Soul

Descartes published his principal work on human emotions, *Les Passions de l'âme*, in 1649, less than a year before his death in Sweden. This book represented a synthesis of earlier piecemeal efforts to describe mind–body interaction— some of which had been developed in correspondence with Princess Elizabeth during the 1640s—and of a 'little treatise' on the passions that had been drafted during the winter of 1645–6 and posted to his royal correspondent in May 1646.[1] However, the relatively late date of its composition does not imply that Descartes's interest in the emotions developed only as a result of the philosophical issues raised by the *Meditations*. The status of the emotions was an issue that had attracted his attention from his earliest writings. He first adverts to the bodily symptoms of various emotional states in the *Cogitationes privatae* and records, in that notebook, the effects of sadness and fear on his sleep and appetite. 'I notice that, if I am sad or in danger, or if I am distracted by disagreeable undertakings, I sleep deeply and eat voraciously. But if I am full of joy, I neither eat nor sleep' (x. 215).[2] From these early comments to the end of his life, Descartes never lost sight of the emotions as a central feature of the mental life of human beings.

Such a theoretical interest in the emotions was not unusual in the seventeenth century. The passions had been the focus of philosophical attention since Aristotle's *De anima*. Their role in the moral and civil life of individuals, especially their potential for disturbing the equanimity that was expected from either a rational philosopher or a Christian believer, gave them a prominence that had certainly not diminished in the early modern period.[3] It was fully in keeping with this well-established tradition, therefore, that a philosopher who initiated a naturalized account of our mental life should address, in a systematic

---

[1] See Descartes to Elizabeth (May 1646) (iv. 407). Descartes wrote to Chanut (15 June 1646) that, during the previous winter, he had 'sketched a little treatise on the nature of the passions of the soul' (iv. 442).

[2] Cf. Descartes to Elizabeth (May 1646): 'I believe that, for many people, sadness takes away their appetite; but since I have always found that it increased mine, I have been guided by that in my discussion' (iv. 409).

[3] See James (1997).

way, the nature of human emotions, the ways in which they are caused, the symptoms by which they are manifested and, in general, their integration into an anthropology that was proposed as both comprehensive and revolutionary.

The range of questions addressed by books on the emotions in the seventeenth century varied considerably from one commentator to another. One of Descartes's contemporaries offers the following taxonomy of perspectives on the passions, at the beginning of *A Treatise of the Passions and Faculties of the Soul of Man*:

Now passions may be the subject of a three-fold discourse; *Naturall, Morall,* and *Civill.* In their *Naturall* consideration, we should observe in them, their essentiall *Properties,* their Ebbes and Flowes, their Springing and Decayes, the manner of their severall *Impressions,* the Physicall *Effects* which are wrought by them, and the like. In their *Morall* consideration, we might likewise search, how the *indifference* of them is altered into Good and Evill, by vertue of the Dominion of right Reason . . . in their *Civill* respects, we should also observe how they may be severally wrought upon and impressed; and how, and on what occasions, it is fit to gather and fortifie, or to slack and remit them, how to discover, or suppresse, or nourish, or alter, or mix them, as may be most advantageous. (Reynolds 1640: 41–2)[4]

If this taxonomy is adopted, then Descartes is primarily concerned with providing a 'natural discourse' that explains how the passions arise and how they affect the human subject. This is confirmed by a letter to an unidentified correspondent that forms part of the preface to the *Passions of the Soul*: 'my plan was not to explain the passions as a rhetorician, nor even as a moral philosopher, but merely as a natural philosopher [*physicien*]' (xi. 326).[5] Descartes concedes that, as a result of adopting this theoretical perspective, he may lose many potential readers who expect another popular self-help book and that only those who are prepared to make the effort required will benefit from reading the book. However, what Reynolds calls a 'moral consideration' was also a secondary consideration for Descartes, especially in the advice he offered in correspondence with Princess Elizabeth.

The other preliminary issue about the Cartesian approach to the passions that merits a brief comment is the methodology used or the way in which the issues to be discussed are ordered. For example, Descartes could have begun with an inductive survey of our experience of various passions and then attempted to construct an appropriate theory; alternatively, he could have

---

[4] Susan James brought this book to my attention.

[5] The opening sentence of the *Passions* argues that the defectiveness of the 'sciences . . . des anciens' is nowhere more apparent than in what they wrote about the passions. Descartes subsequently refers in the same book to explaining (*expliquer*) the passions, and to giving an account of the passion of love (*les raisons de tout ceci*) by identifying the cause of the motions that give rise to it (*la cause de ces mouvements*) (xi. 401, 407).

developed a more general theory first and then applied it to the passions. He chose the latter. The tree metaphor in the Preface to the French edition of the *Principles* (1647) implies that a discourse on the passions would be one of its uppermost branches, and that it should be located within the framework of the natural philosophy that had been developing since *The World*.[6] Descartes and his contemporaries already had available an established literature on the description and classification of various passions. His novel contribution, if any, was to explain how the passions arise as a natural result of various conditions of the human body and how they are expressed, just as naturally, in the symptoms that we traditionally associate with them, such as blushing, perspiring, and so on.

This methodological approach is evident from the initial pages of *The Passions of the Soul*. Although the Cartesian natural philosophy of the body had been written much earlier, it remained unpublished prior to 1649 except for brief summaries in the *Discourse on Method* and *The Dioptrics*. To compensate for this lacuna, the *Passions* provides readers, at the outset, with a ten-page summary of how the human body functions when it is compared with 'a watch or other automaton (that is, some other machine that moves of its own accord) when it is wound up and has in itself the physical principle of the movements for which it was built, together with everything else that is required for its operation' (xi. 331).[7] This includes a review of how the blood circulates, how animal spirits— which are 'very small bodies that move very quickly' (xi. 335)—flow to the brain, and how they function in sensation, imagination, and the stimulation of our muscles to cause appropriate bodily actions. Once this summary of Cartesian physiology is in place, the author can isolate the phenomena that he wishes to classify as passions of the soul.

Thus the Preface to the *Passions* is entirely accurate when it characterizes the author's perspective as that of a *physicien*. Descartes applies to traditional questions about the emotions a physiology that had been developed earlier and independently, and the whole discussion is approached from the perspective of a natural philosopher or scientist who aims to explain the interactive functioning of mind and body, as a result of which a distinctive kind of thought occurs in the soul. The status of the resulting psycho-physiological account is that of a

---

[6] 'The whole of philosophy is like a tree whose roots are metaphysics, whose trunk is physics, and the branches that emerge from this trunk are all the other sciences, which are reducible to three principal sciences, namely medicine, mechanics and morals' (ix-2. 14). The original plan for the *Principles* included, in addition to the four parts that were actually published, two further parts on physiology (Pt. V) and on human beings (Pt. VI), but these were never written. The minimal extent to which the *Principles* addresses questions in moral philosophy is admitted to Chanut on 15 June 1646 (iv. 441).

[7] He returns to this comparison in 1. 16; all our bodily actions occur in the same way 'as the movement of a watch is produced simply by the force of its spring and the shape of its wheels' (xi. 342).

hypothesis, or of a corollary to a more fundamental and more comprehensive hypothesis about how states of the mind are caused by corresponding states in the body.[8] This suggestion had originally been outlined in *A Treatise on Man*, in which passions are compared with internal sensations.

PASSIONS AS INTERNAL SENSATIONS

A Treatise on Man (Part IV) offers a rather speculative explanation of how we come to have internal sensations, such as the sensation of hunger. It claims that our stomachs contain different fluids, each of which is appropriate for dissolving specific kinds of food in much the same way as acids selectively dissolve some metals and not others. If these fluids flow into the stomach very actively and fail to encounter appropriate objects that could dissipate their force, they attack the lining of the stomach instead and transmit messages to the brain from the nerve endings found there. These neural transmissions cause the soul 'when united to this machine, to conceive the general idea of hunger' (xi. 163; W. 139). A similar rather schematic physiological-neural explanation is provided for the sensation of thirst, where a specific 'movement in the brain . . . will make the soul conceive of thirst' (xi. 164; W. 139). Immediately following these explanations of hunger and thirst, Descartes adds: 'Similarly, when the blood which enters the heart is purer and more subtle and is kindled there more easily than usual, this disposes the tiny nerve there in the way required to cause the sensation of joy, and in the way required to cause the sensation of sadness when this blood has completely opposite qualities' (xi. 164–5; W. 140). The account of the passions that follows relies on what later became the standard Cartesian theory of animal spirits that flow from the heart to the brain and, through the nerves, to relevant muscles elsewhere in the body. Descartes argues that all the functions that require an explanation in this section of the *Treatise* depend exclusively on three factors: 'the spirits that come from the heart, the pores of the brain through which they pass, and the way in which the spirits are distributed in these pores' (xi. 166; W. 140). The animal spirits may also vary (1) by being more or less abundant, and their parts may be (2) more or less coarse, (3) agitated, or (4) uniform. These four variables, together with the condition of the

---

[8] In the course of presenting his account of the passions, Descartes advises Princess Elizabeth (15 Sept. 1645) that 'we cannot have certain demonstrations of everything' (iv. 295). The following year he wrote that he did not include all the principles of physics required to give an adequate explanation of the movement of the blood associated with each passion, because that would presuppose an account of how all the parts of the body are formed. 'That is something that is so difficult that I would not dare to undertake it yet' (iv. 407). Thus his physiology is acknowledged to be incomplete and hypothetical.

brain and any possible input from the soul, determine the various humours or natural inclinations of the body. For example, an exceptionally abundant flow of spirits excites a movement associated with generosity, liberality, or love. Other variations in the animal spirits stimulate movements that are associated with promptitude, diligence, malice, timidity, and so on. The text distinguishes between these 'humours' and 'the passions to which they dispose us', but the link between them is very close. For present purposes, it is enough to notice that Descartes wishes to explain how the food we eat, the air we breathe, and the condition of our liver, gall bladder, and spleen all affect the condition of our blood and consequently those features of our animal spirits that cause different passions. 'In short, whatever can cause a change in the blood can also cause one in the spirits' (xi. 169; W. 142) and, consequently, in our passions.

Apart from variations in animal spirits, the other factors mentioned above are the condition of the brain and relevant inputs from either the external senses or the mind. The role of the external senses in causing passions is discussed in the context of the Cartesian account of automatic reactions, such as spontaneously withdrawing one's hand from a flame that burns it. The main focus of this discussion is how the external senses normally cause brain states or ideas that are sufficiently specific to stimulate a definite sensation in the mind. In autonomic responses, however, the normal occurrence of ideas and thoughts is short-circuited so that, prior to having any thought, one spontaneously withdraws one's hand from a flame. This can happen only if the fibres of the brain are disposed to conduct the spirits directly to the relevant muscles needed for action, and such a disposition may be either acquired or natural (xi. 192; W. 162). What is 'natural' is the result of God's planning, when he designed the human body so that it automatically performs actions that are consistent with our 'natural instincts'. For example, the most immediate result of feeling pain in one's hand is to move the hand or the whole body, and to turn one's head in the appropriate direction to identify the cause of the pain (see Fig. 8). In parallel, nature also arranges for a spontaneous flow of spirits 'towards the heart, the liver, and so on', which are normally associated with 'inner emotions' and are usually caused by pain. Finally, a third spontaneous flow of spirits causes the symptoms that usually witness to the inner emotions, such as tears, crying, or different facial expressions.

These interconnected flows of spirits, which reflect the design of nature, depend on our spontaneous 'pursuit of desirable things or . . . the avoidance of injurious things' (xi. 193; W. 163). They result in external actions of flight and so on, and 'internal movements that are commonly called passions' (xi. 193; W. 163). Nature has also disposed the brain so that the internal motions are adapted to support appropriate external movements. For example, if we need to use our

Fig. 8

strength to avoid some evil and if the passion of anger would support such an effort, then an appropriate flow of spirits occurs to stimulate the emotion of anger. Descartes suggests that external symptoms of the passions are caused only by chance, since the spirits flow accidentally through the nerves that cause laughter or crying when they are rushing to stimulate the appropriate internal emotion.

This psycho-physiology of the emotions seems to attach the name 'passions' to the flows of spirits that cause our feelings, the symptoms of specific passions (such as laughter in the case of joy), and the feelings that are excited in a manner that resembles the causality of internal sensations such as hunger or thirst. The extent to which the passions are integrated into the physiology is shown from the example of factors that may interfere with our sleep; these include 'noise and heat . . . which forcefully move the internal parts of the brain . . . and joy and laughter and the other passions that greatly agitate the spirits' (xi. 199; W.

167). In this case, passions agitate a corresponding flow of spirits. When Descartes summarizes his account of the machine of the body, at the conclusion of what was planned as one section of the *Treatise* and before describing 'the rational soul',[9] he reflects that he has 'postulated' only such organs and systems as are likely to be found in human bodies and 'in various animals lacking reason'. He hopes to have persuaded readers that, since 'nature always acts by the simplest and easiest means', the hypotheses he had suggested will be accepted as the most plausible available. Among the functions he claims to have explained in this way Descartes lists digestion, blood circulation, and other similar physiological functions; the reception of impressions from the external senses, the impression of ideas on the common sense and the imagination (and their retention in memory); and, finally, 'the internal movements of the appetites and the passions' (xi. 202; W. 169). To explain these functions, he argues, it is not necessary to postulate a vegetative or sensitive soul. They can all be explained simply by 'the disposition of the organs as wholly naturally as the movements of a clock or other automaton follow from the disposition of its counterweights and wheels' (xi. 202: W. 169). According to this summary, therefore, passions cannot be exclusively thoughts in the mind, for no mind has yet been introduced into the theoretical body that is being described at this point in the *Treatise*.

This predominantly physiological perspective is reflected in the suggestion made to Regius, in 1641, that the 'seat of the passions must be taken to be the part of the body that is most affected by them, which is undoubtedly the heart' (iii. 373). The central role of animal spirits in this account is also consistent with the passions being potentially disruptive or threatening to our self-control. Accordingly, when Descartes was attempting to console Princess Elizabeth about the illnesses that disturbed her, he wrote in 1645: 'I know also that the best minds are usually those in which the passions are most violent and act most strongly on their bodies' (iv. 236). From this perspective, the passions are extremely active rather than passive.

DEFINING THE PASSIONS

These initial discussions in *A Treatise on Man* remained unpublished, and hence Descartes had a new opportunity to develop them further in correspondence with Princess Elizabeth after 1645, and later again in *The Passions of the Soul*. In

---

[9] The *Treatise* was incomplete, unpublished during the author's life, and the promised section on the soul was never written.

the latter, he defines human emotions within a framework of concepts that had earlier been adopted for independent reasons and in which the basic categories are those of (1) agent and patient, and (2) body and mind. If one thing affects another, the former is said to be the agent and the latter the patient. The concept of agency is explained by reference to local motion, where the paradigm is borrowed from causal interactions between bodies. This was another issue on which the unfortunate Regius had been accused of misrepresenting the Cartesian position. In response Descartes wrote that, in the case of bodies, all actions and passions consist simply in local motion; 'we call it [a motion] an "action" when considered in the body that imparts the motion, and a "passion" when considered in the body that is moved' (iii. 454–5). He also suggested that, when applied to immaterial things, the terms 'action' and 'passion' are used only by analogy with physical agency. However, in the case of either material or immaterial realities, the event by which a causal exchange takes place is *both* an action and a passion, so that the choice of what to call it depends on the perspective from which it is viewed. 'Although the agent and the patient are often very different, the action and passion must always be the same thing, which has these two names because of the two subjects to which it can be attributed' (xi. 328). This provides an initial general concept of a passion as anything that is caused to or in something, even if the efficient cause or agent in question is also the thing affected (that is, the patient).

That 'the action and passion must always be the same thing' opens up the possibility of a double-aspect analysis of the passions according to which passions, despite their name, are very active. In fact, it might seem in advance of considering the Cartesian account that any viable theory of passions must include activities in the mind–body composite that disturb our tranquillity, provoke us to what are often incautious actions, and in general are consistent with the etymology of their description as emotions. I return to this below.

The other relevant distinction that had been adopted in previous writings is that between what is bodily and what pertains to the mind. The reader is reminded of this at the beginning of *The Passions of the Soul*: 'Thus because we do not conceive of the body as thinking in any way, we have reason to believe that every kind of thought that occurs in us belongs to the soul' (xi. 329). Without further argument, it is assumed that all thoughts—or, at least, all human thoughts—are attributable to the mind rather than to bodies. This may be a careless telescoping of a number of theses into one. It begs the question of how animals have passions, since that had been accepted in *A Treatise on Man* and was frequently reiterated by Descartes in correspondence. The status of human passions, then, in so far as they are thoughts, is that they are caused in the mind in some manner that remains to be explained. However, it is also worth mentioning that Descartes emphasizes, at the beginning of the *Passions*, that the distinction between the body of a living person and a dead body is analogous to the difference between a watch that is wound up and the same watch when it is broken and the principle of its movement is no longer active (xi. 331). This does not suggest that the distinction depends on the addition of another reality or substance, such as the soul, but merely on some disposition of its parts when they function properly.

Based on these distinctions between action and passion, and between mind and body, Descartes provided two versions of his definition of the passions that are equivalent in all relevant respects. These are found in a letter to Princess Elizabeth (6 October 1645), and in Part I (Articles 19–29) of *The Passions of the Soul*. He accepts that some of our thoughts are actions initiated by the mind itself—for example, when we decide to do something or other. But many thoughts are passions or perceptions—that is, thoughts that are caused in the mind when it is passively receptive to the effects of some extra-mental cause. Among the latter, the mind acting on itself may cause some perceptions; but many are evidently the result of a causal activity that originates in one's body or elsewhere, and these include a class of perceptions that rely on the nerves to transmit effects to the pineal gland and thence to the mind. Such neurally caused perceptions may be subdivided into three groups, depending on the remote causes to which we attribute different thoughts: (1) perceptions that we refer to external objects and events, which are called sensations; (2) perceptions that we attribute to states of the body that are known by internal sensation, such as hunger or pain; and (3) perceptions that are attributed to the soul itself. The third category includes 'perceptions that are referred [*qu'on rapporte*] to the soul alone . . . whose effects are felt as if they were in the soul itself, and of which one usually does not know any proximate cause to which they can be referred' (xi. 347). Accordingly, the passions of the soul, in a strict sense, are defined as follows: 'perceptions [*perceptions*], or feelings [*sentiments*], or emotions [*émotions*] of the soul that are specifically referred to the soul and are caused, maintained, and strengthened by some movement of the animal spirits' (xi. 349).

The subdivision that identifies passions in a strict sense is shown in Fig. 9. This classification of thoughts suggests that passions, in a strict sense, are limited to those mental states that result from some condition of the body and are transmitted to the soul through the nerves. However, Descartes had already agreed (in Article 26) that the same thoughts may be stimulated in the mind either by perceptions that are transmitted through the nerves or by the random movements of animal spirits through the brain that cause imaginings. While conceding that the thoughts that are stimulated in this way are usually less vivid or

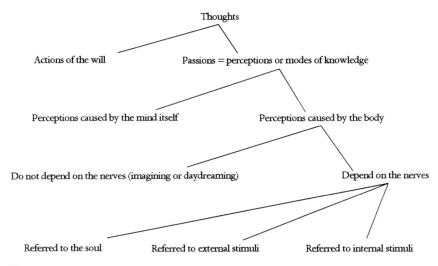

Fig. 9

strong than those that result from veridical perceptions, Descartes must agree that we can experience equally genuine passions, such as sadness, on the occasion of merely imagined realities.[10]

This definition is expanded in Articles 28 and 29. The passions are best called emotions, Descartes contends, because they are more likely than any other thoughts to disturb or agitate the soul. As indicated above, this provides a description of the emotions as being simultaneously both passively received in, and very active in their effects on, the soul. The second phrase, about the role of animal spirits, is included to identify the proximate causes of such thoughts. The suggestion here, already explained in Articles 23 and 24, is that emotions are thoughts that resemble sensations in the way in which they are caused (where the latter result from either external or internal senses). In contrast with sensations, however, the passions are not referred to either external objects or states of the body. It must be admitted that, at this stage of the presentation, it remains unclear why they should be referred simply to the soul, as if the soul originated the action that causes some of its own states called emotions in a manner that parallels the external or internal causality of sensations. The solution is to understand Descartes's definition very literally. It is not that the passions are *caused* by the soul, in the same way that external or internal sensations are caused by stimuli that are external or internal to the body. The point is, rather,

---

[10] The comments of an anonymous reader for the Press persuaded me to disagree with the taxonomy proposed by the editors in Descartes (1985–91: i. 338 n. 1). While this taxonomy reflects the distinctions proposed in the text, it suggests inaccurately that passions in a strict sense always involve the transmission of images by the nerves.

that we often cannot readily identify what causes them; and, even if we could identify the cause of a particular passion—for example, what made us angry or happy on a particular occasion, or what caused us to experience fear—it would not make sense to refer the feeling of anger or happiness to the experience that provoked it. Thus passions are 'referred to the soul', but they are 'caused, maintained and strengthened by some movement of the animal spirits'.

The concluding articles of Part I develop the standard Cartesian account of the interaction between mind and body and the role of the pineal gland and the animal spirits in this interaction. The opening article of Part II confirms the ambiguity about the causality of emotions:

The most proximate cause of the passions of the soul is nothing other than the agitation by which the animal spirits move the small gland that is in the middle of the brain . . . However, although they may sometimes be caused by the action of the soul when it determines itself to conceive of one object or another, and likewise by the mere temperament of the body or by the impressions that occur by chance in the brain, as happens when one feels sad or happy without being able to say why, it seems nonetheless . . . that all these passions may be equally excited by the objects that affect the senses, and that these objects are their more usual and principal causes. It follows that, in order to discover all the passions, it suffices to consider all the effects of these objects.   (xi. 371–2)

This only succeeds in confusing the matter further. The definition proposed in Part I, Article 27, identified the passions in a strict sense as those thoughts that (1) are passively caused in the mind and supported and strengthened by the movement of animal spirits, and (2) can be referred to the mind in contrast with the other two recognized sources of perception. But it now seems as if the remote causes of the passions may be any one of the following: (a) the action of the soul when it decides to think about something; (b) the temperament of a particular body; (c) impressions that are stored in the brain that accidentally trigger a passion in the soul; or (d) objects that cause external sensations. It also seems as if the usual and principal causes of various passions are precisely the *same external objects that cause our sensations*. The special character of the passions, therefore, needs to be explained in some other way.

The specificity of passions is obscured by the apparent suggestion that they result in the mind from various kinds of neural transmissions to the centre of the brain. However, as already indicated, Descartes acknowledges that we may experience the same passion—for example, fear—when we see some fearful object and when we merely imagine the same thing while daydreaming or while asleep. He also concedes that two people may see the same object (for example, a lion) and may be affected differently; one of them may experience fear while the other may not. Thus, it cannot be merely the perception of a lion that causes fear or the imagined perception that occurs when they are merely dreaming about lions. The specificity of emotions must be explained, therefore, in terms of the subjective assessment by the perceiver of whatever images they receive, and the role of animal spirits in causing, maintaining, and strengthening a passion must be additional to the contribution of animal spirits in the nerves when a passion-inciting image is transmitted from a perception. This is explained in Article 36. If a given image stimulates fear in someone, then the spirits move through the nerves that cause the agent to turn their back and flee. There is also a natural connection between the feeling of fear and the motion of animal spirits to the heart so that the brain continues to be supplied with animal spirits that sustain the actions appropriate to fear. This natural loop—between feeling fear, the activity of fleeing, and so on, the stimulation of the nerves in the heart to cause the heart to produce more animal spirits, which sustain the passion and its associated actions and symptoms—explains the role of animal spirits in the causality of the emotions. For the passions themselves, as already indicated, are thoughts in the soul, but they are different from ordinary passively received perceptions.

One of the suggestions made in *The Passions of the Soul*, to distinguish passions from internal or external sensations, is that we cannot be mistaken about emotional feelings. We may feel thirsty when we are not genuinely so, and we may think we perceive some external object when we are merely dreaming. But we cannot be similarly mistaken about our own passions; they are 'so close and so internal to our soul that it cannot possibly feel them otherwise than as they truly are' (xi. 348). The metaphor about closeness to the soul translates as: we do not attempt to identify any specific cause of emotions, and therefore cannot be mistaken, in the same way that we think of some internal or external state of affairs as the proximate cause and apparent object of a perception. It is in this sense that the passions are 'attributed' to the soul even though they are not caused by it. However, the most plausible way of distinguishing the passions depends on Descartes's theory about their natural function. While our sensations reflect variations in the objects that stimulate our senses, the very same objects may excite different passions in different people because they may appear harmful or beneficial to them. Thus the passions are useful for this alone; 'they dispose the soul to will those things that nature dictates are good for us, and to persist in this willing' (xi. 372). Besides, the same motion of the spirits that causes the passions also triggers actions on our part that are appropriate to implementing our choices. This presupposes some account of what is naturally good for us, and of how the thoughts that are called passions act on the soul to provoke or support appropriate acts of the will.

'TAUGHT BY NATURE'

Given the widespread reluctance among natural philosophers of the seventeenth century to invoke nature as an explanatory concept—most clearly articulated in Boyle's systematic critique, *A Free Enquiry into the Vulgarly Received Notion of Nature*—it might seem a retrograde step on Descartes's part to appeal to nature as a source of reliable instruction. Nonetheless, this is precisely what he does throughout the Sixth Meditation, where he addresses the unity of the human being and the significance of what we spontaneously judge on the basis of what we learn from our sensations. Despite initial appearances to the contrary, however, there is no danger that nature is being introduced here as a novel and dubious theoretical entity. Descartes claims that, by 'nature' in this context, 'understood in a general way, I understand nothing but God himself or the co-ordinated system of created things that was established by God' (vii. 80; M. 63).[11]

Nature in this sense teaches me 'that I have a body' (vii. 80; M. 63), 'that I am not present in my body only in the way that a pilot is present in a ship' (vii. 81; M. 64), and 'that various other bodies exist in the vicinity of my body' (vii. 81; M. 64). However, I also seem to be taught by nature many other things, which are found subsequently to be either untrue or doubtful. It is therefore necessary to 'define more carefully what exactly I understand when I say that I am taught something by nature' (vii. 82; M. 65). Nature, in the general sense already adopted, includes things that I learn exclusively either from my mind or from my body. Descartes thus wishes to narrow the scope of the term so that it refers only to 'those things that were given me by God in so far as I am composed of a mind and body' (vii. 82; M. 65).

'Nature in this sense, therefore, teaches me to flee from things that cause a sensation of pain and to seek those that cause a sensation of pleasure, and so on' (vii. 82; M. 65). The key distinction to be introduced, at this point in the *Meditations*, is between (1) nature as a teacher of truths about the external sources of my sensations, and (2) nature as a guide to what is usually beneficial or harmful to me in so far as I am a mind–body composite. Descartes invokes his usual disclaimer to the effect that our sensations cannot be trusted to provide sensations or ideas that resemble the stimuli that cause them. Thus, for example, although I feel heat when I approach a fire and feel pain if I go too close to it, these experiences do not provide any reason to believe 'that there is something in

---

[11] Cf. his critique of what Seneca might have meant by living according to nature (Descartes to Elizabeth, 18 Aug. 1645). Descartes accepts that 'nature' might mean 'the order established by God', but he contends that it 'explains nothing' to recommend that one should live one's life in accordance with nature in that sense (iv. 273–4).

the fire that resembles that heat any more than that there is something in it that resembles the pain' (vii. 83; M. 65). Sensations are therefore not reliable indicators of the objective nature of the realities that cause them. However, Descartes does wish to claim that we can rely on the function of sensations, with respect to harms and benefits, to provide some reliable knowledge. 'For sensory perceptions, strictly speaking, were given by nature only to signify to the mind what is beneficial or harmful for the composite of which it is a part and, to that extent, they are sufficiently clear and distinct' (vii. 83; M. 65).

Evidently, even with this limited claim about what we are taught by nature, there remains the possibility of mistaken judgements. 'It is not unusual for us to be mistaken about things to which nature inclines us' (vii. 84; M. 66). For example, I may be misled by nature to swallow something with a pleasant taste that I later discover is poisonous, or to drink water because I feel thirsty even though, if I have dropsy, this aggravates my condition. The only conclusion possible is that God has designed nature so that, when my body is affected by some stimulus, it triggers 'the specific sensation that, among all the sensations that it could possibly trigger, is conducive most often and to the greatest extent to the conservation of human health' (vii. 87; M. 68). Therefore, unless God were to intervene on the occasion of every sensation of every human being to correct possibly misleading information, the only option available to the creator that is consistent with his goodness and immutability is always to join, by nature, the same sensation with the same stimulus and, among the possible sensations that result from a given stimulus, to choose those that usually provide reliable guides to a creature's self-protection.

What we are taught by nature (*a natura doctus*) can hardly realize the degree of indubitability required to avoid the sceptical doubts of the First Meditation. It seems more likely that these claims should be understood merely as plausible hypotheses; they are thus consistent with our experience of sensations sometimes misleading us into doing things that cause us harm. At the same time, the content of what we are taught by nature is something that we share with animals,[12] and it is most improbable that Descartes would have described animals as learning from nature in the sense of acquiring reflective knowledge. It is more consistent with the Cartesian account of animals' behaviour and of how they survive in their natural environment to think of them as being designed by nature (or by God) so that their sensations guide them, for the most part, towards what is beneficial to them. The same applies to human beings.

---

[12] 'All the motions of the spirits and of the gland that excite the passions in us are also found in them [i.e. animals]' (xi. 369). 'All animals that lack reason conduct their lives merely by performing physical actions that are similar to those that, in our case, usually result from the passions and to which the passions encourage our souls to consent' (xi. 431).

Thus 'taught by nature' means: on the assumption that animal natures have been designed to facilitate their survival, we should think of natural appetites and sensations as being appropriately matched to increase the probability of an animal's survival. This is equally true of all animals. Human beings, however, may also reflect on their natural propensities and thereby draw inferences about what, in most cases, is likely to be beneficial or harmful. This is a kind of reflective awareness of an elementary natural programming of responses to particular sensations that also leaves open the possibility of subsequent training or habit formation.

A MORAL DISCOURSE

There was a theological tradition associated especially with the name of St Augustine, and with theories of Original Sin, which attempted to find in human nature symptoms of Adam's fall from grace that underpinned the soteriology of the schools. According to this tradition, human nature reveals signs of what is otherwise a purely theological condition that is usually described as a lack of grace. These signs include weakness of the will, or various internal impediments to implementing our moral choices. Descartes integrates a secularized version of this tradition into his account of the passions by adapting his doctrine of clear and distinct ideas to explain how passions may be deceptive. This in turn provides scope for a moral discourse or supplementary moral reflection on the passions.

Cartesian passions are exactly similar to all other sensory impressions, in so far as they are perceptions that result from our bodily condition. What we feel during an emotional experience is not the flow of animal spirits in our nerves or the tightening of the heart that results from it, but something that we describe as love, anger, fear, and so on. This is consistent with the general principle that had been proposed in the French edition of the *Principles* (iv. 190): 'All the various feelings depend, firstly, on the fact that we have many different nerves and, secondly, on the fact that there are different movements in each nerve' (ix-2. 311). Descartes refers back to this text, in a letter to Chanut in the same year, when explaining the distinction between love as a passion and a purely intellectual or rational love. He reminds Chanut that there is nothing surprising in the fact that 'certain motions of the heart' are naturally connected 'with certain thoughts that do not in any way resemble them' (iv. 603). Thus the passion of love, which is linked with a specific flow of animal spirits in the heart, is a thought in the mind that bears no resemblance whatever to the flow of spirits that causes it.

This kind of love 'is nothing but a confused thought, aroused in the soul by some motion of the nerves' (iv. 603), and such confused thoughts are comparable to feelings of hunger or thirst. 'Just as in thirst the sensation of the dryness of the throat is a confused thought that disposes the soul to desire to drink, but is not identical with that desire, so in love a mysterious heat is felt around the heart and a great abundance of blood in the lungs that makes us open our arms as if to embrace something . . . ' (iv. 603). Descartes argues that the thought by which we feel heat is likewise different from the thought that joins the soul to its object of desire. We may have the feeling of love and not have any clearly identifiable object of our affection, and we may have a specific object of desire without the characteristic warm feeling that we normally expect. If the latter is rational love, the former is 'the corresponding passion' (iv. 603). Later in the same letter, Descartes describes four basic passions as 'sensations or very confused thoughts' (iv. 605).

These 'confused thoughts' are not expected to provide us with accurate information about our environment, as already indicated above in the discussion of what we are taught by nature. Nor are they as inactive, in the total life of an individual, as the term 'passion' might suggest. The extent to which they disturb the soul was developed in a number of letters to Princess Elizabeth in 1645. In May or June of that year, Descartes explained how one could become sad or ill by watching tragedies, even though we know, intellectually, that they are nothing more than theatrical pieces. They affect us emotionally because they affect the imagination, which, in turn, affects the flow of spirits in the body. He returns to this theme in another letter on 1 September, in which he discusses the distinction between intellectual pleasure and the contentment that results from practising the virtues. In our pursuit of pleasure, for example, we can be misled into believing that some object of desire will provide much more pleasure than it does provide. As a general rule, then, 'passion often makes us believe that certain things are much better and more desirable than they really are' (iv. 284). In fact, all the passions 'represent the goods to which they tend with greater splendour than they deserve, and in that way they are all deceptive' (iv. 285).[13] The passion of love, for example, may so affect the lover that his or her judgement is impaired. The recommended cure, when we feel moved by some passion, is to suspend judgement until the potentially distorting effects of the passion abate.

---

[13] This is repeated in another letter to Elizabeth two weeks later: 'all our passions represent to us those goods towards which they drive us as being much greater than they really are' (iv. 294–5). The same idea is found in the *Passions* (ii. 138): 'Besides, they [the passions] nearly always make both the goods and evils that they represent appear much greater and more important than they are' (xi. 431).

In this respect, the passions are no more deceptive than other impressions that result from our sensations. The novel factor in the case of the passions is that they also move the subject to act in a certain way, for their principal effect is to move or dispose the soul to want things for which they prepare the body. One might then wonder whether the passions could so dominate reason or free will that the power of the latter to control one's life is suspended completely. In a letter to Elizabeth (1 September 1645), Descartes acknowledges that there are various diseases that 'take away the power of reasoning' (iv. 282). In order to pursue our happiness we need to be able to discern where our true happiness lies, and such extreme bodily indispositions may prevent someone's 'will from being free'. Since our eternal happiness in the afterlife depends on making appropriate choices in this life, it seems consistent with the religious beliefs of his royal correspondent when Descartes claims that to lose one's reason is more serious than to lose one's life, and that the worst thing that can happen to us is to be attached to a body that 'takes away one's freedom'. The passions, however, usually stop short of this worst case.

Thus, among the factors that are impediments to exercising our free will are bodily conditions that alter one's humours or make us unusually subject to 'sadness, or anger, or some other passion' (iv. 283). We are misled by our passions for two related reasons: (1) they misrepresent the value of certain things to which we are naturally attracted; and (2) they interfere with the freedom of our choice by moving us towards actions that are not in our best interests. The cure for both defects depends on using one's reason, although its application in the second case must be indirect.

Despite these comments on how our passions may mislead us, Descartes's evaluation of their role and influence is not generally unfavourable. For example, he wrote to Chanut that, in examining the passions, 'I have found almost all of them to be good' (iv. 538). This coincides with a similar evaluation in the penultimate article of *The Passions of the Soul*: 'We see that they [the passions] are all good in their own nature' (xi. 485). When they mislead, it is initially the role of reason to evaluate impartially the merits of various things to which the emotions incline us. Accordingly, it is not necessary to free oneself completely from the influence of the passions; it is enough 'to subject one's passions to reason' (iv. 287).[14] This should be sufficient to prevent us losing our 'free judgement' (iv. 411).

However, even if one's estimate of the object of one's love or anger is clinically accurate, this in itself may not be enough to change the flow of animal

---

[14] Cf. Descartes to Elizabeth (3 Nov. 1645), where he commends the passions on condition that they are 'subject to reason' (iv. 331).

spirits that characteristically accompanies a passion and inclines us to misguided action. Since we are trying to change a natural process here, the only mental option available is to imagine other thoughts that are normally associated with passions that have the opposite effect on the flow of spirits. Accordingly, Descartes recommends that Princess Elizabeth try to direct her imagination away from distressing thoughts and that she even consider using medication to thin the blood at the same time (iv. 219–20). This is not a situation in which it is enough simply to know, intellectually, what is true or false (which is the scope of theoretical knowledge). One also needs what Descartes calls practical knowledge and, in an otherwise unusual compliment to the scholastics, he admits that they were right to claim that the virtues are habits (iv. 296).[15] The control of the passions, therefore, requires some training in the exercise of reason, and a creative use of the imagination so that we cause ourselves to have thoughts whose accompanying flows of animal spirits can counteract the misleading effects of the emotions.

It should also be acknowledged that, according to this theory, there are significant variations between individuals in the emotions generated by particular thoughts and in the strength of those emotions even when they are similar. Descartes suggests that our first emotions were probably formed in the womb or in our infancy, and were associated with the satisfaction experienced in being adequately fed or the sadness of the opposite experience.[16] These earliest experiences establish a pattern so that some people, later in life, can hardly experience any love without the recurrence of the same heat in the heart that accompanied their initial satisfaction when they were well fed. Thus the differences between the emotional responses of various individuals reflect their personal histories. Descartes accordingly speculates about different possible emotional responses among the people of a besieged town. Although all the inhabitants may concur in their analysis of the danger, they are not all equally affected by the emotion of fear. The degree of their fear depends on their personal inclinations or 'habits' (iv. 312). The judgement or impression of imminent harm triggers a flow of spirits and, in some people, this causes both the impression of fear in the mind and the symptoms of fear, such as becoming pale, trembling, and feeling cold. Those who experience more fear are those in whom the disposition of their bodies causes a different flow of animal spirits than in the case of others who are brave.

---

[15] Cf. *Passions* (III. 161): 'It should be noted that what are usually called virtues are habits in the soul that dispose it towards certain thoughts; although they are distinct from such thoughts, they are able to produce them and reciprocally may be produced by them' (xi. 453).

[16] See Descartes to Elizabeth (May 1646) (iv. 409), and Descartes to Chanut (1 Feb. 1647) (iv. 605–6).

A DOUBLE-ASPECT ANALYSIS

It is evident from the texts considered so far that the subjective states identified by the Cartesian theory as emotions or passions—for example, anger, love, fear, hatred, and so on—are the same as those found in traditional classifications of the passions, and that they are as active as they had been described in earlier treatises on the subject. At the same time, Descartes unambiguously classified the emotions as states of mind that *passively* result from various conditions of the agent's body, especially the flow of animal spirits through the nerves. This emphasis on passivity might lead one to think of the passions merely as mental after-effects of extremely active bodily conditions, and might support the comment by Lyons (1980: 4–5) that, according to this theory, 'emotion was like an after-thought or epiphenomenon to the basic causal nexus from perception to bodily reaction and purposive action'. However, it is a mistake to think of the passivity of our thoughts, including the passions, as implying that they are either inactive or epiphenomenal. It is not as if Descartes constructed a 'brilliant account' of the emotional mind–body interaction and then relegated it to a mere 'preamble to emotion', while he simultaneously 'invented a special epiphenomenon in the soul as the real emotion' (Lyons 1980: 5). This interpretation points to a need for some explanation of what otherwise seems like an inconsistent or confusing conflation of suggestions from disparate sources—namely, a definition of emotions as passive mental conditions that are extremely active.

Descartes had explained, in the letter to Regius quoted above, that the model on which the distinction between an action and passion is based is local motion. The standard Cartesian definition of motion is a relativist one, according to which whether something is described as being in motion or at rest is determined by the framework that one accepts as being at rest. The same body may be at rest relative to one framework and in motion relative to another. The example given by Descartes is of a sailor sitting on a moving boat; he is at rest relative to the boat but in motion relative to the shore. Descartes normally defines a body as being in motion when it changes place relative to the other bodies in its immediate environment.[17] Any example of such differential motions between adjacent bodies requires the intervention of some force. Therefore the distinction between being passive and being active depends on the local interaction between bodies—that is, whether one impacts on another and causes it to change its current condition of motion or rest, rather than on some absolute framework such as Newtonian space. According to this way of

---

[17] See e.g. *Principles* (II. 25) (viii-1. 53–4).

understanding motion, almost all bodies are constantly in motion in a perpetual flux and are therefore active. They can be described as passive only relative to a given impact or received causal influence from another body. Hence a body that is moved by the impact of another body is the passive recipient of a motion that, in itself, is active.

Although thoughts are described as actions or passions of the mind they are evidently not local motions. They may be described by analogy with active or passive motions only because they resemble them in being causes or effects. The passions of the soul are typical of other similar mind–body interactions in the Cartesian theory, because they are both physical and mental, and they are both active and passive. They are part of a complex interactive network in the human subject. There is no absolute beginning—except, perhaps, before God imparted motion to matter when creating the universe—at which one could describe some reality as being completely at rest. Human bodies are themselves complexes of many distinct parts that are already in motion as soon as we are born, and they interact physically with their environment in an ongoing active–passive causal negotiation. Thus, no matter how early one examines the life of an individual subject, it is causally interactive with its environment and the results of those events reverberate within the body. One particular case of such environmental causality is the way in which we perceive realities that are external to ourselves. But it would evidently be a mistake, according to Descartes, to think of the human body as being exclusively a passive recipient of external influences, as being similar to the passive minds or *tabulae rasae* of Locke's *Essay*. Our bodies are extremely active, both within the skin of each human body and in seeking in their environment whatever is necessary for their survival. Descartes takes for granted that human beings have various natural desires as a result of which we seek food, avoid pain, and so on. There is an obvious sense, then, within Cartesian physics, in which the human body is an active part of the physical environment in which it lives and that it moves, in some ways, independently of its environment.

This perspective on the passions is readily available from the most basic principles of Cartesian physics. According to these principles, various parts of our body are constantly being moved by other internal and external bodies. The motions of animal spirits associated with perceptions and passions are no exception. They follow the same laws of nature as any other body. It is equally clear that Descartes took for granted that mind and body interact, and that they are included in causal exchanges.[18] Given the causal interaction in both directions between a human body and its environment, there is a sound theoretical basis in

---

[18] Descartes to Arnauld (29 July 1648) (discussed below in Chapter 5).

Cartesian physics for claiming that every action is equally a passion, depending on the perspective from which it is described.

The double-aspect description of phenomena as being both active and passive thus extends from bodies in motion, as the paradigm, to mind–body interactions by analogy.[19] At the limit, one could even think of changes that occur completely within the mind as being active and passive from different points of view. For example, Descartes describes volitions as the principal activities of the soul (xi. 339), and argues that it is impossible to make decisions without being aware of doing so. However, while the thoughts by which we perceive (namely, perceptions) are passions in the soul, the (passive) thought by which we perceive a volition is identical with the (active) thought by which we make a decision. 'Because this perception and this volition are, in reality, identical, it is always described by what is most noble in it, and thus it is customary to call it not a passion, but only an action' (xi. 343). In a word, volitions are thoughts that are both active and passive from different points of view.

The interactive causal loop described by Descartes when analysing how an individual may come to have the experience of fear involves the following factors: (1) having an impression or making a judgement about an imminent harm; (2) the physical flow of spirits towards the heart in a pattern that is usually associated with such impressions; (3) the feeling of fear that results from such a flow of spirits, and that is distinct from the original impression merely of an imminent harm (for one could react to a perception of harm in different ways, by anger, by bravery, and so on); (4) the appearance of physical symptoms of fear, such as a white pallor, shivering, and so on, and, possibly, behaviour that is consistent with fear, such as flight. According to this hypothesis, the feeling of fear is both passive and active. It is passive because it is felt by the subject as an effect of some prior impression or judgement; in that sense its passivity is similar to the way in which we feel thirst or other internal sensations. At the same time, it is evidently active because it causes the agent to act in appropriate ways and stimulates various symptoms that are natural signs of the relevant emotion.

This double-aspect description of the passions explains how a commentator such as Louis de la Forge, who set out to present Descartes's own theory of mind faithfully by quoting from his writings, could classify the passions as modalities of the will rather than of the understanding.[20] La Forge thinks of the

---

[19] Descartes applies a similar double-aspect description to the movement associated with a desire, which may be seen as pursuing a good or avoiding the opposite evil. 'It seems to me that it is always one and the same movement that brings us to pursue a good and at the same time to avoid the evil that is its opposite' (xi. 393).

[20] La Forge (1997: 100–1): 'No one should object if I quote various passages from Mr Descartes in this way, since I only claim to borrow his ideas here and to provide a supplement to what he would have said about the nature of the mind at the end of his *Treatise on Man*, if death had not prevented him from completing it.'

human mind as being both active and passive, and in so far as it is active it is called the will. According to him, the will is the power of the mind 'to move itself and to determine itself', or 'the principle of all our determinations and judgments and, generally, of everything which is active in the mind's operations' (La Forge 1997: 71, 192). However, the Saumur physician warns us that the language of distinct powers or faculties in the mind should not be understood as if the will and understanding were two separate realities. Instead he cautions that 'these two faculties are not distinct from the mind or the power of thinking . . . they are not really distinct from each other either . . . these two faculties are just the thing itself which thinks, which sometimes knows and sometimes determines itself' (La Forge 1997: 69). Given that the mind is both active and passive, and that the passions are passively received states that stimulate specific actions, La Forge is not really modifying the Cartesian account when he classifies the passions as emotions of the will. 'All our natural appetites and passions can also be understood as so many streams which flow from this great source [namely, the will], not insofar as they are each obscure perceptions of the soul—for in this sense we have classified them as internal sensations—but insofar as they provoke the mind to will those things for which they prepare the body or to which the body is already disposed'(La Forge 1997: 71–2).[21] In this reclassification, the passions are said to function in exactly the same way as Descartes had proposed, but they are here described from the perspective of how they affect the subject (actively) rather than how they are themselves caused in the mind (passively).

This double-aspect or integrated perspective on the passions follows directly from the underlying account of causal interactions that is implicit in Cartesian physiology, and from the concept of a real distinction that is made explicit in the *Principles* (I. 60) (and discussed further in Chapter 9 below). This should be sufficient to rescue the passions from the status of mere epiphenomena that are causally inactive with respect to our behaviour, a kind of mental after-image of flows of animal spirits. But it does not protect them against a more fundamental objection that, as mental states, they seem to be causally disconnected from all physical states. This is an issue to which I return below. The detailed attempt to provide a physiological analysis of specific passions is an indication of the extent to which Descartes was serious about the systematic causal interaction of the mental and the physical.

---

[21] Cf. La Forge (1997: 192): 'Thus the will is subject to two different kinds of emotion. The first kind depends only on the mind, while the other is stimulated by the disposition of the body. . . . they are only different modes of willing and are all stimulated by certain perceptions of the mind, either those to which the soul applies itself freely or those which originate in the senses.'

DISTINGUISHING THE PASSIONS

One of the standard objections to a theory of the emotions, such as Descartes's, is that it presents the emotions merely as vague feelings that lack any cognitive content. According to this objection, a subject experiences them as mere feelings, such as feeling hot or cold; 'they do not by themselves connect up to behaviour' (Lyons 1980: 7). In fact, the comparison accepted by Descartes between passions and internal sensations might suggest that Cartesian emotions are nothing more than mere states of awareness of physiological conditions of a subject's body. On this view, the emotion of fear tells us nothing about the world or about our attitude to it, but merely registers 'our physiological changes and bodily movements'(Lyons 1980: 6).[22]

A first response to this objection is that it collapses the distinction between a phenomenology of the emotions and a scientific explanation of their occurrence. It must be conceded that, when I fear a wild animal, for example, I experience a distinctive emotion that is very different from love or anger. The Cartesian explanation of what is happening in the subject of such emotions includes a reference to flows of animal spirits, the tilting of the pineal gland in a certain direction, and so on. But there is no suggestion that I feel those physiological processes any more than, when I perceive the moon, I can be said to feel flows of animal spirits from my optic nerves or, when I hear a musical tune, I could describe my subjective state as being aware of vibrations in the tympanum. Descartes emphasizes this in the *Passions* (I. 23):

When we see the light of a torch, and when we hear the sound of a bell, this sound and this light are two different actions . . . which provide the soul with two different sensations. We refer the latter to the subjects that we assume are their causes in such a way that we think we see the torch itself and that we hear the bell, and not that *we merely perceive the motions that come from them.*   (xi. 346; emphasis added)

It is one of the fundamental principles of the Cartesian account of the mind that we should not confuse the subjective state that we are attempting to explain and the states of the body or mind that a scientific hypothesis suggests as their causes. Thus fear of a lion cannot be felt subjectively as an internal sensation of flows of animal spirits, and so on. The fear of a lion feels like fear.

On the other hand, it seems like an exaggeration of the specificity of our feelings to claim that, merely by introspection, we can distinguish clearly between

---

[22]   Lyons comments (1980: 7) that 'Descartes is forced to grant not merely that the subjective awareness of the bodily movements and physiological changes following on a perception of something such as a frightening animal is an emotion, but also that the subjective awareness' of similar bodily states that result from ingesting a drug are also emotions.

emotions such as fear or anxiety, love or desire, and that, in the case of bouts of very strong emotion, we can decide whether we are shaking from fear or anger or both. This might suggest that we distinguish within any emotional state between its cognitive content and its bodily symptoms. This is particularly plausible in cases where, for example, we are in an emotional state that is not expressed in any observable symptoms. We might hate someone without any of the usual symptoms of emotions, such as redness of the cheeks, perspiring, and so on. If this distinction depended on the availability of language to specify the cognitive content of a given emotion, one might think of human beings as alone being capable of specific emotions, because they alone have a language with which to conceptualize the distinctions required. On this account, anticipating the Cartesian account of language that is discussed below in Chapter 6, animals would lack the linguistic prerequisites for having many emotions. They may run from a threatening master with a stick, but they do not conceptualize the danger involved sufficiently to warrant our describing their condition as fear. Likewise, they might wait indefinitely for the return of their absent master, but their behaviour could not then be described as motivated by affection. The cognitive content of emotions would have to be supplied by a language-dependent understanding, while flows of spirits and so on could provide the appropriate concomitant feeling and actions.

This might seem like an obvious way out for Descartes, and it is consistent with another suggestion in *The Passions of the Soul*, to the effect that there are six basic passions (xi. 380, 443). The hypothesis of a limited number of basic passions might be understood as the suggestion that there are six kinds of bodily state associated with the emotions. These bodily states would distinguish the emotions into six genera, and the specificity of different emotions would then be a function of their cognitive content (which is supplied by understanding). The effect of this suggestion would be to introduce a form of dualism into each emotion; the cognitive content would be provided by our understanding of a particular situation and our reaction to it, while the accompanying physical symptoms would depend on a limited range of bodily conditions. But Descartes does not adopt this solution. His suggestion, instead, is to link the whole range of distinct emotional states with a correspondingly large range of distinct physical states of the subject. He also recognizes the almost insuperable challenge involved in implementing such a research project. Thus he writes to Elizabeth, May 1646:

I did not include [in the draft *Passions of the Soul*] all the principles of physics that I used to distinguish the movements of blood that accompany each passion, because I would not have been able to deduce them properly without explaining the formation of all

parts of the human body. That is something so difficult that I would not dare to undertake it yet, even though I have almost satisfied myself about the truth of the principles
that I used in that work . . . It is true that I had difficulty in distinguishing the relevant
movements for each passion, because they never occur alone. However, since the same
passions do not always occur together, I tried to notice the changes that take place in the
body when they occur in different combinations. Thus, for example, if love were always
joined with joy, I could not know which of them to associate with the heat and dilation
that they cause us to feel around the heart. But because love is sometimes joined with
sadness and, in that case, one still feels the warmth but no longer the dilation, I judged
that the heat belongs to love and the dilation to joy. Although desire almost always
accompanies love, they are not always together to the same extent because, even if one
loves greatly, one desires little as long as one has little hope. And since one does not then
have the diligence and promptness one would have if our desire had been greater, one
can judge that they arise from desire and not from love.   (iv. 407–9; M. 165)

What is significant about this passage is not its success or otherwise in providing
an explanation of distinct emotions, but the fact that Descartes chooses to link
each passion with a corresponding specific bodily state. This implies a much
more systematic and comprehensive kind of mind–body correspondence than
is likely to be proposed by philosophers who rely on introspection or understanding to discriminate between the emotions. The rigour of the match
between brain states and thoughts is acknowledged in the letter just quoted:
'Thus if the same movements are triggered again by some external cause, they
will also trigger in the mind the same thoughts and, reciprocally, if we have the
same thoughts again, they produce the same bodily movements' (iv. 408; M.
165).[23]

On this account, there is a complete parallelism between thoughts and bodily
states, and Descartes is confident that the body can undergo a sufficiently wide
range of distinct states to correspond to the range of thoughts we may have.
The fact that he was unable to identify those bodily states precisely, as we still are
today, only helps to underline the conviction with which he proposed what
seemed, in the absence of success in the seventeenth century, like a vain hope.
This need not imply a degree of specificity in the cognitive content of emotions
that would make them comparable to perceptions. For example, if I fear a lion,
it may not be the case that, apart from its intensity and the associated tendency
to flee, and so on, fear of a lion is experienced as specifically different from fear
of a tiger. The emotions may be exactly similar, and the unfortunate subject
may even misidentify the immediate cause of their fear. For this reason,

---

[23] The *Passions* (1. 34) defends a similar one-to-one correspondence between physical conditions of the
pineal gland and thoughts in the mind: 'it [the soul] has as many different perceptions as there occur different movements in this gland' (xi. 354).

Descartes defines emotions in such a way that they are attributed to the soul rather than to the specific object that stimulates them. What we describe as fear of a lion may be a combination of an emotion that is specific enough to be fear, combined with a perception (or even a misperception) of a lion.

In this analysis the specificity of the emotional experience is defended against any attempt to reduce the emotion to a mere perception that triggers appropriate behaviour. When Hobbes suggested that fear of a lion was reducible to the perception of a lion and the behaviour of fleeing, and so on, and that the perception was the only thought involved, Descartes replied: 'It is self-evident that seeing a lion and being afraid of it is different from merely seeing it' (vii. 182–3). The passion of fear is a distinctive thought that may or may not accompany one's perception of a lion, even if the perception is followed by flight. One could perceive a lion, flee from it for safety, and not experience any fear.

EXPLAINING THE PASSIONS

Descartes claims in *The Passions of the Soul* (ii. 136) that there is a single principle underlying everything that he had written about the causes and effects of the passions. That principle is 'that there is a link between our soul and our body such that, if we have once joined some physical action with some thought, neither one of them will occur in us subsequently without the other also occurring, and that it is not always the same actions that are joined with the same thoughts' (xi. 428).[24] The first part of this principle assumes some kind of innate programming of certain passions with specific physical actions, while the second part allows for establishing new mind–body connections as a result of experience and thereby introducing significant variations, between individuals, in their emotional responses to similar stimuli.

The first part of this principle attributes to nature, or to God, the spontaneous desires and aversions—for example, to pleasure or pain—on which the whole theory of the passions depends.

the objects that move the senses do not excite passions in us because of all the differences among them, but only because of the various ways in which they may harm or benefit us or, in general, because of the different ways in which they may be important for us. The function of all the passions consists in this alone, that they dispose the soul to want those things that nature dictates are useful for us and to persist in this volition; and the same movement of the spirits which usually causes the passions disposes the body towards those actions that serve to achieve those things.   (xi. 372)

[24] The same principle is invoked in I. 50, and II. 107 (xi. 369, 407).

The hypothesis is that there are six basic or generic passions that are built into our nature, and that all the others are species that are composed of various combinations of primitive passions. Hence, if human nature has evolved or been created in such a way that the passions of wonder, love and hatred, desire, joy and sadness, are natural reactions to our perceptions of whether various things are harmful or beneficial to us, then all the other passions are composed of these or are species of them.[25] Thus each of the six primitive passions is explained as a spontaneous natural response to the impressions made on our brain and nervous system by perceptions. For example, wonder is a passion caused by an impression (*impression*) on the brain, and by the consequent flow of spirits to the appropriate part of the brain to maintain that impression as it was formed. All other passions are then explained by various combinations of the flows of spirits that are characteristic of those associated with the primitive passions. For example, generosity results from a combination of the flows of spirits that normally give rise to wonder, joy, and love.[26]

The second part of the principle quoted above acknowledges that the life history of different individuals may establish varying emotional responses to different stimuli. Accordingly, one individual may have been frightened in their cradle by a cat or may have got a headache from the smell of roses, and this experience in their infancy may result in a lifelong aversion to cats or roses. Descartes describes this effect as the idea (*idée*) of the aversion remaining imprinted in the brain (*cerveau*) (xi. 429). As a result of personal experiences of different individuals, the sight of a cat may stimulate an emotional response in one person and not another, but for any given individual the same thoughts or emotions normally co-occur in response to the same actions.

Causal interactions between a perceiving subject and their environment can be hypothesized without any mention of the soul or mind. The principle 'of all these functions' is the 'animal spirits and nerves which contribute to actions and to sensations' (xi. 333). The natural interactions between a subject and its environment result not only in dispositions such as desire or aversion, but also in appropriate responsive actions by the subject and usually in various symptoms of otherwise hidden dispositions. The latter are listed in *The Passions of the Soul* (II. 112) as 'external signs of the passions', and they include 'actions of the eyes and the face, changes in colour, trembling, listlessness, fainting, laughter, tears,

---

[25] It follows that every passion must have some natural function in terms of supporting the life and survival of the individual, although Descartes is hard pressed to think of a natural function for the passion of timidity (xi. 462).

[26] *Passions* (III. 160): 'This passion is produced by a movement [of the spirits] composed of those of wonder, joy and love—both of the love one has for oneself and of the love one has for the thing that causes self-esteem' (xi. 451).

groans and sighs' (xi. 411). From the perspective of the underlying causal connections between impressions made on the perceiver and the responses that they stimulate, there is nothing passive about the passions. In fact, their function in relation to the body implies that they are very active:

As regards their function, it should be noted that, by a natural institution, they all relate to the body and are given to the soul only in so far as it is united with the body. Thus their natural function is to stimulate the soul to consent and contribute to actions that can help to protect the body or make it more perfect in some way. From this perspective, sadness and joy are the two primary passions that are used. For the soul is immediately informed about things that harm the body only by means of the feeling of pain that it has, which produces in it . . . a desire to get rid of it. In the same way the soul is immediately informed of things that are beneficial to the body only by some kind of titillation, which produces in it . . . a desire to acquire whatever can make it continue in this joy. (xi. 430)[27]

This naturally instituted coordination between our sensations, the passions they generate, and the relevant behavioural response can operate without any intervention of the soul or mind. 'These movements that are produced in the blood by the objects of the passions follow so promptly solely from the impressions made in the brain and the disposition of the organs, even though the soul contributes nothing at all to them, that there is no human wisdom that can resist them as long as one is not adequately prepared for it' (xi. 486). For example, many people cannot prevent themselves from laughing when they are tickled, even if they find it unpleasant and would prefer not to laugh.

One might suspect that, with this theory of the passions and their integration into a general account of the interaction between a body and its environment, the passions will be effectively independent of the mind and its operations. There are clear reverberations of this conclusion in the way in which the mind cannot affect the passions except indirectly. Accordingly, when Descartes discusses the soul's power with respect to the passions (I. 45), he argues: 'Our passions likewise cannot be directly aroused or removed by the action of our will, but this can be done indirectly by the representation of things that are usually linked with the passions that we wish to have or opposed to the passion we wish to remove' (xi. 362–3). For example, we cannot suppress our fear merely by willing to do so. We have to use our imagination to reduce the cause of our fear, or imagine reasons for being brave, and so on, and hope that passions that are usually associated with those thoughts will help suppress those that we wish to avoid.

[27] Cf. *Passions* (II. 74): 'It is easy to know from what has been said so far that the usefulness of all the passions consists only in this: that they strengthen and prolong in the soul those thoughts that are good for the soul to keep and that would otherwise be easily erased from it' (xi. 383).

In summary, then, the emotions or passions are states of mind that are programmed by nature in response to various things that we perceive or imagine. The primary function of this natural programming is to support the survival of any given organism. Thus the basic emotions are designed by nature to help guide us towards what is good for us, and to steer us away from what is harmful. Because emotions are stimulated in a manner that is similar to other sensory perceptions, especially to what Descartes calls internal sensations, they are confused thoughts that may be deceptive in particular cases. However, their failure in individual cases does not undermine their regular primary function, which is to act as general guides. Given the degree to which they are innate, each subject finds that they must adjust to a range of emotions that occur spontaneously within themselves and are to a great extent outside their direct control. Our spontaneous emotional reactions—for example, of fear of something that is perceived as dangerous—are as automatic as our blood circulation or the increase in heart rate that they sometimes cause. What is natural or automatic here is not just the physiological response of the organism but equally the emotion or passively impressed thought that accompanies it. Descartes acknowledges, as already indicated, that the specific stimuli for different emotions may vary from one subject to another, depending on their personal histories, and thus new stable connections may become established between certain stimuli and corresponding emotions. But even this is subject to an underlying natural or pre-established connection between basic emotions and the way in which we perceive various things as being harmful or beneficial. Once stimulated, the emotions affect the subject by supporting the subject's choices, and by triggering appropriate behaviour. This account has obvious implications for a Cartesian account of the will, which is discussed below in Chapter 5. It also accommodates easily a 'moral discourse' that addresses traditional questions about how someone may strive to control the impact of the emotions on their moral decisions.[28] Finally, this account of the emotions assumes that it is possible to provide parallel accounts, as in the case of sensory perception, of how similar emotions occur in human and non-human animals.

[28] In *Passions* (II. 147) Descartes is so concerned about this issue that he introduces a reference to 'internal emotions [*emotions interieures*]' that are stimulated in the soul itself and on which our well-being is said primarily to depend. Such internal emotions are not genuine emotions at all, but states of mind that are associated with acts of the will.

CHAPTER 5

The Will as a Power of Self-Determination

I argued in Chapter 1 that there is a distinctive Cartesian model of scientific explanation, and that any explanation of our mental life must at least attempt to satisfy the demands of that model. The preceding chapters have examined the extent to which sensation, memory, imagination, and the emotions were included in the Cartesian explanatory project. Despite the traditional faculty language used to classify these forms of thinking, Descartes offers a primitive theory of how they occur as a result of activities in the brain. However, even in the course of speculating about the brain activities that cause them, Descartes leaves in place a form of dualism according to which something called the mind is reserved as the apparent ultimate locus of mental events. The Cartesian discussion of voluntary actions follows a similar pattern of explanation in which the voluntariness of human actions is both explained by reference to brain activities and, at the same time, classified as a feature of the mind in so far as it is active. While Descartes is content to use traditional faculty language in describing such actions, it is clear that the term 'will' does not denote a something, however mysterious it may be. 'Will' is used in the Cartesian context as shorthand for a distinctive power or ability that human agents have and in virtue of which some of their actions are subject to moral evaluation. The principal question here, then, is to say what 'will' or 'free choice' means in Descartes's writings, and to explore the extent to which voluntary human actions can be accommodated within the scientific project of explanation that underpins much of his work.

If one adopted from the outset a standard substance dualist interpretation of Descartes, one could say that willing is a type of activity that is characteristic of the soul, whereas the causality of local motion is characteristic of the physical world. This raises the well-known difficulty of explaining how voluntary actions that take place in the soul might affect motions of the body and vice versa. This difficulty could be resolved, at least temporarily, by insulating both kinds of action in their respective separate but parallel worlds. If they appear to be frequently well coordinated, one could stretch the limits of credulity and assume some version of occasional causality according to which God has preordained the harmony between both worlds without any genuine interaction between them. Descartes, however, seems not to support such an account of completely separate, harmoniously arranged, but non-interacting worlds. For example, he wrote to Arnauld (July 1648) about the interaction of mind and body: 'Nonetheless, that the mind, which is incorporeal, can move the body is something that we are shown, not by any reasoning or comparison with other matters, but by the most certain and evident everyday experience. This is one of those self-evident things that we obscure when we try to explain them in terms of other things' (v. 222).[1] The context of this remark was not a discussion of whether it is possible for our minds to move our bodies, but the inappropriateness of certain ways of conceptualizing the obvious reality of mind–body interaction. That our decisions somehow affect our behaviour is so evident, as is the complementary reality that bodies affect our minds in sensation, that the only problem is to find a language for expressing these realities, and a model for explaining them, that do not compromise the distinctive natures of mind or body.[2]

At the same time, this response to queries from Arnauld does not override a fundamental assumption of Cartesian natural philosophy, to the effect that a body can be moved (*impellere*) only by a force imparted by another body, and that the natural world of bodies is a self-contained world in which forces or their effects are simply redistributed, without addition or loss, once the creator adds an initial quantum of motion to matter.[3] Thus, if one were to consider the human body from the perspective of natural philosophy, one would assume that its various motions are scientifically explicable, and one would expect to

---

[1] Cf. Descartes to Elizabeth (6 Oct. 1645): 'You already know how I conceive of various impressions being formed in the brain . . . in the case of human beings, by the action of the soul, which has some power to change the impressions in the brain, just as these impressions in their turn have the power to stimulate some thoughts in the soul that do not depend on its will' (iv. 310). Descartes also mentions, in the *Principles* (ii. 26), that we are inwardly aware of the fact that our bodies are moved by our will (viii–1. 54). However, the context of this comment is that this experience may lead to a mistaken judgement. We find that we cannot move our bodies without effort, whereas no effort is required in order not to move them. Descartes wishes to block the mistaken conclusion in physics that a force is required to move a body, but that none is required to stop a moving body. Despite our personal experience, he argues, it requires as much force to stop a moving body as it does to initiate movement in another body of the same size.

[2] Descartes's argument here is that scholastic philosophers think of heaviness as if it were a substantial quality; according to Descartes, that is equivalent to thinking of it as a substance. They also think of heaviness as 'incorporeal'. Thus their explanation of why heavy bodies move towards the centre of the earth involves an incorporeal substance pushing an extended body. Descartes concludes: 'Therefore it would be no more difficult for us to understand how the mind would move the body than it would be for others to understand how such heaviness would move a stone downwards' (v. 222–3). Apart from the rhetorical benefits of such a comparison, the underlying positive suggestion is that neither Cartesians nor scholastics should think of bodies as being shoved along by an incorporeal substance that operates as if it were a body.

[3] Descartes's physics evidently predates the formulation of the second law of thermodynamics, but that is irrelevant to the issue raised by the manner in which the will operates.

find Descartes reasserting that basic claim, especially in his principal work devoted to this topic, *The Description of the Human Body*. One is not disappointed in this regard. The relevant text is unambiguous.

We can also see that when parts of our body are harmed—when a nerve is pricked, for example—the upshot of this is that, not only do they stop obeying our will (which is what they normally do), but often they even have convulsive movements which are quite opposed to it. This shows that the soul can cause no movement in the body unless all the corporeal organs required for that movement are properly disposed. Besides, when the body has all the organs disposed for this movement, it does not need the soul to produce it. Consequently all those movements that we do not experience as depending on our thought must not be attributed to the soul but only to the disposition of our organs; and even those movements that are called 'voluntary' proceed principally from this disposition of the organs, for they cannot have been produced without it, no matter how much we will it, and even though it is the soul that determines them.   (xi. 225; W. 171)

The first claim—that an appropriate disposition of one's body is a *necessary* condition for voluntary action—seems uncontroversial. If the nerve connections to my legs, for example, are not functioning, no amount of willing on my part will cause me to walk. The second part of the paragraph is more surprising on first reading, because it seems to say that the correct disposition of our bodily organs is also *sufficient* for voluntary actions and that implies that the contribution of the will to voluntary actions is redundant. However, on closer inspection, that is not quite what the text says. Instead it claims that the correct disposition of our organs is sufficient to produce all the motions of which human bodies are capable, including those that sometimes result from acts of the will. Hence the appropriate disposition of our organs is a necessary and sufficient condition only for those bodily movements 'that we do not experience as depending on our thought'. In the case of movements that are called 'voluntary', the same kind of bodily condition is 'principally' their cause, and the soul is said to 'determine' them.[4]

The word 'determine' is a technical term in Cartesian physics, which has a special function within the analysis of the motive forces that explain why bodies move as they do. Descartes thought that, in the case of collisions between hard bodies, no force is expended in changing merely the direction in which a body in motion moves (on condition that its speed remains unchanged). Thus the

---

[4] Descartes makes this clear a few lines later in the same text, where he concedes that 'it may be hard to believe that the disposition of organs alone is sufficient for the production in us of all the movements that are not determined by our thought' (xi. 226; W. 171). Cf. *Passions* (1. 16): 'Thus all the movements that we make without our will contributing to them (which happens often when we breathe, when we walk . . .) depend only on the disposition of our limbs and on the route that the animal spirits follow naturally in the brain, in the nerves and in the muscles' (xi. 341–2).

determination of a body's motion, or, at least, that feature of the determination that is usually described as its direction, may be changed without any expenditure of force.[5] This may seem to leave room for an intervention by thought to modify the determination of the motion of animal spirits in the brain and, as a result, the movements of a human body that result from them. This suggestion would involve the soul merely 'determining' bodily motions without expending any force, while the force of motion in virtue of which our bodies move would derive, as it usually does in Cartesian physics, from the motion of other bodies.[6] However, even that resolution breaches the principle proposed in the letter to Arnauld—namely, that, when we conceive of the way in which thought influences our bodily motions, we should not think of the soul as if it were another body or as if it operated like a body. Therefore, to suggest that thought merely determines the motion of animal spirits without causing their motion is only marginally less unsatisfactory than claiming that the mind pushes the body about. In both cases, thought or mind is acting as if it were a body. It would be preferable to find an alternative solution to the problem of how willing, as a kind of thinking, can affect our bodily motions. That would require interpreting the term 'determine' in a non-physicalist sense, by analogy with its literal meaning in Cartesian dynamics. Before I do so, a brief review is required of Descartes's description of the will and its activities.

THE EXPERIENCE OF FREEDOM

Descartes often claims that we experience freedom of the will and that we are aware of this when we reflect on our inner mental life. For example, he wrote in response to Hobbes's Objections to the *Meditations* that 'I have not assumed anything about freedom here apart from what all of us experience in ourselves; it is very well known by the natural light . . .' (vii. 191).[7] This is made even more

---

[5] I include the parenthetical qualification here to avoid controversy with those who think that Cartesian determination is a vectorial quality that includes both speed and direction. In Cartesian physics, the direction in which a body moves can be changed by impact with another body, without any expenditure of force or loss of what he calls 'quantity of motion' by the second body. Cf. Clarke (1977) and Gabbey (1980).

[6] I avoid discussion of whether Leibniz attributed this view to Descartes. Garber (1983) argues that Leibniz was mistaken in claiming that Descartes held this position, and he offers an alternative resolution to reconciling the causality of motion by the mind and the Cartesian principle of conservation. Garber's resolution is to argue that the causal activity of finite minds is not subject to the apparent universality of the law of conservation of the quantity of motion.

[7] In the Fifth Replies, Descartes rejects Gassendi's comments about the indifference of the will, because the latter is 'obvious', and he refers his description of human freedom to 'what I have experienced and what anyone else may experience in themselves' (vii. 377).

explicit in the *Principles* (1. 39), when he refers to our ability to refrain from making judgements based on doubtful or inadequate information.

Freedom of the Will is self-evident:
That there is freedom in our will and that we are able to assent or not assent, in many cases arbitrarily, is so evident that it should be counted among the first and most common notions that are innate in us. This was most evident above when, attempting to doubt everything, we reached a point at which we imagined some most powerful author of our origin who tried to deceive us in every way. Despite that, we experienced such freedom in ourselves that we were able to refrain from believing whatever was not fully examined and certain.   (viii-1. 19–20; M. 126)[8]

This is so certain, according to Descartes, that, even though we cannot understand how it is consistent with God's universal causality, it would be absurd to doubt 'something of which we have a profound understanding and which we experience in ourselves' (viii-1. 20; M. 127) just because we cannot understand something else (namely, God's activity) that we have independent reasons to believe is beyond our comprehension. I return to the compatibility of human and divine freedom below.

It would help explain what Descartes means here if he were to say more about those inner experiences of which he claims to be so certain that there could be nothing else 'more self-evident' (viii-1. 20; M. 26). The most striking feature of his discussion is that freedom of the will is most clearly experienced in making judgements (or in refraining from making them), although the judgements range over what to believe or what to do. In fact, the will is defined in the extended analysis, in the Fourth Meditation, in terms of its role in making judgements.

For the will consists in this alone, that we can either do or not do something (that is, affirm or deny something, seek or avoid it); or rather, it consists in this alone that we bring ourselves to affirm or deny, to seek or avoid, whatever is proposed to us by our intellect in such a way that we feel that we are not determined by any external force [*a nulla vi externa nos ad id determinari sentiamus*].   (vii. 57; M. 47)

There is a significant difference between (1) not being determined by any force and (2) not feeling so determined, and this text excludes only the feeling of determination by external forces in certain well-defined circumstances. This suggests that we look more closely at the Cartesian understanding of the will as

---

[8] Cf. *Principles* (1. 6): 'we experience in ourselves a freedom such that we can always refrain from believing things that are not fully investigated and certain . . .' (viii–1. 6; M. 113).

a form of thought and that we leave open the possibility, as he does, that free will is compatible with being determined by appropriate *internal* forces.[9]

Before we do so, it may help to make explicit the significance of the external force that is excluded in the Fourth Meditation. One of the epistemological worries that motivates the *Meditations* is that we may be forced, without being aware of it, to believe false propositions by some evil genius or manipulative demiurge. If that were to happen and we were not even aware of it, we would have no way of escaping from false beliefs. Thus it is of primary concern at this point in Descartes's argument that he establish the independence of the mind when it reviews beliefs that may have been introduced into it by a suspect causal route. In the text quoted above from the *Principles* (I. 39), he concluded that we are able to resist such beliefs, even if they originate from a most powerful external cause, and that we experience the freedom to withhold assent from 'whatever is not fully examined and certain'. This is reiterated two articles later, in *Principles* (I. 41), in which we are said to be aware of our 'freedom and indifference'.[10] In this text, freedom and indifference are interchangeable as the object of our experience, and they are classified as a single entity. This is the same point that is being made in the *Meditations* text quoted above. In affirming or denying a proposition, he claims, we experience our independence and conclude that we are not determined by any external force or power.[11]

None of the texts mentioned so far provides convincing evidence of some inner experience of freedom to which we have access by reflection. They rely on a particular interpretation of the experience we have when we defer making a decision about believing something, or when we decide to question apparently plausible propositions and thereby exercise our freedom. For, as already indicated, the fact that we do not experience being compelled by causes (of which we are possibly unaware) does not imply that they are not present or active. However, it does help clarify what Descartes means by freedom. It is a necessary condition for a judgement to be free, it seems, that it not be determined by powers or forces (including God) that are external to the individual

---

[9] Evidently, one also needs to specify the scope of the reality relative to which the forces are said to be internal or external.

[10] The Latin text is: 'libertatis autem & indifferentiae, quae in nobis est, nos ita conscios esse, ut nihil sit quod evidentius & perfectius comprehendamus' (viii–1. 20). The corresponding text in French is: 'nous sommes aussi tellement assurez de la liberté & de l'indifférence qui est en nous qu'il n'y a rien que nous connoissions plus clairement' (ix–2. 42).

[11] Cf. Descartes to Regius (24 May 1640). Regius had suggested that rashness in making judgements results from some innate or acquired disposition of the body. Descartes replies that, if that were true, 'the freedom and breadth of our will would be taken away' (iii. 65). The objection is that any outside force (such as one's body) that determines our judgement would compromise human freedom. Thus without deciding whether we really are free, in this sense, to be free means to make judgements that are not determined by extra-mental forces.

human mind. Descartes's claim is that we are aware of being free, in this sense, in the indifference that we experience when we suspend our judgement about some proposition. That leaves open the possibility that the mind is determined by forces that are internal to itself.

One of the clearest features of the Cartesian theory of the will is that acts of the will are modes of thought and that, in the division between modes of thought and modes of extension, the will is firmly on the side of the former. Thus, in the *Principles* (1. 32): 'all modes of thinking that we experience in our-selves can be referred to two general types, of which one is perception or the operation of the intellect, and the other is willing or the operation of the will' (viii-1. 19; M. 124).[12] Descartes claims that 'thought' is not a universal that includes a number of distinct types or species of thought, such as sensing, imag-ining, reasoning, willing, and so on. Rather, thought is something that may assume different modes of being, just as extension may assume different shapes. 'By "thought", therefore, I do not mean a universal thing that includes all modes of thinking, but a particular nature, which receives all those modes, just as extension is a nature which receives all shapes' (v. 221). The language of 'modes of the same nature' helps to re-enforce the unity of the human mind in its inter-action with different realities. This is an issue that had been taken up, in the correspondence with Regius in 1641, at a time when Descartes was still merely counselling him about how best to express the Cartesian view rather than accus-ing him of subverting it by intentional misrepresentation. On that occasion Descartes explained that he preferred to say that willing and understanding differ only as the activity and passivity of the same substance. 'For understand-ing is, strictly speaking, the passivity of the mind and willing is its activity; and because we never will anything without simultaneously understanding it and we hardly ever understand anything without simultaneously willing some-thing, we do not easily distinguish passivity from activity in such cases' (iii. 372).[13] The conclusion suggested by these texts is that the human mind is not equipped with faculties that are so distinct from each other that there could be problems of communication between them. Thus there could not be a genuine philosophical problem about how our understanding provides what is needed for the will to make its decisions. There is no real distinction between the mind and its faculties. 'Willing' and 'understanding' are simply traditional terms used

---

[12] Cf. *Comments on a Certain Manifesto* (viii-2, 363; M. 199).

[13] Cf. Descartes to Hyperaspistes (Aug. 1641), where he discussed the influence of a physical cause after it has ceased to operate or even to exist: 'I have always thought that it was one and the same thing that is called an action when it is referred to a *terminus a quo* and a passion when referred to a *terminus ad quem* or in *quo*. Thus it is clearly impossible to have an action without a passion, even in the shortest period of time' (iii. 428).

to describe the same mind in so far as it is active or passive. Whether these latter terms can provide any explanatory light remains to be seen.

The Cartesian paradigm of passivity, in this context, is the way in which we acquire thoughts that result from external or internal sensations. This was the basis of the argument, in the Sixth Meditation, to show that external physical things exist. The argument was that a thinking subject is often aware of having experiences, especially of unpleasant ones such as a sharp pain, over which they have no control. Therefore I must have a 'passive faculty for sensing' by which I acquire some ideas 'when I am not cooperating and even in spite of me' (vii. 79; M. 62). It is not within our power to decide whether we have these ideas that arise from sensation.[14] This shows that, with respect to the occurrence of at least some ideas, we are passive rather than active. However, Descartes extends the scope of passivity to all cases of understanding, even to thoughts that do not result from sensation, although he also accepts that the mind may also be the active source of some of the ideas that are 'passively' received in the understanding.

Once the understanding is passively impressed with various ideas, the term 'will' is used to denote the ability of the mind to make an appropriate response. Here, too, the extent to which the mind's response is within our power is limited. Descartes is unambiguous in conceding that, whenever the evidence provided to the understanding is sufficiently strong, the mind cannot withhold its assent. For example, in the Fourth Meditation, he claims (in relation to the *Cogito* argument) that the conclusion 'I exist' cannot be avoided once I see how it follows from 'I think'. 'This was not because I was coerced into it by some external force (*ab aliqua vi externa*), but because a strong inclination of the will followed from a great light in the understanding and, as a result, I believed it much more spontaneously and freely in so far as I was less indifferent to it' (vii. 58–9; M. 48). Likewise, if something is presented as good, the mind cannot fail to want it. For this reason, Descartes can argue that 'judging well is sufficient to do well' (i. 366), because the will automatically responds favourably to what is presented as good. The same thesis is developed at greater length in a letter to Mesland, in May 1644: 'thus when we see very clearly that something is good for us, it is very difficult and even impossible, I believe, to stop the course of our desire as long as one remains in this thought' (iv. 116). The only way out, suggested by the concluding phrase, is to change one's thoughts from one subject to another and thereby escape the ineluctable attraction of what is perceived as good.

---

[14] Cf. Descartes to Mersenne (3 Dec. 1640): 'I have never said that all our thoughts were in our power, but only that if there is anything absolutely in our power, it is our thoughts, that is, those that come from our will and free choice . . . I wrote that only to explain that our free will has no absolute jurisdiction over any bodily thing, which is obviously true' (iii. 249).

Accordingly, Descartes rejects one of the traditional ways of analysing freedom of the will in terms of indifference between two or more options. In some circumstances the will is free even though it is not indifferent.

THE INDIFFERENCE OF THE WILL

I suggested above that the term 'indifference' was used to describe the inner experience of suspending judgement when the evidence in favour of a particular judgement is not compelling. What we experience in such examples, according to Descartes, is 'freedom and indifference'. However, indifference may be merely a symptom of the underlying reality of freedom and it may not be a necessary condition for the voluntariness of a given act. Descartes addresses the question of the relation between freedom and indifference on a number of occasions: in the Fourth Meditation, in the Replies to Objections, and especially in correspondence with Father Mesland. He also approaches it indirectly by contrasting the role of indifference in human and divine freedom.

The text in the Fourth Meditation that aroused queries, among both contemporary readers and recent commentators, is as follows:

> Nor is it true that, in order to be free, I must be capable of moving in either direction; on the contrary, the more I am inclined in one direction the more freely I choose it, either because I clearly recognize it as being true or good or because God so disposes my innermost thoughts. Surely neither divine grace nor natural knowledge ever diminishes freedom; instead, they increase and strengthen it. But the indifference I experience when I am not moved one way or another by any consideration is a lower degree of freedom, and it does not indicate perfection in our freedom but merely some kind of defect or something lacking in our knowledge. For if I always saw clearly what is true and what is good, I would never deliberate about what judgement to make or what to choose and thus, although I would obviously be free, I could never be indifferent.   (vii. 58; M. 47)[15]

Michelle Beyssade (1994) has argued that there are two alternative senses of 'indifference' at issue here, and that Descartes changed his mind about this question between the Latin edition of the *Meditations*, which is translated above, and the French edition of 1647. The two senses to be distinguished are: (1) a power or ability to choose either of two contrary options; and (2) a psychological state of being undecided between alternatives because the agent lacks sufficiently strong reasons to persuade them either way. Beyssade argues that Descartes

---

[15] This text raises a question that was very much disputed at the time but that Descartes fails to address. If God 'disposes my innermost thoughts' by means of 'divine grace', would that not constitute a controlling external force that compromises my freedom? He seems to assume that God's intervention is so obviously beneficial that it merely helps us to choose freely what is true or good in the same way that a clear understanding determines our choices without negating our freedom.

changed his mind, between 1641 and 1647, about whether the first kind of indif-ference is a necessary condition for free will. 'Freedom then, in 1641, does not require a two-way power, but consists merely in being unconstrained: it is the spontaneous movement towards something. By contrast, what Descartes, in the French text [i.e. in 1647], regards as not necessary for human freedom . . . *is the state of indifference or wavering or balance* due to ignorance' (Beyssade 1994: 194). While Beyssade has identified a difficulty experienced by Descartes in ar-ticulating his position, I think the texts can support a consistent reading that does not imply a change of mind on the author's part. On this alternative reading, the power to choose between alternatives is essential to freedom but it is also time sensitive.

In a letter to Father Mesland (9 February 1645) Descartes distinguishes between two kinds of indifference, and makes the second one, (2) above, ex-plicit. 'It seems to me that indifference, when understood strictly, means the state of the will when it is not moved one way rather than another by any per-ception of truth or goodness. I understood it in this way when I wrote that it was the lowest degree of freedom by which we determine ourselves to things to which we are indifferent' (iv. 173). In other words, to be indifferent with respect to some judgement is to lack sufficiently strong reasons for making a positive or negative judgement. We could describe ourselves as indifferent in this sense if, for example, we lack sufficiently clear evidence to choose which route to take on a journey or if we are offered a selection of beverages and none of them seems more attractive than another.

Descartes also identified another sense of the term 'indifference'—(1) above—in reply to Mesland's queries.

But perhaps others understand 'indifference' as a positive faculty of determining oneself to either of two contraries, that is to say, to pursue or avoid, to affirm or deny. I did not deny that there is such a positive faculty in the will. Indeed, I think that it has such a posi-tive faculty with respect to those actions to which it is not moved by any evident reasons towards one side rather than the other, but also with respect to all other actions; so much so that, when a very evident reason moves us in one direction, although morally speak-ing we can hardly move in the opposite direction, absolutely speaking we can. For it is always possible for us to turn back from pursuing a clearly known good, or from admit-ting a clearly perceived truth, on condition merely that we think that it is good to bear witness, by doing so, to the freedom of our will.   (iv. 173)

Descartes is admittedly attempting to be conciliatory here and to share as much common ground as possible with a sympathetic Jesuit correspondent who explained human freedom in terms of indifference. The compromise was to distinguish two senses of the term 'indifference' and to reject only one of them.

This reflects accurately the point Descartes had made in the *Meditations*, quoted above, that it is not a necessary condition for being free that the agent be equally attracted to two (or more) alternative options. This latter vague phrase means: in the case of judgements about what is true, it is not necessary to believe that the evidence in support of a proposition is as weighty as the evidence against it; and in choosing what is good, it is not necessary to believe that two alternative things are equally good for us. Even when we are completely convinced that something is true or good and we are not the least indecisive about which option to choose, our action may still be voluntary.

The other sense of 'indifference', (1) above, is used to describe the power or ability we have, as free agents, to say 'yes' or 'no' to whatever is presented to us. This is still too vague to specify what is at issue, for it seems to depend on our uttering words, even silently. Descartes had defined the relevant power, in the *Meditations*, as follows (in the text quoted above): 'we can either do or not do something (that is, affirm or deny something, seek or avoid it); or rather, it consists in this alone that we bring ourselves to affirm or deny, to seek or avoid, whatever is proposed to us by our intellect in such a way that we feel that we are not determined by any external force.' If one accepts that this definition is intended primarily to exclude determining influences from outside the mind, the power of the agent to decide voluntarily is a power of self-determination that depends on factors that are internal to the mind itself. This kind of self-determination might equally well be called autonomy or spontaneity. The question that remains unanswered, of course, is whether this process of self-determination is such that the agent always remains capable of assenting or not assenting to propositions, or of seeking or not seeking what is believed to be good.

In writing to Mesland, Descartes answers this question by introducing a distinction between what is possible at different temporal stages of decision making. Before we make a decision about something, freedom entails indifference in sense (1) but not in sense (2). Descartes here exploits the distinction between external and internal influences. Thus we may say that we are less free in making decisions when someone else commands us (although, as he recognizes, their commands and our own contrary preferences may put us in a state of indifference in the second sense). But, he argues, we cannot apply the same analysis of competing forces to our own internal deliberations and then claim that we are more free when we are less influenced by reasons or evidence, as if they were also extraneous interfering factors. 'If we choose something that seems to have more characteristics of what is good, we determine ourselves more easily' (iv. 174). As long as we have not made a decision, it is true of us as agents that we may or may not assent to something, even in those cases where we are very strongly moved by reasons, and so on. However, once we have made a decision, the voluntariness of our decision implies neither kind of indifference. It consists simply in the facility with which we do something. 'At that point, acting freely, spontaneously, and voluntarily are clearly identical. It was in this sense that I wrote that, to the extent that I was moved towards something by more reasons, I was moved more freely; for it is certain that our will moves itself then with greater facility and force' (iv. 175).

These suggestions imply that, for Descartes, freedom of the will never requires indifference in sense (2) above—that is, being undecided between alternative options because the reasons that support them are evenly balanced. Voluntariness requires merely that a decision be made on the basis of what is presented by the understanding, and, even if the reasons are overwhelmingly in favour of one decision rather than another, that does not diminish the voluntary character of the resulting decision.

Indifference, then, in sense (2) above is not *necessary* for freedom of the will. But it may be *sufficient* in the sense of providing reliable evidence of the exercise of freedom. The context of this discussion of indifference is the Cartesian explanation of how we come to make mistaken judgements. We can decide to believe propositions for which we have inadequate evidence or of which we have an inadequate understanding. As long as the evidence is not compelling, we are indifferent about what judgement to make. 'This indifference extends not only to things that are not known at all by the understanding but generally to anything that is not understood clearly by it at the precise time that the will deliberates about it' (vii. 59; M. 48). Descartes wants to claim that our indifference is removed by compelling evidence, but that the absence of such indifference does not imply that we are not free. This interpretation is confirmed by his reply to one of the objections submitted by Mersenne.

Besides, knowing something to be true is not the only thing that is independent of the will; so likewise is believing or giving one's assent. For we believe, whether we wish to or not, whatever is proved by valid arguments or is reported credibly. It is true that affirming and denying, defending and rejecting propositions, are acts of the will; but it does not follow that our internal assent depends on the will.   (vii. 192)

Despite the initial strangeness of this comment, Descartes is evidently arguing that our assent is voluntary even when we cannot refrain from assenting to propositions that strike us as manifestly true. This is a form of being compelled by an internal force that is compatible with human freedom.

Finally, the indifference that characterizes human freedom may be contrasted with the indifference that applies to God. Evidently, it cannot be the case that Descartes first knows about God's freedom directly and then explains human freedom by comparison or contrast with that of God. The reverse is the case. One must specify what is meant by human freedom prior to applying the same concept, by analogy, to God. Any Cartesian description of God's freedom, therefore, should be understood as presupposing what is meant by human freedom. Descartes addresses the question about the indifference or otherwise of God's actions in reply to Mersenne's objections to the *Meditations*. In the Sixth Replies, he argues that God's freedom is very different from ours, because the indifference that applies to God is very different from what applies to human beings. If God were indifferent, that would imply some condition of God's will in virtue of which it could be affected by truths or goods that are prior, logically or naturally, to God making a decision about them. However, according to the standard Cartesian account, God's will is the source of all goods and all truths, and therefore there is nothing independent of God that could cause him to be indifferent about a decision. In the case of human beings, by contrast,

since they find that the nature of every good and every truth has already been determined by God and that their wills cannot tend toward anything else, it is clear that they embrace what is good or true more willingly and therefore more freely in so far as they perceive it clearly, and that they are never indifferent except when they do not know what is better or more true, or when they do not see the distinction between them so clearly that they are unable to have any doubt. Thus the indifference that applies to human freedom is very different from that which applies to divine freedom.   (vii. 432–3; M. 100)

This confirms the suggestion that Descartes wishes both to acknowledge an indifference in many human decisions, in so far as they may be determined by inadequately conclusive guidance by the intellect, and that this kind of indifference is not a necessary condition for human freedom. Since such an indifference reflects a lack of knowledge or understanding in the human case, and the consequent failure of the will to be determined uniquely by the intellect, God's freedom cannot be characterized either by imperfect knowledge, or even by a perfect understanding of realities that are in some sense independent of his omnipotence.

CARTESIAN COMPATIBILISM

The range of things that fall outside the power of our will is so extensive that, by a process of elimination, the identification of its limited scope becomes almost uncontentious. In mind–body interactions, we cannot normally decide what signals will come into our minds and cause us to have sensations. If external or internal stimuli are sufficiently strong and if our nervous system is functioning properly, we cannot (for example) avoid feeling pain or seeing colours on certain occasions.[16] Likewise, in sending signals in the opposite direction from the mind to our body, we cannot decide arbitrarily what physical actions to perform; when we try to impose our will on our bodies, they frequently fail to comply with our ineffectual commands. For these two reasons, our own bodies are largely independent of our minds. Even if we omit all reference to our bodies and remain within the scope of the mind's own activities, we are still not completely in control. For example, we cannot withhold assent from things that seem to be beyond doubt, and we cannot stifle a desire for things that are presented as unconditionally good. The limited scope of the will must be demarcated, therefore, by looking more carefully at what it does when it functions in its characteristic way. According to Descartes, 'to will, understand, imagine, sense, etc. are only different ways of thinking' (i. 366). Not surprisingly, then, 'there is nothing entirely within our power except our thoughts'.[17] Willing is, therefore, one form of thinking over which we have control and which is efficacious in determining at least some of our actions. Consequently a Cartesian explanation of the will should include an account of how, as a result of having certain thoughts, we succeed in determining the relatively limited range of actions that are said to be voluntary.

There is no suggestion that Descartes thinks of free actions—such as taking a walk when we are not being forced by threats or otherwise—as being exceptions to the general principle of causality. Free actions are caused. In fact, one of the dangers in his account is the overdetermination of human actions rather than the contrary, since they are caused both by God and by the mind of the agent. Thus there are two questions about the compatibility of the mind's causality with the agency of other causes: (1) if God causes everything, is there still a role for the human mind to act as a cause of voluntary actions; (2) can the mind be said to cause some human bodily actions, such as walking, that are also caused by other material causes? Descartes may be described as a compatibilist if the answer to either question is positive (Chappell 1994). The texts suggest that Descartes is a compatibilist in both senses. Once that is accepted, the question then becomes: how can thinking determine voluntary actions that are otherwise caused?

There are no a priori reasons for rejecting the possibility that a single event has more than one cause. The concern about how thinking can be a cause

---

[16] *Passions* (i. 46): 'The soul can prevent itself from hearing a slight noise or feeling a slight pain by being very attentive to something else, but it cannot in the same way prevent itself from hearing thunder or feeling a fire that burns the hand' (xi. 363–4).

[17] Descartes to Reneri for Pollot (April or May 1638) (ii. 35). He repeats the same sentiment at ii. 37: 'Nothing exterior, then, is in our power except in so far as it is at the command of our soul, and nothing is absolutely in our power except our thoughts.' Here Descartes is discussing the claim made in the *Discourse* the previous year, that 'there is nothing that is completely within our control apart from our thoughts' (vi. 25; *D*. 20).

becomes clear only when some background assumptions are made explicit. One such assumption is that thoughts are immaterial and that bodily movements are material, and we lack any understanding of causal interactions between the material and the non-material. A second underlying question may be: if a human mind causes some action, is the mental act in turn caused by some other prior cause in a series, or is it a first cause that is an exception to the model of the universe that underlies Cartesian physics and physiology? According to this model, every event is caused as a result of prior events or states of the relevant part of the universe. Among physical causes, therefore, there is nothing perplexing in the concept of a series of causes, each of which in turn is an effect of other causes. In contrast, arguments against compatibilism seem to assume that the will cannot be free and, at the same time, caused to act as it does—that it functions as an uncaused or undetermined cause of those actions that are called voluntary. One could find an answer to the first question, about mind–body interactions, by extrapolating the Cartesian account of thoughts as brain events. The second question, about mental events as genuine causes despite being caused in turn by other events, requires a theory of what it is to be a subject.

Before developing the Cartesian account of how our actions are caused by thoughts, it may be appropriate to comment briefly on the compatibility of human voluntary actions with God's universal causality. Descartes claims that God's causality is involved in all causal relations that obtain at any level lower than the divine. He even claimed, in writing to Princess Elizabeth, that God causes all human free actions.

> All the reasons that prove that God exists and that he is the primary and immutable cause of all the effects that do not depend on human free will seem to prove, in the same way, that he is also the cause of all those that do depend on human free will . . . philosophy teaches us that it is impossible for the least thought to enter the human mind unless God wills it and unless he has willed it from all eternity . . . God is the universal cause of everything in such a way that, at the same time, he is their total cause and therefore nothing can occur without his will. (iv. 314; M. 160)

This introduces a major issue about how best to understand occasional causality in Descartes, and it is not something that can be resolved in a few paragraphs. However, there are reasons to think that it is not necessary to answer this question satisfactorily before constructing an account of voluntary human action (Clarke 2000).

In a text already quoted above from the *Principles* (i. 41), Descartes suggests that we should not entertain doubts about human freedom (which is something of which we are certain from experience) simply because we cannot explain how it is compatible with divine freedom (which we know we cannot comprehend). This is a sound suggestion rather than a mere evasion of a difficult problem. It is not clear how Descartes uses the concept of a cause. It was a familiar term within a traditional system of philosophy that he inherited, and there are many problems beneath its surface appearance even in the context of physical causes and their operations. More importantly, all concepts used in reference to God are constructed by analogy with concepts that apply within our human experience.[18] Thus, apart from the general principle that God and his operations are incomprehensible to mere human minds, the way in which we may coherently adapt the concept of a cause to describe God's actions remains ill-defined. Both the source of our concepts in experience and their analogical application to God support the suggestion that we hold fast to what we know of human freedom rather than reconsider the latter because we cannot construct a satisfactory metaphysics of God's activity—any description of which presupposes the availability of a language with which to speak of human freedom.

This argument in favour of caution suggests that we not turn something that we do not understand adequately into a firm conviction from which it would then be possible to draw reliable conclusions. Accordingly, when Descartes makes some metaphysical comments on God's immutable act of creating and conserving the world, he must do so in such a way that the causality of secondary causes is compatible with the unique causality of the divine cause. The logic of these considerations is that we first understand causal relations between the realities of our experience, and that this understanding requires the addition of a transcendent cause that underpins the causal efficacy of created causes. It cannot be an implication of this argument that the latter then becomes redundant. Thus, as long as one is giving 'local area' causal accounts of events in the world, the significance and mode of operation of God's causality may be simply acknowledged and omitted.

If all else fails, one could invoke Frankfurt's arguments about free will (1988: 1–10) to show that voluntary actions do not presuppose that the agent in question could have done otherwise. The only kind of determinism that would compromise the moral responsibility of agents would be one that provides a reason for doing a particular action. If agents do something because they wish to do it, it is irrelevant to whether or not they should be held responsible that, without their knowledge and without affecting their choice, it would have been impossible for them to have done otherwise. Therefore, even if God were to operate a background set of constraints as a result of which we cannot do otherwise than

---

[18] Cf. Descartes to More (15 Apr. 1649): 'Although I think there is no way of acting that applies univocally to God and to creatures, I confess, nevertheless, that I find no idea in my mind that represents the way in which God or an angel can move matter apart from that which shows me the way in which I am conscious of being able to move my body by my thought' (v. 347; M. 180).

we do, the question about free will is one that arises in the thoughts, considerations, and decisions of a particular agent, within the wider framework of nature or God's plans. Descartes seems to have been grasping for a resolution along these lines when he wrote to Princess Elizabeth about this issue in January 1646 (iv. 353–3; M. 163). He relies on an analogy (*une comparaison*) of a king who gives a general order against duelling, and at the same time commands two individuals (whom he anticipates will duel if they encounter each other) to undertake errands that cause them to meet and duel. The king thus issues a general command against duelling and a specific command that, he anticipates, will result in a duel. The distinction between two levels of willing in the king that result in contrary effects can hardly be transferred to God, as Descartes suggests, for there are no real distinctions within God. This attempted reconciliation of God's causality with human voluntariness is also complicated by God's foreknowledge, which is likely to introduce other insoluble paradoxes that are irrelevant to the king's commands. For present purposes, then, it would be preferable to think of the Cartesian account of God's causality as being a background theory of how the natural world (including human beings) came to be as it is, and to focus on questions about human freedom as a narrower question of explaining how one's thinking can determine one's voluntary actions.

VOLUNTARY HUMAN ACTIONS

One way into a Cartesian account of the will is through the emotions or passions. Some of these are innate and some are acquired, as explained in Chapter 4. The fundamental passions provide an innate guide for the responsiveness of an individual to their changing environment. Admittedly, it merely moves the question back one stage, to nature or God, to claim that we have innate emotional responses, but that is enough for present purposes. Assuming the passions as natural responses of an organism to certain kinds of stimuli, and assuming the processing of information in the brain according to the outline suggested above for sensation, memory, and imagination, Descartes's use of the metaphor of a pilot or a fountaineer to describe the role of the mind, when it is exercising the power of willing, is not as misleading as it might initially appear.[19]

The best account of how the will functions, in relation to the body, is provided in *The Passions of the Soul*. Here Descartes repeats a comment that he had

---

[19] In *A Treatise on Man* Descartes writes about the rational soul in the machine of the body as follows: 'And finally, when a rational soul is present in this machine it will have its principal seat in the brain and will reside there like the fountaineer, who must be stationed at the tanks to which the fountain's pipes return if he wants to initiate, impede, or in some way alter their movements' (xi. 131–2; W. 107).

made on numerous occasions, to the effect that acts of the will are those thoughts of the soul that are 'absolutely within its power', in contrast with many of its perceptions that are passively and involuntarily received from extra-mental causes. If we assume control of these thoughts, then 'the entire activity of the soul consists in this: that by the mere fact that it wills something, it makes the little gland to which it is closely joined move in the manner required to produce the effect that corresponds to the volition' (xi. 360). However, as long as the thoughts in question are acts of the soul, the proposed explanation seems to dodge the fundamental question of how one's mental decision is implemented in appropriate bodily actions. It seems to leave unanswered the question: how do mental events connect with, and causally affect, a part of the brain? Part Two of the *Passions* provides an answer to this question.

I derive an explanation of all this from what was said above, namely that our soul and our body are so linked that, if we have once joined some bodily action with a certain thought, one of them does not occur afterwards without the other also occurring. We see this, for example, in those who have taken some medicine with great revulsion when they were ill, and cannot afterwards eat or drink anything that tastes similarly without immediately feeling the same revulsion. Likewise, they cannot think of their revulsion from medicines without the same taste returning in their thought.   (xi. 407)

This explanation is based, for the most part, on conditioning; the qualification 'for the most part' applies because some mind–body connections are innate and do not require any training or conditioning. However, whether the connections involved are innate or acquired, Descartes claims that many thoughts are associated with corresponding brain states, and that there is no mystery in principle about how thoughts can influence bodily actions.

The association between a thought and a motion in the pineal gland may have been established in our earliest experiences, or it may have been acquired through subsequent experiences and reinforced by habit. Descartes gives the example of the reaction of infants to pleasant food. The infant is conscious of the food, responds very positively to its taste, and its primitive emotion (that is, a love of food) is expressed in behaviour that makes it easier for the body to acquire more food in the same manner. These elementary connections between sensations, basic emotions, and appropriate actions are innate. However, many thought–brain–muscle associations are acquired much later, and the appropriate trigger may be something as abstract as a word or phrase.[20] This hypothesis is independent of what we eventually think thoughts are. All one needs to

---

[20] Greenfield (2000: 175) discusses the phenomenon of immune conditioning by which the immune system can be conditioned so that it responds to a stimulus that could not possibly have any direct chemical effect on it. For example, a mere photograph of a hayfield triggers a hay fever reaction.

accept, at this stage, is that many thoughts are associated, by nature or training, with changes in the brain, and we succeed in causing voluntary actions only in those cases in which such an appropriate, prior association has been established. There is no implication that we are conscious of the connection between having certain thoughts and the occurrence of corresponding motions in our brains. It is not as if, self-consciously, we had to move the animal spirits through certain pores in order to cause the desired effect. As Descartes commented in a letter to Arnauld, this happens 'because of the appropriate disposition of the body . . . and because of the union of the mind with the body'.[21]

It follows that our volitions may not always be effective in producing a physical change even in our own bodies. Descartes illustrates this phenomenon in the *Passions* by referring to attempts to enlarge the pupils of our eyes (xi. 361–2). If we try to do so directly, merely by willing that it should happen, we fail. But once we realize that the pupils expand when we look at a distant object, we can exploit the connection—established by nature—between looking at a distant object and the corresponding enlargement of our pupils in order to achieve the same result indirectly. Likewise, when we wish to say something, we do not decide to move our muscles in all the complex ways required to express our thoughts. Instead we think only of what we want to say and this achieves the desired result indirectly. In this case, Descartes thinks, the action of the will has become associated 'by the habits acquired in learning to speak' with the meaning of the words rather than with the words themselves, and the latter usually follow if our learning has been successful.

The limitations on the scope of the will in moving our bodies, therefore, result from the limited number of connections between our thoughts and bodily movements that have been established (by nature or by conditioning) prior to a given decision. Since the passions arise in the soul as a direct result of various bodily conditions, our control over them is equally limited and indirect. Thus, as long as the bodily condition continues that causes or maintains a particular passion, the emotion itself will also continue to be felt. Accordingly, the passions cannot be either 'aroused or suppressed directly by the action of our will' (xi. 362), but they may be controlled indirectly by imagining things with which other passions are already associated. For example, we cannot usually overcome our fear simply by willing to be brave, but we can direct our thoughts

---

[21] Letter for Arnauld (29 July 1648): 'We are conscious, however, of the whole action by which the mind moves the nerves, in so far as such an action is in the mind, where it is nothing more than the inclination of the will towards one movement or another. The flow of spirits into the nerves, and everything else required for the movement in question, follows this inclination of the will. This occurs because of the appropriate dispositions of the body, of which the mind may not be aware, and because of the union of the mind with the body, of which the mind is clearly aware' (v. 222).

to considering the probability and significance of the danger that caused the fear. We could even whistle in the dark, assume brave behaviour, and hope that the corresponding feeling of bravery will be stimulated in our minds.

This understanding of the passions provides a Cartesian gloss on the role of morality in moderating our passions, and on the kind of internal conflicts that had been described by some earlier authors as a struggle between different parts of the soul. Having presented reasons for making a 'sensitive soul' a redundant theoretical entity, it cannot be the case that the sensitive soul is in conflict with the rational soul. All such conflicts, according to Descartes, result exclusively from the opposing movements in the same parts of the brain (especially the pineal gland), which result from competing forces impressed on them by the body and will (indirectly). In this conflict of forces, we can refer to strong souls or, in contemporary English, to a strong character if someone has acquired habits through which they can tame their passions and impose their voluntary decisions on the competing influences of the body. One way of doing this is to use our imagination, as indicated above, to trigger another passion that could neutralize the one that threatens our freedom. But that is likely to lead to a loss of control or to an oscillation between the competing influences of different passions. Descartes recommends, instead, that we have recourse to what he calls the 'proper weapons' of the will. These are 'firm and determined judgements concerning knowledge of good and evil' (xi. 367).

One could misread this suggestion as another element in a rationalist exaggeration of the role of judgements in controlling our passions. However, this is a proposal about practical judgements, and it is consistent with the limited and indirect power that is being claimed here for the will. In the *Passions* (ii. 144), Descartes discussed the role of desire in our lives as agents. While the passions cause us to have specific feelings over which we have little control, they 'cannot bring us to perform any action except by means of the desire that they stimulate' (xi. 436). If we wish to control them, therefore, we should focus on these desires 'and here lies the primary usefulness of morality'. There are two kinds of desires, in this context of exercising control. There are those that depend only on us—that is, on our will—and there are those that depend on various factors over which we have little direct control. In keeping with a well-known tradition in moral theology, Descartes argues that 'we can be praised or blamed justifiably only for those actions that depend on free will' (xi. 445). The implications of this analysis for a theory of morality are neither rationalist nor implausible.

Descartes had argued as early as the *Discourse on Method* that 'our will moves naturally to desire only those things that our understanding represents to it as in some way possible' (vi. 25–6; *D*. 21). Thus a necessary propaedeutic to any morality is to distinguish between what we are capable or incapable of doing, and in particular to exclude any references to 'fortune' as some kind of all-powerful cause that controls our fate.[22] Within the range of actions of which we are capable, we then need to distinguish between what is good and evil. 'For since our will cannot follow or flee from anything except in so far as our understanding represents the thing in question as good or evil, judging well is enough to do good, and judging as well as possible is enough to do one's best, that is, to acquire all the virtues and, with them, all the other goods that one is capable of acquiring' (vi. 28; *D.* 22). The immediate effects of correct judgements about what is good or evil are nothing more than new thoughts in the mind. Descartes has conceded, frequently, the limited extent to which thoughts may indirectly moderate the passions (including desire) and control our actions. There are trailing connotations of Stoicism in these suggestions in the *Discourse*, and in the advice given on more than one occasion to Princess Elizabeth. They present a picture of human beings who are very much caught in a web of causal connections, over which they have little power or control. Hence the advice to learn what is possible, since attempting the impossible leads only to frustration. Admittedly, 'one needs long practice and a frequently repeated meditation to get used to seeing everything from this perspective' (vi. 26; *D.* 21). Within the range of what is possible, we should emulate those ancient philosophers who became convinced that 'there was nothing so completely in their power, apart from their own thoughts' (vi. 26; *D.* 21). Morality, therefore, involves a habit of making wise judgements about what is good or evil, and an associated training—for acquiring the virtues—in implementing those judgements despite the obvious influence and distractions of the passions.

In introducing Cartesian compatibilism above, I mentioned two issues that require an explanation or resolution. The first was how what is 'merely a thought' can affect our physical behaviour—for example, how deciding to walk can result in walking. The Cartesian answer to this is that some mental states are connected, by nature or by training, with some physical states, and we exercise our freedom by exploiting those connections to perform the actions that we wish to perform. In this sense, the physical or mechanical explanation of any human action that involves bodily movement depends on the motion of parts of matter in a way that is consistent with Cartesian physics. Human nature (or God) has equipped us with various natural or innate responses to things, some of which were mentioned above in Chapter 4. Such responses can be explained physically, and they are associated by nature with various feelings or sensations, both of which are forms of thought, that provide the initial connection between

---

[22] *Passions* (II. 145), where fortune is described as a chimera that results from misunderstanding and should be replaced with an appreciation of the role of divine providence.

the mental and the physical. Once this is established, the development of rationality in an adult provides a method of assessing the benefits of what is presented to us as goods, of applying experience to estimate the probability of achieving certain results, of comparing one good with another, and, generally, of making practical judgements. This is significantly facilitated by the acquisition of language and the improved powers of thinking that result from this complex manipulation of conventional signs. In this sense, the metaphor of a pilot in a ship, or of a fountaineer who manipulates the forces at work in a fountain, are entirely apt to describe the function of the will. According to these analogies, the will is nothing more than a very sophisticated power of self-regulation, a feedback mechanism that is capable of learning but whose basic programme has been written by nature (or God). The critical contribution of the will is, as Descartes frequently emphasized, to make judgements. The efficacy of these judgements depends on the innate or natural connections that are already established, at birth, between our most basic needs and our awareness of the feelings and sensations associated with their satisfaction.

This perspective helps dissipate the impression that might be given, in speaking of free actions, of a will as an 'uncaused cause', as an active agent in the physical universe without being itself in any way affected by other relevant causes. Descartes's suggestion is that a human body is involved, as any other physical body, in the constantly changing interactive environment in which it is historically placed. What is distinctive about it, as a human agent, is its capacity to make judgements by using language to manipulate the information that it gathers and stores, and to feed those judgements back into behaviour—only in a limited number of circumstances, as indicated—by exploiting innate or acquired connections between thoughts and brain states. This is a form of determination by means of factors that are *internal* to the agent. In that sense, and to that rather limited extent, the human agent is free.

The second question raised above about the compatibility of voluntary actions with natural causes was the apparent implication, in traditional theories of freedom, that the self who causes voluntary actions is not affected by other causes. That picture makes it seem as if the self is a first cause rather than a member in a complex series of interacting causes. Even if the self were understood as a distinct substance, as in the standard account of Cartesian dualism, it is difficult to understand how the self could be a first cause that is so insulated from other causes that it initiates new causal chains without being affected by others itself. I defer until Chapter 8 a more extended discussion of Cartesian dualism. Here it may be enough to suggest an alternative way of thinking of the self, or at least of those features of the self that are relevant for voluntary actions.

Once we acquire a language and learn all the things that a language makes possible, each individual builds up over time a personal store of experiences, rules of thumb for making judgements, desires, skills, and so on. This constitutes their individual character. One can think of this character as being a significant factor in the judgements and decisions made by an agent, without introducing a new kind of entity that is linked in some inexplicable way with the world of material things and events. This 'self' is the locus of free will. However, neither the self nor its will involves new mysterious entities. The will, on this account, is the very limited power of self-regulation or self-determination that is possible for human beings who are born with innate desires, who are aware of these from their earliest experiences (which, according to Descartes, probably begin in the womb), who acquire a sophisticated language with which to conceptualize their experiences, and who learn to make judgements that steer human agents towards the satisfaction of their desires. One could then think of the sum total of accumulated mental dispositions, memories, habits, virtues, and so on as the character or self of an agent in virtue of which they make their decisions or judgements.

On this account, the will is supervenient to the body. It is consistent with the comment made by Descartes, in the *Passions* (i. 6), that death never occurs in human beings because the soul departs, but only because some essential part of the body ceases to function.

Let us judge that the difference between the body of a living human being and that of a dead human being is the same as that between a watch or another automaton (that is, another machine that is self-moving), when it is wound up and contains within itself the bodily principle of the movements for which it was constructed, together with everything else that is required for its action, and the same watch or other machine when it is broken and the principle of its movement stops working. (xi. 330–1)

If the self is an acquired complex of mental dispositions, as suggested, then it can function only as long as the human body in which it exercises its actions is appropriately disposed.

CHAPTER 6

Human Language

Descartes wrote comparatively little about language. Many of his comments on the significance of language for the enterprise of doing philosophy parallel the critical remarks he frequently made about the senses and the circumstances in which sensory information may be misleading. Both facts point towards one standard way of understanding his philosophy of language, to the effect that ordinary language is a function of our uncritical, sensory experience of the world, that it almost always shares the ambiguities and misleading character of the latter and that, even though it is necessary for communication between people, it is no substitute for clear and distinct ideas of which it is a mere external, corporeal, and inadequate expression. On this view, the thoughts or ideas that result from pure understanding are the only reliable guide to knowledge, while language is a secondary or dependent phenomenon that adds nothing to what is already provided by thought.

Hans Aarsleff, for example, assumes this standard interpretation of the Cartesian view of language in contrast with what he presents as the novelty of Condillac's theory. Aarsleff argues (1993: 169) that 'Descartes was determined to conduct his thinking in a silent and wordless world that would allow undisturbed reliance on intuition'. Intuition—understood here as a direct inspection by the mind of its own ideas—provides a reliable access to the truth or, at least, to the seeds of truth that are naturally implanted in the human mind and can be developed by pure reasoning. If 'seeds of truth' are understood as innate ideas, then the most unerring route to the truth for human beings is to reflect directly, individually, and wordlessly on the content of our own minds and to avoid the accumulated misrepresentations of traditional learning that cling to the well-worn words of language. 'In the Cartesian view, innateness owes no debt to social intercourse . . . the wordfree discourse of the mind is the only guarantor of true knowledge' (Condillac 2001: pp. xii, xiv). The focus of Descartes's interest, therefore, is 'the radical failure of language rather than its role in the advancement of knowledge' (Aarsleff 1993: 175). Human language is fundamentally compromised by the lack of clarity and distinctness of the senses. The unique path to scientific knowledge, on this account, requires the purification or turning way from the senses that is recommended in the *Meditations*.

Since Descartes wrote so little about language, it is inevitable that one interprets his relatively infrequent comments on the subject in the light of a more fundamental and comprehensive view of his epistemology, his theory of ideas, and the significance or otherwise of his scientific work for understanding his theory of knowledge. In the following pages, I shall present an alternative interpretation of the Cartesian theory of language that is consistent with the evidence introduced so far about his naturalized account of mental functions. From this perspective, language is essential for metaphysical or abstract thinking, although all languages are not equally suitable for the task. The implication of the *Meditations* is not that language, as such, compromises our metaphysical thinking but only a language that is inappropriately dependent on unsophisticated experience.

SIMPLE IDEAS AND BASIC TERMS

Descartes's earliest discussions of language, in correspondence with Mersenne, reflect the theory of simple ideas with which the *Rules* hoped to construct a method for acquiring scientific knowledge. He wrote to Mersenne at length (20 November 1629) criticizing suggestions about the development of a universal language. He repeated the claim, already outlined but unpublished in the *Rules*, that the ordering of our thoughts and their separation into clear and distinct ideas is a prerequisite for acquiring scientific knowledge. He then continued:

If someone explained correctly what are the simple ideas in the human imagination out of which all human thinking is composed [*les idées simples qui sont en l'imagination des hommes, desquelles se compose tout ce qu'ils pensent*], and if that explanation were accepted by everyone, I would then dare to hope for a universal language that would be very easy to learn, to pronounce, and to write; and the primary benefit would be that it would assist one's judgement by representing everything to it so distinctly that it would be almost impossible for it to go wrong. As it is, our words have only confused meanings, and the human mind is so accustomed to them that there is hardly anything that it can understand perfectly. Now I maintain that such a [universal] language is possible, and that it is possible to discover the science on which it depends . . .   (i. 81)

This is consistent with the assumption, in the *Rules*, that most of our ideas originate in the imagination, and that knowledge is acquired when we combine simple ideas appropriately into compound ideas that correspond to the realities that they are supposed to denote. If the ideal language envisaged by its proponents were mapped onto an accurate ordering of basic and compound ideas, and if the simple ideas in question were sufficiently widely shared by different human beings, then such a universal language would assist communication and help avoid confusion. In contrast, Descartes argues, many familiar languages include words that have 'confused meanings', and this in turn obstructs both clear understanding and unambiguous communication.

Of course the standard objection to this suggestion is that it seems to assume a theory of language acquisition similar to that attributed by Wittgenstein to Augustine.[1] According to this, each individual language-user could begin the task of mapping words onto simple ideas and, even in the absence of social agreement or convention, could avoid or correct the accumulated confusions of our inherited languages. Descartes, however, seems to reject this naive view when writing to Mersenne the following year (4 March 1630): 'Children who are reared together would not learn how to speak all by themselves, except perhaps a few words which they would invent themselves and which would not be any better or more appropriate than ours; whereas our words, having been invented as they are at the beginning, have been and continue to be corrected and improved daily by usage' (i. 125–6). Before we develop further the conventional features of language, it is important to underline the extent to which Descartes thought of linguistic signs as representing something that is abstracted from our experience of the world.

As indicated in Chapter 3, Descartes claimed in his early works that most of our thought originates in sensation and imagination, and that the generation of so-called pure ideas depends on the abstraction involved in their distillation from the 'matter' of brain states. The discussion of the role of the imagination in Rule 14 showed the extent to which we should rely on the imagination to form 'true' ideas of physical realities, rather than risk being misled by the meaning of a word that may have resulted from an abstraction in which features of something that are inseparable in reality are separated in thought. In that context Descartes warned that, 'even though the intellect attends precisely only to what a word means, the imagination ought to form a true idea of the thing, so that the same intellect can turn to other conditions that are not expressed by the word, if the need arises, and without ever judging foolishly that they have been excluded' (x. 445; D. 175). The text in the *Rules* provides examples of the kind of mistake to be avoided. Those who wish to focus their attention merely on numbers will devise names for the numbers and will abstract from the numbered things. But

---

[1] Wittgenstein (1958: Pt. I, §§1–2, 33). Wittgenstein's arguments about the impossibility of a private language are well known. In §33, he interprets Augustine's suggestions as presupposing that a child learning a language from ostensive definitions is already equipped with an ability to think or to talk privately to him/herself.

they should not draw the conclusion 'that the numbered thing is excluded from our concept'. Likewise, we may wish to discuss merely the shape or surface area of a body, but we should not conclude, from the fact that we have a distinct word to denote it, that the shape or surface of something is really distinct from a three-dimensional body. Descartes's use of the term 'true idea' in this context, and the whole context of his discussion, suggest that abstraction is both necessary and possibly misleading, and that the words we use often camouflage the extent to which they are based on a familiar but unacknowledged abstraction.

Given the context in which Descartes was writing to Mersenne, therefore, in 1629, his comments on an ideal language should not be understood as if they were addressing the question raised by Wittgenstein at the beginning of the *Philosophical Investigations*.[2] The focus of his remarks is, rather, the problem that is explicitly addressed in the *Rules* by its author—namely, how to devise a method for acquiring scientific knowledge. Descartes suggests that all our knowledge derives from only two sources, intuition and deduction (x. 368; D. 123), and that intuition relies on sensation and imagination in the case of physical realities. The kind of methodological rules that are needed, therefore, must guide those in search of scientific knowledge to find the truth, not only in purely mathematical disciplines, but also in those that presuppose experiential access to physical phenomena. Descartes does not argue, in the *Rules*, that all knowledge should be modelled on mathematics but that all knowledge, including mathematics, is based on fundamental relations between properties or realities that can be expressed in clear and distinct ideas. The surprising feature of this proposal, for those who are familiar almost exclusively with the *Meditations*, is that the kind of abstraction involved in forming universals is likely to mislead us in most areas apart from metaphysics, and that the words we usually use—especially the words used traditionally in scholastic philosophy and endorsed by centuries of usage—merely reflect the abstractions of our predecessors in their quest for wisdom. Descartes's initial comments on language in 1629–30 should, therefore, be understood as reflecting his general unease about traditional concepts, about the extent to which words are parasitic on underlying concepts and thus reflect their abstractness, and on the need to return to the origin of our ideas in experience in order to test the validity of the deductions that are built on possibly insecure abstractions.

Evidently, none of these suggestions implies that innate ideas are a special class of ideas that are available to human beings independently of experience, or that we can think about ideas without having any words with which to express

---

[2] I take Wittgenstein's question to be: ostensive definitions might explain how we associate names with named things, but names are only a small part of language and therefore naming is inadequate to explain how we learn to count, to use logical connectives, and so on.

them. The theory underlying the incomplete and inchoate suggestions of the *Rules* is that there are different types of experience that are relevant to different types of knowledge, and that we are more likely to succeed in our search for knowledge if we adapt our method to the type of knowledge sought. In fact, the innateness of ideas does not imply that language is redundant in forming concepts but, as Noam Chomsky has notoriously argued, that our linguistic competence must be both innate and structured in some way prior to language learning. Once we deny, as Descartes did, that all our ideas are supplied readymade in our mind and that they are there prior to language learning, like pictures in a gallery, awaiting the attention of the mind's intuitive gaze,[3] the question that is implicit in the *Rules* acquires a new significance: assuming that our faculties of sensation, imagination, and memory function as described in Rule Twelve, what kind of abstraction is appropriate for different kinds of knowledge, and what precautions are necessary to avoid being misled by our own abstractions or by the words in which they are expressed?

The only suggestion about language that is found in the systematic exposition of Cartesian philosophy in the *Principles* (i. 74) is that concepts are more important than words in gaining knowledge, that they may be more or less confused, and that an appeal to ordinary or familiar technical language is no substitute for clarifying our concepts.[4] Here Descartes argues that we normally link all our concepts with words and that we store them both in memory together. Words and ideas tend to remain linked in this way and, of the two, words are easier to recall. Over time, then, words come to assume the role that Descartes thinks should be assigned primarily to concepts, so that 'people often assent to words that they do not understand, because they think that they once understood them or that they learned them from other people who understood them properly' (viii-1. 37–8; M. 143). This does not assume the possibility or preferability of wordless thought, but implies that we are usually constrained by very linguistically dependent thinking and that our language may both include conceptual confusions and camouflage their presence by the familiarity of the words in which they are expressed. The fact that we must be careful with language, especially the inherited philosophical language of the schools, does not imply that we can do philosophy without any language.

---

[3] In the annotations to the *Principles*, Descartes rejects the suggestion that innate ideas 'are always actually depicted in some part of our mind, in the way in which many verses are contained in a book of Virgil' (xi. 655). The Third Replies make explicit the extent to which innate ideas are merely dispositions or powers to acquire ideas: 'When we say that some idea is innate in us, we do not think that it is always present to us; in that sense no idea would be innate. We mean only that we have within us a power to produce the idea in question' (vii. 189; M. 89).

[4] The marginal title for Art. 74 is: 'The fourth cause of error is that we link our concepts with words that do not correspond accurately to things' (viii-1. 37).

NATURAL AND CONVENTIONAL SIGNS

Descartes adverted to a distinction between natural and conventional signs at about the same time as his first comments on language already mentioned above, and he continued to appeal to it in all his subsequent discussions of language. For example, he wrote to Mersenne (18 December 1629) about the distinction between conventional signs and natural expressions of pain or joy.

> As regards words that naturally signify, I accept as a valid explanation that whatever strikes our senses in such a way causes us to emit some sound; for example, if we are struck, that makes us cry out; if someone does something pleasant to us, that makes us laugh; and the sounds that one emits, in crying or laughing, are similar in all languages. But when I see the sky or the earth, I am not constrained to name them in one way rather than another and I believe that this would still be the case even if we were in the state of Adamic innocence.   (i. 103)

This is consistent with the theory of animal functioning that was part of the Cartesian scientific agenda during this period, according to which many of our responses to external stimuli are purely automatic and are common across a given animal species. In *A Treatise on Man*, Descartes hypothesizes various established dispositions or patterns in the fibres that constitute the substance of the brain and he distinguishes, among such dispositions, those that are natural from those that are acquired. Among the former he proposes a link, established by the creator, between certain kinds of external stimuli and the nerves that cause us, for example, to avoid a painful stimulus. This 'natural disposition' means that, if a fire burns our hand, the animal spirits move spontaneously to the part of the brain that causes us to turn our eyes towards the source of the pain and to withdraw our injured hand. 'And they also enter even those nerves causing the external movements which bear witness to these, such as those that excite tears, or wrinkle the forehead and cheeks, or dispose the voice to cry' (xi. 193; W. 163). This example is expanded, on the next page, to include both crying and laughing. 'As for other external movements which serve . . . to bear witness to the passions, such as those consisting of laughing or crying, these occur only by chance [*par occasion*]' (xi. 194; W. 164). The phrase 'by chance' means that the connection between the sensation of pain, for example, and the cry we emit is not a result of any decision made by the subject of the relevant experience. Rather, the flows of spirits that cause such spontaneous expressions of emotion are directed primarily to the causation of the appropriate internal sensations, and they just happen to be linked with the nerves that result in corresponding external signs. Consequently, without any intention or decision on the part of someone who is burned, the unlucky subject spontaneously or 'naturally' emits a characteristic sound.

The natural causality of cries or laughter as expressions of passions is contrasted, in the first chapter of *The World*, with the way in which conventional signs communicate ideas.

> You are well aware that words do not in any way resemble the things they signify; that does not prevent them from causing us to think about those things, often without us even noticing the sound of the words or their syllables. Thus it can happen that we hear a speech and understand its meaning very well, but we are unable later to say what language was used in making the speech. Now if words—which have meaning only as a result of a human convention—are enough to make us think about things that do not resemble them in any way, why is it not possible that nature may also have established a particular sign that would make us have the sensation of light, even though such a sign contains nothing in itself that resembles the sensation? And is this not the way in which it has established laughter and tears, to make us read joy and sorrow on people's faces? (xi. 4; *D*. 85)

The familiar examples of laughter and tears reappear in the final sentence of this paragraph, as natural signs established by nature to testify to other people's internal passions, but without the signs in any way resembling the passions. The focus of the argument, in this context, is not how we succeed in reading such natural signs or how we learn their standard meaning. The point is merely that tears bear no resemblance to the internal feeling of pain that they express. There is a natural, causal connection between feeling pain and crying, or between pain and groaning, and we spontaneously associate both phenomena, as cause and effect, so that one is a natural sign of the other. However, in the case of most words, the link between a word and its meaning is purely a matter of human convention. Yet this degree of arbitrariness does not compromise the reliability with which we can infer the thoughts of others from the words they use.

Descartes appeals to this distinction between natural and conventional signs on all subsequent occasions on which he addresses the distinctiveness of human language. For example, in the *Discourse on Method* (Part V), he borrows from the unpublished *World* to give an outline of his argument for human rationality. In the course of this argument he concedes the possibility of machines that use language in a way that could be explained naturally.

> For one could easily conceive of a machine that is made in such a way that it utters words, and even that it would utter some words in response to physical actions that cause a change in its organs—for example, if someone touched it in a particular place, it would ask what one wishes to say to it, or if it were touched somewhere else, it would cry out that it was being hurt, and so on.   (vi. 56; *D*. 40)

The theory of natural expressions of pain and pleasure, and the machine analogy that underpins the early work on animal physiology, combine here to imply that machines could be designed to utter words in response to specific stimuli. However, Descartes advises readers that 'one should not confuse words [*paroles*] with the natural movements that express passions and that can be imitated both by machines and by animals' (vi. 58; *D.* 41).

The same contrast between conventional signs and signs as natural expressions of passions is used whenever Descartes addresses the fundamental difference in kind between human and animal languages, and the hypothesis of a rational mind that is linked with this distinction. Chapter 2 discussed the Cartesian account of sensation in animals; it is appropriate at this point to return to the principal feature, in the analysis of animal intelligence, about which Descartes disagreed with Montaigne and Charron.

HUMAN AND ANIMAL LANGUAGE

Pierre Gassendi pinpointed a central issue in the Cartesian theory of mind in the Fifth Objections—namely, the claim that there is a difference in kind, rather than merely in degree, between the human mind and the corresponding faculties in other animals. Gassendi raised this objection in response to the Second Meditation, even though Descartes had not mentioned animals at all there. However, the target of Gassendi's concern is implicit in the claim made by Descartes that a human being is essentially 'a thing that thinks'. Thus Gassendi objected: 'although human beings are foremost among animals, they still belong to the same class' (vii. 269). Gassendi anticipates the standard Cartesian reply, which relies on the difference in linguistic competence between human beings and animals, since this had already been published in the *Discourse* four years earlier. Accordingly he expands his objection by proposing merely a difference of degree between animals and human beings, based on the relative sophistication of their linguistic competence:

You may say that they [animals] do not speak. But, although they do not use human words—because they are not human—they still speak their own words and they use them as we use ours. You may claim that even a mad person can put together various words to express something, but that the wisest of the animals cannot. But look and see if you are being fair if you demand human words from animals and do not consider their own words. (vii. 271)

Descartes's reply on this occasion is rather dismissive and evasive. Instead of answering the objection, he says simply that 'what you ask about animals is not appropriate in this context [i.e. in the context of the Second Meditation], because the mind when meditating can experience in itself that it thinks, but it cannot experience whether or not animals think' (vii. 358). However, Gassendi has accurately identified a close connection, in the Cartesian theory of mind, between thinking and using language in a certain way. This is the factor that Descartes exploits a number of times between 1637 (when the argument was first published in the *Discourse*) and 1649 (in reply to queries from More). Descartes also exploits the same connection between thinking and using a language when replying to those who doubt that we have an idea of God, since thinking about God is linked in some way with having a word for God. It remains to be seen whether Descartes merely claims, as he suggests in reply to Gassendi, that the use of language provides an a posteriori argument in support of the presence of thinking in other creatures, or that thinking is itself a form of using language.[5] I return to this question below.

In the *Discourse* (Part V), Descartes offers readers a brief summary of some of the scientific work that he claims to have completed in an earlier treatise that remained unpublished (i.e. *The World*). He summarizes his theory of animal machines and then claims that 'if there were machines that resembled our bodies and if they imitated our actions as much as is morally possible, we would always have two very certain means for recognizing that, none the less, they are not genuinely human' (vi. 56; *D*. 40). The two criteria proposed were: (1) the use of language, and (2) the adaptability of reason as a universal instrument that can be used in unpredictable or unprogrammable ways.

The Cartesian argument about the distinctively human use of language is presented as follows in the *Discourse*:

> The first is that they [i.e. machines] would never be able to use speech, or other signs composed by themselves, as we do to express our thoughts to others. For one could easily conceive of a machine that is made in such a way that it utters words, and even that it would utter some words in response to physical actions that cause a change in its organs—for example, if someone touched it in a particular place, it would ask what one wishes to say to it, or if it were touched somewhere else, it would cry out that it was being hurt, and so on. But it could not arrange words in different ways to reply to the meaning of everything that is said in its presence, as even the most unintelligent human beings can do.   (vi. 56–7; *D*. 40)

The core of this argument depends on assumptions that Descartes had already made about animal machines in his earlier work. These include the apparent sensitivity of animals to a potentially indefinite variety of external stimuli, where the range of responses and the variety of stimuli with which they can

---

[5] The meditating mind 'will investigate subsequently, only in an a posteriori manner based on their operations' whether or not animals think (vii. 358).

cope are limited only by the complexity of their bodies and of the storage and processing capacity of the brain. The Cartesian account of memory and imagination, as outlined in Chapter 3, explicitly allows for some degree of learning in the responses that a machine-like body could make. For example, it would be a modest extrapolation from what Descartes says to claim that his theory envisages the possibility of a machine learning to recognize strings of sounds, and to respond to parts of those strings or to modified versions of them after a sufficiently long training period, because the flow of animal spirits through the brain would be facilitated by similarities in linguistic stimuli. This suggests that one could expect a Cartesian machine to be able to do the following.

1. To react in a predictable way to any physical stimulus that falls within its sensitivity range. The text quoted above refers to the machine being 'touched' and responding to 'physical actions that cause a change in its organs'. Such contacts between the stimuli and the machine could take the form of contact between some external body and the surface of the machine, as when someone hits a robot with a stick. But the 'touching' may be more subtle and less obvious to the naked eye. The Cartesian understanding of sound is that it involves small particles of matter moving and making contact with the inner ear of an animal machine, and this kind of physical touching is enough to cause an appropriate response in a sufficiently sensitive machine. The argument in the *Discourse*, therefore, although written in 1637, anticipates the possibility in principle of machines responding (inflexibly) to spoken instructions. This is exactly what happens, according to Descartes, when a dog responds to its master's voice. It exhibits a motion that is explained 'mechanically' as a result of the impact of noises on its ears and the complex processing of the information provided through the brain. All these suggestions are contingent on an appropriate fit between the incoming signal and the sensitivity of the machine's sensors.

2. To utter words even when there is no relevant external stimulus. However, Descartes assumes that such utterances are caused by appropriate internal stimuli and that therefore either they are a 'natural' expression of an emotion, comparable to laughter or tears, or they result from some form of training that causes an animal machine to repeat what it had learned. 'One should not confuse words with the natural movements that express passions and that can be imitated both by machines and by animals' (vi. 58; D. 41).

The same type of argument is constructed in a letter to Newcastle (23 November 1646), where the focus of the discussion is whether we have any convincing evidence to attribute 'understanding or thought [*de l'entendement ou de la pensée*]' to animals in order to explain their behaviour. Here Descartes is trying to specify what is special about the use by human beings of 'spoken words, or other signs that are relevant to subjects they encounter, but are not related to any passion' (iv. 574). The *relevance* of one's utterances is included, as a necessary condition, in the specification of human speech 'to exclude the speech of parrots', because a trained parrot might utter the phrase 'Good Morning' in inappropriate circumstances. The second condition, independence of any passion, is meant 'to rule out not only cries of joy and sadness and the like, but also whatever can be taught to animals by training' (iv. 574). The argument here seems to be that we can train a magpie to say hello to its mistress, or we can train dogs, horses, and monkeys to perform, but in all such cases our training relies on establishing an association between their linguistic actions and various passions in the animals, such as their need for food, their fear of punishment, and so on. Consequently, their actions may imitate human actions or even human utterances, but ultimately they are merely 'expressions of their fear, their hope or their joy' and therefore can be performed 'without thought' (iv. 574–5).

The same style of argument is used again, without significant modification, in reply to queries from Henry More in 1649. Descartes wrote to More about this topic on two occasions (5 February and 15 April). The argument is briefer and clearer in these letters; it follows directly from the theory of animal machines that had been developed in the 1630s and was reused in the treatise on the passions that he was about to publish. 'I hope to publish this summer a small treatise on the passions from which it will be clear how I think that, in our own case, all the movements of our limbs that accompany our passions result not from the soul but solely from the machinery of the body' (v. 344; M. 178).[6] This idea is developed at length in the letter of 5 February, which distinguished two principles that may explain all our actions. 'One is completely mechanical and physical, relies solely on the force of animal spirits and the structure of the organs, and could be called a physical soul' (v. 276; M. 173). For example, the natural expression of emotions, in cries or similar expressions, is explained in this way. All animals 'signify to us their natural impulses, such as anger, fear, hunger and the like, by using their voice or other bodily movements' (v. 278; M. 174). As long as new items of behaviour are merely substituted for what animals already do 'naturally', there is no reason to appeal to any higher-level explanation. The key to deciding what kind of 'soul' is appropriate is the relative invariance of the responses, or the consistency of behaviour that makes it amenable to mechanical explanation.

---

[6] *The Passions of the Soul* (1. 50) discusses how animals can be trained to substitute different actions for those that they are naturally disposed to perform (x. 368–9).

When, however, Descartes attempts to characterize what defines human speech, he writes in the *Discourse*: 'a machine . . . could not arrange words in different ways to reply to the meaning of everything that is said in its presence, as even the most unintelligent human beings can do' (vi. 56–7; *D*. 40). The same kind of argument is offered to More: 'no brute animal has so far ever been observed that reached a level of perfection at which it used genuine speech, that is, by indicating something by its voice or signs that could be referred exclusively to thought and not to some natural impulse' (v. 278; *M*. 174). The assumptions that are built into the Cartesian explanation of words uttered as mere expressions of passions, when combined with the hints in the texts just quoted, imply that the defining feature of human speech is that it cannot be explained mechanically. This is in danger of degenerating into a circular argument or a purely analytic claim, unless its apparent conclusiveness is qualified to produce something like moral certainty. If that modification is made, the argument is as follows.

Wherever there is a constant conjunction between two types of event, one may assume that there is some kind of causal connection between them. Thus, even in the case of natural phenomena such as the tides, where the causal link has not been observed, there must be some mechanical connection between the motion of the moon and the tides in the sea. If we do not know what that mechanism is, Descartes is willing to construct a rather speculative hypothesis in order to connect them appropriately. In a similar way, he appeals to the relative uniformity, within any given species, of behaviour patterns (including cries or groans associated with pain) to argue that these are mere natural effects of various bodily conditions and that they should therefore be classified as natural signs of the passions to which they testify. Here, as in the example of the tides, the extremely speculative character of the hypothesis does not compromise the validity of the evidence that supports it. There is a constant conjunction in animals between, for example, wounds and pain behaviour and therefore there must be some connection between them at the micro-level. However, the uniformity displayed in such natural or behavioural patterns is radically disrupted in the case of human speech. There is no constant conjunction between what is said to human speakers and what they meaningfully reply. There is no fixed pattern in the choice of words, or even in the way in which words are arranged in a sentence (although there are limits to the grammatical structures available). Besides, there is no evidence to suggest a correlation between what people say and any bodily dispositions or passions that might be considered as their proximate causes. Instead words seem to be selected to refer to realities that are outside the speaking subject, and the selection seems to be guided by the speaker's intention to communicate and the meaning that is to be communicated. In a word, it seems most implausible that the complex patterns of speech that are familiar even among relatively unintelligent human beings could be explained mechanically by reference to factors that are either internal to the speaker or located in their environment.

The lack of any such constant conjunctions is also supported by our personal experience of speaking. Descartes claims, in his reply to Gassendi quoted above, that we are often aware in our own case of the intentions we have and of the flexibility we enjoy in choosing what we wish to say and how to express it. One of the questions raised by critics and correspondents was whether we should assume the same capacity on the part of animals. Descartes's conclusion here is unusually but appropriately hesitant. He makes explicit the distinction between failing to prove that animals think and proving that they do not think. 'Although I think it has been demonstrated that it cannot be proved that there is any thought in brute animals, I do not think that it is therefore possible to prove that there is none, because the human mind does not reach into their innermost lives' (v. 276; M. 173). The only conclusion that one can draw from the evidence, therefore, is that it is most improbable that animals think as we do. 'This seems to me a very strong argument to prove that the reason why animals do not speak as we do is . . . that they have no thoughts' (iv. 575).

The fundamental premiss that supports this conclusion, that human linguistic behaviour is incapable of being explained mechanically, was shared by many of Descartes's contemporaries. For example, Digby argued in the *Two Treatises* (1644: 319) 'that there is no true language among beasts: their voices not being tokens of divers thinges or conceptions, but merely the effects of divers breathings, caused by divers passions'. Pierre Chanet, in *De l'instinct et de la connoissance des animaux* (1646), defines the concept of 'instinct' as the general direction of the first cause that helps guide secondary causes that lack a specific natural faculty for realizing a given objective. Accordingly, he denies trying to explain all the behaviour of animals simply by reference to instinct.

Thus we do not attribute all the actions of animals to instinct. We know that they have whatever faculties they need for most of their operations; that they have some faculties in common with plants; that they have as many external senses as we have; that they also have an imagination, a memory and a faculty for moving; that, without instinct, they know, they remember and are capable of learning.   (Chanet 1646: 4)

Despite all these concessions, Chanet argues at length that animals do not use language in a way that is comparable to human beings, because the sounds made by animals are natural signs of their passions whereas words, by definition, are *conventional* signs. 'A word is a kind of sound or gesture which is not natural, and which has no other meaning apart from what has been imposed on it by an accord and agreement made by those who use it' (Chanet 1646: 162). Thus, while animals succeed in communicating their thoughts by making sounds, they are not using a language, no more than young babies who cry or smile could be said to be using a language, although they are definitely communicating their thoughts (Chanet 1646: 165). The core of Chanet's argument, which could be transferred almost without modification to Descartes, is as follows:

> Animals do not speak at all, because the variety in their vocal sounds results from nature and not from a convention. Secondly, they express their passions by this variety without having any intention [*intention*] of expressing them. Thus our question is not whether animals make known their thoughts and the diversity of their passions by their voice, or by means of other signs, because we are agreed about that; but we deny that they use these signs intentionally [*à dessein*] to express their thoughts, and that they know that these are signs and means by which they can make themselves understood.   (Chanet 1646: 163)

Finally, the distinction between natural and conventional signs, and the distinction between rational and non-rational animals that depends on it, is a central feature of the *Port Royal Logic*. In Part I, Chapter 4, Arnauld and Nicole introduce a number of distinctions between things and signs of things, the third of which is

> between natural signs, which do not depend on human fancy, as an image that appears in a mirror is a natural sign of what it represents, and others that are only instituted or conventional, whether they bear some distant relation to the things symbolized or none at all. Thus words are conventional signs of thoughts, and characters are conventional signs of words.   (Arnauld and Nicole 1996: 36–7)

In the decades following its initial publication in 1662, this text became a standard and influential source for disseminating Cartesian theories from which many other authors borrowed, including Gerauld de Cordemoy (1968). In time, the distinctive character of conventional signs came to be recognized as the most reliable index of rationality.

LANGUAGE AND RATIONALITY

Descartes's comments on the link between the use of conventional signs and rationality are clear enough to conclude that the latter is a necessary condition for the former, and that the use of conventional signs is confined to human beings. 'It seems to me very remarkable that speaking, once it is defined in this way, is something that applies only to human beings' (iv. 575). Descartes rejects completely the suggestions made by Montaigne and Charron that animals have their own languages that we do not understand, or that they have some kind of language that is more primitive than ours. He argues instead that the use of conventional signs, even minimally, is a sure sign of rationality. Thus he concludes in the *Discourse* 'not only that beasts have less reason than human beings, but that they have none at all. For it is clear that, to know how to speak, very little reason is required' (vi. 58; *D.* 41).[7] This suggests that rationality might be defined or explained in some way in terms of the human capacity to use conventional signs.

There are indications in these discussions that Descartes is stretched to the limits of his conceptual scheme in attempting to identify what precisely is involved in human language use. In *The Passions of the Soul* (I. 50) he argues that animals 'lack reason, and perhaps even thought [*pensée*]' (xi. 369), which suggests that thought includes anything of which we are conscious, and that animals may have some degree of consciousness or awareness as a necessary condition for having sensations.[8] In his letter to Newcastle, he contrasts the lack of reason that is evident in the speech of mad people with the rationality that is assumed in their capacity to speak. Here the linguistic behaviour that requires a special explanation includes 'the speech of mad people, which does not fail to be relevant to what is presented to them, even though it does not follow reason' (iv. 574). This implies that the rationality involved is not intrinsic to the content of what is said, at least when so-called mad people speak without making sense; rather, the relevant rationality is presupposed in the very capacity to learn a language and to manipulate conventional signs in order to signify realities that otherwise are completely unrelated to them.

One indication of how Descartes conceives of the role of reason with respect to speech is found in the same context, in the *Discourse*, in which he develops the argument that depends on the human use of conventional signs. Descartes had argued that there are two 'very certain means' of recognizing the distinction between human beings and complex automata. The second of these was that machines do not act 'on the basis of knowledge, but merely as a result of the disposition of their organs. For whereas reason is a universal instrument that can be used in all kinds of situations, these organs need a specific disposition for every particular action.' He concludes that 'it is morally impossible for a

---

[7] Cf. the conclusion in Descartes to Newcastle (23 Nov. 1646), which considers the possibility that there is some kind of thinking in animals, of a much lower degree of perfection than in human beings. 'I have nothing to reply to this, except that, if they thought as we do, they would have an immortal soul as we do. This is not likely . . .' (iv. 576).

[8] 'Thought' (*cogitatio*) is defined, in the replies to the Second Objections, as 'everything that is in us in such a way that we are immediately conscious of it' (vii. 160; *M.* 85).

machine to have enough different dispositions to make it act in every human situation in the same way as our reason makes us act' (vi. 57; *D*. 41). The human use of conventional signs displays this fundamental characteristic of reason as a universal instrument—that is, it does not assume a predetermined link between varying stimuli and appropriate linguistic responses. This argument depends, ultimately, on the Cartesian account of explanation and could be made more explicit as follows.

A scientific explanation of linguistic responses requires an account (no matter how hypothetical) of the mechanisms by which a language-using animal utters appropriate responses to what is said or done in its presence. Consistent with this, one should assume that the limited repertoire of signs used by animals is an expression of their needs or passions, and that one could train them to expand their repertoire or to respond non-linguistically to commands or signals. However, given the assumption that each stimulus–response must be explained in terms of a 'mechanical' disposition in the animal, the total number of responses that could be programmed is limited by the physical capacity or com-plexity of the animal's brain and nervous system. In contrast, the number of lin-guistic responses that are appropriate to any given sample of human speech is indefinitely large, and the number of linguistic stimuli to which human beings can respond is equally large. Hence the conclusion that it is morally impossible for any machine (that is, anything that is to be explained mechanically) of limited size to be so programmed that it could store and produce a range of appropriate responses that would match the creativity and flexibility of human beings.

There is an interesting contrast between Descartes's trust in the resourceful-ness of mechanical explanations for all natural phenomena, even in cases where very little was known from observations about the mechanisms involved, and his conclusion that the same type of explanation could not cope with the range and variety of human linguistic behaviour. The general logical structure of his argument, therefore, must be similar to that developed by Noam Chomsky. In an argument towards the best explanation, Chomsky hypothesizes innate lin-guistic structures in human beings because otherwise it would be impossible to explain how, from their limited exposure to linguistic stimuli, they succeed in learning the almost indefinitely large number of possible combinations of words that are syntactically consistent with the rules of a natural language. The direction of the Cartesian argument is similar. We know from experience that competent human beings can understand what is said to them and can respond appropriately by combining words to form meaningful sentences that express their intentions. Nothing like this could be produced by a machine, unless it were a machine of almost infinite capacity. To explain this phenomenon, there-fore, one must postulate in human beings a capacity that it not amenable in prin-ciple to mechanical explanation.

This evidently leaves open the question about what kind of power or faculty would be required to bridge the explanatory deficit that this argument identi-fies. If one assumed the addition of a non-material soul, then the mechanical limits on which the argument depends would immediately become irrelevant. Descartes makes this clear in the argument about language use that he devel-oped for the Marquess of Newcastle, when replying to the suggestion that animals may have some thoughts that are similar in kind to ours. Here he con-cludes: 'I have nothing to reply to this, except that if they thought as we do, they would have an immortal soul as we do. This is not likely, because there is no reason to believe this about some animals without including all of them, and many of them are too imperfect for this to be credible about them, such as oysters, sponges, etc' (iv. 576). The second part of this conclusion is implausible. If the relevant feature to be explained in animals is complex linguistic behaviour, then some animals might display this phenomenon while others lack it com-pletely, and the apparent need to postulate immortal souls for individuals in every species is averted. But it is evident from the first sentence that Descartes assumes that the creativity of linguistic behaviour implies an immortal soul.

The interim conclusion is that the flexibility of human linguistic responses is such that it is implausible to think that this capacity could be explained mecha-nically, except by postulating a machine whose capacity for pre-programmed responses, or what Descartes calls bodily dispositions, would far exceed the limits of any familiar physical machine.

WORDS AND IDEAS

The theory of sensation and imagination developed by Descartes in the 1630s suggests, as already indicated, that the imagination is a crucial faculty for study-ing mathematics and natural philosophy. More accurately, the way in which we ought to think about the objects of mathematics and physics is appropriately called 'imagining', although there is no separate reality called the imagination. In contrast, the kind of thinking required to study metaphysics is hindered, rather than helped, by this way of thinking. This is not a surprising claim for readers who are familiar with the *Meditations*; but it would be a mistake to project onto the whole of human knowledge this relatively negative evaluation of the contribution of the imagination to metaphysics. The special character of metaphysical thought is made explicit in a letter to Mersenne (13 November

1639): 'The imagination, which is the part of the mind that most helps mathematics, is more of a hindrance than a help in metaphysical speculation' (ii. 622). If this is not understood as a comment on parts of the mind or on distinct faculties, since the mind has no parts and there is no real distinction between its faculties, it raises a more general query about why Descartes should appeal to the traditional faculty language to express his convictions about acquiring clear and distinct ideas about different objects of knowledge.

One way of making sense of the Cartesian alignment of different faculties with different disciplines is to take seriously the suggestions about abstraction that were already mentioned above. The benefit of using the imagination, according to the *Rules*, is that it protects the enquirer from misleading abstractions. However, the limitations of the imagination are uppermost in the *Meditations* when, for example, Descartes discusses the impossibility of imagining a chiliagon, clearly and distinctly, in the Sixth Meditation. The conclusion there was that, once we are not required to construct a distinct picture of such a multisided geometrical figure in our imagination, we have no difficulty in specifying the content of such a concept by using simultaneously the concepts of a closed geometrical figure, a side, and a thousand.[9] Descartes does not suggest that we could never acquire a concept if we lacked an appropriate word with which to express it. But he seems to acknowledge that it is easier for us to have clear and distinct ideas when we form the corresponding images in our imagination, and that it is easier to fix the definition of a concept or idea if we have agreed words with which to demarcate their extension. This implies that, in some very abstract cases, having appropriate words may be a necessary condition for acquiring the corresponding concepts. One way of testing this suggestion is to consider what Descartes says about the idea of God.

The relationship between the meaning of a word and the idea that is required to underpin its meaning is most acute in the case of 'God'. Descartes admits the difficulty in replying to Gassendi, in the Appendix to the Fifth Replies: 'If one has no idea—that is, no perception—that corresponds to the meaning of the word 'God', it is no use saying that one believes that *God* exists; that is the same as saying that one believes that *nothing* exists, and hence one remains in the abyss of impiety and in extreme ignorance' (ix-1. 210). There are other weighty theological concerns in the background here. For example, Descartes's contemporaries were concerned about the relationship between faith and the meaning of

---

[9] Given the analogy between picturing and imagining, Descartes is on firm ground when claiming that we could not recognize on sight a picture of a chiliagon. We could notice immediately that it had many sides, but we would have to mark one of them and count up to a thousand before identifying it as a picture of a chiliagon. Thus, while we can easily close our eyes, imagine a triangle, and count its three sides, we cannot hold a chiliagon steadily in our imagination to count accurately up to a thousand sides.

propositions to which believers were invited to assent.[10] This was especially a problem in the case of doctrines, such as the Trinity, that had traditionally been presented as mysteries and were therefore in some sense incapable of being understood by mere human minds. Descartes adverted to these questions while attempting to respect the limited scope for theological speculation that he enjoyed in the post-Reformation church. One of the distinctions on which he relied was between understanding something in a limited way and understanding it fully. If the term 'comprehend' is used for the latter, then Descartes claimed to have avoided some of the problems involved with mysteries by arguing, in the Third Meditation: 'Nor does it matter that I do not comprehend the infinite or that there are innumerable other things in God that I do not comprehend and that may be completely outside the scope of my thought' (vii. 46; M. 39). Thus God or the infinite, in so far as it is infinite, 'cannot be comprehended [*nullo modo comprehendi*]. But it can still be understood [*intelligi*]' (vii. 112). Whether this Thomistic distinction can do the work required in this context remains debatable. These issues can be deferred here, to focus instead on the alleged relation between having an idea (that is, having even a limited understanding of something) and having the appropriate words with which to express the content of the idea.

Descartes notoriously claimed, most clearly and frequently in the *Meditations*, that he had an idea of God and that this idea provided the basis on which he constructed his proofs of God's existence.[11] This is consistent with his reply to the First Objections that, 'according to the true laws of logic, one should never ask about anything "does it exist" unless one first understands "what it is"' (vii. 107–8). Thus, any discussion of God's existence presupposes some understanding of what is meant by the term 'God'. When pressed to say what he meant by 'God', Descartes offered a definition that reflected the Christian tradition to which he belonged. 'By the word "God" I understand some infinite substance, which is independent, supremely intelligent and supremely powerful, and by which both I, and everything else that exists (if anything else exists), were created' (vii. 45; M. 38). The question, then, is how the author of the *Meditations* came to possess this idea or concept, especially since he nowhere relies on a direct experience of God. This difficulty is rendered even more acute by defin-

---

[10] This concern was expressed sharply by Toland (1696: 28) as follows: 'Now if we have no ideas of a thing, it is certainly but lost labour for us to trouble our selves about it; for what I don't conceive, can no more give me right notions of God, or influence my actions, than a prayer delivered in an unknown tongue can excite my devotion.' Cf. John Locke (1695: 255, 302). The issue is also discussed in Moise Amyraut (1641), a book published the same year as the *Meditations*.

[11] For example: 'Since I am a thinking thing and I have some idea of God . . .' (vii. 49; M. 41); 'it must absolutely be concluded from the mere fact that I exist and that I have some idea of a most perfect being—that is, of God—that it is very clearly demonstrated that God exists' (vii. 51; M. 42).

ing God as an infinite substance, because Descartes denies that he can comprehend the infinite. In fact, he claims, 'the incomprehensibility [*incomprehensibilitas*] of the infinite is contained in its formal nature' (vii. 368).

The concept or idea of God, therefore, is not available to the human mind from experience, nor can the concept of anything infinite be comprehended. If we have such an idea, it must be constructed from some other sources. Descartes argues that we have a direct awareness of our own thinking, and this awareness can be described as having an idea of what it means to think. We also recognize that our thinking is subject to various limitations. To construct the idea of God, then, involves a simple logical step of denying the limitations associated with my idea of myself, as a thinking thing, thereby generating the idea of an unlimited thinking thing. This step-by-step process was explained to Hobbes, one of the most insistent objectors to this part of the Cartesian project. 'For who is there who does not perceive that there is something that they understand? Who therefore does not have the form or idea of understanding and, by extending this indefinitely, does not form the idea of God's understanding, and by a similar procedure an idea of the other attributes of God?' (vii. 188). A similar answer had been penned for a more sympathetic Mersenne, in reply to the Second Objections: 'I go further and freely confess that the idea we have, for example, of the divine intellect does not differ from the idea we have of the human intellect, except in the same way that the idea of an infinite number differs from the idea of a number to the power of two or four. The same applies to the various attributes of God of which we recognize some trace in ourselves' (vii. 137).

Thus, although the idea of God is said to be innate in human minds, it is innate only in the very attenuated sense that we find in ourselves the basic ideas out of which to construct it. We know what it means to understand something from our inner experience of understanding. This basic concept, which is derived by introspection rather than from any experience of the external world and in that sense is innate, provides the foundation on which to construct an idea of God. Descartes does not need to assume that everyone has taken these constructive steps and is already equipped with the same idea of God that he has. But if someone denies that they have such an idea, he argues that they can acquire it easily in the manner suggested, and therefore that any subsequent attempt to deny that they have an idea of God would involve them in denying that they understood the meaning of the words used in the process outlined for constructing the concept.

But if we take the word 'idea' in the way in which I said very explicitly that I was taking it . . . then one could not deny having some idea of God, except by saying that one does not understand what is meant by the following words: 'the most perfect thing that we can conceive of' . . . It involves going to unusual extremes, in order to make objections, to say that one does not understand the meaning of the most commonly used words. (ix-1. 209)

This is not the claim often attributed to Wittgenstein, to the effect that to have an idea is equivalent to being able to use a word or phrase appropriately. Descartes's argument is that having an appropriate idea is a necessary condition for knowing the meaning of a word or phrase, and therefore one would have to deny the latter to deny the former.

Thus, in the case of realities that are not directly accessible to our experience, such as God, we can acquire the corresponding concepts by an appropriate combination of concepts derived from experience. Even in the case of the Trinity, Descartes must maintain his original principle that there is no belief without an adequate concept, and that the concept of the Trinity can be generated from our conceptual resources in order to support belief in the doctrine of the Trinity. Accordingly, in reply to a query from Burman, he argues:

Although that idea [i.e. of the Trinity] is not so explicitly innate that it represents the Trinity to us, none the less the elements and rudiments of the idea are innate in us, since we have an innate idea of God, of the number three, and of similar things. We easily form an adequate idea of the mystery of the Trinity from these elements, supplemented by the revelation of the Scriptures; once the idea is formed in this way, we conceive of the Trinity.   (v. 165)

In the case of abstract concepts such as that of God, therefore, Descartes argues that our acquisition of the concept depends on using language to combine elements abstracted from other basic concepts. To deny that we have such concepts implies that we lack the linguistic resources required to construct them.

The Cartesian theory about the relationship between thought and language is neither that suggested by Aarsleff nor the contrary. Descartes does not argue that we could, in principle, successfully pursue all our thinking in the privacy of our own minds without any reliance on language. It is implausible to think that we could come to have an idea of complex conceptual constructions without having the words required to delimit the constituent parts from which such concepts are constructed. On the other hand, it is equally implausible to characterize Descartes as if he were a proponent of the view associated with the later Wittgenstein, to the effect that having an idea is simply using a linguistic sign appropriately. Descartes's position is much closer to that of Locke. Our consciousness of both internal states and external realities provides us with primitive experiences from which basic concepts result. The capacity of the human mind to construct novel concepts, either by abstraction from basic concepts or by combining them creatively, is part of what is meant by 'reason'.

Once a distinction is granted between the ideas in the mind and the words with which we express them, the language-user is provided with some degree of independence in the choice of words to be used. The first source of such independence is in the conventionality of the signs used. Since there is no natural or causal connection between a concept or idea and the term used to express it in a given language, there is no necessary connection between inner states of the language-user and specific kinds of linguistic behaviour. But, more importantly, the existence of two parallel and similarly structured systems, of concepts and of signs, provides an almost unlimited flexibility to a competent language-user to express inner thoughts in appropriate linguistic behaviour. Descartes's intuition here is that, once the meaning of a question is understood, a genuine language-user may: (1) refuse to answer; (2) tell a lie; or (3) exploit the resources of language in other unpredictable ways. Signs of irrationality may appear in what is said by human beings, but signs of linguistic incompetence are more likely to appear in predictable or inflexible utterances (which could, in principle, be explained mechanically) rather than in untruthful or inconsistent expressions.

This first-person experience of what we can do with language is not used to show that we have thoughts that accompany our utterances. Descartes argued in reply to Gassendi that we already know from our own experience that our thoughts accompany our utterances, at least on most occasions. This is not to prejudge the question, at this stage, about the most appropriate explanation of our own inner mental life. The case raised by animals is completely different. Here the question is: are there any instances of animal behaviour, including their use of sounds, signs, or words, that would justify the hypothesis that they enjoy an inner life of thought or understanding that is comparable to ours? This question could be transformed into a question about degrees of sophistication of animal faculties if it were possible to have stages of development in thought. Descartes, together with many of his correspondents, takes for granted that human thought presupposes having a mind, and that having a human mind is not a matter of more or less. Thus the dichotomy between having/not having a human mind is matched with a radical difference in kind between using/not using conventional signs to express one's thoughts.

The Cartesian theory of language thus straddles any dichotomy, in the relationship between thought and language, which implies that we either can or cannot think without words. It suggests instead that human beings have a limited capacity for thinking without words, and that this is considerably enhanced by the acquisition of linguistic skills. The foundation of all our mental life, therefore, is the cluster of characteristic ideas that are initially formed in the brain. These are primitive acts of awareness of current objects of perception. The ideas thus formed are sufficiently isomorphic with the sensations that cause them for the perceiver to establish an intentional connection between an idea and its intentional object. From such primitive beginnings, the brain develops associations between perceptions; it recognizes similarities between different sensations and stores in memory a residue of impressions that have made a sufficiently strong impression on its receptive faculties. While awareness or thought—what Descartes calls *pensée*—is fundamental to the whole process, reason contributes the manipulation and linguistic expression of thought that signals a radically novel addition to the powers of perception that are common to all animals.

CHAPTER 7

Describing Thought: The Subjective View

The comprehensive extension of the Cartesian term 'thought', which includes an apparently disparate range of phenomena, is explicit from the early pages of the *Meditations*. For example, Descartes gives the following reply in the Second Meditation to his own question about what is meant by a thing that thinks: 'A thing that doubts, understands, affirms, denies, wills, does not will, and senses' (vii. 28; *M.* 26).[1] Remembering is also included in some versions of this list, which is evidently not meant to be comprehensive—a point urged against Regius when he seemed incautiously to propose an exclusive list.[2] So likewise is dreaming.[3] Chapters 2–5 outlined rather schematic Cartesian *explanations* of how different kinds of thinking occur, where the classification borrowed the traditional language of distinct faculties such as sensory perception, imagination, memory, the will, and the passions. These explanation sketches are inevitably limited by the theoretical repertoire within which Descartes worked and by a lack of detailed knowledge of the brain, the central nervous system, the senses, and so on—all the factors on which thinking normally depends.

However, it is clear from even a cursory reading of Cartesian texts that Descartes also devotes considerable time and resources to attempting to *describe* various kinds of thinking from the perspective of the thinking subject, and that the language in which these descriptions are expressed is often imbued with

---

[1] Cf. vii. 78, where imagination and sensory perception are included, and *Principles* (I. 32, 53; IV. 189) (viii-I. 17, 25, 316). Descartes to Reneri (Apr.–May 1638) explains that the word 'thought' is used 'to cover all the operations of the soul, so that not only meditations and acts of the will, but the activities of seeing and hearing and deciding on one movement rather than another, as far as they depend on the soul, are all thoughts' (ii. 36).

[2] *Principles* (I. 65): 'understanding, imagination, memory, volition, etc.' (viii-I. 32); *The Description of the Human Body*: 'our soul . . . thinks, that is to say, understands, wills, imagines, remembers, and has sensory perceptions' (xi. 224); Descartes to Mersenne (May 1637): 'willing, understanding, imagining, and sensing, etc. are just different ways of thinking' (i. 366); *Comments on a Certain Manifesto*: 'He then enumerates only sensing, remembering and imagining among the types of perception' (viii-2. 363; *M.* 199).

[3] *A Treatise on Man* (xi. 173); Descartes to Elizabeth (6 Oct. 1645): 'those [thoughts] that depend solely on the traces left by previous impressions in the memory and the ordinary movement of the spirits are dreams, whether they are real dreams in sleep or daydreams in waking life' (iv. 310–11); Descartes to Arnauld (29 July 1648): 'Thus we do not have any thoughts in sleep without being conscious of them at the moment they occur' (v. 221–2).

dualist connotations. In this chapter, I examine some of these descriptions of thought, which provide the first steps towards the kind of dualism that I attribute to Descartes. The emphasis here is on describing what various kinds of thinking are like from the perspective of the subject who thinks, while leaving open (in theory at least) the question of what kind of explanations may eventually be appropriate to account for them. In other words, one must first identify the mental phenomena that require an explanation, and the only way available to identify them is to describe them from the perspective of a thinking subject.

It must be acknowledged, from the outset, that such a descriptive phenomenology of thought cannot be provided in a neutral language that avoids all theoretical or ontological commitments. For any author in the early seventeenth century who wished to describe what it is like to think, there were only two options available, as there are in any period: to invent a whole new technical language, or to use the resources already available in some established language (with appropriate amendments if necessary). Pascal took the first option, at least with respect to his enigmatic use of the term *cœur*. Whatever that term meant for him, it did not mean a heart that is part of the body. For Descartes, however, for whom communication with other philosophers across Europe was paramount, the second option was more appropriate. Latin had not been spoken outside the academy and the Christian churches for centuries, but it remained the standard language for writing and teaching in universities. Its advantages for international communication, however, were counterbalanced by significant disadvantages in its relative inflexibility as a dead language. One possible compromise, then, was to write in Latin and to adjust the meaning of the limited range of terms it provided by appropriate qualification. Descartes explicitly adopted this strategy in Rule Three of the *Rules* (discussed above in Chapter 2): to adapt the Latin of the schools as best he could to express his thoughts. This justifies more charity than might otherwise be warranted in reading Descartes's Latin so that it is not burdened with all the scholastic implications of the Latin terms that were used, by default, to describe the experience of thinking.[4]

The need for caution and charity when reading Cartesian Latin is best illustrated by a relevant example from the Second Meditation. The intuition that resulted from 'I am, I exist' implied that the subject of this intuition knew nothing about itself, at that stage of the meditation, except that it was a thinking subject. Descartes expressed this conclusion in various ways, one of which was: '*sum igitur praecise tantum res cogitans*' (vii. 27; M. 25). One natural translation of

---

[4] The problems associated with using an inherited scholastic Latin without endorsing some of its theoretical implications are discussed in Dear (1988: 229).

this is: 'Therefore I am in a strict sense only a thinking thing.' Despite the apparent exclusiveness of the term '*tantum*' (only), Descartes raised a question in the subsequent paragraph about the possibility that this thinking activity might take place in a body or in association with a body. 'Is it possible that these very things, which, I am supposing, do not exist because I have no knowledge of them, are not in fact distinct from the me that I know? I do not know, and I am not discussing that issue for the moment' (vii. 27; M. 25). In other words, despite the fact that I am suspending claims to know anything about bodies, and that I know nothing about myself except that I am a thinking thing, it may still be the case that my thinking is an operation that depends on something bodily. When challenged about this apparent inconsistency by Gassendi, Descartes replied as follows in a letter to Clerselier (12 January 1646):

I said in one place that while the soul is in doubt about the existence of all material things, it knows itself *praecise tantum*—'in the strict sense only'—as an immaterial substance. And seven or eight lines further down I showed that by the words 'in a strict sense only' I do not at all mean an entire exclusion or negation, but only an abstraction from material things. For I said that in spite of this we are not sure that there is nothing corporeal in the soul, even though we do not recognize anything corporeal in it.   (ix-1. 215)

One might argue that Descartes is being disingenuous here, and that he is avoiding a valid objection by relying on a subtle and somewhat contrived rereading of the original Latin text, which could be translated in either of two ways: (1) 'I am therefore, in a strict sense, only a thinking thing'; or (2) 'I am therefore, in a strict sense only, a thinking thing.' Although the term '*tantum*' might be read more naturally as qualifying '*res cogitans*' rather than '*praecise*', it is more consistent with the structure of the argument in the *Meditations* as a whole to read the text as its author proposed. The Second Meditation had established only that the meditator is a thinking something; whether the meditator has other essential features, including possibly a body, remained to be decided later.

This suggests a need for a general caution in reading texts that apparently make definitive, exclusive claims on behalf of the mind and its various operations. In particular, it implies that, when describing human thought from the perspective of the thinking subject, Descartes is likely to abstract from bodily realities on which at least some kinds of thinking depend. In fact, a strict observance of the distinction between describing and explaining would preclude any determination of the realities on which our thinking depends. Some kinds of thinking may appear to the subject to be more or less *independent* of factors outside the control of the thinker. Other thoughts may be experienced by a thinking subject as depending on various extra-mental realities. Descriptions of such dependent thoughts are likely to involve speculative hypotheses about the factors on which they depend or, more likely, generally assumed theories that are implicit in the very words used to name them, such as 'sensing'. Despite these problems about the theory-ladenness of descriptions of thought, Descartes can be read as offering an elementary phenomenology of thinking in which the activity of thinking appears more or less independent of, or abstracted from, the environmental conditions that allegedly trigger some thoughts in the human mind.

If we assume, therefore, that Descartes is sometimes merely *describing* what thinking is (or what different kinds of thinking are) from the perspective of the subject, we should be cautious about reading into such descriptions implications that are either unfounded or inconsistent with the general theory that he proposed. The basis for due caution is twofold: (1) the distinction between describing and explaining; (2) Descartes's choice of Latin as the language in which he wrote his principal metaphysical works (the *Meditations* and the *Principles*), and the extent to which he used Latin creatively and without endorsing all its apparent ontological commitments.

DEFINING THOUGHT

Despite misgivings about the possibility of defining thought, Descartes seems to offer a definition, or something close to one, in the Second Replies:

By the term 'thought' [*cogitatio*] I mean everything [*illud omne*] that is in us in such a way that we are immediately conscious of it. Thus all operations of the will, intellect, imagination, and the senses are thoughts. But I added the word 'immediately' to exclude whatever follows from these operations; for example, although a voluntary motion has some thought as its principle, it is not itself a thought.   (vii. 160; M. 85)

The *Principles*, written three years later, repeats essentially the same definition: 'By the word "thought" I understand all the things that we are aware of as occurring in us, in so far as we are aware of them. Thus not only understanding, willing, and imagining, but even sensing is the same as thinking in this context' (viii-1. 7; M. 114).[5] Neither definition is adequate to clarify many of the issues raised by them. What seems clear initially is that thought (*cogitatio*) is some kind of activity or operation that takes place within us and of which we are aware as it is taking place. This definition fails to exclude physical activities that take place

---

    [5] Both texts were originally written in Latin, as follows: '*Cogitationis* nomine complector illud omne quod sic in nobis est, ut eius immediate conscii simus. Ita omnes voluntatis, intellectus, imaginationis & sensuum operationes sunt cogitationes.' The text in the *Principles* is: 'Cogitationis nomine, intelligo illa omnia, quae nobis consciis in nobis sunt, quatenus eorum in nobis conscientia est. Atque ita non modo intelligere, velle, imaginari, sed etiam sentire, idem est hic quod cogitare.'

within us and of which we are aware while we perform them, such as walking accompanied by an awareness of walking. The addition of the qualification 'immediately' was supposed to tidy up that loose end. However that alone does not resolve the problem. One could be immediately aware of walking too (it is not as if one needs to look at oneself in a mirror to become aware of it), and the sensory awareness in virtue of which we are aware of it is evidently a thought. Perhaps 'immediately' has connotations of indubitability. Thus when it was objected, in the Sixth Objections, that we could as easily argue: 'I walk, therefore I exist' as 'I think, therefore I exist', Descartes replied as follows: 'I cannot argue: I walk, therefore I exist, except to the extent that being conscious of my walking is a thought' (vii. 352; M. 96). I may imagine that I am walking when I am merely sitting in my chair and daydreaming. In that case my (mistaken) thought that I am walking is still secure, but I cannot be said to be aware of walking. This suggests that thoughts are peculiar activities in virtue of which we are aware of something and, at the same time, incorrigibly conscious of our awareness. The 'immediately' of the proposed definition applies to the second kind of self-awareness. Thus 'thought' applies to those operations, such as sensing, dreaming, and so on, that we are immediately aware of as they occur in us.

The term 'thought' is also ambiguous by ranging over a number of interdependent acts and powers. Hobbes had objected that Descartes had conflated the activity of thinking with the faculty responsible for thinking, and even with the reality that possesses that faculty. Descartes's reply endorsed rather than qualified the wide extension of the term because 'thought', he claimed, may be used in different ways: 'thought is sometimes understood as an action, sometimes as a faculty, and sometimes as the thing of which it is a faculty' (vii. 174; M. 88). He might have added that his use of the term 'thought' was also ambiguous between a 'thought' as an event (a particular act of thinking by a given subject) and 'thought' as the object of such acts of thinking. In the latter sense, thoughts are whatever we think about when we are thinking—that is, the contents of our thoughts. I return to this ambiguity below, under the discussion of intentionality.

It may be that these difficulties arise from the very attempt to define thinking, or at least to define it in terms of necessary and sufficient conditions. *The Search for Truth* suggests that some realities are best known by acquaintance and that attempts to define them make them more obscure than they already are. Thus 'doubt, thought, and existence can be regarded as belonging to the class of things that have this sort of clarity and that are known just on their own' (x. 524). If this is accepted, then the most appropriate strategy for identifying thought would be to invite people to reflect on their own inner experience of thinking (with hints about where to look), to provide different words to distinguish various forms of thinking that may require different explanations, and to leave the futile task of trying to define thought, as Descartes suggested, 'to someone who wants to be a professor or to debate in the Schools' (x. 523). This suggestion about the indefinability of 'thought' is consistent with the suggestion made to Princess Elizabeth (21 May 1643) that 'thought' is a 'primitive notion' (iii. 665; M. 149) that cannot be defined by reference to any other more basic concept.

If we agree that a definition in terms of genera and species is either impossible or uninformative, we would still need some clear pointers to the phenomenon on which so much of Descartes's metaphysics depends. Here are some suggestions. One acceptable approach to theorizing about thought is, initially, to give different examples of thinking and then to identify those features of thinking that are relevant to a particular enterprise. The Third Meditation includes a classification of thoughts into two general categories. Some thoughts 'are like the images of things' while others 'have additional forms; for example, when I will, fear, affirm, or deny, I always grasp something as the subject of my thought but I include in my thought something more than a resemblance of the thing in question' (vii. 37; M. 32). When I have a sensation, I am aware of something that seems to affect my internal or external senses. Likewise, when I imagine something, my awareness is apparently triggered by some kind of image in my brain. The images themselves are not thoughts; however, 'when the mind imagines or turns towards those impressions, its operation is a thought' (iii. 361). According to these proposals, a thought is the *act* in virtue of which we are aware of something real or imagined, or the more complex act in virtue of which we are both aware of something and adopt some kind of propositional or emotional response to it. This explains why Descartes had no difficulty in classifying brain patterns as ideas; they have a role with respect to imagination similar to that of external stimuli in the case of sensation, because they help specify the content of different thoughts.

When reflecting on typical examples of thought, some of which are listed above, Descartes claims that, not only are we immediately aware of various thinking operations, but there can be nothing in our minds of which we are completely unaware. Arnauld objected plausibly that there might be things in the mind of which the subject is not aware. Indeed, if there were such, by definition we would not be aware of them. But the Cartesian reply was that the original claim was self-evident.

As regards the claim that 'there can be nothing within the mind *in so far as it is a thinking thing* of which it is not aware', that seems to me to be self-evident [*per se notum*], because we do not understand that anything is in the mind, understood in this way, which is not a thought or which does not depend on thought. Otherwise it would not belong to the mind in so far as it is a thinking thing, and we cannot have any thought in us of which we are not aware at the time we have it.   (vii. 246: M. 93; emphasis added)

This reply shows up the ambiguity of the definition in the *Principles*, that 'thought' applies to whatever we are aware of as occurring within us, in so far as we are aware of it. This could mean: (1) if we are thinking of something O, then we are aware of O; or (2) if we are thinking of something O, we are also aware of the activity of thinking of O. The claim about self-evidence points towards (1), although Descartes's 'definition' of thought and some of his claims elsewhere suggest (2).[6]

One of the most notorious cases of arguing from the fact that I am not aware of O to the conclusion that O is not present in my mind occurs in the Third Meditation, where Descartes asks whether he has the power to cause himself to continue to exist from one moment to the next. He argues that, in so far as he is a thinking thing, he is not aware of any such power in himself. 'Since I am only a thinking thing or, at least, I am discussing only that part of me which is specifically a thinking thing, if I had such a power I would undoubtedly be aware of it' (vii. 49; M. 41). Since he is not aware of such a power in himself, he concludes that his continued existence must depend on something other than himself considered *as a thinking thing*. On first reading, one spontaneously suspects that there may be many things 'in' a human mind of which the mind is not actually aware, especially if the things in question are described, as they are here, as powers. This distinction between acts and powers is adopted, for example, in the Fourth Replies to Arnauld, where Descartes claims that we are always aware of acts or operations of our mind, but we are not necessarily aware of faculties or powers of which we become conscious only when we use them. 'But it should be noted that while we are always actually conscious of acts or operations of our mind, we are not always conscious of faculties or powers, except potentially; thus, when we apply ourselves to using some faculty, if that faculty is in our mind we become actually conscious of it immediately, and in this way we could deny that it is in our mind if we are not able to become conscious of it' (vii. 246–7). If one applies this distinction to the issue raised in the Third Meditation, it would be possible for Descartes to have various powers of which he is not aware, and even powers of which he would not readily become aware simply by asking himself the question: do I have such a power?

The simplest way out of the muddle is to focus on the Cartesian concept of thought as being primarily an *act*. Acts of thought are necessarily thoughts about something or other, O. Thus we cannot be thinking of O and not be aware of O, though it may happen that we are not self-consciously aware of the fact, as

---

[6] Some of these are discussed by Wilson (1978: 150 ff.).

we are thinking, that we are thinking of something. If one accepts that Descartes used the phrase *'praecise tantum res cogitans'* in the Second Meditation as narrowly and carefully as he subsequently claimed, then he can support the claim about self-evidence as follows. I am either thinking of something, *O*, or I am not. If I am thinking about *O*, then I must be aware of *O*. If I am not thinking about it, then it is not in my mind 'in so far as it is a thinking thing'.

Assuming the degree of hermeneutic charity already proposed, this fits with the various claims Descartes makes about being aware of what he thinks about. For example, he claims in the Second Replies that 'there cannot be anything in me of which I am not conscious in any way' (vii. 107). But this was preceded by a similar qualification to that mentioned above: he was asking about himself 'not in so far as I consist of a mind and body but only in so far as I am precisely a thing that thinks'. Thus there cannot be anything in me, precisely in so far as I am thinking, of which I am not in some way aware, because the only way in which something can be present in me, in so far as I am a thinking thing, is for me to think about it. But then I must be conscious of it. Likewise, when Descartes wrote to Mersenne that 'nothing can be in my mind of which I am not conscious' (iii. 273), he needs nothing more than the understanding of thought as an act of the mind, and as the only way in which things can come into the mind, to reach the conclusion that if I am thinking of something, I must be aware of it. In this sense, the reply to Arnauld about the self-evidence of his claim is not as extraordinary as it might originally have seemed.

The most natural reading of these claims about the transparency to my consciousness of whatever is in my mind is to accept them as descriptions of what I perceive when I reflect on my own experience of thinking. In typical cases, whenever I think about something, I am by definition conscious or aware of it. This may be described, in Descartes's terms, as self-evident. But Descartes also implies that, when we are aware of something *O*, we are aware of the fact that we are thinking of *O*. We know today that there are exceptions to this, such as the phenomenon of blindsight—that is, having a perceptual experience without simultaneous self-awareness. However, even this is not something that we know from our awareness of it while it is taking place. Instead, we fail to have any concurrent awareness of the experience and, based on what we subsequently discover that we know, we conclude that we must have had a perceptual experience despite the fact of not being aware of it at the time when we had it. There are two ways in which Descartes can accommodate that exception. One is to acknowledge that, when it occurs, it is an event that is simply not available to us by introspection or 'in so far as I am a thinking thing'. In that sense, there are presumably many things going on in me of which I am not aware and that are not currently accessible to me as a thinking being.[7] A slightly different version of the same response is to limit, by a stipulative definition, the extension of the term 'thought' to whatever I am directly and immediately aware of. This accounts for the extension of the term 'idea' to include acts such as willing or fearing. As explained in the Third Replies, the term 'idea' is taken to apply to 'everything that is perceived immediately by the mind'. Thus 'when I will or fear something, I simultaneously perceive that I will or fear' and therefore 'the volition or fear itself is numbered among my ideas' (vii. 181).[8]

This amounts to claiming that Descartes was both describing the way in which a thinking subject experiences thinking, and borrowing terms to describe that experience, which had potentially significant theoretical implications. Geneviève Lewis (1950: 10) has suggested that, in choosing a language with which to describe the experience of self-awareness, Descartes had at least two ways of describing it, borrowed from either Aquinas or Augustine. For Aquinas, we are initially conscious of some object of thought or perception, and we become aware of ourselves reflexively by being aware of our thinking or perceiving. For the Platonic tradition that came through Augustine, however, the mind is directly accessible to itself without depending on reflective acts of awareness of its own mental acts. If one prescinds from these scholastic theories and focuses exclusively on thought as experienced, in the case of many of our thoughts we are both aware of some object of thought and also aware of thinking. It is plausible to assume that, in this context, Descartes is simply borrowing a familiar Augustinian terminology—though evidently one that is theory-laden—to describe the experience we frequently have of being aware of our own thoughts. To avoid endorsing the theory that was implicit in Augustinian terminology, Descartes would have needed an analysis of thought, similar to his analysis of three degrees of sensation, that would distinguish analytically features of thinking that normally occur together and that may seem necessarily joined. Without such an analysis, Descartes describes his own thinking experiences as acts by means of which he is aware of something and, at the same time, is conscious of being aware of them.

I return below to the question of the relationship between thoughts and ideas, and to the status of innate ideas as a possible exception to the general claim that we are always aware of our own thoughts.

---

[7] Lewis (1950) suggests innate ideas, and a range of dispositional properties such as habits and prejudices that are in some sense present to the mind without it being always actually aware of them.

[8] The Cottingham *et al.* edition of Descartes (1985–91: ii. 127) translates *volo* as 'want'. But it is clear that one might want something and not be aware of one's own wants. Descartes refers to an act of willing, as when I decide to do something, and he assumes that we are normally aware of making such decisions at the time of making them.

Thus, when we have a sensory perception of something or, in plain English, when we see, hear, and so on, we are thinking. Likewise, when we imagine something that is not actually present to our senses and therefore is not (by hypothesis) acting on our senses, we are influenced by something comparable to an external stimulus—namely, an impression in our brain. We do not imagine the brain state, but rather the reality that it represents. The same story can be told, with minor changes, about memory. In all such cases, my inner experience as a thinker is that I am aware of those experiences as they take place in me, although there could evidently be other operations taking place in me of which I am not aware.

Apart from our consciousness of internal operations that are called thinking, Descartes also has available another common feature of thoughts in what he called the 'objective reality' of ideas or, as we would more normally say today, their intentionality.

THE INTENTIONALITY OF THOUGHT

The two perspectives on thought mentioned above—thoughts as acts of awareness, and thoughts as whatever is thought about—recur in the Cartesian discussion of what he calls, in Latin, the *realitas objectiva* of ideas and what I am translating here as the intentional reality of ideas. Descartes makes this distinction in the Third Meditation, using the terms 'formal reality' and 'intentional reality', although he makes the same distinction elsewhere by using different scholastic terminology.[9] Aside from the variable terminology used, the distinction itself is relatively familiar and uncontentious. By the 'actual or formal reality' of an idea, Descartes means whatever a human idea is independently of its specific content. The distinction can be made easily in the case of a sign—for example, the type of sign often displayed by real estate agents outside a property they wish to sell. What Descartes calls the formal reality of the sign is (often) a piece of board, attached to a pole, on which there are various characters painted. The meaning of the sign, of course, is whatever is expressed in English by 'For Sale' or in French by *à vendre*. One could modify the formal reality of the sign without any change in its meaning, for example, by installing a flashing neon sign, 'For Sale', outside a property that is particularly difficult to sell. One

---

[9] Jolley (1990: 13–15) draws attention to the terminological confusion. In the Preface to the *Meditations* Descartes contrasts ideas when considered materially and intentionally (vii. 8; *M.* 13), while in his reply to Arnauld (vii. 232) he makes the same distinction between ideas considered materially and formally. Evidently, 'materially' is used in both of these contexts to mean the same as 'formally' in Meditation Three, and 'formally' is used in reply to Arnauld to mean the same as 'intentionally' in the other texts.

could also modify the intentional reality of the same sign with minimal cost to the vendor, by sticking 'Sold' over the original cardboard notice.

In a similar way, the formal reality of a human idea is an act of thinking on the part of a particular human subject in virtue of which they think about some 'object'. In Descartes's words: 'the reality of the idea is such that, in itself, it requires no more formal reality than what is borrowed from my thought, of which it is a mode' (vii. 41; M. 35).[10] There are few theoretical assumptions built into this description of thoughts as modes, except that they are entities of the kind that typically cannot exist on their own and must be predicated of something else. Nothing need be known at this point in the *Meditations* about the kind of subject of which they are predicated, except that it is a subject that thinks. Descartes calls thoughts modes, rather than qualities or attributes, simply because they may change; the same person can have different thoughts from one moment to another without changing his or her identity.[11] Thus, when we specify the formal reality of any idea, we identify it merely as an act of thinking by a particular subject that can vary over time, without reference to its object or specific content. In many cases, even in those considered in the Third Meditation, such thoughts seem to be (partly) caused by external events or things.

In contrast with thoughts considered simply as acts or modes of a particular thinker, Descartes distinguishes the content of a thought or what a particular thought is about. 'But in so far as one idea represents one thing and another idea represents something else, it is clear that they are very different from each other' (vii. 40; M. 34). The intentional reality of an idea is not the reality itself that is thought about (which may be an objective reality such as the sun, or a non-existent reality such as a unicorn), but that feature of an act of thinking in virtue of which it has a specific content.

This distinction, expressed in traditional scholastic terminology, should have been unproblematic for readers of the *Meditations*. However, Caterus raised a question, at the beginning of the First Objections, about the Cartesian assumption that we need a cause to explain the *realitas objectiva* of a given idea. He argued that, when we think about something such as the sun, our thinking causes no change in the sun. In fact, we can even think about things that do not exist at all. Thus the *realitas objectiva* of ideas seems to be a non-entity or, at most, a mere label that is attached to whatever we think about without changing the latter in any way. Caterus objects that, since thinking about the sun does not

---

[10] Cf. 'For if I consider the ideas as certain modes of thought, and if I do not refer them to anything else . . .' (vii. 37; M. 33); 'In so far as those ideas are simply certain modes of thinking, I do not see any inequality between them and they all seem to originate in me in the same way' (vii. 40; M. 34).

[11] The use of the terms 'mode', 'quality', and 'attribute' is explained in the *Principles* (1. 56).

change the sun, there is no need for a causal explanation of the intentional reality of one's ideas.

Descartes's reply changes the focus of the discussion from the reality or otherwise of what is thought about to the mental state that is the act of thinking. 'An idea is the thing itself that is thought, in so far as it is in the intellect intentionally . . . consequently, "intentional being" means simply to be in the intellect in the way in which objects are usually there' (vii. 102; M. 72). If someone asks what happens to the sun as a result of my thinking about it, it is best to say that nothing happens to it, apart from being named as the object of an intellectual act on my part.

But if someone asks about the *idea* of the sun: what is it? and if the reply is that it is the thing thought about in so far as it is in the intellect intentionally, no one will understand that to be the sun itself . . . 'To be in the intellect intentionally' will mean . . . to be in it in the way in which objects of the intellect are usually there, so that the idea of the sun is the sun itself existing in the intellect—not, however, formally, as it exists in the heavens, but intentionally, that is, in the way in which objects are usually in the intellect. (vii. 102–3; M. 72)

Descartes goes further and attempts to make sense of the extraordinary argument, proposed in the Third Meditation, according to which there is some necessary proportionality between the adequate cause of an idea and the degree of reality that is present intentionally in the idea. The example suggested to Caterus helps explain what the problem was, although the claimed proportionality remains as opaque as ever. Descartes gives the example of someone who has an idea of a very sophisticated or complex machine, and he asks the question: how could we explain the origin of the complexity that is included in their idea of the machine? Among the various acceptable answers are: (1) that the person thinking about the machine has seen a similar one before; (2) that the thinker may have a detailed knowledge of mechanics from which they could have constructed such an idea; or (3) that they have the creative mind of an inventor, which made it possible for them to think about a complex machine that no one had thought about previously. The plausible part of this argument is the interim negative conclusion drawn by Descartes, namely: some explanation is required, even if we are not confident about which one to choose, to account for the fact that someone is actually thinking about a complex machine. It is not a satisfactory account of the complexity of the idea simply to say that the human mind, in virtue of its *im*perfection, caused this idea to arise within itself. 'It is obviously no more probable that the imperfection of our intellect is the cause of our having an idea of God, than that a lack of expert knowledge of mechanics is the cause of our imagining some very complex machine rather than some other machine that is less perfect' (vii. 105; M. 74).

The argument for God's existence in the Third Meditation cannot be rescued by these comments, but Descartes's general account of the intentionality of ideas may fare better. The query about the cause of the intentionality of our ideas can be translated into a request for an explanation of the particular content of a given thought. Descartes assumes that such explanations are readily forthcoming in the case of sensing, remembering, imagining, and so on. In all these cases, the content of our thought is explained, at least in principle, by the kind of theories that were summarized in earlier chapters above. However, even such explanations leave unresolved the disparity in kind between the proximate causes of such thoughts and the thoughts themselves. Thus, a stroke of a sword can cause us to feel pain, and the experience of pain is evidently a thought. But, while we can understand how the motion of one body might cause that of another, we have no understanding of how the impact of one body on another can cause a thought in the mind associated with the latter.[12] This apparently unbridgeable gap in explanation persuaded Descartes to argue, in his *Comments on a Certain Manifesto*, that the ideas of pain, and so on, must be innate because the motions that cause them bear no resemblance to their effects. Thus the demand for adequate explanation is appropriate, not only with respect to the occurrence of a thought, but also with respect to its content. Since some explanation of the content of ideas is required by Descartes, it is plausible to suggest that the appeal to the *realitas objectiva* of ideas is not itself a theory of ideas, but merely a familiar scholastic name for what needs to be explained. In other words, it is part of Descartes's description of the experience of thinking, or a specification of one feature of our thinking, rather than a contribution to explaining how our ideas acquire the specific content they have.

This piece of borrowed scholastic terminology has few redeeming features, but it at least has the merit of focusing attention on the things thought about, the *objects* of our thought. Descartes was very keen to avoid the possible implication that, when we think about something, we are thinking about some intermediate picture or representative that mediates between our thinking and the objects of our thought. That kind of representationalism, which emerges so transparently in Malebranche's *êtres représentatifs*, was not part of the original

---

[12] *Principles* (IV. 197) (viii-1. 320–21). This repeats an argument that had been drafted for *The World*, Ch. 1, but was still unpublished when the *Principles* appeared in 1644. The same argument is repeated in *Principles* (IV. 198), where Descartes acknowledges both the fact and the unintelligibility of bodily motions causing thoughts in sensation.

Cartesian account. Hobbes had proposed something along these lines, in the Third Objections, suggesting that when we reason about things we are actually reasoning about the words that represent the things that we think about. Descartes's reply was uncompromising, possibly because of the source of the objection. He argued that a Frenchman and a German can think about the same thing while using different words to denote it. Likewise in reasoning, we establish connections between the things thought about and not just between the words that stand in for them (vii. 178–9). Unless persuaded by strong counterarguments, therefore, Descartes prefers to begin his account of thinking with a description that assumes our ability to think about things, including nonexistent things, and not simply to think about ideas of them or words that refer to them.

The intentionality of our thought, then, is that familiar feature in virtue of which each act of thinking is about something or has some content, however vague it may be. All thinking is intentional, and the specific content of any given thought is its intentional reality. As Descartes explains in his Second Replies: 'by the "intentional reality of an idea" I understand the reality of a thing that is represented by an idea in so far as it is in the idea . . . For anything that we perceive, as if in the objects of our ideas, is in the ideas themselves intentionally' (vii. 161; M. 85).

Descartes's assumption that all thoughts are in some sense intentional may provoke the kind of 'obvious objection' made by Richard Rorty (1979: 22) 'that pains are not intentional—they do not represent, they are not *about* anything'. Rorty concedes that one could gerrymander the extension of the term 'intentional' so that it includes even pains although, on his account, they have no legitimate claim to be included. The appropriate Cartesian response, however, is not to gerrymander. The concept of representation assumed by Rorty is too narrow, and what is thought about in a pain is just as real as what is thought about in any other sensation. Whatever its merits, this is the position proposed by Descartes in the *Principles*.

The question about the object of perceptions of pain is raised in the *Principles* (Part I), in a context where the author is attempting to explain why we are likely to form mistaken judgements when we make inferences from our thoughts to the realities to which they refer. This happens, familiarly, when we see something red and then naively assume that the cause of our red perception is some external reality that resembles the subjective perception we have. There is no suggestion here that it is mistaken to believe that there is usually an external stimulus that causes our perception. The mistake against which readers are warned is to assume a resemblance between the stimulus and the perception. Likewise, in the case of internal sensations, we make the same mistake if we assume that, when (for example) we feel a pain in our foot, the object of our perception is something in our foot that resembles the experience of pain. 'In order to distinguish what is clear from what is obscure in this context, it must be carefully noted that pain, colour, and other similar things are perceived clearly and distinctly when they are considered simply as sensations or as thoughts' (viii-1. 33; M. 139). It does not follow, however, that this is the end of the matter. Descartes adds: 'Obviously, if we say that we see a colour in some body or feel a pain in some limb, that is the same as saying that we see or feel something there, but it is a something of which we are completely ignorant . . .' (viii-1. 33; M. 139). The parallel discussion of both cases suggests a similar conclusion for each one. Both internal and external sensations are intentional, they are both perceptions of something other than the internal states of the mind, but there is a risk involved in projecting the phenomenology of our perceptions outwards, from the mind, as if we could thereby discover unproblematically the nature of the realities that we perceive. For Descartes, such perceptions involve thoughts that are clear and distinct only as long as we focus on the content of the thoughts. They become obscure and confused as soon as we make judgements about the objects of such thoughts that are based exclusively on their subjective, mental features. Thus pains are as intentional as any other 'thought', including sensations, even if the spontaneous associated judgements that we make are more misleading than usual.

IDEAS AND THOUGHTS

Many readers of Descartes, beginning with his own contemporaries, have expressed frustration at the latitude he exercised in using the same words in different ways or in using traditional scholastic terms in non-standard ways.[13] For example, the terms 'idea' and 'thought' are sometimes used as equivalents, and sometimes as if an idea were the content or object of a particular thought. Much of this confusion can be alleviated, I claim, if one highlights the subjective perspective adopted by Descartes when he was choosing descriptions of his own mental activities with as few theoretical commitments as possible. In this spirit, one could assume initially that the paradigm example of a Cartesian thought is some inner event by which we are aware of something or other. This is consistent with the distinction in the Third Meditation (vii. 37; M. 32) quoted above, between thoughts that merely make something present to us, and thoughts by which we adopt some kind of propositional attitude towards their

---

[13] Among recent authors, Kenny (1969: 98–125) set a pattern.

content. For this reason, there is nothing unusual about using the term 'idea' for a propositional content that is the object of a thought. In fact, if one adopts the degree of ontological agnosticism already proposed, one can think of the term 'idea' as a synonym for the content or object of any thought without commitment to the existence of abstract entities. At least, from the perspective of one's initial description of the phenomenology of first-person experience, one needs some words to refer to all the various kinds of things that we frequently think about without yet having any theory about the nature of such realities or the most appropriate way to explain the occurrence of such thoughts.

This is particularly useful in addressing the confusion created by Descartes's use of the term 'innate ideas'. When the term 'innate' was introduced in the *Meditations*, Descartes had already published a developed account of clear and distinct perception in *The Dioptrics*. But from the perspective of the meditator in the Third Meditation, he had no general theory in place about what ideas are, how they are caused, and so on. For that reason, the classification of ideas into three types is as tentative as one might wish. The text says simply: 'Among these ideas, some seem to be innate, some acquired and some seem to have been fabricated by me' (vii. 37–8; M. 33). This tentative threefold classification is clearly a function of the various possible origins of our ideas, or the various ways in which their occurrence in my mind may have been caused. To say that some ideas seem to be innate, in contrast with the other two options suggested, is merely to say that they may originate in myself or in my own thinking, and that they may not be explained adequately by reference to sensation or the combination of images that takes place in the imagination. This, of course, is not an argument to show that we have any innate ideas. It merely offers one possible source of ideas, and it does not preclude the possibility that some ideas may be partly acquired and partly innate, even if the initial classification might seem to imply that these options are mutually exclusive.

It is well known that Descartes offers a dispositional account of the innateness of ideas. For example, he argues in the Fourth Replies: 'when we say that some idea is innate in us, we do not think that it is always present to us; in that sense no idea would be innate. We mean only that we have within us a power to produce the idea in question' (vii. 189; M. 89). This is consistent with the standard Cartesian account of thoughts as occurrent acts. If 'innate idea' meant something that we actually think about, then no idea could be innate unless we were constantly thinking about it. 'Innate' must refer to the source of some ideas that would become actual only when we exploit our ability to generate them from our own intellectual resources and begin thinking about them. This same point is expressed more sharply in *Comments on a Certain Manifesto*.

By 'innate ideas' I have never understood anything else apart from what he himself [Regius] explicitly claims as true . . . namely: 'that we have in us a natural power by which we are capable of knowing God'. I have never either thought or written that the ideas in question are actual, or that they are species that are in some unknown way distinct from the faculty of thinking. Besides, I am opposed more than anyone else to the completely useless fabrications of scholastic entities, so that I cannot refrain from laughing when I see the large number of arguments that this gentleman . . . has laboriously put together to prove that infants in their mother's womb have no actual knowledge of God, as if he were thereby launching a magnificent attack on me!   (viii-2. 366; M. 201)

For Descartes, the idea of God is innate only in the sense that we cannot acquire that idea from our sensations or construct it from images in the imagination. If we succeed in thinking about God, that happens only because we have reflected appropriately on our own understanding. In this sense, innate ideas are not thoughts at all but merely potential thoughts or a subjective source for the content of some thoughts. As Descartes wrote to Voetius in 1643: 'all those things whose knowledge is said to be naturally implanted in us are not for that reason expressly known by us; they are merely such that we come to know them by the power of our own native intelligence, without any sensory experience' (viii-2. 166). Thus, if 'idea' is taken to refer to the content of thoughts (that is, what is thought about), Descartes uses the term 'innate ideas' to signify: (1) that we are naturally endowed with various dispositions to acquire certain thoughts; (2) that some actual thoughts originate from reflection on our own minds and their activities (approximately equivalent to Locke's ideas of reflection). In each case 'innate' points to the origin of thoughts in the subject, although ideas are involved in a strict sense only when the dispositions assumed in (1) result in some actual thinking by the subject in question.

This rather consistent line on what is meant by innate ideas makes it possible for Descartes to avoid suggesting that infants begin thinking about God from their earliest days, and to defer providing a comprehensive theory about all the sources of ideas. It also allows him to maintain that the paradigm use of the term 'thought' is an act of thinking, and that the content of our acts of thinking are appropriately called ideas, even though the acts of thinking themselves are also called ideas on some occasions.

However, although Descartes is quick to dissociate himself from the suggestion that infants actually think about God, he makes no effort to avoid the implication that, according to his account, we are constantly thinking, even in our sleep. This claim is more than a description of the inner world of our experience. It is evidently a conclusion to which he feels bound because he defines thought as the essential attribute of what is mental. It follows from that definition that we must be thinking when we are asleep, even though we often forget what we have thought. 'There is a distinction between being conscious of our thoughts at the time when we are thinking and remembering them afterwards. Thus we do not think of anything while we are asleep without being conscious of our thoughts at the moment they occur, even if we immediately forget most of them immediately' (v. 221). This kind of concurrent awareness and subsequent forgetting also applies in the case of infants. They have thoughts even in the womb but their thoughts are so dominated by their most basic needs, such as nutrition, that most of what they think is forgotten. 'Consequently I do not doubt that the mind begins to think as soon as it is infused into the body of an infant and, at the same time, that it is aware of its own thought, although subsequently it does not remember this because the impressions of those thoughts do not remain in the memory' (vii. 246). The claim that we are thinking constantly, as long as we are alive, may coincide with our experience of having some minimal level of awareness throughout our lives. But, as already indicated, the strength of the claim exceeds any supporting empirical evidence and it must be understood as a conclusion of some other metaphysical claim, rather than as a description of our first-person experience. In the case of our infancy, evidently, the fact that we forget most of our early mental experiences implies that we cannot describe those experiences from the perspective of the thinker.

PURE THOUGHT OR UNDERSTANDING

When Descartes rehearses, in the *Discourse*, the argument used more extensively in the *Meditations* four years later to show that he knows himself as a thinking thing independently of knowing anything about his body, he concludes as follows: 'I knew from this that I was a substance, the whole essence or nature of which was to think and which, in order to exist, has no need of any place and does not depend on anything material' (vi. 33; D. 25).[14] The *Discourse* claims that the description of the subject, using the language of substances, follows from the indubitability of our knowledge of our own thinking while we are suspending knowledge claims about our body. Whether that conclusion follows, and whether the appeal to substances adds any explanatory value to what is already known, remains to be discussed in the following chapters. Thus, although the *Discourse* text telescopes an argument that is developed at greater

---

[14] Here Descartes anticipates the conclusion of an argument about the mind's relative independence of the body. Towards the conclusion of Part V, he claims that 'our soul has a nature that is entirely independent of the body, and, consequently, it is not subject to dying with it' (vi. 59). Neither this nor the excerpt quoted in the body of the text provides an independent description of the experience of thinking.

length in the *Meditations*, it does not claim that thinking is an activity that is completely independent of the body. Such a description is not available to Descartes as long as he remains faithful to providing merely a description, from the subject's perspective, of what it feels like to be engaged in thinking. Even if that is accepted, however, it must be acknowledged that there are references throughout Descartes's works to something called 'pure' understanding. The total number of such references is relatively few, but they seem to provide an independent phenomenological description that could underpin the conclusion outlined in the *Discourse* text quoted above. In examining these texts, it is important to keep in mind the distinction already mentioned above between describing and explaining thinking, and the caution required in order not to read theoretical or ontological commitments into Descartes's use of a language that was both common in the seventeenth century and endorsed by centuries of usage in the schools.

A number of commentators have understood references to 'pure' understanding as one of the most unambiguous symptoms of (substance) dualism. For example, Margaret Wilson argued for a distinction between twentieth-century dualism, which claims that mental states and brain states occur in parallel, and her understanding of Descartes's dualism, according to which some mental states occur without any corresponding brain states at all. In this version of dualism, 'bodily states are not merely not *identical* with mental states: they are not even *relevant* to a subclass of such states . . . Pure understanding is carried on independently of all physical processes' (Wilson 1978: 181). On the assumption that Descartes is a substance dualist, 'pure understanding' occurs in the mind without any accompanying activity in the brain and, a fortiori, without depending on such parallel bodily events. John Cottingham likewise understands Descartes as claiming that 'an act of thinking or doubting needs no place and depends on no material thing', and he assumes that most people today would consider that view 'ridiculous' (1986: 119).[15] Jolley (1990: 27–8) adopts the same interpretation. But it is not at all clear that this was Descartes's view. The 'purity' of understanding may be understood as a description of the degree of abstraction involved in its content, rather than as a denial of its reliance on the brain as the primary centre of the activity involved.

The first systematic use by Descartes of the Latin phrase *intellectus purus* occurs in the *Rules*, in which various forms of the adjective *purus* and its adverbial Latin equivalent, *pure*, are used in a wide range of different contexts.[16]

---

[15] I am grateful to John Cottingham for bringing to my attention the text quoted above from the *Discourse*, although he acknowledges that the subject of the sentence quoted is 'ce moi' rather than thinking.

[16] Armogathe and Marion (1976) list seven occurrences of *pure* and twenty-two forms of the adjective *purus* in the text.

There is no contradiction in terms involved, for example, when Descartes writes about the imagination as being 'purely bodily' (*pure corporea*) or of some simple natures being 'purely material' (*pure materiales*) (x. 415, 419). These adverbial expressions translate naturally into English as 'completely bodily' or 'exclusively material'. The *Rules* displays a similar latitude in the use of the adjectival form *purus*. Among the realities qualified as 'pure' are: an inference, a nature, an object of study, an intuition, a science, a body, the light of reason, an aether, and so on (x. 365, 381, 365, 440, 385, 415, 373, 424), while the intellect is described as 'pure' on five occasions (x. 416, 419, 432, 440, 444). 'Pure' is often linked with 'simple' to provide a compound adjective, 'pure and simple', that suggests something that is neither complex nor combined with any foreign realities; for example, 'a pure and simple nature' (x. 381) or the 'pure and simple objects of Geometry' (x. 365). One of the best examples to illustrate this non-dualistic use of the adjective 'pure' occurs in Rule Twelve (discussed in Chapter 2 above), where Descartes describes, hypothetically, how shapes or ideas may be transmitted along a series of physical connectors from a sensory organ to the brain. The 'shapes or ideas' are described as being transmitted 'purely and without any body' (*puras et sine corpore*) (x. 414). That means simply that the images are not themselves distinct physical things, although they are transmitted along a physical connector. It seems then as if Descartes's use of the term *purus* must be read, as it usually was in Latin, to indicate that the reality to which it is applied is one that is not contaminated by any extraneous or foreign things, or is a paradigm example of whatever reality is being discussed.[17] We still speak that way in English today. Pure air is an appropriate mix of oxygen and nitrogen, without contamination by carbon monoxide, sulphur dioxide, and so on, and pure water is what one hopes to get when one buys a bottle in the local shop. In general, a reality or action is pure to the extent that it does not involve any mixture of extraneous factors. What then does Descartes mean by 'pure understanding' in the *Rules*?

Rule Twelve speaks about a single cognitive power being used in different ways, in sensation, imagination, memory, and so on. When this cognitive power 'acts on its own [*si sola agat*], it is said to understand' (x. 416). It is almost certain from this context that the purity of the act involved is a function simply of its independence of any accompanying brain state that would determine (even if partly) *the content of the thought*. In contrast, the way in which we think of something while we are having a sensation is limited, in its clarity and distinctness, by

---

[17] There is a good example of this usage in Baillet's report of the title of *The Search for Truth*. The search was to be pursued by using 'la lumière naturelle, qui toute pure, & sans emprunter le secours de la Religion ni de la Philosophie . . .' (Baillet 1691: ii. 406). In this text, the purity of the operation of the natural light implied no reliance on either religion or generally accepted views in philosophy.

many factors that impinge on the perceiver. Likewise, when we imagine a triangle, for example, our thinking is determined partly by the image that is simultaneously in the brain as we are engaged in imagining it, and consequently our capacity to imagine complex geometrical figures is limited by the capacity of the brain to represent them clearly and distinctly. But we can transcend those limitations, in a way that resembles Descartes's proposal in Rule Eighteen for representing quantities raised to the fifth or sixth power in two-dimensional geometrical figures. We simply abstract the concept of a straight side, a plane figure, and any number we wish, and then define a geometrical figure with that number of sides even though we cannot picture it clearly in our imagination. There is no question raised, and no answer suggested, about whether this kind of thinking depends on accompanying brain processing. 'Shapes or ideas' are said to be transmitted *'pura et sine corpore'* through the nerves in a context, in Rule Twelve, in which brain processing is taken for granted. 'Pure understanding', in the same Rule, suggests a form of understanding that takes place as a result of brain activity but does not involve perceiving a physical object or being caused to think by an image in the brain. These examples in the *Rules* are given in a context where Descartes is simultaneously proposing a description and assuming a widely held analysis of these various ways of thinking. There are clearer examples of 'pure understanding' as primarily a descriptive term in the *Meditations*.

At the beginning of the Sixth Meditation, Descartes offers a distinction between imagination and pure understanding (*puram intellectionem*) (vii. 72). The distinction is made before he has established that we are embodied, and therefore at a point when Descartes can do no more than identify and describe a significant difference in our subjective experiences of different kinds of thinking. In his attempt to persuade us that we are already acquainted with different kinds of thinking that merit different names, Descartes offers the well-known example of how difficult it is to imagine complex geometrical figures and how impossible it is to distinguish, in our imagination, between geometrical figures with a very large number of sides. For example, I can imagine a triangle with little difficulty, but I cannot imagine clearly a plane figure with exactly 1,000 sides. In contrast, I can easily understand what is meant by a plane figure with exactly 1,000 sides. This provides the experiential basis for making a distinction between two different kinds of thinking. Simply from the point of view of how I experience what are called understanding and imagining, I notice that, in the case of imagining, 'I need a characteristic effort of the mind that I do not use in order to understand' (vii. 72–3; M. 58). This new mental effort 'shows clearly the difference between the imagination and pure understanding' (vii. 73; M. 58).

There is a similar, equally subjective, distinction later in the same meditation when Descartes describes the difference between having a pain and having the thought or the concept of a pain. From our own experience, we know that we do not experience pain as a sailor observes damage to a ship. If I were not joined intimately to my body, I would not experience pain when my body is injured but 'I would perceive the injury by means of a pure understanding [*puro intellectu*] as a sailor perceives by sight [*visu*] that his ship is damaged' (vii. 81; M. 64). It should be noted, immediately, that the counterfactual pure understanding of my injured body is similar to the way in which a sailor knows about a damaged ship by looking at it. This distinction combines elements of a subjective description and a preliminary explanation. From the point of view of a subject, there is a significant difference between, for example, feeling pain in a tooth and knowing or understanding the source of the pain from the perspective of a dentist. When I reflect on my experience of thinking, I find that I have both kinds of thought and, however I may subsequently explain the difference between them, there is no likelihood that I would fail to notice it. Descartes combines this subjective perception of the difference with elements of his theory of perception developed elsewhere, and interprets the distinction by reference to the role played by brain states in causing our perception of pain.[18] The examples of imagining and sensing, especially internal sensing such as feeling pain or thirst, both testify to the extent to which the content of my thinking is controlled or limited by factors that are not within my power as a thinking thing. These limitations suggest some kind of interference in my thinking by an extraneous reality of some kind, although any attempt to identify that reality and to explain how it functions would go beyond a phenomenology of thinking. It is in this context that Descartes contrasts (1) thinking that is apparently influenced significantly by factors external to the mind and (2) thinking that seems to be completely within my own control as a thinking being. The latter may be called pure understanding.

In the Fifth Replies, Descartes replies to Gassendi:

I have . . . often distinctly shown that the mind can operate independently of the brain; for certainly the brain cannot be of any use for understanding purely [*ad pure intelligendum*], but only for imagining and sensing. And, although the mind is not free to

---

[18] The contrast between our awareness of pain, thirst, hunger, etc. and other thoughts, such as thinking about thought itself, is often described in terms of the concept of pure understanding. See e.g. Descartes to Regius (Jan. 1642), where he denies that we experience pain and other similar sensations 'as pure thoughts of the mind distinct from the body' (iii. 493), and Descartes to Gibieuf (19 Jan. 1642), in which Descartes claims that, when not relying on sensation and imagination, 'we can conceive of the soul entirely pure [*toute pure*]' (iii. 479). In *The Passions of the Soul*, the passions are also classified among those perceptions that are rendered 'confused and obscure' (xi. 350–1) because of the close liaison between body and mind.

understand readily other things when it is affected by a strong image or sensation (for example, when the brain is disturbed), nonetheless we experience that, when the imagination is less strong, we often understand something completely different from it. For example, if we notice that we are dreaming while we are asleep, the imagination is required in order to dream but we need only the understanding to notice that we dream. (vii. 358–9)

The contrast here is between sensing something—for example, a rising sun—which cannot occur unless we are present to and observing a rising sun, and being aware of the fact that we are having such a sensation. From the point of view of the subject, as already argued above, we seem to be immediately aware of our own sensations without any need for a mediating image to come between us and the acts of sensation of which we are aware. If that were not the case, it would begin an infinite regress of images of images, and so on.[19] This still leaves open the question whether, in being aware of our act of sensation or our dreaming, we rely essentially on the brain—which seems entirely plausible. But as long as we are not trying to explain how we are aware of our acts of perception, we describe the awareness subjectively as something that is immediate or apparently independent of any image.

The characteristic feature of so-called pure understanding, therefore, is that the content of 'pure' thoughts is not determined by the simultaneous causal activity of an image or impression of the reality thought about. Descartes explains it, in *Comments on a Certain Manifesto*, as 'an understanding that is not concerned with any physical images' (x. 363–4; M. 199). From the perspective of the thinking subject, the distinction depends on whether, in having certain kinds of thought, the mind relies in some essential way on being stimulated by a certain kind of object (or, what amounts to the same thing, a physical image in the brain). This is made clear in response to Gassendi's objections to the distinction between thought and imagination in the Sixth Meditation. Descartes replies that we understand something by using the mind alone, whereas in imagining we contemplate a bodily image. Although geometrical figures are completely bodily, 'the ideas by which they are understood—when they are not imagined—should not be considered as bodily' (vii. 355). To reinforce the point, Descartes goes on to say that the 'pure understanding of both bodily and non-bodily things is realized without any bodily image' (vii. 387).[20]

[19] Descartes argues along these lines in his conversation with Burman (v. 149), to the effect that we can be conscious of a thought without needing a second thought by which to reflect on a first one and thereby always being one thought removed from the reality of which we are aware.

[20] This coincides with the conclusion of the argument about the piece of wax in the Second Meditation; despite the fact that the piece of wax is obviously a physical thing, Descartes argues that it cannot be perceived in a strict sense by the senses or by the faculty of imagining, but only by the intellect: 'mihi nunc notum [est] . . . non proprie a sensibus, vel ab imaginandi facultate, sed solo intellectu percipi' (vii. 34).

Evidently this type of thinking is peculiarly relevant to metaphysics, as Descartes explains in a letter to Elizabeth (28 June 1643), where he contrasts it with the kind of thinking that works best in mathematics: 'metaphysical thoughts, which exercise the pure intellect, help to familiarize us with the notion of the soul; and the study of mathematics, which exercises mainly the imagination in considering shapes and motions, accustoms us to form very distinct notions of body' (iii. 692). Thus, in contrast with sensation, imagination, or memory, pure understanding is a form of thinking in which the content of our thought is not determined by a concurrent image or impression in the brain. This in turn provides Descartes with a basis for making a distinction between understanding and conceiving.

It is one of the common threads of the Cartesian account of God and the soul that we cannot have an image of such objects of thought. Accordingly, Descartes advises Burman to distinguish carefully 'between understanding, conception, and imagination'. He argues that we cannot imagine or conceive of the perfections of God, but that we can understand them in some limited sense. The only explanatory clue to this use of terminology occurs when he argues that, although we understand God's perfections, 'we do not conceive of them, since we cannot, so to speak, represent them to ourselves' (v. 339). This suggests that, in this context, Descartes reserves the term 'conceive' for types of thinking in which we form a mental image, or an image in the imagination, of whatever is understood. When we are thinking of God or the soul, however, we cannot form such images and the type of understanding we exercise is called pure thought.

Thus thought always involves some content. It would be impossible to think without thinking of something. In most cases—one is tempted to add, in all the primitive cases of thinking that are explicable by reference to our embodiment—thinking involves the manipulation of images or 'ideas' that help determine the content of our thoughts. Such thinking is characteristically limited to individual entities, as when we perceive or imagine a particular house with its colour, shape, and so on. This kind of thinking, at least when triggered by external stimuli, is also characterized by our relative lack of control over the content of our thoughts. We cannot choose to feel something else when we feel a toothache. In this sense, our conscious experience is such that we would spontaneously think of it as being determined by some independent cause during the time when we are having such a thought. In contrast, 'pure thought' seems to depend on the will of the thinker. Descartes uses this index of pure thinking when classifying various kinds of thought in *The Passions of the Soul*: 'when it [the soul] applies itself to consider something that is purely intelligible and not imaginable—for example, in considering its own nature—the perceptions it has of these things depends chiefly on the volition that makes it aware of them' (xi. 225). However, it is also possible to abstract from such concrete ideas some elements that are common to members of a class, and the resulting abstract concepts provide a foothold for metaphysical thinking. The Cartesian use of the term 'pure', in this context, means some kind of independence of matter. In the *Rules* it was used to refer to images that were not themselves material things, but were transmitted through a material connector. In the case of pure think-ing, however, 'pure' means thinking that does not rely on a concurring image to specify the content of one's thought, and is consequently not limited by our ability to form images when the relevant images either are too complex or are unavailable.

If 'pure' understanding is understood in this way, one could avoid its apparent ontological implications by simply renaming it as abstract thinking. The dispar-ity between the particular inputs of information from the senses and the universal concepts with which we think prompted Descartes to argue, against Regius, that the latter could not be transmitted to the mind, without mental processing, from sensory stimuli. 'All such physical movements [by which our sense organs are stimulated] are particular, whereas the common notions are universal' (viii-2, 359). From the point of view of the thinking subject, however, there may be degrees of abstractness that range from, at one end of the scale, feeling a pain, to considering features of objects that we have evidently abstracted from the realities in question (such as their number).

Does this mean that 'pure thought' is an activity that is completely independ-ent of brain processing, a conclusion that Descartes might seem to endorse in the text quoted above from the *Discourse on Method* (vi. 33)? The most plausible answer depends on the order in which various Cartesian theses are established. If one assumes substance dualism from the outset, then all instances of 'pure thought' might be understood as operations of an independent, non-bodily sub-stance that either does not rely on anything material or that takes place exclu-sively in the mind in parallel with corresponding brain states.[21] If, however, one interprets 'pure understanding' as a description of our experience of certain kinds of thought from the perspective of the subject, one especially designed to mark a distinction between abstract thinking and the thought involved in an experience of pain or thirst, then it remains for further discussion whether pure thought involves brain processing or takes place in angelic isolation from the world of bodily things. Evidently, the assumption of substance dualism is

[21] M. Rozemond also interprets 'pure thought' in terms of independence: '[Descartes] is concerned to claim that, unlike sensation and imagination, intellection is *independent* from the body. Intellection is an operation of the mind alone in which the body does not take part' (1998: 41). This is compatible with a parallel processing in the brain since, on this account, intellection occurs in a distinct substance.

conveniently consistent with one interpretation of 'pure understanding'. However, if Descartes did not have available the concept of substance that is required for traditional substance dualism, and if he rejected the suggestion that an appeal to substances could provide a genuine explanation of our mental life, then the corroborative effect of 'pure thought' remains doubtful. In the next two chapters I examine directly Descartes's use of the concept of a substance and the arguments he developed, especially in the *Meditations*, against the reducibility of thinking to matter in motion.

CHAPTER 8

Descartes's Use of the Concept of Substance

There can be no gainsaying the fact that Descartes frequently refers to sub-stances in contexts where the concept appears to have some descriptive or explanatory role. This is particularly true when referring to the human mind. Thus he claims that 'this I which thinks is an immaterial substance' (iii. 247–8), and that 'our natural knowledge teaches us that the mind is distinct from the body and that it is itself a substance' (vii. 153). In fact, he claims to have been the first 'to identify thought as the principal attribute of a non-physical substance' (viii-2. 348; M. 188).[1] Descartes also describes God as an infinite substance: 'The substance that we understand as supremely perfect, and in which we conceive of nothing that involves any defect or limitation of perfection, is called God' (vii. 162). Apart from the mind and God, parts of matter, items of clothing, and parts of a living body are all described in various contexts as substances. One might reasonably assume that the very frequency of its use implies that 'substance' is a technical, philosophical term in Descartes's philosophy and that, once its meaning is defined, it can support the standard account of Cartesian dualism according to which mind and body are distinct substances that are united together in some way.

However, there are strong reasons to doubt whether Descartes's concept of substance is sufficiently coherent to support the disparate roles that such a varied usage requires. One reason is the lack of clarity about what philosophical problem is being addressed when Descartes appeals to substances. The second and, possibly, more fundamental reason is that Descartes argues that we have no knowledge of any substance apart from what we know about its properties. This restriction applies even in the case of our own minds; spiritual substances are just as inaccessible as material substances. Thus, if Descartes claims that human beings are composed of two substances, he could not be understood as claiming some direct or independent knowledge of the substances involved. His references to substances must ultimately revert to claims about the properties that require subjects of predication.

---

[1] Cf. Descartes to Mersenne (Mar. 1637) (i. 349–50).

The standard account of Cartesian dualism also presupposes that, if the concept of substance were used to explain human conscious experiences, the resulting explanation would be immune to the objections marshalled by Descartes against the explanatory value of substantial forms. Despite the distinction drawn by scholastics between substances and substantial forms, however, the arguments outlined in Chapter 1 against substantial forms apply with equal rigour against substances. This implies that Descartes cannot make any progress in explaining why or how we think by postulating a 'thinking substance' and that, in this context, the concept of a substance does no more work than the concept of a thing.

In support of these claims, I review the texts in which Descartes explicitly defines what he means by a substance and I argue against interpreting them as sympathetic to substrata. This is consistent with Descartes's frequently expressed thesis, that we know substances only by knowing their properties. These arguments are further confirmed by examining whether the concept of a substance does any non-redundant work in Cartesian natural philosophy. Descartes notoriously defines matter in terms of extension, so that either extension is the substance of bodies or it is the nearest equivalent in Descartes's conceptual framework to what scholastics called material substance.[2] One might respond that, even if Descartes makes the concept of a substance redundant in the case of material things, it retains an irreducible role in the case of immaterial realities. However, the Cartesian analysis of substances, like Locke's, maintains an exact parity in its treatment of both material and immaterial substances. They are both known only by their properties, and they are each defined by a single essential property.

Despite the logic of his own philosophy, however, Descartes continued to use the traditional scholastic language of substances to articulate a view that would render intelligible the Christian doctrine of the immortality of human souls. This in turn drew him into discussing various ways in which substances may or may not be combined. I review some of these efforts below, especially those in which Descartes searches for appropriate metaphors to envisage the manner in which the mind can interact with the body. I argue that this entanglement by Descartes with scholastic metaphysics was theologically motivated, and that the logic of his metaphysics points in a different direction. Since substances are either unknowable or redundant, the core of the Cartesian theory of mind is the apparent irreducibility of mental properties to the properties of matter as Descartes understood that term, or what I labelled above as matter$_c$. This apparent irreducibility frustrates the construction of a unified Cartesian

---

[2] Guenancia (1976: 26) refers to this as the 'desubstantializing of extension'.

account of the human being, and the arguments that support it are examined in Chapter 9.

THE CONCEPT OF SUBSTANCE

Descartes's appeal to the concept of a substance reflects the range of its disparate uses by other philosophers in the seventeenth century. Ian Hacking (1972) has distinguished a number of the philosophical contexts in which substance had a role. One is the 'problem of creation', where 'substance' refers to entities that are self-caused or whose existence is caused directly by God. The second context is the 'problem of predication', in which a substance is a (special kind of) subject of qualities. The same concept cannot be used without equivocation in both contexts, and the need to resolve ambiguities that result from such a dual role is evident. In the context of predication, for example, Descartes is willing to apply the term 'substance' to a stone or a block of wood. 'For when I think that a stone is a substance, that is, the kind of thing that can exist on its own, and when I also think of myself as a substance . . . they seem to agree in so far as they are both substances' (vii. 44).[3] However, if a mason splits a stone in two, there are then at least two distinct objects of which different qualities can be predicated. But it is hardly consistent with the first concept of substance, which applies in theories of creation, to suggest that a mere human agent can create new substances at will; according to this other concept, a substance is an entity that can come into existence only by being created directly by God. Thus in the Synopsis that introduces the *Meditations*, Descartes argues that 'all substances—that is, things that, in order to exist, have to be created by God—are without exception incorruptible by their nature, and they can never cease to exist unless they are reduced to nothingness by the same God' (vii. 14). In this sense even 'body, considered in general, is a substance and therefore can never perish either' (vii. 14). The natural imperishability that results from God's creation and concurrence (which implies that matter in general is a substance) is a very different feature from whatever makes something like a stone a substance, as a subject of which qualities are predicated.

Before looking in more detail at Descartes's use of the traditional category of a substance, it is appropriate to mention two other contexts in which the term 'substance' is used. One is 'the problem of matter', where the term 'substance' refers in a general way to the stuff of which the universe is composed. Finally,

---

[3] This may be read, of course, as saying: if I were to think of a stone as a substance, it would share the property of being a substance with my mind; but I need not grant the antecedent.

substance language is often invoked when discussing 'the problem of identity', especially when claiming an identity between different temporal stages of the life cycle of something, such as a river, that changes significantly with the passing of time. Descartes uses the term 'substance' or 'substantial form' in both contexts.[4] In the following discussion, I ignore these peripheral uses and focus on Descartes's more explicit comments about substances in the context of creation and predication.

The term 'substance' is defined as follows in the *Meditations*, in the second replies to objections from Mersenne: 'Every thing in which resides, as in a subject [*in subjecto*], or by which exists, everything that we perceive—that is, every property, quality, or attribute of which we have a real idea—is called a *substance*' (vii. 161). There is a similar definition in the *Principles* (Part I): 'By the term "substance" we cannot understand anything other than a thing [*res*] that exists in such a way that it needs nothing else in order to exist' (viii-1. 24). Since this definition may suggest that finite things are capable of existing without God's concurrence, the French version of the text (ix-2. 47) added an extra sentence to the effect that the phrase 'it needs nothing else' may be obscure. The proposed clarification was that all finite substances depend on God, who uniquely is a substance that does not depend causally on anything else in order to exist. Consequently the term 'substance' does not apply to God and to finite substances univocally. On this initial reading, the fundamental problem being addressed by Descartes is the problem of predication. The further subdistinction, between (*a*) God and (*b*) other substances, is secondary and is designed to protect the uniqueness of God.[5]

However, even the concept of substance that results from Cartesian considerations about predication remains obscure. Descartes introduces this distinction explicitly in the *Principles*: 'We think of whatever falls within our perception either as things or as states of things' (viii-1. 22; M. 129). One could readily agree that it makes no sense to speak about a specific size or shape without assuming that it is the size or shape of something. One could mark this distinction by saying that size, shape, colour, and so on are predicables and that the realities of which they are predicated can be called, generically, substances. That leaves

---

[4] In this sense, for example, Descartes refers in *A Treatise on Man* (xi. 173) to the 'substance of the brain' as being soft and pliant. The same phrase, 'la substance du cerveau', occurs at xi. 179, 192. Descartes to Mesland (9 Feb. 1645) discusses the identity of the human body over time despite the fact that no parts of its matter remain unchanged, and he explains its identity by reference to its substantial union with the soul. The problem is similar to claiming that 'the river Loire is the same river that it was ten years ago' (iv. 165), despite the fact that the water and material in the river bank may have changed completely.

[5] Another way to reach the same conclusion is to claim that, as in other contexts, Descartes initially derives the concept of a substance from familiar objects of experience, and then applies it by analogy to God. He cannot claim to have an independent concept of substance from a direct acquaintance with God.

open the possibility that substances have nothing in common apart from being the kinds of realities of which qualities can be predicated. Descartes seems to endorse this conclusion in the sentence immediately following the definition quoted above from the *Meditations*: 'Nor do we have any idea of the substance itself in a strict sense, except that it is the thing in which whatever we perceive exists either formally or eminently, or whatever is present intentionally in one of our ideas, for it is known by the natural light of reason that no real attribute can belong to nothing' (vii. 161; M. 86). The final phrase implies that, if there were no substance available of which one could predicate attributes, the alternative would be to attribute properties to nothing (*nihil*).[6] The same phrase implicitly distinguishes between 'real' (*reale*) and non-real attributes, and relies on a distinction made in the *Meditations* between terms that refer to genuine properties in things, and other terms that seem to name properties but in fact merely indicate the absence of some property. In that context Descartes had contrasted what he called 'a real and positive idea' (*realem et positivam ideam*) of God with a 'negative' (*negativam*) idea of nothingness. This terminology allowed him to classify human error, for example, as a negative reality or (in relation to human beings) as a privation. Error is not therefore 'something real' (*quid reale*) whose existence requires the intervention of a cause: 'a privation . . . does not need God's cooperation because it is a non-entity [*non est res*]; if it is referred to God as its cause, it should not be called a privation but merely a negation [*negatio*]' (vii. 60–1). By using the same classification, Descartes can distinguish negative or non-real attributes, which are not necessarily predicated of a real thing, and real attributes that must be predicated of something that exists.

The definition of substance as a subject of real properties also requires a distinction between first-order properties and other higher-level properties. A first-order property is one that can be instantiated only by a concrete individual.[7] In contrast, even properties have properties, and many realities that are classified by Descartes as abstractions, such as geometrical figures, also have properties. For example, a triangle has a certain size and other characteristic mathematical features, but that does not imply that it is a Cartesian substance in the restricted sense of a real thing. Besides, even if a triangle were described as a substance, it is not the case that a property of its properties—for example, a relation between its sides—implies a Cartesian substance. This distinction supported part of the response to Arnauld, in the Fourth Replies to Objections.

---

[6] The choice between predicating qualities of a substance or of nothing is often used. For example, Descartes argues in the *Principles* that 'there are no attributes or properties in nothingness [*nihil*]' (viii-1. 25).

[7] This may be circular, and may require that we adopt the concept of a concrete individual or a thing as an undefined term.

First of all, although a triangle might be taken concretely to be a substance, the property of having the square on the base equal to the squares on the sides is certainly not a substance. Therefore neither of these may be understood as complete things [*res completa*] in the same sense in which the mind and body are complete; nor can either of them be called a thing [*res*] in the sense in which I said, 'It is enough that I can understand one thing (that is, a complete thing) without another . . . etc.,' and this is clear from the words which follow: 'besides, I find in myself faculties, etc.'. I did not call these faculties things, but I distinguished them carefully from things or substances.   (vii. 224; M. 91)

Thus everything that has a property is not necessarily a thing or substance. There is a relational property (of equality) between the square on the base of a right-angled triangle and the squares on its sides, but the bearers of this property are not concrete things. Nor is a triangle a substance, in the strict sense, although Descartes concedes that it might be such—presumably if a triangular body with three dimensions were involved.[8] Hence only first-order properties unambiguously indicate the presence of a concrete thing or substance.

If the natural light of reason requires us to postulate a substance every time we perceive a first-order 'real quality', it does not thereby provide us with any knowledge of the substance as such: '*neque enim ipsius substantiae praecise sumptae aliam habemus ideam.*' The only thing we know about a substance, as such, is that it is a reality of the appropriate kind of which first-order real qualities may be predicated. This could mean either: (1) that there is a substance underlying the qualities that we perceive or think about, but that it is inaccessible to human understanding; or (2) that we have no idea of any substance *in so far as it is a substance*, but only in so far as it is a concrete thing of a particular kind that has the qualities that we know about. The first alternative assumes the existence of an unknowable something, a bare particular, whereas (2) implies that there is no limit in principle to knowing anything we wish about substances or things, on condition that all such knowledge is reducible to knowing their qualities. In the second sense, to talk about a substance is not to talk about a new kind of unknowable particular, but to talk about something that can be known through its qualities and to classify it as a concrete individual entity.

Some commentators have adopted the first interpretation, which construes substance as a propertyless substratum. For example, Louis Loeb (1981: 108) attributes to Descartes a theory of what he calls 'substance$_s$', 'an unobservable-substratum-in-which-qualities-inhere'.[9] Substance$_s$ can be understood in two

---

[8] Jubien (1992: 4) uses the term 'physical' to describe the two-dimensional face of a three-dimensional 'material' cube.

[9] This interpretation is also consistent, as Loeb acknowledges, with Descartes's claim about our inability to know substances otherwise than through their properties. 'We cannot immediately apprehend, cognize, or observe substances$_s$ themselves; rather, we immediately observe only the qualities which immediately inhere in a substance$_s$, and then infer . . . that a substance$_s$ exists' (Loeb 1981: 80).

different ways. On one reading, the substratum is identical with the substance. On the second reading, a substance is a substratum together with the properties that are predicated of it. Neither reading is sufficiently coherent to attribute to Descartes, unless the textual evidence is compelling and there is no more plausible reading available.[10] The principal objection to the concept of a substratum is that it exemplifies no properties. But every entity, of necessity, exemplifies some properties, minimally the property of being an entity. The concept of a bare substratum seems to be self-contradictory. For if anyone were to speak about it, they must presuppose that they attribute to a substratum the property that other properties can inhere in it, that it is a concrete entity, that it can subsist, and that (paradoxically) it has no properties. Despite the apparent connotations of Descartes's language, the concept of a bare particular is so problematic that one would be well advised to find a more promising interpretation of the relevant Cartesian texts.

The alternative reading, (2) above, is that the term 'substance' is used by Descartes to designate concrete particulars that are known only by means of their first-order properties, and that there is no other underlying reality apart from concrete particulars such as a human being, a mountain, or a parrot. The texts are not decisive between the two interpretations. Part of the argument, therefore, must depend on a more general account of what theoretical benefit Descartes thought he could derive from the concept of a substance, and on ancillary arguments about the role of properties in providing us with information (or ideas) about various realities. The argument at this point is simply that the texts are consistent with this second interpretation, (2) above, and that the principle of charity requires that we not impose on the texts a manifestly implausible interpretation.

If the concept of a substratum were eliminated as irrelevant to Cartesian substances, it would still be true that we know substances only by knowing their properties. Descartes often makes this claim. For example, in reply to Arnauld's objections to the *Meditations*, he wrote: 'We do not know substances immediately . . . but only because we perceive various forms or attributes that, in order to exist, must inhere in some thing and we call the thing in which they inhere a substance' (vii. 222). Likewise, in reply to Hobbes's objections: 'we do not come to know a substance immediately through itself, but only in so far as it is a subject of certain acts' (vii. 176). Finally, Descartes wrote in the Fifth Replies to Gassendi, who was consistently critical of Descartes's apparent claim that one could know a substance apart from the attributes or properties that are predicated of it: 'But as far as I am concerned, I have never thought that anything else

---

[10] For the following arguments, see Hoffman and Rosenkrantz (1997: 18–19).

is required to reveal a substance apart from its various attributes, so that the more we know the attributes of some substance the more perfectly we understand its nature' (vii. 360).[11] The *Principles* endorses the same view, that substances cannot be known directly and that our knowledge of them is limited to what we know of their qualities. 'A substance cannot be recognized initially from the mere fact that it is an existing thing because this alone, on its own, does not impinge on us. But we recognize it easily from one of its attributes, by using the common notion that there are no attributes, or no properties or qualities, in nothingness' (viii-1. 25; M. 131). Substances as such do not impinge on our cognitive faculties. We are affected only by various qualities and we then rely on the 'common notion' that qualities must inhere in some thing to claim that we know the thing or substance of which those qualities are predicated.

This way of thinking of substances is also consistent with the Cartesian understanding of the relation between qualities and substances. Descartes uses the general term 'quality' to refer to all those features that, in order to exist, must inhere in something else. While some qualities are essential to things of a certain type, others may vary without any change in the thing itself and these are called 'modes'. 'We understand the term "modes" here in exactly the same way as the terms "attributes" or "qualities" are understood elsewhere. However, when we think of a substance as being changed or modified by them, we call them "modes"' (viii-1. 26; M. 133). Some qualities of a substance can evidently change; there is no suggestion that all features of a given substance are necessary in the way in which mereological essentialism stipulates that things have their parts essentially. For example, the speed of a moving body can vary from zero to the upper limits envisaged for moving bodies in a Cartesian universe, and the direction of the motion can vary also. However, any change in a mode involves automatically a change in the substance of which it is a mode. There is no real distinction, in the Cartesian sense of 'real distinction', between a mode and the substance of which it is a mode.[12] The reason is that there is no possibility in this metaphysics for some kind of propertyless substratum that can acquire or lose different properties while remaining the same substance throughout.

The suggestions that we have no idea of substance as such, because there is nothing there to be known apart from the properties of any given substance, is

---

[11] Cf. *Principles* (1. 11): 'it is very well known by the natural light of reason that nothingness has no attributes or qualities and that nothing can happen to it. Therefore, whenever we encounter some qualities, there is necessarily some thing or substance to which they belong, and the more qualities we find in some thing or substance the more clearly we know it' (viii-1. 8).

[12] A 'real distinction' is defined in the *Principles* (viii-1. 28; M. 135), and is discussed in Chapter 9. Descartes admits in the Fourth Replies (vii. 249) that God might be able to separate modes from a substance, but we cannot understand how that is possible.

confirmed by an otherwise strange reply to a query from Burman in 1648. Burman asked about the apparent implications of a sentence in the Second Replies, where Descartes had written that 'it is a greater thing to create or conserve a substance than to create or conserve the attributes or properties of a substance' (vii. 166). Burman's query was: surely the attributes are the same as the substance, and thus it is not clear how it could be a greater achievement to create the latter rather than the former. The reply confirms at least the assumption underlying the query: 'All the attributes, when considered collectively, are indeed identical with the substance [*omnia attributa, collective sumta, sunt quidem idem cum substantia*] but not when considered individually and distributively. Thus it is greater to create a substance than its attributes, that is, than individual attributes, one now, another later, and all of them in succession' (v. 155).

The thesis that there is no real distinction, in the Cartesian sense, between a thing and its properties is also reflected in Descartes's controversial discussion of the Tridentine theology of the Eucharist. The teaching of the Council of Trent assumed that the underlying substance of bread and wine could be changed without any modification in their observable appearances. This change of substances might be described as intelligible but miraculous (in the sense of something that does not happen naturally, but is realized only by God's power) if a substratum account of substance were adopted. But the Cartesian understanding of substances made this account seem both miraculous and unintelligible. Descartes had the temerity to propose an alternative interpretation of Trent, which, in his view, would make less unintelligible the manner in which Christ could be present in the Eucharist without any of the normal properties of that concrete, historical person.[13] The unfortunate consequences of his dabbling in theological controversy are well known. For present purposes it is enough to acknowledge that Descartes had independent reasons for avoiding theological controversy about this extremely sensitive issue, and that the only reason for his involvement was to explain how his explicitly adopted theory of substances was not inconsistent with Trent. If modes are inseparable from the substance of which they are modes, it would be unintelligible to attach the modes of one substance to a different substance. If a piece of bread and a cup of wine are substances, in the sense of concrete individuals, Descartes evidently does not think of them as having substrata that could be substituted, even by the power of God, without any corresponding change in their observable properties.

There is nothing in the arguments considered so far that provides an independent and satisfactory account of substances and properties. It may be that

---

[13] See Fourth Replies to Objections (vii. 252–4) and Descartes to Mesland (9 Feb. 1645) (iv. 165). The standard account of this controversy is Armogathe (1977).

the concept of a property and of a substance are so interdependent that neither one can be clarified without reference to the other or without assuming one member of the pair as a basic, unexplained concept. It also seems clear that the concept of a bare substratum is so problematic that the burden of proof must be on those who wish to attribute that position to Descartes. The texts examined above concerning the Cartesian understanding of modes, the theology of the Eucharist, and Descartes's response to Burman all indicate that Descartes never appealed to a substratum, even in the context of philosophical problems where it might have done some useful work or at least helped him to avoid theological controversy. When addressing the problem of predication, then, Descartes uses the traditional distinction between things (or substances) and their properties, but he avoids endorsing bare substrata or substances that are really distinct from concrete individuals.

As indicated above, Descartes also tried to define substances in terms of their capacity to exist without being causally dependent on anything else apart from God.[14] There are supporting texts for the latter; for example, in the Fourth Replies: 'This is the very notion of a substance, that it can exist through itself, that is, without the assistance of any other substance' (vii. 226).[15] These texts suggest a distinction between God as a primary or basic substance and other entities, such as human agents, animals, planets, and so on as secondary or non-basic substances.[16] Thus, if secondary substances, or substances other than God, are defined as follows: 'x is a secondary substance if it is possible for x to exist without being caused to exist by any other entity existing, apart from God,' and if a primary substance is defined in a similar way without the phrase 'apart from God', one could define a substance as anything that is either God or a secondary substance. This interpretation of substances has the unwelcome implication that, if any secondary substance exists, then God exists. It also implies, equally implausibly, that a secondary substance such as an animal could exist even if other relevant secondary substances did not exist. But it is difficult to make sense of that suggestion since the existence of any animal depends on the

---

[14]   Peter Markie (1994) distinguishes three concepts of substance rather than two. A substance as an independent existent is defined as either God or something that exists without being dependent on the causal power of other created things and without being a quality of something else. Substance as a subject is defined as whatever perceivable qualities exist in. Pure substances are independent substances that have no substantial parts.

[15]   Cf. Third Meditation: 'a substance, that is, the kind of thing that can exist on its own' (vii. 44); and the *Principles*: 'Physical substance and mind (or created, thinking substance) can both be understood under this common concept, in so far as they are things that need only God's conservation in order to exist' (viii-1. 24–5; M. 31).

[16]   Loeb (1981: 97) and Markie (1994: 67–9) distinguish between primary and secondary substance, while Hoffman and Rosenkrantz (1997: 22) opt for the language of basic and non-basic substances.

existence of those that gave birth to it and on the existence of many other things in its environment, including food. To avoid these implications it would be preferable to think of Descartes's comments on this issue, not as a contribution to analytical metaphysics that attempts to define the concept of a substance, but simply as consequences of the Cartesian understanding of God's role in creation. His point is that, if God exists and is understood in the traditional Christian sense, then God creates everything apart from himself, including things, their qualities, eternal truths, and so on. If in turn the contents of that creation are distinguished into substances and their properties, and if the latter depend on the former, then the comprehensiveness of God's creative causality can be expressed in terms of the ultimate dependence even of otherwise apparently independent or complete things, called substances, on God's causal activity.

The texts reviewed above indicate that Descartes used the concept of a substance in a way that reflected a range of disparate philosophical concerns that were current in the seventeenth century. Apart from those contexts in which he was concerned about God's role in creation, he might just as readily have used the term 'thing' (*res, chose*) in every context in which he used 'substance' as a count-noun. The apparent synonymy of these terms is reflected in many texts. For example, in the Third Meditation, he claims that 'I am a thinking thing or substance [*res sive substantia*]' (vii. 48), and in reply to Gassendi he substitutes the phrase 'thinking thing [*res*]' for 'thinking substance [*substantia*]' (vii. 355).[17] This linguistic variation, however, does not imply an unresolved ambiguity in a term that was significant for his philosophical project; for Descartes, the concept of a substance is redundant. This is most explicit in his natural philosophy, in which one might expect to find as much clarity as he promised in its metaphysical foundations.

MATERIAL SUBSTANCE

I argued above that, for Descartes, there is no underlying, propertyless substrate that is independent of its modes and that might be described, in the words of Gassendi's objection, as a 'bare, hidden substance' (*nuda et occulta substantia*) (vii. 273). In the case of material things, therefore, it would certainly be a mistake to think of their substance as some kind of reality that is independent of their properties. If misguided philosophers 'distinguish a [physical] substance from

---

[17] Cf. *Comments on a Certain Manifesto*, 'res existens sive substantia' (viii-2, 354; M. 193); Descartes to [Silhon] (May 1637) (i. 353); Replies to the Fourth Objections, where Descartes distinguished faculties 'from things or substances [*a rebus sive substantiis distinxi*]' (vii. 224).

extension or quantity, they either understand nothing at all by the term "substance" or they have only a confused idea of an incorporeal substance that they falsely attribute to physical substance' (viii-1. 45). The substance of a material object, such as a tree or an animal, is not a substratum, nor is it similar to an 'incorporeal substance' (whatever that turns out to be). Descartes's positive hints all point towards equating the substance of material things with their extension, or substituting extension in Cartesian natural philosophy for the role played by substance in scholastic metaphysics.

I have already summarized, in Chapter 3, the Cartesian approach to this issue in the *Rules* and the use of imagination in avoiding the pitfalls of abstraction. Descartes returns to this question in the *Meditations* and the *Principles* under the guise of identifying the essential properties of material and immaterial things. The distinction between essential and inessential qualities is assumed when discussing the piece of wax in the Second Meditation. The wax example is introduced initially to counter the apparent obviousness of the assumption that physical things, which are known through sensation, are known more clearly or reliably than our own minds. The argument is, in outline: if we consider a piece of wax, we can observe its colour, shape, size, smell, and so on. But these properties are all subject to change once the wax is heated; despite these changes, 'the same wax remains' or, at least, 'no one thinks otherwise' (vii. 30). Descartes suggests that we therefore need a distinction between those features of the wax that can change without the wax ceasing to be wax, and those that are so essential that, without them, it would no longer be wax at all. I assume he means here that if, for example, the wax were not only heated but were burned and turned into ashes, it would no longer be a piece of wax. But if one stops short of that kind of fundamental change, we could remove conceptually 'whatever does not belong to the wax' (vii. 31) or, in another metaphor, we could 'consider it as if it were bare and without its clothes on' (vii. 32). At that point, we would realize that nothing remains except 'something that is extended, flexible, and changeable' (vii. 31). A similar analysis of what is essential to a stone, in the *Principles*, concludes that 'nothing remains in the idea of the stone except that it is something extended in length, breadth, and depth' (viii-1. 46). Descartes did not have available in 1640 even an elementary version of contemporary chemistry. But one may borrow some empirical details from his contemporary, Robert Boyle, without being anachronistic and without importing into the Cartesian world elements that were conceptually incompatible with it. If pressed about the defining features of wax, in contrast (for example) with a stone or a piece of wood, Descartes would have appealed to a specific combination of the three kinds of corpuscles that were proposed in his physics. What makes something a piece of wax, rather than a piece of wood, is the characteristic combination of parts of matter of which it is constituted. The point being urged in the Second Meditation was that the essence of wax could not be known simply from a survey of its observable properties, because these can vary without the wax ceasing to be wax.

This is not the same question that is addressed in the *Principles* (I. 53), where Descartes argues that there is one principal attribute of every substance. Before reading this text one might anticipate that each type of thing has a single defining attribute that specifies the natural kind to which it belongs. For example, among material things, we might attempt to specify the essence of various things, such as a table, a mountain, or gold, by identifying a single defining property in virtue of which each of these realities is classified as being the kind of thing it is. Descartes does not address that question in the *Principles*. Instead he divides all substances into two general types, and distinguishes between them by reference to two essential attributes.

While a substance can be known from any one of its attributes, there is still one principal property of every substance, which contains its nature and essence and to which all the other properties are referred. Extension in length, width, and depth constitutes the nature of physical substance, and thought constitutes the nature of thinking substance. For everything else that can be attributed to a body presupposes extension, and is merely a certain mode of an extended thing; likewise, all the things that we find in the mind are merely different modes of thinking.   (viii-1. 25; M. 132)

Descartes goes on to explain, in Article 56, that the kinds of reality to which the terms 'attribute', 'mode', and 'quality' apply are all equivalent, and that he chooses different names depending on the connotations of each word. Why then does Descartes claim that there is one principal property for each type of substance?

The examples given in the *Principles* do not suggest that he is attempting to define the essence of salt, wax, a tree, a mouse, and so on. Instead he is dividing all substances into two general types, and then claiming to find one property in common between all members of the same class. His conclusions here cannot be supported merely by conceptual analysis, although the presentation of the results might suggest this. It is more plausible to think of Descartes as proposing that the most fundamental quality of all material things—that is, the quality that is presupposed by all other qualities—is extension, and in that sense extension is essential to matter. If the quality called thinking is irreducible to extension or other material properties, then the subject of such qualities must be a different kind of substance. The apparent irreducibility of thought to the fundamental attribute of material things provides Descartes's unique access to knowledge of immaterial substances.

IMMATERIAL OR SPIRITUAL SUBSTANCES

Descartes's proofs of God's existence in the *Meditations* imply that he has an idea of God and, since God is a spiritual substance, that he has an idea of this incorporeal substance. He writes: 'this idea of God . . . has the highest clarity and distinction and contains more intentional reality than any other idea' (vii. 46; M. 39).[18] Likewise, he claims to have 'an idea of a substance from the very fact that I am a substance myself' (vii. 45; M. 38), and that he has a sufficiently clear and distinct idea of his own mind as a thinking substance to conclude that he is nothing other than a thinking thing: 'when I discover that I am a thinking substance, and form a clear and distinct idea of this thinking substance . . .' (vii. 355). However, on further examination, it becomes clear that Descartes has no idea of his own mind apart from the properties that, he claims, identify the substance in question. Since having an idea of God depends, in turn, on having an idea of his own mind, the status of both claims can be decided by examining the latter.

Descartes never claims to have knowledge of the spiritual substance that is his mind independently of the qualities by which that substance is known. His initial efforts to define what he is, in the *Meditations*, conclude as follows: 'But what, then, am I? A thinking thing [*res cogitans*]. And what is that? A thing that doubts, understands, affirms, denies, wills, does not will, and that also imagines and senses' (vii. 28; M. 26). The suggestion that the mind or self is only a something that thinks is often made in the subsequent meditations: 'I, who am nothing but a thinking thing' (vii. 81); 'when I reflect on the mind, or on myself in so far as I am simply a thinking thing' (vii. 86). In reply to Hobbes, Descartes makes explicit the relationship between thought and the mind as that of an act to the subject that acts. Hobbes had complained about the triviality of the conclusion 'I exist' once the truth of 'I think' is granted. He argued that this is simply another example of a more general principle to the effect that 'we are incapable of thinking any act whatsoever without its subject; for example, of dancing without a dancer, knowing without a knower, or thinking without a thinker' (vii. 173). Descartes accepted this characterization of his insight: 'He then says, correctly, that we cannot conceive of any act without its subject; for example, we cannot conceive of thought without a thinking thing because whatever thinks is not nothing [*non est nihil*]' (vii. 175).[19] He disagreed, however, with Hobbes's conclusion that the mind must therefore be a body.

---

[18] There are many texts in the *Meditations* where Descartes claims to have an idea of God. For example: 'I have some idea of God' (vii. 49); 'I have some idea of God' (vii. 51); 'a clear and distinct idea of God occurs to me' (vii. 55); 'I have a real and positive idea of God, or of a supremely perfect being' (vii. 54); 'I find in myself an idea of God' (vii. 65); 'true ideas that are innate in me, among which the idea of God is the primary and principal one' (vii. 68).

[19] Here again, the alternatives considered are (1) that thinking is attributed to nothing, or (2) that it is attributed to what can be called a substance.

The logic of this position is that we are initially aware, by reflection, of our own activity of thinking. We are directly conscious of thinking, and we recognize it as a quality that must belong to something or other. From being aware of thinking we conclude that we are thinking substances. Our idea of God is then constructed by analogy with our concept of ourselves as a thinking substance that is finite. 'I confess that the idea we have of the divine intellect . . . does not differ from that which we have of our own intellect except in so far as the idea of an infinite number differs from the idea of a number raised to the second or fourth powers' (vii. 137). A similar analogy is suggested in reply to Hobbes: 'Is there anyone who does not perceive that they understand something, and who does not therefore have the form or idea of understanding from which, by indefinitely extending it, they can form the idea of God's understanding and thereby ideas of all his other attributes?' (vii. 188). The disanalogy between God and the human soul derives from the fact that our ideas of human features cannot be applied univocally to God (vii. 137). Consequently, it is impossible for a finite intellect such as ours to comprehend God's nature or to acquire an idea that is adequate to the reality involved (vii. 52, 55, 107, 112, 114). Despite the amount of conceptual manœuvring and analogical reasoning involved here, these claims are consistent with the notorious description, in the *Meditations*, of our idea of God as innate. If God created me, he could have left his trademark on the result of his creative work. But it is not 'necessary that the mark be distinct from the work itself' (vii. 51). The resemblance between God and myself is grasped 'by means of the same faculty by which I perceive myself' (vii. 51). In other words, in so far as I can form an idea of the activity of thinking by introspection, I can form by analogy an idea of God's thinking. Secondly, in so far as I understand that my own thinking must be the activity of some finite thinking substance, I can equally form, by analogy, an (inadequate) idea of an infinite thinking substance. My idea of God is innate only in the limited sense in which my idea of myself is innate. It is acquired by reflection on my own conscious experiences rather than on any information acquired through sensation.

Descartes's claims about finite or infinite thinking substances add nothing new to our knowledge of substances as such. In both cases, he is claiming no more than what is supported by the natural light of reason—namely, that, if thinking is occurring, there must be a thinking thing of which the act of thinking is predicated. There is no independent knowledge of the human mind or of God. 'We can see that our soul, in so far as it is a substance distinct from body, is known to us solely from the fact that it thinks, that is to say, understands, wills, imagines, remembers, and senses, because all these functions are kinds of thoughts' (x. 224; W. 170–1). Since our limited knowledge of God, without revelation, is constructed by analogy with what we know of our own thinking, our indirect knowledge of immaterial substance leaves intact the general thesis already defended for material substances—namely, all our knowledge of substances reduces to what we know about the qualities of which we have ideas, because we cannot avoid thinking of qualities without some subject of which they are predicated.

We do not know substances immediately, as indicated elsewhere, but only by perceiving certain forms or attributes that, in order to exist, must inhere in some thing [*alicui rei*] and consequently we call the thing [*illam rem*] in which they inhere a substance. If, however, we subsequently wished to strip that substance of those attributes by which we know it, we would destroy all our knowledge of it; and thus we might still be able to apply various words to it, but we would not perceive their meaning clearly and distinctly. (vii. 222)[20]

Evidently, in the case of the activity called thinking, it follows that the activity is predicated of a thinking substance, but the conclusion is analytic.

COMBINING SUBSTANCES

If the problems associated with God and creation are provisionally left aside, then substances may be understood merely as ultimate subjects of predication or as concrete things, and they can come into existence or cease to exist without God's intervention. In this sense of the term, then, two 'substances' may be combined to form one, and one substance may be subdivided to form two or more substances. If I have a bag of flour and some eggs before I begin to make a cake, I can attribute to each one separately various qualities that are not truly predicable of the others. For example, I can attribute to the eggs their characteristic shape, and to the flour its usual powdery quality or its weight. If I combine them with other ingredients and bake the mixture, I can attribute to the results of my culinary exercise various attributes that were not true of the separate items before combination and cooking. There is nothing deeply metaphysical or mysterious about this; a kilogram of flour has properties that a cake does not have.

It follows that any argument designed to show that substances (in the sense of subjects of predication) cannot be combined would have to take the form of showing that their properties are incompatible. Evidently, some properties of two substances may be incompatible while others are not. Arguments against the possibility of combining substances that rely on knowledge of their proper-

---

[20]   Cf. the *Principles* (1. 63): 'In fact, we understand extended substance or thinking substance more easily than substance on its own—which involves omitting the fact that a substance thinks or is extended. For there is some difficulty in abstracting the notion of substance from the notions of thought and extension because there is only a distinction of reason between them . . .' (viii-1. 31; *M*. 137).

ties may be either empirical or conceptual, but for the reasons already mentioned there is no independent access to substances themselves that could reveal their compatibility or otherwise. Descartes's use of substance language in the context of mind–body interaction includes an assumption that the relevant substances may be combined. One could think of this combination as taking either of the following forms: (1) a combination in which each substance maintains its original identity, and the result is a mere joining-together of two separate entities that remain separable; (2) a combination in which the original identity of the substances is lost and the result is a new substance with, usually, new attributes that were not present in either of the former substances. To the extent that two substances are incompatible, a combination of both would have to be of the first type. Descartes argues explicitly in his correspondence with Regius in 1641 and 1642 against understanding the union of mind and body according to (1). He frequently argues instead, even by his very choice of descriptive metaphors, in favour of (2).

Regius had defended a number of theses at the University of Utrecht in which, among other things, he had claimed that the unity of body and mind in human beings is an accidental union or, as he expressed it, that a human being is an *ens per accidens*.[21] Descartes's letter to Regius in December 1641, in response to his views about mind–body unity, was very clearly a damage limitation exercise. He warned his supportive colleague that he could hardly have said anything more objectionable to scholastic philosophers, and advised him how to put a plausible retrospective interpretation on his theses, since it was too late to retract them completely. The advice assumed that Regius would be able to persuade his critics that the term 'accident' could be used in different ways. 'For we apply the term 'accident' to anything that is present or absent while the subject [in which it is present] remains, even if it were a substance when considered on its own, as an item of clothing is for a human being' (iii. 460).[22] If this analogy is to work, Descartes has to accept that our clothes are substances in their own right. However, when used to clothe our bodies, they can be classified as accidents in relation to the body. Similarly, the body is sufficiently independent of the soul that it can exist without the soul, and therefore the soul is accidental to

---

[21] Rozemond (1998: 167) discusses the contrast, in scholastic terminology, between an *ens per se* and an *ens per aliud* (i.e. between a substance and a mode), and between an *ens per se* and an *ens per accidens* (i.e. something that is not essentially or necessarily joined with something else, such as clothing to a clothed body). The soul is an *ens per se* in the first sense, and may be described as an *ens per accidens* in the second sense.

[22] The same argument is used in the Sixth Replies to Objections; 'an item of clothing, considered on its own, is a substance although, when it is referred to a clothed person, it is a quality' (vii. 441–2). Descartes accepts, in the Sixth Replies, that 'the mind, although it is a genuine substance, can nevertheless be said to be a quality of the body with which it is joined' (vii. 442).

the body, and vice versa. Descartes thus encourages Regius to clarify that, despite the latitude allowed in using the term 'accident', he had never claimed that the mind–body combination is an *ens per accidens*. What he meant, rather, was that both body and soul are incomplete substances and that the unity formed by them is an *ens per se*.

Regius did not adopt this advice and, as a result, Descartes returned to the same issue one month later, in his letter of January 1642. He explained that his correspondent had evidently intended only what everyone involved in the dispute accepted—namely, that a human being is composed of two things that are really distinct from each other (*ex duabus rebus realiter distinctis*). However, that was not what was meant by the phrase *ens per accidens* in scholastic philosophy. So, if Regius could not accept the earlier advice, it would be much better simply to acknowledge his mistake in misunderstanding scholastic terminology, and subsequently to take every opportunity, in private and in public, to show that he believed that a human being is a genuine *ens per se*, 'and that the mind is really and substantially united with the body . . . by a real kind of union' (iii. 493). Descartes added that, although everyone admits such a substantial unity, no one is able to explain it and he concludes by suggesting that Regius might consider saying what he himself had claimed in the *Meditations*:

We perceive that the sensation of pain, and all the other sensations, are not pure thoughts of a mind that is distinct from a body, but are confused perceptions of a mind that is really united with it. For if an angel were present in a human body, it would not have sensations like us, but it would merely perceive the motions that would be caused by external objects and in this way it would be distinguished from a genuine human being. (iii. 493)

Descartes then sketches a draft reply to the objections from Voetius, partly in French and partly in Latin, to prevent Regius from simply copying the draft and risking the identification of its original author. In the course of this draft, Descartes reiterates in January the advice given the previous December: that Regius should clarify that he used the phrase *ens per accidens* only in relation to the body and soul when considered separately, and that he meant that, since each can exist without the other, it is accidental for either one to be joined to the other. But when a human being is considered in its totality, then evidently a human being is an *ens per se*. It would be difficult to find a clearer expression, on Descartes's part, of a rejection of the hypothesis that mind and body are united 'by the mere presence or nearness of one to the other'. Instead, they are united 'by a genuine substantial union' (iii. 508).

Descartes emphasizes the unity of human nature in a number of other texts, in words or phrases that reveal the problem involved in describing such a unity without undermining the distinctness of mind and body. For example Part V of the *Discourse on Method*, which summarizes earlier unpublished work, rejects the metaphor of a pilot in a ship to describe the soul in the body. In describing the need for a special creation of 'the rational soul', Descartes writes that 'it is not enough if, with the possible exception of moving its limbs, it is lodged in the human body as a pilot in their ship, but that it has to be joined and united more closely [*jointe et unie plus étroitement*] with the body in order to have . . . sensations and appetites like ours and thus constitute a real human being' (vi. 59).

This theme is taken up more formally in the *Meditations*. The introductory Summary invites readers to find in Meditation Six that the author has successfully shown that, although the mind 'is really distinct from the body', it is 'so closely joined with it that together they form a single entity [*tam arcte illi esse conjunctum, ut unum quid cum ipsa componat*]' (vii. 15; M. 17). This is an accurate reflection of the kind of unity proposed in the final meditation, where the metaphor of a pilot and a ship is used a second time to identify one way in which the mind is *not* related to its body. The sensations of pain, hunger, thirst, and so on show instead that 'I am very closely joined to it [my body] and almost merged with it [*me . . . illi arctissime esse conjunctum & quasi permixtum*] to such an extent that, together with it, I compose a single entity [*unum quid*]' (vii. 81; M. 64). At the end of the same paragraph, he concludes that these sensations of thirst, pain, and so on result from 'the union and, as it were, the thorough mixing together [*ab unione & quasi permixtione*] of mind and body'. Since Descartes frequently uses the term 'substance' to mean the same as 'thing', and since the Sixth Meditation is one of his most explicit and official expositions of the relation between mind and body, the single entity here is equivalent to a single substance. Thus his 'whole self' is a unity that is 'composed of a body and mind', and 'human nature' is 'composed of a mind and a body' (vii. 81, 88; M. 64, 69).[23]

Those readers to whom the text of the *Meditations* was sent prior to publication raised many questions about the nature of the mind–body union. One anonymous correspondent, whose objections reached Descartes after the manuscript had been sent to the printer, was identified as Hyperaspistes in Descartes's reply (August 1641), in which he used his favourite analogy to illustrate the way in which mind and body interact. Those scholastic philosophers, he argued, who described gravity as a 'real quality' had no difficulty in conceding that gravity was able to move bodies towards the centre of the earth. They also thought that such real accidents were 'different in kind' to the matter on which they act. Descartes reports that, according to their proponents, real

---

[23] At vii. 65 Descartes refers to being 'composed of a body and mind' and a 'composite' of mind and body. In the Sixth Replies, he denies that he has ever seen or perceived a human body thinking, but only that the same human beings have thought and a body (vii. 444).

accidents were said to be corporeal if this term meant merely 'capable of acting on a body'. In the same way, the human mind can be said to be corporeal because, evidently, it acts on the body. But if 'corporeal' means 'whatever is 'composed of the substance called body', then neither the mind nor so-called real accidents can be said to be corporeal. Descartes then adds what might seem to be an astonishing conclusion: 'It is only in this latter sense that the mind is commonly said not to be corporeal [*hoc tantum sensu negari solet mentem esse cor-poream*]' (iii. 424–5). In other words, the human mind is incorporeal only in the sense that it is not 'composed of the substance called body'. This would be true of the mind even if it were understood merely as a complex of functions or dis-positions of a body. The same analogy with the status accorded to real accidents in the scholastic tradition had been used in the Replies to the Sixth Objections, and in 1648 in reply to queries from Arnauld.[24] The letter to Arnauld emphasizes the incontrovertible evidence of our everyday experience that 'the mind, which is incorporeal, can set the body in motion'. Here again the analogy with the heaviness of a stone is used, not to show that the mind can move the body (which is taken for granted), but to illustrate that the way in which the mind's effect on the body is no less intelligible, at least for scholastic philosophers, than the way in which heaviness can move stones. This introduces the same kind of analysis of the concept of corporeality as had been offered to Hyperaspistes:

If by the word 'bodily' [*corporea*] we understand whatever belongs to a body, then even the mind—although it is of a different nature—can be called bodily in so far as it is apt for being united to a body. If, however, we were to understand by 'bodily' that which par-ticipates in the nature of a body, then this heaviness is no more bodily than the human mind.   (v. 223)

The human mind is therefore corporeal, because it acts on the human body, and it is incorporeal in the sense that—just like heaviness—it does not have the nature of body.

This degree of unification is also emphasized in a letter to Princess Elizabeth (28 June 1643), which was mentioned above in Chapter 1. Although the style of the letter appears designed to reassure his royal correspondent that her diffi-culty in understanding the unity and distinctness of mind and body results from the conceptual problems involved, rather than from her lack of metaphysical sophistication, Descartes does not exceed anything already claimed in the *Meditations* when he writes:

These meditations were responsible for making you find obscure the notion we have of the union of mind and body, because it seemed to me that the human mind is incapable

---

[24] The analogy between gravity and the soul is developed at vii. 441–2.

of conceiving very distinctly, and simultaneously, both the distinction and union of body and soul. The reason is that, in order to do so, it would be necessary to conceive of them as one single thing [*une seule chose*] and, at the same time, to conceive of them as two things—which is self-contradictory.   (iii. 693; M. 53)

To conceive of mind and body as 'one single thing' is to conceive of them as a single substance. However, even a single substance may be either simple or compound. This distinction is developed in reply to the infamous manifesto of Regius, which provoked the *Comments on a Certain Manifesto* (1648):

An entity is compound if we find it has two or more attributes, each of which can be understood distinctly without the other . . . A simple entity, however, is one in which such attributes are not found. It follows from this that a subject in which we understand only extension and various modes of extension is a simple entity; so, likewise, is a subject in which we recognize only thought and various modes of thought. However, an entity in which we think of extension and thought simultaneously is composite—that is, a human being, consisting of a soul and body, while our author [i.e. Regius] seems to have assumed here that it is only a body of which the mind is a model.   (viii-2. 350–1; M. 190)

This was Descartes's reply to a suggestion from Regius that thought and extension, although they are distinct qualities, might be attributed to the same substance. Descartes seems to insist that each of these two attributes must be predicated of different substances, and at the same time that they might be predicated of one and the same substance on condition that we think of it as a compound substance.

This sharp response to what Descartes took to be a misrepresentation of his views about mind–body relations highlights the apparent ambiguity involved in disputing the extent to which human nature includes one or two substances. If one follows the hermeneutic guidelines suggested to Princess Elizabeth, one should expect to find places where the separate identity of mind and body are emphasized, and other places—few, since he accepted that this was not his primary objective in the *Meditations*[25]—where the unity of mind and body is more clearly acknowledged. But it remains problematic if the two substances of mind and body are not only distinct but lacking the kind of unity required for human experiences.

Descartes offered a few other suggestions about the unity of body and mind in the analogies he chose to illustrate it. For example, he wrote to More (5 February 1649) that he thought of immaterial substances as powers or forces: 'I understand them rather as powers or forces of some kind that are such that,

---

[25] The reason offered on a number of occasions for emphasizing the distinction rather than the unity of mind and body was that no one doubted their unity, but many were tempted to deny their distinction. See e.g. Descartes to Regius (Jan. 1642) (iii. 508).

although they are applied to extended things, it does not follow that they them-selves are extended, just as there is fire in a white-hot piece of iron but it does not follow that the fire itself is iron' (v. 270; M. 169). The analogy between the mind and a force had already been used in the Sixth Replies, where Descartes claimed that he thought of the mind being united with the whole body but capable of acting through one part of it just as gravity is coextensive with a whole body and capable of exercising its force through one part. 'This is how I understand the mind to be coextensive with the body' (vii. 442). These analogies are offered, it seems, to encourage readers not to think of the mind as something like another body, but as a distinctive power that can act in a body while remaining otherwise unobservable.[26] In that case the pineal gland should not be thought of as the part of the body in which the mind is lodged, but as the part of the body through which mental functions are exercised.[27]

The texts reviewed here illustrate the extent to which Descartes attempted to make sense of the unity of human experience by describing human beings as a combination of two incomplete substances, and as an entity that has new prop-erties that are not found in either of the substances when considered separately. The principal examples of such new properties are the 'confused thoughts', such as feelings of hunger, thirst, and so on that are not found in pure spirits, such as angels, but occur only in human beings as creatures in whom bodily and conscious properties coalesce. What Descartes required was a coherent way of describing how apparently incompatible properties could be simultaneously attributed to something that, when described in the language of substances, apparently required to be characterized as two disparate substances. The interim solution adopted in correspondence with scholastic philosophers, and even in advising Regius, was to muddle through with distinctions and qualifica-tions that were unsatisfactory but not explicitly opposed to scholastic philoso-phy. The real solution was to follow the logic of his own position and treat substances as a redundant category in any genuinely explanatory context.

SUBSTANCE AS AN EXPLANATORY CONCEPT

It is commonplace today to distinguish between the ontology of our everyday conceptual scheme and the ontology of a scientific theory, and to acknowledge

---

[26] See the Fifth Replies to Gassendi: 'I did not add that the mind is not extended in order to explain what it is, but only in order to warn those who think of it as extended that they are mistaken' (vii. 388). In the same context he advises Gassendi: 'Thus when you wish to compare the intermingling [*permixtio*] of mind and body with the intermingling of two bodies, it is enough for me to reply that one should not propose any comparison between them because they are completely different . . . ' (vii. 390).

[27] See Descartes to Meyssonnier (29 Jan. 1640): 'My view is that this gland is the principal seat of the soul and the place where all our thoughts are generated' (iii. 19).

the relative independence of the latter (Sellars 1963: 1–40; Churchland 1979). A discussion of substance in contemporary metaphysics therefore should distinguish between (1) articulating various concepts of substance that are assumed in ordinary language, and (2) examining the necessity or otherwise of using such concepts in a given scientific theory. Hoffmann and Rosenkrantz, for example, reject the coherence of any scientific theory that is inconsistent with our common-sense or 'folk' ontology of substances. 'Any ontologist must begin as a point of reference with a consideration of folk ontology . . . It is sometimes alleged that theoretical physics . . . entails that a belief in substance is mistaken. . . . A natural response to the foregoing allegation is that if it is true, then so much the worse for theoretical physics' (Hoffman and Rosenkrantz 1997: 7). Substances are said to be ineliminable from any viable ontology because every scientific theory depends on the evidence that supports it, and the possibility of finding data to support any theory 'presupposes that there are substantial beings, namely, human observers' (Hoffman and Rosenkrantz 1997: 7). However, that objection begs the question about whether human observers, as the source of the relevant data, must be described *within a scientific theory* as individual substances.

An alternative approach to metaphysics, adopted by Jubien (1992), is to think of the whole world as being constituted by matter that is differentiated by its properties. From this perspective, the stuff of the world is spread out indefinitely more or less densely throughout the universe and the portion of it that occupies one part of space–time may or may not be said to be a *thing*, depending on the language we use and the features of its distribution that are relevant in a particular context. This perspective gives ontological priority to properties rather than to things. Accordingly, whether or not certain *things* exist is a matter of convention, but the question about which properties exist is not. Some properties may be redundant, because they can be reduced to or explained in terms of other properties, but the ultimate reality of the world is described in terms of the minimal number of properties required to explain it adequately. Thus, 'in a certain sense, there are no things, but, partly as a consequence, there are as many things as we like' (Jubien 1992: 1).

Descartes's theory of the matter of the universe adapts naturally to the latter ontology. For Descartes, 'there is no real difference between space and corporeal substance' (viii-1. 46), and 'this world, or the universe of corporeal substance, has no limits to its extension' (viii-1. 52), Thus, using the term 'indefinite' rather than 'infinite' (where the latter is reserved for God (viii-1. 114–15)), the Cartesian world could be described as an indefinitely extended mass of matter. This otherwise uniform matter or stuff is divided into particles of three kinds, which are distinguished by their size and the speed of their relative motion. In this world, the things that we ordinarily distinguish as distinct things, such as a stone or a piece of wax, share a fundamental common nature of being a piece of material that is defined by its extension. While all physical objects share the same fundamental property of being extended, different kinds of material objects are distinguished as combinations of parts, of varying sizes, of material substance.

One of the principal issues that arises immediately for this concept of matter is how to individuate parts of matter such as a stone or a piece of wax, which in ordinary language are classified as things, and whether Descartes's parsimonious metaphysics includes enough theoretical entities to explain the multiplicity of natural phenomena that require explanation. Descartes's relativized concept of motion implies that any parts of matter that move together, against a background environment of other parts of matter, can be said to be a body. Thus 'motion is the transfer of one piece of matter [*pars materiae*] or one body [*unus corpus*] from the vicinity of the other bodies that are in immediate contact with it, and that are regarded as being at rest, to the vicinity of other bodies' (viii-1. 53). Whether such separable parts of matter would ultimately require some kind of internal cohesive forces to help maintain their unity is a question that need not be addressed here. Cartesian natural philosophy seems not to cope well with this problem. However, this merely helps to support the conclusion that physical objects in Cartesian physics are mere parts of matter, and that the number of basic properties of matter that are available for explanatory purposes is very meagre and inadequate to the task at hand. Yet, despite this explicitly constructed theory in the *Principles*, Descartes shows no reluctance about describing such parts of matter as substances.[28] The question then is: does the concept of substance have some extra explanatory value, in physics, that adds to the resourcefulness of the concepts already available in terms of which the properties of matter are described? It is impossible to avoid a negative reply. This suggests a further, equally unavoidable, question: why does Descartes introduce or rely on a traditional philosophical concept, such as the concept of substance, when it clearly has no explanatory function in his natural philosophy?

Descartes's attitude towards the categories of the scholastic tradition is well expressed, at an early stage of his philosophical career, in Rule Three of the *Rules*: 'I am not thinking at all about the way in which certain words have been used in recent times in the schools . . . All I do is to notice what particular words mean in Latin, so that, whenever I lack appropriate words, I shall transfer to my own meaning whatever words seem most suitable' (x. 369; D. 123). In other

---

[28] Descartes to Gibieuf (19 Jan. 1642), where parts of matter are described as 'complete substances' (iii. 477).

words, Descartes uses whatever term, in Latin or French, is closest to what he wishes to express without necessarily adopting its scholastic meaning. One might suspect that this may have been merely an interim arrangement, in his relative youth, and that it does not adequately describe his subsequent use of philosophical language in his maturity. However, the strategy of using traditional scholastic language with a new meaning, and, especially, of not rejecting explicitly the concepts used by opponents, remained unchanged even during the 1640s. Thus Descartes wrote to Mersenne (January 1641) that the *Meditations* contained all the foundations of his physics but that his correspondent should refrain from revealing his secret, lest it make it more difficult for supporters of Aristotle to accept them. 'I hope that those who read my principles will unconsciously become used to them, and will recognize their truth before realizing that they destroy those of Aristotle' (iii. 298). The same kind of toleration is commended to Regius in 1642. Here Descartes suggests to his embattled correspondent, who was the target of serious objections from the Rector of his university, that he not propose any novel opinions but retain all the traditional theories 'in name only'. Once new arguments are introduced, readers will then recognize that the ancient theories are redundant or unworkable, and they will take the initiative to change their allegiance without Regius being held responsible for their philosophical apostasy.

The focus of that dispute between Regius and Voetius was the status of substantial forms. Descartes argued, on that occasion, that there was no need for a substantial form (understood as something that satisfied all the conditions for being a substance) to be joined with matter (considered as a mere potency to form bodies):

Lest there be any ambiguity in the word it should be noted here that, when we reject substantial forms, we understand that term to mean some substance that is joined to matter and, together with it, constitutes some complete entity that is merely corporeal and that, no less than matter and even more than it—since it is called an act, while matter is called only a potency—is a true substance or a self-subsisting thing. (iii. 502)

Descartes gave two reasons for omitting such substantial forms. In each case, he began his objection with a principle or assumption that was accepted by Voetius. The first was linked with the commonly accepted role of God in creating new substances. 'It is clearly inconceivable that some substance would begin to exist *de novo* unless God creates it *de novo*' (iii. 505). But physical bodies come into existence and disappear again every day, and no one thinks that God's creative intervention is required on each occasion. Hence the concept of a substantial form cannot apply to such changes in matter. The second reason was drawn from the explanatory purpose envisaged for substantial forms by their proponents. In Descartes's view, scholastic philosophers introduced them to 'give an account of the proper actions of natural things, of which this form would be the principle and root' (iii. 506). But the complete failure of their explanatory function implies that we could simply omit them from our onto-logical categories. The conclusion is difficult to avoid. While the language of substances might be maintained by those trained in Aristotelian philosophy to account for the characteristic features of natural phenomena, Cartesian natural philosophers could achieve at least comparable results without relying in any way on the concept of a substantial form. The same arguments hold if one substitutes 'substance' for 'substantial form'.

This programmatic suggestion coincides exactly with the contents of Carte-sian natural philosophy. Descartes never appeals to the concept of a substance to explain any natural phenomenon, although the term appears often in his natural philosophy, with the same meaning as the word 'thing'. That usage is compatible with parts of a substance being substances in their own right, but whether we choose to call them complete or incomplete substances is merely a matter of the reference frame. We cannot coherently say that something is a substance (that is, a thing that can subsist on its own), and at the same time describe it as incomplete (that is, 'not possessing the power to subsist' on its own). One is then forced to rely on a mere verbal manœuvre by talking about complete and incomplete substances, in which the latter term does not imply that the reality in question is not a genuine substance. 'Thus a hand is an incom-plete substance when it is referred to the whole body of which it is a part; but it is a complete substance when it is considered on its own' (vii. 222).

Even if the concept of a substance drops out as redundant from Cartesian natural philosophy, it might be objected that it serves an irreducible explanatory role in the case of spiritual substances. But Descartes maintains an exact parity between the two kinds of substance.[29] Both spiritual and material substances are known only through their respective attributes and it is impossible to say anything meaningful about them without talking about the properties that justify their postulation in the first place. This suggests that the most plausible way of reading Descartes's use of substance language is to think of substances merely as things, and to understand the distinction between material and spiritual substances as being based exclusively on the irreducibility of mental properties to material properties.

---

[29] One might compare this with the argument used by Locke in the *Essay*, II. xxiii. 5: ''Tis plain then, that the *Idea* of corporeal *Substance* in Matter is as remote from our Conceptions, and Apprehensions, as that of Spiritual *Substance*, or *Spirit*; and therefore from our not having any notion of the *Substance* of Spirit, we can no more conclude its non-Existence, than we can, for the same reason, deny the Existence of Body; It being as rational to affirm, there is no Body, because we have no clear and distinct *Idea* of the *Substance* of Matter; as to say, there is no Spirit, because we have no clear and distinct *Idea* of the *Substance* of a Spirit.'

It would then be arbitrary, or a matter of convention, whether or not we think of different parts of matter as distinct substances. Evidently, as parts of matter, they have distinct properties, and properties are always properties of something. Thus we could think of two parts of matter, when joined together, as forming a single thing and, when separated, as forming two things. The predication of thinghood would follow the properties that are the focus of attention. However, in the case of everyday objects that can be disassembled and reassembled again, such as a bicycle, one need not think of a bicycle as a substance that goes out of existence and returns mysteriously into existence when it is disassembled to fit it into a compact space, such as the boot of a car. As a typical example of a mereological sum, the bicycle as such has various properties that its distributed parts do not have. These properties are the properties of the bicycle. Likewise, parts of matter have properties that their mereological sum does not have, and one can talk coherently about either the parts or the sum as things, depending on which properties are at issue. In this sense, what counts as a thing or, in Descartes's borrowed scholastic language, as a substance, depends on which properties are used to specify the thing in question. Things or substances depend on properties. This would explain why there is no philosophical problem in Descartes's variable usage in describing both material objects and their parts as substances. Nor is there any metaphysical problem if the same place is occupied by a number of different things simultaneously, in so far as the matter occupying a place can be simultaneously a thing in its own right and a part of a larger unit.

It would be an exaggeration to conclude that Descartes had resolved, to his own satisfaction, all the philosophical problems to which the scholastic concept of substance was applied. He seems rather to have abandoned some of them or, in some contexts, to have addressed different problems. In particular, he took a crucial step that was later exploited by Locke by arguing that we know nothing about substances apart from their properties, and that there is only a distinction of reason between a substance and its properties. Given their epistemic inaccessibility, all claims about Cartesian substances can therefore be translated into claims about their properties. Not surprisingly, Descartes also claimed that substances could not be used to explain anything, except in the provisional sense outlined in Chapter 1. The characteristic role of an explanation is to give an account of why some phenomenon has a certain property. For example, a theory of mind should ideally explain how we think, how we dream, how we are conscious of our sensations, and so on. None of these questions is answered by claiming that we are thinking substances or things, just as we cannot explain how sleeping powder works by saying that it has a dormitive power. Thus we would expect Descartes's attention, in philosophy of mind, to focus on a hypothetical account of how the activity of thinking is produced by creatures like us with the properties that we have and know about. If that enterprise encounters insurmountable difficulties, he may revert to the kind of empty explanation sketch that he was attempting to avoid—namely, we succeed in thinking because we are thinking beings. But that is not substance dualism as a theory of the human mind, but a temporary recourse to the scholastic language of substances to mark the point at which explanation has come to a provisional stop. Before accepting that conclusion, however, Descartes must examine whether it is possible to provide the kind of structural explanation of thinking that his philosophy required. His inability to provide such an explanation is camouflaged by arguments for property dualism, and these are examined in the next chapter.

CHAPTER 9

Property Dualism

One of the principal conclusions of Chapter 1 is that a Cartesian explanation of any reality cannot be merely a description, or redescription in a different language, of the reality to be explained. Nor can some phenomenon be explained adequately by constructing a law of nature, in the form of a universal statement, from which a description of the phenomenon follows logically as an instantiation of the general law. Cartesian explanations are structural in the sense that they describe a hypothetical micro-structure and its associated mechanisms that cause observable phenomena. Thus an explanation of the motion of hands of a clock requires a description of its internal parts and of how they are structurally related and move to produce the hands' motion. There must, therefore, be an appropriate gap (which I shall call an explanatory gap) between what is offered as an *explanation* of some phenomenon and what is available as its pre-theoretical *description*.

Another conclusion, most explicit in the Cartesian account of sensation, is that there is often a difference between how something appears to us and how (we hypothesize) it is independently of our perceiving. The distinction between appearance and reality suggests that, in many cases, we should expect to have two alternative descriptions of the same reality. This difference, which corresponds to what Wilfrid Sellars (1963: 1–40) called the 'manifest image' and the 'scientific image', implies that we can fix the reference of a referring expression in two different ways. For example, if we begin from our experience of how hot things feel, we can identify heat indirectly as whatever features of some external reality cause us to have a sensation of heat. If we also hypothesize that heat is something like the mean kinetic energy of molecules in the thing in question, we arrive at that description as a conclusion from a scientific theory. Those who then claim that heat is identical with the mean kinetic energy of molecules in motion may appear to have adopted a trivial identity claim rather than an insight that might be part of an explanation. The appearance of triviality, or of making no progress in explanation, is supported by Kripke's well-known argument (1982) that such an identity claim, if true, is necessarily true, so that there is no real distinction between the realities to which both phrases in English apply.

However, there is nothing trivial about such an identity claim and, despite its necessity (if it is true), it is something that has to be discovered by the range of strategies, both empirical and conceptual, that normally characterize the work of scientists. Another way of expressing the same point is this: the identity between heat and the mean kinetic energy of molecules is not something that can be discovered or confirmed simply by considering the meanings of the words used in the identity claim. Thus, once an identity claim is accepted, the theory-derived description on one side of the identity statement either facilitates or presupposes the construction of an explanation in the usual sense anticipated by Descartes.[1] Scientific explanations need not result in such identity statements. If they do, however, they assume an account of the phenomenon in question in terms that do not rely in any circular way on one's initial description of the explanandum.

It is worth making explicit that the kind of identity statement envisaged here, which provides an appropriate link between two languages or descriptions that have developed independently, is not itself an explanation. There is an obvious sense in which the required explanation is developed within an independent theoretical framework, in what Sellars calls the 'scientific image'. The relevant identity statement merely provides a translation or link between two different languages. If the evidence supports a claimed identity, then the required explanation of a phenomenon is provided once the bridge is crossed successfully from familiar ordinary language to a new scientific language.

It follows from the theory of explanation that underpins the Cartesian enterprise in natural philosophy that a genuine theory of mental activities could never be simply a description of how such activities are experienced subjectively, although that is an obvious first necessary step in the process. But neither can it be a mere redescription of mental activities that depends essentially on our subjective experience and adds nothing more than conclusions from that description. This has significant implications for what could count as a Cartesian *explanation* of mental phenomena. Such explanations may not include as part of the *explanans* a description of what it is like, subjectively, to feel, think, and so on. Evidently, there is a major problem in deciding whether a proposed explanation is adequate or otherwise, but it would be a mistake in principle to fix the price of adequacy so high that an *explanans* is required to include a pre-theoretical description of the phenomenon to be explained.

---

[1]   This is not to suggest in any way that the order of discovery is first an identity statement, and then some account of how molecules move, etc. The order is probably the reverse. But the reason why the identity statement is a non-trivial element in an explanation is that it is shorthand for the underlying account of the kinetic energy of molecules in motion.

The 'identity theory' of mind was a familiar alternative in the seventeenth century to the position proposed by Descartes, although it was not described in that way then. A typical identity theorist claims an identity between the referents of two different descriptions, one of which denotes a mental event or a type of mental event as experienced by a human subject, while the second description cannot be circularly dependent on such a description. Secondly, such an identity statement avoids the Cartesian objection to the circularity or triviality of Scholastic explanations because one side of it includes (at least in principle) the possibility of developing an account of how mental states are caused.

In recent years Thomas Nagel (1989, 1995) has extensively discussed this question, about the minimal requirements for a viable theory of mind. Nagel argues that no theory of mind is remotely plausible if it omits from its *explananda* those first-person experiences that we have as conscious beings, such as feeling a pain, and so on. 'A theory of consciousness that doesn't include mental events among the data is like a book about Picasso that doesn't mention his paintings' (Nagel 1995: 88).[2] This means that descriptions of all relevant facts about human consciousness must eventually be included among the explananda of an adequate theory of the mind. However, this is not enough to specify the minimal conditions for what could count as an *explanation* of such phenomena (admittedly described in the familiar, ordinary, and first-person language that has become available to us from tradition). Nagel seems to demand such a degree of coincidence between the descriptions of conscious events as experienced by a subject and the descriptions of the same events from the perspective of an independent observer that the subjective description reappears in its integrity in the scientific explanation. That sets the price of an adequate explanation so high that it is unrealizable. It also implies that, if it were feasible, it would be trivial in the sense highlighted by Descartes.

In contrast, Descartes's account of scientific theory focused attention on external phenomena that are described, in a functional manner, as the causes of our sensations. For example, I have a sensation of heat and I postulate some kind of external cause of that sensation that is also called 'heat'. The structure of an explanation is described as follows in the *Discourse on Method* (Part VI):

If some of the issues that I have spoken about at the beginning of *The Dioptrics* and *The Meteors* shock people initially, because I call them assumptions and seem not to want to

---

[2] In a sympathetic review of Searle, Nagel summarizes part of Searle's argument and endorses at least the first premiss of this argument: 'No theory that leaves out consciousness can claim to be a theory of the mind, and no analysis of consciousness in non-mental terms is possible; therefore, no materialistic reduction of the mental can succeed' (Nagel 1995: 100–1).

prove them, they should have the patience to read the whole text attentively . . . For it seems to me that the arguments are interconnected in such a way that, as the last ones are demonstrated by the first, which are their causes, the first arguments are demonstrated reciprocally by the last, which are their effects. It should not be imagined that, by doing so, I commit the fallacy that logicians call a 'vicious circle'; since experience makes most of these effects very certain, the causes from which I deduce them are used not so much to prove as to explain them; but, in exactly the opposite direction, it is the former that are proved by the latter.   (vi. 76; D. 53)

This passage refers to the hypothetical causes of some phenomenon, and the relationship between a description of those causes and a description of the corresponding effect. If the latter are designated, respectively, as *E* (for explanation) and *D* (for description), the arrows symbolize the relations that Descartes calls 'explaining' and 'proving':

Thus one begins with a description of one's sensation of heat (*D*), and one explains it with a description of the hypothetical cause of the sensation (*E*). The Cartesian objection to scholastic explanations was that no explanatory progress would be made if the content of *E* were completely dependent on *D*. For example, if we knew nothing more about the cause of heat except that it is a 'heat-causing phenomenon', then the apparent circularity about which Descartes was concerned would be resolved by substituting for the complexity of explanation and confirmation something closer to a biconditional: $E \leftrightarrow D$. This gives rise to what may initially appear paradoxical, that *E* succeeds in explaining *D* only to the extent that *E* is independent of *D*. The same condition applies even if *E* and *D* are both descriptions of objective phenomena. For example, if I wish to explain the motion of the planets, I make no progress by postulating a planet-motion-producing power about which nothing further is known except that it is the kind of power that makes planets move in their characteristic elliptical orbits.

However, in making explicit a priori one of the requirements for an adequate theory of the human mind, Nagel closes the explanatory gap entirely and demands that the penultimate step of any explanation include a description of mental events that duplicates the way in which we describe them from the perspective of the subject. 'The subjective features of conscious mental processes—as opposed to their physical causes and effects—cannot be captured by the purified form of thought suitable for dealing with the physical world that underlies the appearances' (Nagel 1989: 15). This point can be illustrated by comparing the role of identity statements in physical theory with their counterparts in a theory of mind.

According to (a simplified version of) current theories of heat, we fix the referent of phrases that refer to the cause of our sensation of heat in two parallel ways. In the 'manifest image', we work from our sensation of heat to some external phenomenon whose nature is unknown and which is called 'heat'. The term 'heat' at this stage means nothing more than 'whatever it is in hot things that causes my sensation of heat'. In the 'scientific image', we use current molecular theory to derive a description of one property of molecules in motion, namely, their mean kinetic energy. When these two cases of reference-fixing are placed in parallel, we can hypothesize a link between the two descriptions in the form of an identity claim.

Molecular theory	Description of sensation of heat
↓	↓
Description of mean kinetic energy	Derivative description of heat

Once an identity claim is made: 'heat = mean kinetic energy', then the identity claim drops out as part of the explanation of why we have the sensation of heat, and we can work directly from a general theory of molecules, to their mean kinetic energy, to their causing us to have a sensation that we call 'heat'. The molecular theory is a plausible hypothesis that explains the experiences we have on the occasion of being exposed to hot things. Nagel's argument is that nothing like this is possible, in principle, for a theory of mental events because the corresponding diagram would be:

Scientific theory of the brain	Description of the experience of pain
↓	↓
Description of some brain state	Description of pain

The problem is that there is no distinction on the right side of this diagram between a pain and the experience of pain. The alternative suggested by Descartes is that pain is an 'internal' sensation that makes us aware of some damage to our body, in the same way that heat is an 'external' sensation that makes us aware of some condition of the external environment. If so, the corresponding diagram for an identity statement about pain should be:

Scientific theory of the brain	Description of the experience of pain
↓	↓
Description of a brain state	Derivative description of pain-causing events

Nagel's argument derives some plausibility from an objection to some types of explanation sketch that is the converse of the Cartesian objection and that motivated the Newtonian worries described in Chapter 1. Newton had constructed in the *Principia* an extremely successful mathematical model of how postulated gravitational forces of a certain kind could predict planetary motions, but there remained a niggling worry about how, precisely, planets could causally affect each other across great distances. His reply was that part of the story remained to be provided, and he anticipated that it could be supplied by a description of contact action between unobservable particles or some similar hypothesis. Meantime, he assumed that he had made some progress towards providing the kind of explanation required. Here the legitimate worry was that the explanatory gap may be so wide that the proposed bridge is no more than a vague promissory note—although in some cases we may have to accept promissory notes when nothing better is offered. The corresponding objection in Nagel's argument is expressed as follows:

We can *see* how liquidity is the logical result of the molecules [of water] 'rolling around on each other' at the microscopic level. Nothing comparable is to be expected in the case of neurons, even though it is empirically evident that states of consciousness are the necessary consequences of neuronal activity . . . we do not really understand the claim that mental states are states of the brain: we are still unable to form a conception of *how* consciousness arises in matter, even if we are certain that it does.   (Nagel 1995: 106)

This seems to be a version of Newton's worry. If so, it can be accommodated in the same way as Newton dealt with his concerns in the 1680s. It may also be a completely different objection, about how subjective states can ever be explained by any objective discourse, even one in which the resources of traditional substance dualism are made available.

These reflections on the seventeenth-century account of scientific explanation suggest two conclusions:

1. that a genuine explanation must involve some explanatory gap between the description of an *explanandum* and the corresponding descriptions in the *explanans* of apparently distinct phenomena;
2. that too large a gap would compromise the plausibility of any proposed explanation, because of the amount of theoretical work that remains to be done.

It also follows from this concept of explanation that identity statements are not themselves explanations. They merely provide a link between two descriptions (of the same phenomenon) whose referents are specified in two different ways. Once in place, an identity statement can drop out of the final explanation, so that one could move (in the example used) from a molecular theory → a description of the mean kinetic energy of molecules → a description of the sensation of heat. In the case of mental events, the question that philosophers (including Descartes) have traditionally asked is: are identity statements of this kind possible or plausible in a theory of mind? One response is to argue that identity statements are impossible in this context, although such a position must acknowledge that impossibility claims typically require extremely strong arguments. Alternatively one could argue that, although they are possible in principle, we do not currently have sufficient work done in our understanding of the brain that would result in a promising though incomplete explanation sketch. It is worth underlining that the work that needs to be done is in constructing a plausible theory. An identity claim comes later, when one's new theory is placed alongside the pre-theoretical description of the relevant phenomena—in this case, mental events as experienced by the thinking subject.

I argue in the following sections that Descartes was persuaded, by the evidence available to him, that the gap between the subjective description of mental events and the objective description of brain states was so great that there was no way in which it could be bridged, and that this apparently unbridgeable gap was presented in terms of a real distinction between the properties of mental events and physical things. In other words, Descartes used the only option available to him when genuine explanation ran into apparently insurmountable obstacles: he resorted to postulating a mental reality as the subject of mental acts, while acknowledging the obvious limitations of that provisional ploy.

A REAL DISTINCTION: DESCARTES'S REPLIES TO OBJECTIONS

The apparent scandal of Cartesian metaphysics is the argument, in the *Meditations*, from the fact that I do not know if I have a body to the conclusion that I am not identical with my body, or that having a body is not part of what I am in so far as I am a thinking being. Descartes acknowledged this problem as one of two major objections to which he wished to draw attention in the Preface to the *Meditations*. He accepted that readers objected as follows: 'from the fact that the human mind reflecting on itself does not perceive itself as anything other than a thinking thing, it does not follow that its nature or essence consists merely in the fact that it is a thinking thing, where the word "merely" excludes everything else that might be said to belong to the nature of the soul' (vii. 7–8; M. 12). The standard Cartesian reply was that the inference from what we perceive to what is the case was not made in the Second Meditation, as many critics claimed, because it would have been illegitimate at that stage of the argument. However, he also claimed that this inference was proved beyond doubt in the Sixth Meditation, and that the key premiss that underpins the argument is the real distinction between the mind and the body.[3] I argued in Chapter 8 that Descartes does not have available any independent knowledge of substances, and that he cannot support any form of dualism by appealing directly to knowledge of different kinds of substance. The logic of his argument is the opposite: we know what substances are like only by examining their properties. The crucial claim in his whole philosophy of mind, therefore, is what he calls a 'real distinction' between mental and bodily properties.

Another way of clarifying the same point is this. Descartes knows from experience that he thinks and he concludes, by the natural light of reason, that he is a thinking thing. He also knows that he has other physical properties and, by a similar argument, that he is a physical thing.[4] Evidently, if he stops the list at that stage he must be assuming some general classification of properties into only two types, physical and mental. Otherwise, he could continue by showing that he is a walking thing, a fencing thing, a daydreaming thing, and so on. There are independent theoretical arguments for not multiplying the total number of 'things' of which he is composed. Therefore the minimal number of things that need to be postulated in order to explain the full range of properties of which he is aware in himself depends on whether or not those properties are compatible in the same thing.

This approach is acknowledged in response to Hobbes's objections. Hobbes urged that the mental properties that we experience subjectively are to be explained by some unknown motion of parts of matter. Descartes replied that we know substances only through their acts, and that we cannot reasonably decide in advance that everything is or is not material. We should consider what we know first—namely, the actions or properties of whatever we are discussing. We may temporarily give different names to each action that appears to be distinct, without prejudice to whether they are found subsequently to belong to the same thing or to two different things.

Since, however, we do not know a substance itself immediately through itself, but only by the fact that it is the subject of certain acts, it is very reasonable and in keeping with common usage that we apply different names to those substances that we recognize as

---

[3] Descartes mentions a number of times that the inference from ideas to reality is made only in the Sixth Meditation; see vii. 226, 355.

[4] The two parallel arguments, from the possession of two different kinds of faculties (*facultates*) to the existence of two substances as the necessary subjects of those faculties, are developed in the Sixth Meditation (vii. 78–9; M. 62).

the subjects of completely different acts or accidents, so as to examine later whether those different names signify different things or one and the same thing.   (vii. 176)[5]

Descartes accordingly concedes that Hobbes may initially use any term he wishes to denote the substance of which are predicated acts that fall under the concept of thought, perception, or consciousness, on condition only that he not identify it a priori with bodily substance. That would be to beg a question that should remain open. The argument about whether we need one or two substances then comes later.

There is nothing surprising in the fact that Hobbes pressed this objection. But Mersenne also raised it (twice), and so did Caterus, Gassendi, and Arnauld. Thus every one of the six sets of objections that accompanied the first edition of the Meditations includes either a query or an objection to the inference made by Descartes. The replies to these critics help explain the meaning and motivation of the Cartesian position.

Mersenne had raised this concern in the Second Objections, in which he suggested that 'the whole system of your body . . . or some parts of it, for example the brain, may concur to form those motions that we call thoughts. I am, you say, a thinking thing, but who knows whether you are a bodily motion or a body that is moved' (vii. 123). Descartes replied by defending his proposed criterion of a real distinction and inviting Mersenne to offer a better alternative. 'Is it not sufficient that we understand clearly one thing without another in order to recognize that they are really distinct?' (vii. 132). Mersenne might have assumed that perceiving one thing in the absence of the other might be a more reliable criterion. But such perceptions themselves are thoughts: 'perceiving one without the other is nothing other than having an idea of one thing and understanding that idea is not the same as the idea of the other thing' (vii. 132). Descartes argues that the alternative view, 'that parts of the brain concur to form thoughts', is based not on any positive argument but on the fact that people have no experience of not having a body and that they often have the experience of their mental operations being impeded by bodily conditions. This, however, is as contingent as the experience of someone whose feet have been shackled from birth, who might equally be tempted to conclude, from the experience of their constant concurrence, that shackles are required for walking (vii. 133).

Mersenne was not impressed by this response and he returned to the same query when he submitted further objections, collected from different sources,

---

[5] Cf. Descartes to Reneri for Pollot (Apr./May 1638): 'Of course one may wonder whether the nature that thinks may perhaps be the same as the nature that occupies space, so that there is one nature that is both intellectual and corporeal' (ii. 38).

in the Sixth Objections. On this occasion he also added that the Cartesian argument had won few converts. 'Someone might maintain . . . that you are nothing else but bodily motion. For no one has yet been able to comprehend your demonstration, by which you think you have demonstrated that no bodily motion can be what you call thought . . . Can you show us—for we are attentive and, we think, sufficiently intelligent—that it is impossible for thoughts to emerge from those motions?' (vii. 413). Descartes provides a more extensive and explicit reply on this occasion, and reveals the extent to which his concept of a real distinction has modal connotations. The Cartesian position involves two steps: (1) to discover whether two properties are distinct; and, if the answer is yes, (2) to find out whether such distinct properties can occur in the same reality.

The identity or distinctness of properties is decided by examining their clear and distinct ideas. If someone knows that they think, and if they understand what motion is, then 'since they clearly have an idea or notion of thought that is different from their idea of bodily motion, it is necessary that they understand one as different from the other' (vii. 422–3). Descartes concedes that one may not be able to convince others of the validity of this distinction because it 'is understood from this alone, that the notion of a thinking thing and of an extended or mobile thing are completely different, and are independent of each other, and it would be inconsistent if those things that are understood clearly by us to be different and independent could not be made separate, at least by God' (vii. 425). I return below to the modal connotations of the last phrase here.

Assuming for the sake of argument some kind of *conceptual* distinction between properties (that is, a distinction in the meanings of the phrases used to describe them), Descartes admits that even distinct properties may be found in the same subject. This may happen in two ways: (1) by what he calls 'a natural unity and identity', or (2) 'by a mere unity of composition'. For example, we have different ideas of shape and motion, of understanding and willing, or of bones and flesh. We 'see clearly that the same substance that is capable of being shaped is also capable of being moved, so that being shaped and mobile are one and the same by a unity of nature' (vii. 423). The same applies in the case of willing and understanding. 'But we do not perceive the same about something that we think about under the form of bone and a thing that we think about under the form of flesh; therefore, we cannot take them to be one and the same thing by a unity of nature, but merely by a unity of composition, in so far as it is one and the same animal that has bones and flesh' (vii. 423). Descartes concludes that we cannot see any more 'affinity or connection' between thinking and extension than between flesh and bone. This supports the conclusion that thought and extension 'are said to be one and the same only by a unity of composition, in so far as they are found in the same human being, as flesh and bone are found in the same animal' (vii. 424).

Gassendi raised the same objection as Mersenne by challenging Descartes to prove that matter in motion could not provide an explanation of thought: 'you have to prove that neither a vapour nor any other mobile, pure and rarified body can be organized in a way that would make it capable of thought' (vii. 355). Descartes's initial reply, plausibly enough, was that he did not have to prove every negative claim he made. 'In order to philosophize correctly, it is not necessary that we prove false all those things that we do not accept because we do not know if they are true' (vii. 354). Thus, if Descartes knows he is a thinking thing, and if his concept of what it is to think includes nothing that belongs to the concept of a bodily substance, 'that is clearly enough to affirm that I, in so far as I know myself, am nothing other than a thinking thing' (vii. 355). The qualification 'in so far as I know myself' implies a conditional reference to my current epistemological state. I have no reason to believe that thinking is identical with the motion of some body and I do not need a proof of such a denial. The onus of proof is on those who make a positive claim in the opposite direction. One could readily accept this point from Descartes but still be concerned, however, at the relative equanimity with which he claims, as if the point were completely obvious, that we are subjects of properties that are really distinct and that the real distinction between thinking things and bodily things follows necessarily. The apparent certainty of the conclusion was challenged by Arnauld.

Arnauld's objection refers to the attempt, in the Preface to the *Meditations* quoted above, to explain the argument against an identity theory of mind in two stages, and he acknowledges that the conclusive part of the argument appears only in Meditation Six. The relevant section of this meditation, part of which is quoted by Arnauld in his objection, is as follows:

I know that everything that I understand clearly and distinctly can be made by God in the same way that I understand them; therefore it is enough that I understand one thing, clearly and distinctly, without another in order to be certain that one thing is distinct from another, because it is possible for them to be separated at least by God. Therefore from the fact alone that I know that I exist and that, at the same time, I notice absolutely nothing else that belongs to my essence or nature apart from the simple fact that I am a thinking thing, I correctly conclude that my essence consists in this alone, that I am a thinking thing. And although I may (rather, as I shall say soon: I certainly) have a body that is joined very closely to me, since I have on the one hand a clear and distinct idea of myself in so far as I am a thinking, non-extended thing, and on the other hand, I have a distinct idea of the body as it is merely an extended, non-thinking thing, it is certain that I am really distinct from my body and that I can exist without it.   (vii. 78; M. 61–2)

Arnauld rightly identifies 'these few lines' as containing 'the core of the whole difficulty' (vii. 200).

Arnauld's objection focuses on the adequacy or otherwise of concepts to reflect the realities of which they are predicated. To make his point he borrows part of an earlier reply by Descartes to Caterus, which acknowledged the possibility that we may confuse a real distinction with a *modal* distinction,[6] and that we might think that motion, for example, is really distinct (in Descartes's sense) from a body in motion. Arnauld illustrates his objection by referring to someone who has a limited knowledge of geometry. Such a mathematical neophyte might understand some features of a geometrical figure and not others, and might mistakenly deny the necessary connection between two of its properties.[7] Likewise, he argues, it is possible that Descartes understands the concepts of thought and extension only as inadequately as the inexpert mathematician understands the concept of a triangle, and that he therefore fails to see a connection between them. 'Why could I not possibly be mistaken in believing that nothing else belongs to my nature—which I certainly and distinctly know is a thinking thing—other than that I am a thinking thing, when it may also possibly belong to it that I am an extended thing?' (vii. 203).

In reply Descartes defines knowledge as adequate if it includes 'absolutely all the properties of the thing known' (vii. 220). Since we can never know if our knowledge has achieved this degree of adequacy, it would be self-defeating to require it as a prerequisite for making claims in philosophy. He therefore proposes a less strict and apparently circular criterion; knowledge is adequate when 'the power of knowing is adequate to the thing to be known' (vii. 220). There are background issues here related to the warrant of our epistemic faculties, which had been addressed earlier but unsatisfactorily in the *Meditations*. Even if these issues could be avoided, there remains the problem of using what are normally adequate or appropriate epistemic faculties in an inadequate manner—for example, using our eyes to see macroscopic bodies. Without resolving any of these problems, Descartes claims simply that our knowledge would be adequate to the task at hand if it avoided being *in*adequate as a result of making a misleading intellectual abstraction.

For the most part, Descartes's reply to the argument from geometry is to reject the analogy between a geometrical figure and a substance, and to challenge the claim that one could have a clear and distinct idea of a right-angled tri-

---

[6] Descartes uses the term 'modal' to describe a distinction between the modes of a substance and the substance itself. The same term is used today to refer to discussions that involve questions about necessity, possibility, etc. To avoid confusion, I shall italicize the term *modal* whenever it is used in the Cartesian sense.

[7] For example, someone knows that a triangle formed on the diameter of a circle, whose apex is on the circumference, is a right-angled triangle; but he doubts or denies that the square on the hypotenuse is equal to the sum of the squares on the other two sides.

angle without knowing the relation between the squares on its sides. But that leaves unanswered the principal source of concern: how 'from this alone that I understand one substance clearly and distinctly without another, I am certain that one excludes the other' (vii. 225–6).

In many ways, the Cartesian argument at this point seems to be circular, or at least as bootstrapping as Quine (1953) famously claimed about traditional attempts to define analyticity. For example, when faced with the query: how can you argue from a clear distinction of substances to the conclusion that one excludes the other? Descartes's immediate response is: that is exactly what we mean by a substance—namely, something that can exist by itself. If we perceive two things as substances through two distinct concepts, we claim that they are 'really distinct'. There may have been residual doubts in the Second Meditation, about whether our ideas are reliable enough to support such inferences. But, once such general sceptical worries about the reliability of knowledge claims are removed, he argues, there is no further reason to doubt that things that are identified by different attributes are really distinct. This is a separate, epistemo-logical concern that may be left aside here. The metaphysical question being addressed is that substances are understood as entities that exclude each other: 'for this is the nature of substances, that they mutually exclude each other' (vii. 227). The argument can move in either direction, from mind to body or vice versa. 'When I examine the nature of body, I find nothing at all in it that has con-notations of thinking. There can be no better argument for a real distinction between two things than that, when we look at either of them, we find nothing at all in one that is not different from the other' (vii. 227). Since being a body does not include having mental properties, it follows that being physical is really distinct from being mental.

The following interim conclusions result from the *Objections and Replies*:

1. Descartes admits that we initially name properties, such as thinking and bodily motion, as if they were distinct properties (in some sense to be defined), and that we must leave it to subsequent investigation to deter-mine whether or not they happen to name the same feature of reality, or whether they refer to different properties that are compatible or incompatible in the same reality.

2. There are two ways in which properties may occur together in the same entity. It is beyond doubt that thinking and bodily motion are attributes of the same creatures, human beings. The open question is whether they co-occur 'through a natural unity and identity' or by 'composition'.

3. In the case of thinking, willing, perceiving, and other forms of thinking, Descartes rejects the suggestion that these are different species of generically similar phenomena. Instead he classifies them as modes or

manifestations of the same phenomenon—namely, thought. The question of a real distinction, then, is whether some complex motion of matter is the same phenomenon as thinking, or whether it is really a distinct phenomenon that is contingently associated with thinking in human experience.

To clarify this question, one needs to have a closer look at the Cartesian concept of a *real* distinction.

REAL DISTINCTION

The Cartesian understanding of a real distinction, despite the obscurity that may result from the Scholastic terminology in which it is expressed, is unambiguously modal. It is defined in the *Principles* (1. 60), in a strict sense, as a distinction between two or more things or substances. 'There is a real distinction, in a strict sense, only between two or more substances. We perceive that substances are really distinct from each other simply from the fact that we are able to understand, clearly and distinctly, one substance without the other' (viii-1. 28; M. 135). However, Article 61 also admits another kind of real distinction that depends on the strict version just defined; according to this, there is a real distinction between one substance and the mode of another substance, or between the modes of one substance and those of a different substance—for example, between body B and the motion of body C, or between the motion of B and the shape of C. Different substances are said to be really distinct if we can understand one of them, clearly and distinctly, without the other. The relevant criterion is what we can distinguish in thought. Thus, even if there were no matter in the universe, our concept of matter is such that, if God created matter, 'every part of matter that is defined in thought is really distinct from the other parts of the same substance [*eiusdem substantiae*]' (viii-1. 28; M. 135). Likewise, the motion of one body is really distinct from the motion of another, because we cannot understand either motion without reference to the really distinct substances of which they are modes.

  The criterion for recognizing a real distinction, therefore, is not whether the distinct realities are substances. In the text just quoted, 'parts of the same substance' are said to be really distinct; and, if that is not conclusive, it is certain that modes of two substances may be really distinct, although they are by definition not substances. Thus a real distinction depends on whether we conceive of the allegedly distinct realities in such a way that one could exist without the other. This criterion is expressed in terms of the power of God. Even if God always joined two qualities T and M together so that we have no experience of T occurring without *M*, 'he cannot lose the power that he had previously to separate them or conserve one in existence without the other' (viii-1. 29; *M.* 135). Despite initial appearances to the contrary, the conceivability or otherwise of the distinction of *T* and *M* does not rely on a description of God's powers. Descartes cannot claim to know what God can or cannot do. Therefore it is impossible to resolve a question about whether two realities are really distinct by starting with a reliable description of God's powers and then working towards a conclusion about what is or is not really distinct. The argument goes in the opposite direction, as Descartes explained in a letter to More (5 February 1649): 'I never determine anything about God's power. I only consider what may or may not be conceived by me . . . [and] boldly claim that God is capable of doing everything that I perceive as possible. But I do not rashly deny, on the contrary, that he can do what I cannot conceive; I say simply that it involves a contradiction' (v. 272; *M.* 170). Thus there is no independent information available about God's power that would help determine which things are really distinct. Any reference to what God can do is merely a theological expression of what Descartes can conceive, clearly and distinctly, as possible. What Descartes conceives as possible is possible for God, although things that Descartes thinks are impossible may still be possible for God.

I also argued in Chapter 8 that Descartes has no independent access to or knowledge of substances as such. Thus, he can no more appeal to his knowledge of substances to decide in a given case whether a distinction is real than he can rely on independent knowledge of God's powers. Here too the argument runs in the opposite direction. We know which substances are distinct by first knowing their properties and then arguing that such properties can or cannot be predicated of the same substance.

Thus references to God's power or to the reality of substances are a distraction from the core of the argument. Descartes is unflinching in his claim that the only way to know if two realities are really distinct is by consulting our ideas of them, as he explained to Mersenne (21 January 1641):

To say that thoughts are merely movements of the body is as perspicuous as saying that fire is ice, or that white is black; for no two ideas that we have are more different than those of black and white, or those of movement and thought. Our only way of knowing whether two things are different or identical is to consider whether we have different ideas of them, or one and the same idea . . .   (iii. 285)[8]

---

[8] Cf. Descartes to Reneri for Pollot (Apr. / May 1638): 'From the very fact that we conceive clearly and distinctly the two natures of the body and the soul as different, we know that in reality they are different and consequently that the soul can think without the body . . . ' (ii. 38); Descartes to Regius (June 1642): 'The only criterion by which we know that one substance differs from another substance is that we understand one without the other' (iii. 567); Descartes to an unknown correspondent (1645/6) (iv. 349–50).

This can hardly be the trivial suggestion that the only way that we know anything is by consulting our ideas, because Descartes acknowledged many ways in which a distinction between our ideas does not correspond to a real distinction between the realities to which they refer. For example, he had pointed out, as early as the *Rules*, the danger of abstracting in thought some feature of a reality that is incapable of existing independently of that reality. He returns to this question in the *Principles*, where he introduces, in addition to real distinctions, two other types of distinction. There is what he calls a *modal* distinction, of which there are two kinds. One is between a thing and its own modes; for example, the distinction between the shape of a body and the body itself is *modal* because we cannot envisage the shape existing without the body of which it is the shape. But we could envisage the same body existing with a different shape or motion. The other kind of *modal* distinction is between two modes of the same substance, such as between the shape and motion of the same body. There is a third type of distinction that is even less real than a *modal* distinction, and this is called a distinction of reason. Descartes classified universals as modes of thinking rather than as modes of the realities to which we attribute them. For example, we can distinguish in our thought between something and its existence or its duration, but in reality there is no distinction between them. Likewise the thought by which I think of someone called Peter is *modally* distinct from the thought by which I conceive of him as a man, but in Peter himself 'being a man is nothing other than being Peter' (iv. 350), and the distinction between the realities to which my thoughts correspond is merely a distinction of reason.

Thus there are at least three ways in which we distinguish different features, in our thinking or talking about things, and in two of them it would be a mistake to infer, from that fact that our thoughts are distinct, to the conclusion that the realities to which our thoughts refer are really distinct. This general rule is expressed as follows in the course of classifying different kinds of distinction: 'nothing seems to cause a difficulty in this context except that we do not distinguish adequately the things that exist outside our thought from the ideas of things that are in our thought' (iv. 350). That implies a general embargo on arguing from a distinction in thought to a real distinction, unless there is some extra evidence to support the objective reality of the distinction.

This leads naturally to the question that is basic to Descartes's dualism: is the distinction between mental attributes (such as sensation) and physical attributes (such as motion) a real or a *modal* distinction? To the extent that the same body may change its shape or motion, such qualities are classified as *modes* of the thing of which they are predicated. Descartes goes on to warn readers of the danger involved in transgressing the boundaries of what we perceive clearly and distinctly. For example, we best perceive motion if 'we consider nothing but local motion and do not enquire into the force by which it is produced' (viii-1. 32; M. 138). The same applies to modes of thought. They are 'perceived clearly if we are very careful not to make any judgements about them apart from what is included precisely in our perception and of which we are inwardly aware' (viii-1. 32; M. 138). Descartes accepts the parallel between our perception of motion and our perception of pain. In the case of sensations, the demarcation line between clarity and obscurity coincides with the distinction between subjective experience and the objective causes of our experience. 'In order to distinguish what is clear from what is obscure in this context, it must be carefully noted that pain, colour, and other similar things are perceived clearly and distinctly when they are considered simply as sensations or as thoughts' (viii-1. 33; M. 139). Matters become obscure, he argues, when we move incautiously from our thoughts to claims about some extra-mental reality, although it is legitimate to claim that there is something 'of which we are completely ignorant' that causes our sensation. If Descartes blocks the move from a perception of red to the conclusion that there must be something in what is perceived that resembles our red perceptual experience, he is not blocking the logic of postulating an appropriate, though not necessarily resembling, cause of our perceptual experience. But we are still faced with a complete lack of resolution about the fundamental issue: assuming that we have distinct *ideas* of thought and of matter in motion, how can we decide that the *realities* to which they refer are really distinct? Descartes has not established this conclusion in the replies to objections to the *Meditations*.[9] Although the concept of thought has nothing in common with the concept of matter in motion, an explanation of thinking may rely essentially on a description of the human brain and its operations. Descartes seems to have been convinced that this was so implausible a possible development that it did not need an explicit discussion.

MIND–BODY IDENTITY

The principle of the indiscernibility of identicals is that realities that are identical have all their properties in common, including their modal properties. When Descartes considers the properties of matter and thought, his immediate reaction is that they have almost no properties in common. Thus the version of the identity thesis proposed in all the Objections to the *Meditations* involves taking

---

[9] Here I agree with Secada (2000: 241) that Descartes never provided a proof of the real distinction of mind and matter.

for granted something very implausible that requires an argument. The question is, then: what kind of argument or evidence would be appropriate to bridge the explanatory gap between mental properties and physical properties?

As already indicated above, Saul Kripke argued that an identity statement, if true, is necessarily true if the relevant referring expressions in the identity statement are rigid designators, such as proper names. Thus if 'Hesperus' and 'Phosphorus' are alternative names for exactly the same referent (otherwise known as Venus), then the identity statement 'Hesperus = Phosphorus' is necessarily true (that is, true in all possible worlds). One can make sense of this kind of transworld identity on the assumption that the words used to express it are rigid designators, and that the referent is such that it maintains the same properties long enough to support the rigidity of the connection between a name and (at least a time slice of) the reality named. This implies, that if one could conceive of one referent having any property that is not shared with the other referent, they are not necessarily identical. For example, if votes in the US presidential election had been counted differently in Florida in November 2000, 'George W. Bush = the forty-second President of the United States' would not be true. Thus this should be understood as expressing a true but merely contingent identity, because the right side of the equivalence sign is a definite description rather than a rigid designator.

As described by Kripke, the Cartesian argument involves two steps: (1) mental states can exist without physical states or vice versa; and (2) therefore they are not identical.[10] Since (2) follows from (1), those who reject the Cartesian position would have to reject (1). It is not clear how to establish the possibility that thoughts could exist without the physical states with which they are allegedly identical or vice versa. In the case of contingent identities, this is done by describing a coherent possible world in which the two sides of the identity statement refer successfully to two different realities. The challenge, then, is to do this coherently for either token–token or type–type identity theories of mind. Assume, for example, that we name a particular occurrence of a mental state M, and that we use P to name a physical state. A token–token identity claim could be expressed as $M = P$ (assuming that we had named the appropriate events in each case). If Kripke is correct about the status of M and P as rigid designators, then it is necessarily true that $M = P$, since the two terms simply name the same unique event from two different points of view. Therefore, if someone wished

---

[10]   This is shorthand for a longer, more carefully expressed argument. There is no dispute about the possibility of physical things and events taking place without any associated mental events. But this would show only that *some* physical events are distinct from mental events. The question is whether the precise physical events with which identity theorists wish to identify mental events could exist without the corresponding mental events, and vice versa.

to avoid the Cartesian conclusion (that *M* and *P* are distinct), it would be necessary to deny (1) above and accept that *M* could not occur without *P* or vice versa. In other words, for any mental event, there are two alternative linguistic items that belong to parallel languages and are found to name the same reality, so that the identity claimed on behalf of their referents is necessary. I return to this possibility below.

The status of type–type identity theories is less promising. Davidson's argument (1970) in favour of anomalous monism shows that, even if mental states were identical with physical states, there is no reason to hope that we could construct laws that linked some types of event described in physical terms with other types of event described in mental terms. The justification for this claim is similar to the reasons why propositional attitudes cannot be defined in terms of specific kinds of behaviour. Mental terms belong to an unavoidably intensional language, and cannot be abstracted from that context so that they can feature, one at a time, in laws that link together the physical and the mental. 'Just as we cannot intelligibly assign a length to any object unless a comprehensive theory holds of objects of that sort, we cannot intelligibly attribute any propositional attitude to an agent except within the framework of a variable theory of his beliefs, desires, intentions, and decisions' (Davidson 1970: 96). To describe an event in mental language, therefore, is to apply to it a background theory such that the content of any propositional attitude attributed to the agent depends essentially on the theory of which it is part and, more importantly, on the flexibility allowed in reassigning descriptions so as to save as much as possible the kind of rationality that is essential to describing the agent as rational. Anomalous monism, therefore, suggests that mental descriptions cannot be reduced to physical descriptions, and that there is no reason to hope for laws that would underpin any kind of type–type identity theory; at the same time, there is no reason to believe that there are two distinct types of reality corresponding to the two languages that fail to be linked nomologically.

This suggests a reconsideration of token–token identity as the only plausible option available for identity theorists. It reopens the question about whether one can provide a coherent expression of such a theory and, if so, what kind of evidence would be required either to support it or to argue in the opposite direction.

PROPERTY DUALISM

Kripke's analysis of identity statements apparently raises the theoretical cost of identity claims and, by implication, seems to make less demanding the kind of evidence that would support the reasonableness of the Cartesian position. This impression is supported by the conclusion that the kind of identity statements in which an identity of mind and physical events could be expressed must be either necessarily true or false. It is difficult to establish the truth of a necessarily true statement, and much easier to cast doubt on it. For example, Kripke comments (1982: 146) on a sample token–token identity claim, which suggests an identity between a specific brain state and a specific occurrence of a pain: '*prima facie*, it would seem that it is at least logically possible that *B* [a brain state] should have existed . . . without Jones feeling any pain at all, and thus without the presence of *A* [a mental state].' If it is logically possible for a brain state to occur without the mental state with which it is allegedly identical, then it follows from Kripke's analysis of the necessity of identity statements that the brain state in question is not identical with the associated mental state. Thomas Nagel makes a similar claim about the *conceivability* of a distinction between brain states and mental states, and argues that it is implausible to deny the conceivability of such a distinction, since Descartes claims to have conceived of mental states without the associated physical states. 'Clearly it would not content Descartes to be told that he cannot be certain that the disembodied occurrence of those sensations is *in*conceivable, for he is certain that it *is* conceivable, having conceived it' (Nagel 1995: 79). However, both arguments are mistaken and they provide no support for what they assume is the Cartesian position.

What is logically possible is irrelevant to deciding whether token–token identity statements are true, although it would be relevant to deciding whether a given statement is analytic. One of the significant implications of Kripke's analysis is that some identity statements, which turn out to be both true and necessary, are discovered only by scientific research and are therefore known *a posteriori*. Before doing the relevant scientific research, one cannot decide whether heat is identical with the mean kinetic energy of molecules by asking whether it is logically possible for one to occur without the other. All one needs to know, before doing the relevant scientific research, is that it is *not logically impossible* for heat to be identical with the mean kinetic energy of molecules. Whether or not they are identical is a matter of fact that, if it turns out to be true, is necessarily true because we are naming the same reality twice.

Likewise Nagel's argument does not establish that, since it is conceivable that a specific brain event is not identical with the occurrence of a specific thought, they cannot be necessarily identical and therefore (by Kripke's argument) they are not identical at all. This argument confuses epistemic possibility and the kind of semantic (or metaphysical) necessity that is relevant to Kripke's argument. This point can be illustrated by a simple example. In the history of science, before the acceptance of currently adopted theories of heat, one could think of a contemporary of Descartes or Boyle arguing as follows. 'Heat' is a name that is applied to two related phenomena. It names one of our sensations, and it names whatever external events cause us to have sensations of heat. Since we do not yet understand what these latter events are, it is conceivable, *from the perspective of our present state of knowledge*, that heat is not identical with the motion of small parts of matter. Such an epistemic conceivability evidently does not imply that, when the theory of heat is eventually formulated in the eighteenth century, a proto-Nagel could have argued: the proposed identity of heat with the motion of molecules is, if true, a necessary identity. But we could conceive of one without the other, and in fact some early theorists have done so in the past. Therefore, whatever the connection between these distinct phenomena, they are not identical.

This brings the discussion back appropriately to the nub of the issue. Whether or not any identity claim turns out to be true (and then, in retrospect, necessarily so) is a function of the state of development of the relevant scientific theory. The question faced by Descartes was: is there any reason to believe that our mental descriptions of thoughts could turn out to be alternative descriptions of phenomena that are also describable by physics? If not, what is the status of our belief that one is not identical with the other?

I argued in Chapter 1 that the Cartesian concept of matter is notoriously inadequate to accommodate subsequent developments in scientific theory. Theories of matter change as a function of the kinds of theoretical entity admitted into one's explanatory repertoire. The extreme theoretical parsimony of Descartes's physics caused insurmountable problems in attempting to explain even phenomena that were widely accepted in the seventeenth century as physical, such as attraction between bodies at a distance or the elasticity of various bodies. Thus any proposal to explain thoughts in terms of the motion of parts of matter had to face an almost unbridgeable explanatory deficit, and the apparent gap between *explanans* and *explanandum* was increased by the weight of traditional arguments in the opposite direction. When it was necessary to identify some of the more obvious discrepancies between the properties of thoughts and the properties of physical things, Descartes argued (for example) that pieces of matter necessarily have parts, but it does not even make sense to talk about the parts of a thought or the parts of the mind. This is the kind of argument that, when articulated in contemporary terms, is similar to Davidson's argument (1970: 93) that 'mental and physical predicates are not made for one another'. The two languages in which such predicates naturally occur are incommensurable in the sense that there can be no neat one-to-one translation from one language to the other. In that sense, the terms pick out different properties.

Descartes's way of describing this feature of concepts was by reference to the way in which they cluster around basic notions. Thus concepts such as sensing, believing, affirming or denying, remembering, understanding, and so on all denote various ways in which we think. The alternative cluster, including words that refer to the size, shape, speed, and so on of bodies, all presuppose the fundamental concept of extension or a type of entity that has parts. There is little in common between the two groups, and they both equally refer to properties of human beings the existence of which would be extremely implausible to doubt. The minimal conclusion, it would seem, for Descartes is some kind of dual-aspect theory of language.[11] However, his recourse to the language of substances might seem to imply a stronger conclusion than this.

CONCLUSION: DESCARTES'S DUALISM

When we think about realities that are sensed or otherwise thought about, Descartes's most consistent intuition was that our thoughts may fail to reflect the nature of those things or that the realities may turn out to be very different from how we initially conceived of them. It is difficult to see how he could have avoided making the same distinction in the case of thought itself. If a person P is conscious of any object O, Descartes's standard claim is that P's consciousness is an unreliable guide to the nature of O. If P then reflects on his own thinking or is conscious of his act of consciousness, the same principle applies: one's thinking is not guaranteed to depict accurately the reality that one thinks about. It might seem impossible in the case of some experiences, such as pain, to have any conceptual distance between one's thought and one's awareness of having that thought. How could one have a pain without being conscious of it? But this seems to be obvious only because we normally understand 'having a pain' as being already a self-conscious thought. According to the Cartesian analysis in the *Principles*, when we have a pain we perceive, obscurely, the object of our sensation—that is, a damaged part of our body—and at the same time we are aware of this sensation (which is the characteristic feeling of pain). But it would be possible, in principle, to have a similar perception of the same object without the associated pain.[12]

If one keeps in mind the general Cartesian caution against making illegiti-

---

[11]   I intentionally modify this phrase from a dual-aspect theory of the mind to a way of thinking about language, since the dual-aspect analysis is not in any sense an explanation of how mental events or thoughts occur.

[12]   For a recent attempt to distinguish between pains and their subjective perception, see Hardcastle (1999).

mate inferences from acts of consciousness to the nature of what we are conscious of, Descartes must conclude that we cannot draw any reliable inference from our subjective conscious experiences to the nature of the realities, events, or processes that cause them. Such inferential moves are necessarily hypothetical.

At the same time, when Descartes consults what he thinks is the best available theory of the physical world, the properties attributed to the theoretical entities used in that theory have nothing in common with the properties of which he is subjectively aware in his experience of thought. There is a lack of fit between the concepts used in both languages, and it would therefore be premature either to merge them forcefully (as Hobbes proposed) or to declare them incompatible in principle. Descartes's reply to Mersenne (in the Sixth Replies), discussed above, was that he could not understand how mental properties can fit with physical properties. That means that he could not provide any *theory*, no matter how tentative and incomplete, of how mental properties may be caused by physical properties.

The conclusion to which he was forced, therefore, is the only option left open by his theory of explanation and his inadequate concept of matter. When we attempt to explain any given phenomenon, sooner or later we encounter the limits of our efforts and it is appropriate at that point to signal having reached those limits by an uninformative appeal to the way things are. Such explanatory limits are encountered almost immediately if we look for a theory of thought or mental acts by beginning with our subjective experience of thinking. We have a concept of what this is like, and we attribute the corresponding properties to a 'something that thinks'. As in the case of Molière's sleeping powder, this is both true and uninformative. The usual strategy in the case of objective phenomena in need of explanation, such as the dormitive power of sleeping pills, is to hypothesize some kind of chemical microstructure in the powder that could cause the effect to be explained. In the case of conscious or mental events, however, Descartes lacked even the first intimations of such a theory.

The type of argument deployed by contemporary critics of identity claims does not affect this unresolved issue. Davidson's anomalous monism is, essentially, a critique of a certain kind of reductionism that assumes or demands nomological links between two independent languages. A similar point was made by Nagel (1995: 77), in his critique of Armstrong's materialist theory of mind: 'why should a materialist theory of the operation of human beings correspond closely enough to any mentalist picture to permit identification of items between the two theories?' If one accepts that the intentionality of mental language cannot be reduced to or explained in terms of the extensional languages typically available in traditional physical theories, one has already accepted the first step towards Descartes's dualism.

However, this argument does not support the claim that it is impossible in principle to develop a scientific theory of human mental events. Even if Kripke's account of identity claims is adopted, it merely implies that such identities are usually not knowable a priori. Nagel may argue that he cannot see how descriptions of neuronal activity can explain the experience of consciousness, but that points merely to a gap in our theory that may or may not be filled with advances in scientific theory. Descartes's dualism was an expression of the extent of the theoretical gap between a science of matter in motion, within the conceptual limits of Cartesian physics, and the descriptions of our mental lives that we formulate from the first-person perspective of our own thinking. The properties that feature in these very different perspectives are sufficiently different to make implausible any Hobbesian, ad-hoc, or a priori claim of identity. But they are not sufficient to justify the conclusion that it is impossible, in principle, to develop an explanation of human thought by including new theoretical entities in one's concept of matter. The underlying support for Descartes's property dualism was not a metaphysical theory of substances, or a plausible argument about the distinctness of properties, but an impoverished concept of matter. The resolution to the question, therefore, depends not on new philosophical arguments but on developments in a science of the mind.

Was Descartes, then, a substance dualist? Yes and no. He was not a substance dualist if that means that one explains the human mind by reference to a non-material substance. For Descartes, substances as such are non-explanatory. We speak about different substances in the same way as we speak about different things or the subjects of properties that are theoretically irreconcilable. Descartes acknowledged that he had no theory about the way in which thinking might be caused or explained by the known properties of matter, and he was persuaded that such a theory was most implausible. For that reason he was a property dualist. However, he also argued unconvincingly in the *Meditations* that the implausibility of finding a theoretical link between thinking and the properties of matter implied a 'real distinction' between the substances to which such properties belong. Cartesian dualism, therefore, is not a theory of human beings but a provisional acknowledgement of failure, an index of the work that remains to be done before a viable theory of the human mind becomes available.

REFERENCES

Primary Sources

Amyraut, Moise (1641). *De l'élévation de la foy et de l'abaissement de la raison en la créance des mystères de la Religion.* Saumur: Jean Lesnier.

Aristotle (1986). *De Anima,* trans. Hugh Lawson-Tancred. London: Penguin.

Arnauld, Antoine (1990). *On True and False Ideas,* trans. and ed. S. Gaukroger. Manchester and New York: Manchester University Press (1st edn. 1683).

——and Nicole, Pierre (1996). *Logic or the Art of Thinking,* ed. Jill Vance Buroker. Cambridge: Cambridge University Press (1st edn. 1662).

Baillet, Adrien (1691). *La Vie de Monsieur Descartes.* 2 vols. Paris: Daniel Horthemels.

Bos, Erik-Jan (2002). *The Correspondence between Descartes and Henricus Regius.* Utrecht: Zeno (Leiden-Utrecht Research Institute of Philosophy).

Boyle, Robert (1996). *A Free Enquiry into the Vulgarly Received Notion of Nature.* Cambridge: Cambridge University Press (1st edn. 1686).

——(1999–2000). *The Works of Robert Boyle,* ed. M. Hunter and E. B. Davis. 14 vols. London: Pickering & Chatto.

Chanet, Pierre (1646). *De l'instinct et de la connoissance des animaux.* La Rochelle: Toussaincts de Govy.

——(1648). *Esclaircissement de quelques difficultez touchant la connoissance de l'imagination.* La Rochelle: Toussaincts de Govy.

Charron, Pierre (1654). *De la sagesse trois livres.* Leiden: Jean Elzevier.

——(1729). *Of Wisdom Three Books,* trans. George Stanhope. 3 vols. 3rd edn. London.

Condillac, Étienne Bonnot de (2001). *Essay on the Origin of Human Knowledge,* trans. and ed. Hans Aarsleff. Cambridge: Cambridge University Press (1st edn. 1746).

Cordemoy, Gerauld de (1968). *Discours physique de la parole* (1st edn. 1668), in P. Clair and F. Girbal (eds.), *Œuvres philosophiques.* Paris: Presses universitaires de France.

Cureau de la Chambre, Marin (1648). *Les Characteres des passions.* Paris: Rocolet.

——(1662). *Traité de la connoissance des animaux, où tout ce qui a esté dit pour, & contre le raisonnement des bestes est examiné.* Paris: Jacques d'Allin.

——(1665). *The Art How to Know Men,* trans. John Davies. London: Thomas Dring.

Descartes, René (1859–60). *Œuvres inédits de Descartes,* ed. Foucher de Careil. 2 vols. Paris: Auguste Durand.

——(1985–91). *The Philosophical Writings of Descartes,* trans. and ed. J. Cottingham, R. Stoothoff, D. Murdoch, and A. Kenny. 3 vols. Cambridge: Cambridge University Press.

——(1996). *Le Monde, L'Homme,* intro. by Annie Bitbol-Herpériès. Paris: Éditions du Seuil.

——(1998). *The World and Other Writings,* ed. Stephen Gaukroger. Cambridge: Cambridge University Press (1st edn. 1664).

Digby, Sir Kenelme (1644). *Two Treatises in the one of which, The Nature of Bodies; in the other, the Nature of Mans Soule: is looked into: in way of discovery, of the Immortality of Reasonable Soules.* Paris: Gilles Blaizot.

Galilei, Galileo (1957). *Discoveries and Opinions of Galileo,* trans. Stillman Drake. New York: Doubleday.

——(1967). *Dialogue concerning the Two Chief World Systems.* 2nd edn., trans. Stillman Drake. Berkeley and Los Angeles: University of California Press (1st edn. 1632).

Hobbes, Thomas (1991). *Leviathan,* ed. Richard Tuck. Cambridge: Cambridge University Press (1st edn. 1651).

La Forge, Louis de (1997). *Treatise on the Human Mind (1666),* trans. D. M. Clarke. Dordrecht: Kluwer.

La Mettrie, Julien Offrat de (1996). *Machine Man and other Writings,* ed. Ann Thomson. Cambridge: Cambridge University Press (1st edn. 1747).

Locke, John (1695). *The Reasonableness of Christianity, as Delivered in the Scriptures.* London: Awnsham & Churchill.

——(1975). *An Essay concerning Human Understanding,* ed. Peter H. Nidditch. Oxford: Clarendon Press (1st edn. 1690).

Malebranche, Nicolas (1997). *The Search after Truth,* trans. T. M. Lennon and P. J. Olscamp. Cambridge: Cambridge University Press (1st edn. 1674–5).

Molière, J.-B. P. de (1971). *Œuvres complètes,* ed. Georges Couton. 2 vols. Paris: Gallimard.

Montaigne, Michel de (1991). *The Complete Essays,* trans. and ed. M. A. Screech. London: Penguin (1st edn. 1595).

Newton, Isaac (1952). *Opticks, or A Treatise of the Reflections, Refractions, Inflection & Colours of Light.* New York: Dover (4th edn. 1730).

Reynolds, Edward (1640). *A Treatise of the Passions and Faculties of the Soul of Man.* London: Bostok.

Rohault, Jacques (1723). *Rohault's System of Natural Philosophy,* illustrated with Dr Samuel Clarke's Notes, trans. John Clarke. London: Knapton (1st edn. 1671).

Toland, John (1696). *Christianity not Mysterious.* London.

Willis, Thomas (1664). *Cerebri Anatome: cui accessit Nervorum Descriptio et Usus.* London: Martyn & Allestry.

——(1965). *The Anatomy of the Brain and Nerves,* ed. William Feindel. 2 vols. Montreal: McGill University Press.

Secondary Sources

Aarsleff, Hans (1993). 'Descartes and Augustine on Genesis, Language, and the Angels', in M. Dascal and E. Yakira (eds.), *Leibniz and Adam.* Tel Aviv: University Publishing Projects, 169–95.

Arbini, Ronald (1983). 'Did Descartes Have a Philosophical Theory of Sense Perception?' *Journal of the History of Philosophy,* 21: 317–37.

Ariew, Roger, et al. (1998) (eds.). *Descartes' Meditations: Background Source Materials.* Cambridge: Cambridge University Press.

Armogathe, Jean-Robert (1977). *Theologia Cartesiana: L'Explication physique de l'eucharistie chez Descartes et Dom Desgabets*. The Hague: Nijhoff.

——and Marion, Jean-Luc (1976) (eds.). *Index des Regulae ad Directionem Ingenii de René Descartes*. Rome: Edizioni dell'Ateneo.

Baker, Gordon, and Morris, Katherine J. (1996). *Descartes' Dualism*. London: Routledge.

Beyssade, Michelle (1994). 'Descartes's Doctrine of Freedom: Differences between the French and Latin Texts of the Fourth Meditation', in Cottingham (1994), 191–206.

Bitpol-Herpériès, Annie (1990). *Le Principe de vie chez Descartes*. Paris: Vrin.

Blackwell, Richard J. (1991). *Galileo, Bellarmine, and the Bible*. Notre Dame, IN: University of Notre Dame Press.

Chappell, Vere (1994). 'Descartes's Compatibilism', in Cottingham (1994), 177–90.

——(1997a). 'Descartes's Ontology', *Topoi*, 16: 111–27.

——(1997b) (ed.). *Descartes's Meditations: Critical Essays*. New York: Rowan & Littlefield.

Churchland, Paul M. (1979). *Scientific Realism and the Plasticity of Mind*. Cambridge: Cambridge University Press.

Clarke, Desmond M. (1977). 'The Impact Rules of Descartes' Physics', *Isis*, 68: 55–66.

——(1982). *Descartes' Philosophy of Science*. Manchester: Manchester University Press.

——(1989). *Occult Power & Hypotheses: Cartesian Natural Philosophy under Louis XIV*. Oxford: Clarendon Press.

——(1992). 'Descartes' Philosophy of Science and the Scientific Revolution,' in Cottingham (1992), 258–85.

——(1996) 'The Concept of *vis* in Part III of the *Principia*', in J.-R. Armogathe and G. Belgioioso (eds.), *Descartes: Principia Philosophiae 1644–1994*. Naples: Vivarium, 321–39.

——(2000). 'Causal Powers and Occasionalism from Descartes to Malebranche', in Gaukroger et al. (2000), 131–48.

——(2001). 'Exorcising Ryle's Ghost from Cartesian Metaphysics', *Philosophical Inquiry*, 23: 28–36.

——(2002). 'Explanation, Consciousness, and Cartesian Dualism', in Randall A. Auxier and Lewis E. Hahn (eds.), *The Philosophy of Marjorie Grene. Library of Living Philosophers*. Chicago: Open Court, 471–85.

Cottingham, John (1986). *Descartes*. Oxford: Blackwell.

——(1992) (ed.). *The Cambridge Companion to Descartes*. Cambridge: Cambridge University Press.

——(1994) (ed.). *Reason, Will, and Sensation: Studies in Descartes' Metaphysics*. Oxford: Clarendon Press.

——(1997). *Descartes: Descartes' Philosophy of Mind*. London: Phoenix.

——(1998) (ed.). *Descartes*. Oxford: Oxford University Press.

Davidson, Donald (1970). 'Mental Events', in L. Foster and J. W. Swanson (eds.), *Experience & Theory*. London: Duckworth, 79–101.

Dear, Peter (1988). *Mersenne and the Learning of the Schools*. Ithaca, NY: Cornell University Press.

Denzinger, Henricus (1960). *Enchiridion Symbolorum*, ed. K. Rahner. Fribourg: Herder.

Des Chene, Dennis (1996). *Physiologia: Natural Philosophy in Late Aristotelian and Cartesian Thought*. Ithaca, NY: Cornell University Press.

Des Chene, Dennis (2000). *Life's Form: Late Aristotelian Conceptions of the Soul*. Ithaca, NY: Cornell University Press.

——(2001). *Spirits and Clocks: Machine and Organism in Descartes*. Ithaca, NY: Cornell University Press.

Foti, Véronique M. (2000). 'Descartes' Intellectual and Corporeal Memories', in Gaukroger et al. (2000), 591–603.

Frankfurt, Harry G. (1988). *The Importance of what we care about: Philosophical Essays*. Cambridge: Cambridge University Press.

Gabbey, Alan (1980). 'Force and Inertia in the Seventeenth Century: Descartes and Newton', in Gaukroger (1980) (ed.), 230–320.

——(1990). 'Explanatory Structures and Models in Descartes' Physics', in G. Belgioioso et al. (eds.), *Descartes: il metodo e I saggi*. Rome: Istituto della Enciclopedia Italiana, i. 273–86.

Garber, Daniel (1983). 'Mind, Body, and the Laws of Nature in Descartes and Leibniz', *Midwest Studies in Philosophy*, 105–33, repr. in Garber (2001), 133–67.

——(1992). *Descartes' Metaphysical Physics*. Chicago: University of Chicago Press.

——(2001). *Descartes Embodied*. Cambridge: Cambridge University Press.

Gaukroger, Stephen (1980) (ed.). *Descartes: Philosophy, Mathematics and Physics*. Sussex: Harvester Press.

——(1998) (ed.). *The Soft Underbelly of Reason: The Passions in the Seventeenth Century*. London: Routledge.

——(2002). *Descartes' System of Natural Philosophy*. Cambridge: Cambridge University Press.

——Shuster, J., and Sutton, J. (2000) (eds.). *Descartes' Natural Philosophy*. London: Routledge.

Gibson, James J. (1966). *The Senses Considered as Perceptual Systems*. London: Allen & Unwin.

Greenfield, Susan (2000). *The Private Life of the Brain*. London: Penguin Books.

Grene, Marjorie (1985). *Descartes*. Minneapolis: University of Minnesota Press.

Guenancia, Pierre (1976). *Du vide à Dieu. Essai sur la physique de Pascal*. Paris: François Maspero.

Hacking, Ian (1972). 'Individual Substance', in Harry G. Frankfurt (ed.), *Leibniz: A Collection of Critical Essays* (New York: Doubleday), 137–53.

Hardcastle, Valerie G. (1999). *The Myth of Pain*. Cambridge, MA: MIT Press.

Hatfield, Gary (1992). 'Descartes' Physiology and its relation to his Psychology', in Cottingham (1992), 335–70.

Hoffman, Joshua, and Rosenkrantz, Gary S. (1994). *Substance among other Categories*. Cambridge: Cambridge University Press.

————(1997). *Substance: Its Nature and Existence*. London: Routledge.

Hoffman, Paul (1986). 'The Unity of Descartes's Man', *Philosophical Review*, 95: 339–70.

James, Susan (1997). *Passion and Action: The Emotions in Seventeenth-Century Philosophy*. Oxford: Clarendon Press.

Jolley, Nicholas (1990). *The Light of the Soul: Theories of Ideas in Leibniz, Malebranche, and Descartes*. Oxford: Clarendon Press.

Jubien, Michael (1992). *Ontology, Modality, and the Fallacy of Reference*. Cambridge: Cambridge University Press.

Kenny, Anthony (1969). *Descartes: A Study of his Philosophy*. New York: Random House.

——(1972). 'The Homunculus Fallacy', in Marjorie Grene (ed.), *Interpretations of Life and Mind*. London: Routledge & Kegan Paul, 65–74.

Kripke, Saul A. (1982). *Naming and Necessity*. Oxford: Blackwell.

Lennon, Thomas (1980). 'Representation, Judgment and Perception of Distance', *Dialogue*, 19, 151–62.

Lewis, Geneviève (1950). *Le Problème de l'inconscient et le Cartésianisme*. Paris: Presses universitaires de France.

Loeb, Louis E. (1981). *From Descartes to Hume: Continental Metaphysics and the Development of Modern Philosophy*. Ithaca, NY: Cornell University Press.

Lyons, William (1980). *Emotion*. Cambridge: Cambridge University Press.

——(1995). *Approaches to Intentionality*. Oxford: Clarendon Press.

McGuire, J. E. (1967). 'Transmutation and Immutability: Newton's Doctrine of Physical Qualities, *Ambix*, 14, 69–95.

——(1968). 'Force, Active Principles, and Newton's Invisible Realm', *Ambix*, 15: 154–208.

MacIntosh, J. J. (1983). 'Perception and Imagination in Descartes, Boyle and Hooke'. *Canadian Journal of Philosophy*, 13: 327–52.

MacKenzie, Ann W. (1989). 'Descartes on Life and Sense'. *Canadian Journal of Philosophy*, 19: 163–92.

——(1992). 'Descartes on Sensory Representation'. *Canadian Journal of Philosophy* (Supplement), 16: 127–46.

McMullin, Ernan (1978a). 'Structural Explanation', *American Philosophical Quarterly*, 15: 139–47.

——(1978b). *Newton on Matter and Activity*. Notre Dame, IN: University of Notre Dame Press.

——(1978c). *The Concept of Matter in Modern Philosophy*. Notre Dame, IN: University of Notre Dame Press.

Margolis, Joseph (1980). 'The Trouble with Homunculus Theories', *Philosophy of Science*, 47: 244–59.

Marion, Jean-Luc (1975). *L'Ontologie grise de Descartes*. Paris: Vrin.

Markie, Peter (1994). 'Descartes's Concepts of Substance', in Cottingham (1994), 63–87.

Matthews, Gareth B. (1992), *Thought's Ego in Augustine and Descartes*. Ithaca, NY: Cornell University Press.

Menn, Stephen (1995). 'The Greatest Stumbling Block: Descartes' Denial of Real Qualities', in R. Ariew and M. Grene (eds.), *Descartes and his Contemporaries: Meditations, Objections, and Replies*. Chicago: University of Chicago Press, 182–207.

——(1998). *Descartes and Augustine*. Cambridge: Cambridge University Press.

Nagel, Thomas (1989). *The View from Nowhere*. New York: Oxford University Press.

——(1995). *Other Minds: Critical Essays 1969–1994*. New York: Oxford University Press.

Olivo, Gilles (1993). 'L'Homme en personne', in Verbeek (1993), 69–91.

Quine, W. V. O. (1953). 'Two Dogmas of Empiricism', in *From a Logical Point of View*. Cambridge, MA: Harvard University Press, 20–46.

Reiss, Timothy J. (1996). 'Denying the Body? Memory and Dilemmas of History in Descartes'. *Journal of the History of Ideas*, 57: 587–607.

Rodis-Lewis, Geneviève (1990). *L'Anthropologie cartésienne*. Paris: Presses universitaires de France.

——(1993). 'Problèmes discutés entre Descartes et Regius: L'Âme et le corps', in Verbeek (1993), 35–46.

Rorty, Richard (1979). *Philosophy and the Mirror of Nature*. Princeton: Princeton University Press.

Rosenfield, Leonora Cohen (1968). *From Beast-Machine to Man-Machine. Animal Soul in French Letters from Descartes to La Mettrie*. New enlarged edn. New York: Octagon Books.

Rosenthal, David M. (1997). 'Will and the Theory of Judgment', in Chappell (1997*b*), 129–58.

Rozemond, Marleen (1998). *Descartes's Dualism*. Cambridge, MA: Harvard University Press.

Ryle, Gilbert (1949). *The Concept of Mind*. London: Hutchinson.

Secada, Jorge (2000). *Cartesian Metaphysics: The Late Scholastic Origins of Modern Philosophy*. Cambridge: Cambridge University Press.

Sellars, Wilfrid (1963). *Science, Perception, and Reality*. London: Routledge & Kegan Paul.

Sepper, Dennis L. (1996). *Descartes's Imagination: Proportion, Images, and the Activity of Thinking*. Berkeley and Los Angeles: University of California Press.

Simmons, Alison (1999). 'Are Cartesian Sensations Representational?' *Noûs*, 33: 347–69.

Slowik, Edward (2001).'Descartes and Individual Corporeal Substance', *British Journal for the History of Philosophy*, 9: 1–15.

Sutton, John (1998). *Philosophy and Memory Traces: Descartes to Connectionism*. Cambridge: Cambridge University Press.

Verbeek, Theo (1992). *Descartes and the Dutch: Early Reactions to Cartesian Philosophy, 1637–1650*. Carbondale and Edwardsville, IL: Southern Illinois University Press.

——(1993) (ed.). *Descartes et Regius: Autour de l'explication de l'esprit humain*. Amsterdam and Atlanta, GA: Editions Rodopi.

Voss, Stephen (1994). 'Descartes: the End of Anthropology', in Cottingham (1994), 273–306.

Westfall, Richard S. (1980). *Never at Rest: A Biography of Isaac Newton*. Cambridge: Cambridge University Press.

Wilson, Margaret D. (1978). *Descartes*. London: Routledge & Kegan Paul.

Wittgenstein, Ludwig (1958). *Philosophical Investigations*, trans. G. E. M. Anscombe. Oxford: Blackwell.

Wolf-Devine, Celia (1993). *Descartes on Seeing: Epistemology and Visual Perception*. Carbondale and Edwardsville, IL: Southern Illinois University Press.

Woolhouse, Roger (1993). *Descartes, Spinoza, Leibniz: The Concept of Substance in Seventeenth-Century Metaphysics*. New York: Routledge.

Yolton, John (1983). *Thinking Matter: Materialism in Eighteenth-Century Britain*. Oxford: Blackwell.

——(1991). *Locke and French Materialism*. Oxford: Clarendon Press.

Zeki, Semir (1993). *A Vision of the Brain*. Oxford: Blackwell Scientific Publications.

INDEX